During the second half of the eighteenth century, the pace of London's concert life quickened dramatically, reflecting both the prosperity and the commercial vitality of the capital. The most significant development was the establishment of the public concert within the social and cultural life of fashionable society. The subscription concerts that premiered symphonies by J. C. Bach and Haydn were conspicuous symbols of luxury, even though they were promoted on broadly commercial lines. It was a lucrative environment that attracted many other foreign musicians, including the Mozart family in 1764 and virtuosi like Clementi, Dussek and Viotti, whose influential music deserves greater recognition. At the same time London supported two alternative musical cultures. One was based around the English music of composers such as Arne and Boyce. The other was dedicated to the preservation of older repertoire, culminating in the massive Handel Commemoration of 1784. Drawing on hitherto untapped archival sources and a comprehensive study of daily newspapers, this book analyses audiences at venues as diverse as the Hanover Square Rooms, Vauxhall Gardens and City taverns. The musical taste of the London public is investigated in the light of contemporary theories of aesthetics; and there is detailed discussion of the financial and practical aspects of concert management and performance, in a period that encouraged enterprise and innovation.

*Concert life
in London from
Mozart to Haydn*

Concert life
in London from
Mozart to Haydn

SIMON McVEIGH

Lecturer in Music,
Goldsmiths' College, University of London

CAMBRIDGE
UNIVERSITY PRESS

Published by the Press Syndicate of the University of Cambridge
The Pitt Building, Trumpington Street, Cambridge CB2 1RP
40 West 20th Street, New York, NY 10011-4211, USA
10 Stamford Road, Oakleigh, Melbourne 3166, Australia

First published 1993

Printed in Great Britain at the University Press, Cambridge

A catalogue record for this book is available from the British Library

Library of Congress cataloguing in publication data

McVeigh, Simon.
Concert life in London from Mozart to Haydn / Simon McVeigh.
p.   cm.
Includes bibliographical references and index.
ISBN 0 521 41353 2 (hardback)
1. Music – England – London – 18th century – History and criticism.   2. Concerts –
England – London – History – 18th century.   3. London (England) – History – 18th
century.   I. Title.
ML286.8.L5M28   1993
780.78′421′09033–dc20 92–565 CIP

ISBN 0 521 41353 2 hardback

To my parents

Contents

Illustrations

Plates

Plans

Preface

London's importance in the early development of the public concert has been recognised since the eighteenth century itself. The main outlines – from the modest City origins of the late seventeenth century through to the fashionable subscription concerts of Salomon and Haydn at the end of the eighteenth – are well enough known. But the only extensive study of London's concert life in the second half of the eighteenth century remains C. F. Pohl's *Mozart und Haydn in London*, published in German as long ago as 1867. Furthermore, the history of the public concert has often been misinterpreted as a smooth progression of middle-class commercial endeavour, leading directly from John Banister's concerts at his Whitefriars music-school in 1672 to the symphony concerts at today's Festival Hall. In fact the process was by no means so smooth; nor is the role of the middle classes, however defined, nearly so straightforward.

Undoubtedly music played its part in the 'commercialisation of leisure', to quote the title of J. H. Plumb's 1972 Stenton Lecture which has had such an influence on eighteenth-century studies in general. Music-publishing and instrument-selling are clear examples of a luxury product spreading into new middle-class markets. The rise of the public concert has traditionally been regarded in the same light. In fact London's concerts developed in a quite different manner. Certainly they were commercialised, in the sense that tickets were sold by enterprising impresarios, who sought to attract audiences by strenuous advertising and by all kinds of attention-seeking publicity ruses. But the price and ticketing systems of the principal subscription concerts and benefits were specifically designed to maintain social exclusivity, a cachet reinforced by the novelty of the entertainments on offer – usually the latest foreign music and the most prestigious soloists. London's early concert life in reality developed somewhat fitfully; the main achievement of the later eighteenth century was the establishment of public concerts in the fashionable calendar of high society. Concerts remained at the forefront of London's entertainments at least from the mid 1760s to the mid 1790s – the successful years of J. C. Bach and Abel, of the Pantheon and the Professionals, of Salomon. The extent of bourgeois participation, whether by attendance at the top concerts or by emulation elsewhere, is open to debate, as will be seen. But it would certainly be a mistake to attribute the rise of the modern symphony concert to a welling-up of middle-class energies. In this respect, the study of concert life evidently contributes to the current debate about the relative roles of the aristocracy and the middle classes in British political and social life. The realignment of the upper classes is particularly manifest within the 'ancient-music' movement, investigated in detail by William Weber in his recent study *The Rise of Musical Classics in Eighteenth-Century England* (Oxford, 1992), to which this book, with its emphasis on London's modern musical culture, is intended to be complementary.

The second half of the eighteenth century forms a convenient period for reasons other than mere chronology. In the early 1750s London witnessed a sudden explosion of concert activity, and Charles Burney regarded the arrival of Felice Giardini in 1751 as the start of a new era in the instrumental music of the capital. Indeed the foundation of the modern symphony-concert series in London can effectively be dated to that very year, coinciding with the introduction of Italian symphonies in an early Classical style. The end of the century, perhaps surprisingly, forms a natural end to the cycle: the departure of Haydn in 1795, among other factors, brought about a temporary decline in the vitality of London's concert life, which was only resuscitated by the foundation of the Philharmonic Society in 1813.

Various limitations have deliberately been imposed on this study. The term 'concert' is interpreted rather loosely to incorporate public subscription series, benefits, oratorios and performances at the pleasure gardens, as well as meetings of orchestral societies and private or court concerts. But glee clubs and other convivial groups have been excluded from detailed discussion, and no attempt has been made to cover all those myriad occasions in eighteenth-century London when music played an ancillary part – from odes for anniversary dinners through elaborate church services to wind-bands playing on Thames barges. Nor has any comparison been offered between London's musical life and that of other European capitals, in view of the insuperable obstacles as yet involved. Certainly one is tempted to speculate that London's concert life was unrivalled in Europe for the volume and range of its activities, if not always for its creative achievements. My database *Calendar of London Concerts 1750–1800* (Goldsmiths' College, University of London) lists nearly 5,000 public concerts – and this without several hundred unadvertised concerts at the two ancient-music societies and many more at the pleasure gardens, not to speak of private concerts. It is unlikely that such a figure could be rivalled by Paris, and it could certainly not be matched by Vienna, with its predominantly salon-concert culture. Comparison with provincial British music must also remain a subject for further inquiry. Music outside London operated within a different type of social framework, and with some notable exceptions it did not inspire new repertoire of the highest quality. But undoubtedly a fascinating network of cultural links remains to be disentangled, both within Britain and outside it: after future research London's music will surely appear to be only part of a much broader social and musical picture.

Much of this book is dependent on hitherto untapped newspaper sources. There are dangers in the use of such material – not only because newspaper reports are often simply unreliable, but also because editors with an eye to commercial gain made no pretence whatsoever of impartiality. Malicious gossip about musicians sold newspapers and (for a fee) it could also be planted by a rival. Nevertheless newspapers provide a much more comprehensive picture than any other single source; furthermore, the nature of advertisements and reviews gives a direct insight into the attitudes of both promoters and audiences. My research in this area has benefited greatly from the support and enthusiasm of Rosamond McGuinness. The computerised *Register of Musical Data in London Newspapers 1660–1800* (Royal Holloway College, University of London) has not yet reached 1750, but I am most grateful to her and to Ian Spink for kindly making available to me the college's newspaper microfilm resources.

I should like to acknowledge in particular the generous assistance given by William Weber and Cyril Ehrlich, whose advice and comments on sections of the manuscript were invaluable in encouraging me to view the subject in the widest perspective. Many other scholars have kindly responded to requests for information and in some cases shared research materials, among them Mark Argent, Robert Bruce, Donald Burrows, H. Diack Johnstone, David Wyn Jones, Leanne Langley, Zaide Pixley, Curtis Price, Stephen Roe and Tony Trowles. Edward Olleson skilfully guided my research during its early stages at Oxford in the late 1970s; and on one occasion he casually suggested that I might glance at a few eighteenth-century London newspapers, with consequences that even he cannot have foreseen. The archivists of the institutions acknowledged below have given unstintingly of their time; and I have also been assisted by the staff of the British Library, the Royal College of Music, the Greater London Record Office, the Guildhall Library, Marylebone Library, Lambeth Archives Department, the Theatre Museum, the Museum of London, the Bodleian Library (Oxford), the Pendlebury Library (Cambridge), Leeds Central Library, the Library of Congress (Washington) and the Beinecke Rare Book Library (Yale University). I should like also to record my gratitude to the staff of Cambridge University Press, in particular to Victoria L. Cooper and Penelope Souster, who have carefully overseen the production of this book at every stage.

Finally I should like to express my thanks to my wife Alice, without whose tireless encouragement and search for the *mot juste* this book would be immeasurably the poorer.

Acknowledgments

I am indebted to the following institutions for permission to reproduce extracts from their archives: the United Grand Lodge of England (Freemasons' Hall records); the Royal Academy of Arts Library (Society of Artists); the Royal Bank of Scotland plc (Drummond's Bank); the Royal College of Surgeons of England (Lock Hospital); the Royal Society of Musicians; the Thomas Coram Foundation for Children (Foundling Hospital).

The following have kindly supplied photographs and granted permission for their reproduction: the Hulton Picture Library (plate 1); the Yale Center for British Art, Paul Mellon Collection (plates 2, 7); Westminster City Archives (plate 3); the Archive Department, Royal Opera House Covent Garden / trustees of the late Robert Eddison (plate 4); Trustees of the National Gallery, London (plate 5); Board of Trustees of the Victoria and Albert Museum, London (plate 6); the British Museum, London (plates 8, 9); the British Library, London (plate 10); University of London Library (plan 1).

Abbreviations

Contemporary newspapers

Full titles vary slightly from year to year

DI	*The Diary, or Woodfall's Register*
DUR	*The Daily Universal Register* (becomes *The Times*)
GA	*The General Advertiser*
GZ	*The Gazetteer*
MC	*The Morning Chronicle*
MH	*The Morning Herald*
MP	*The Morning Post*
OR	*The Oracle*
PA	*The Public Advertiser*
TB	*The True Briton*
TI	*The Times*
WO	*The World*

Others

BL	British Library, London
Bodl.	Bodleian Library, Oxford
CPL	Pendlebury Library, University Music School, Cambridge
CUL	University Library, Cambridge
EM	*Early Music*
GSJ	*The Galpin Society Journal*
IRASM	*International Review of the Aesthetics and Sociology of Music*
JAMS	*Journal of the American Musicological Society*
JRMA	*Journal of the Royal Musical Association*
LS	*The London Stage* (see bibliography)
ML	*Music & Letters*
MQ	*The Musical Quarterly*
MR	*The Music Review*
MT	*The Musical Times*

P(R)MA	*Proceedings of the (Royal) Musical Association*
QMMR	*The Quarterly Musical Magazine and Review*
RCM	Royal College of Music, London
RMARC	*Research Chronicle*, published by the Royal Musical Association
RSM	Royal Society of Musicians

Currency

One pound (£1) = twenty shillings (20*s.*)
One shilling (1*s.*) = twelve pence (12*d.*)
One guinea (1 gn.) = £1 1*s.*
10/6 = ten shillings and sixpence (half a guinea)

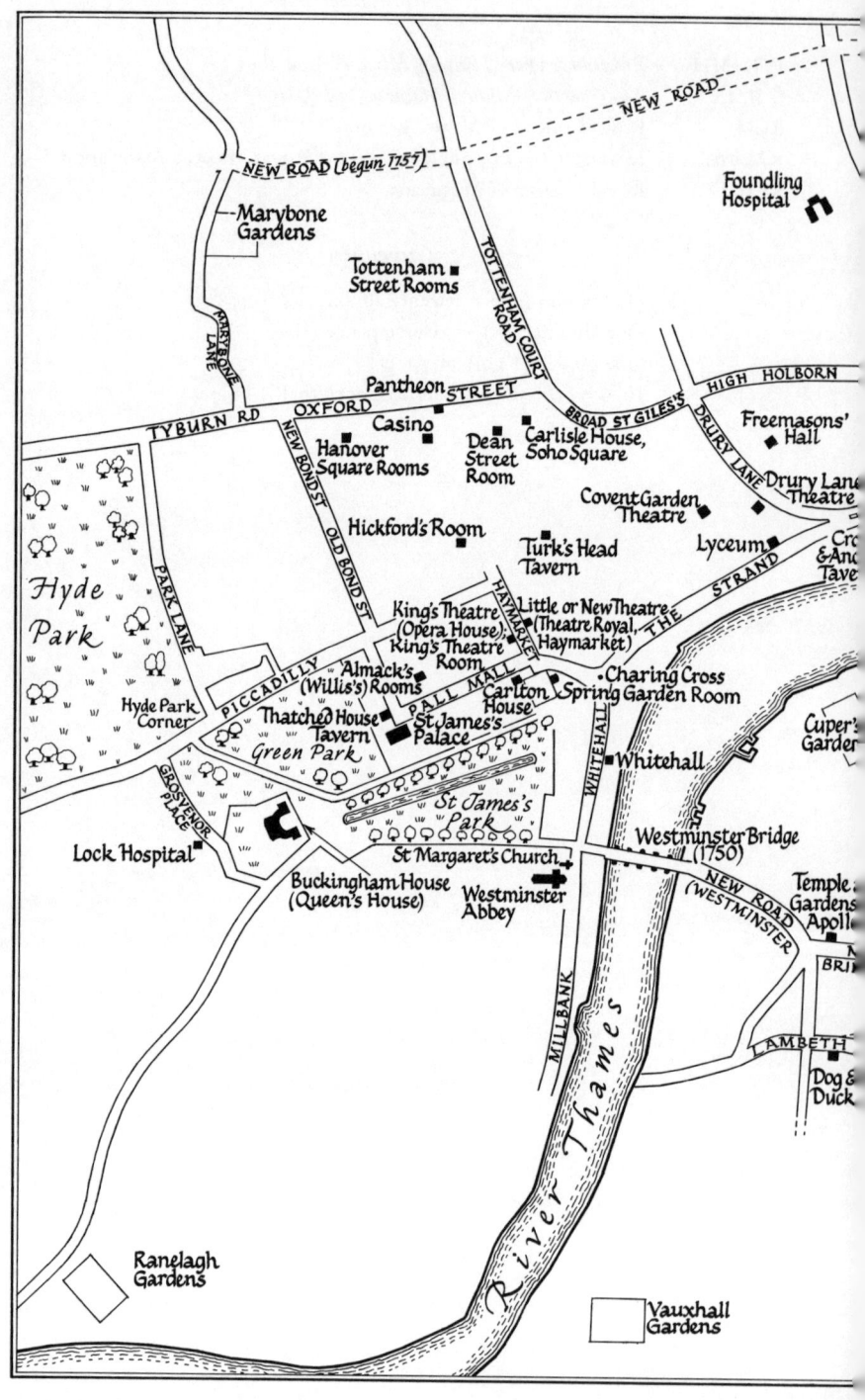

Map of London in the second half of the eighteenth century, showing the principal concert venues.

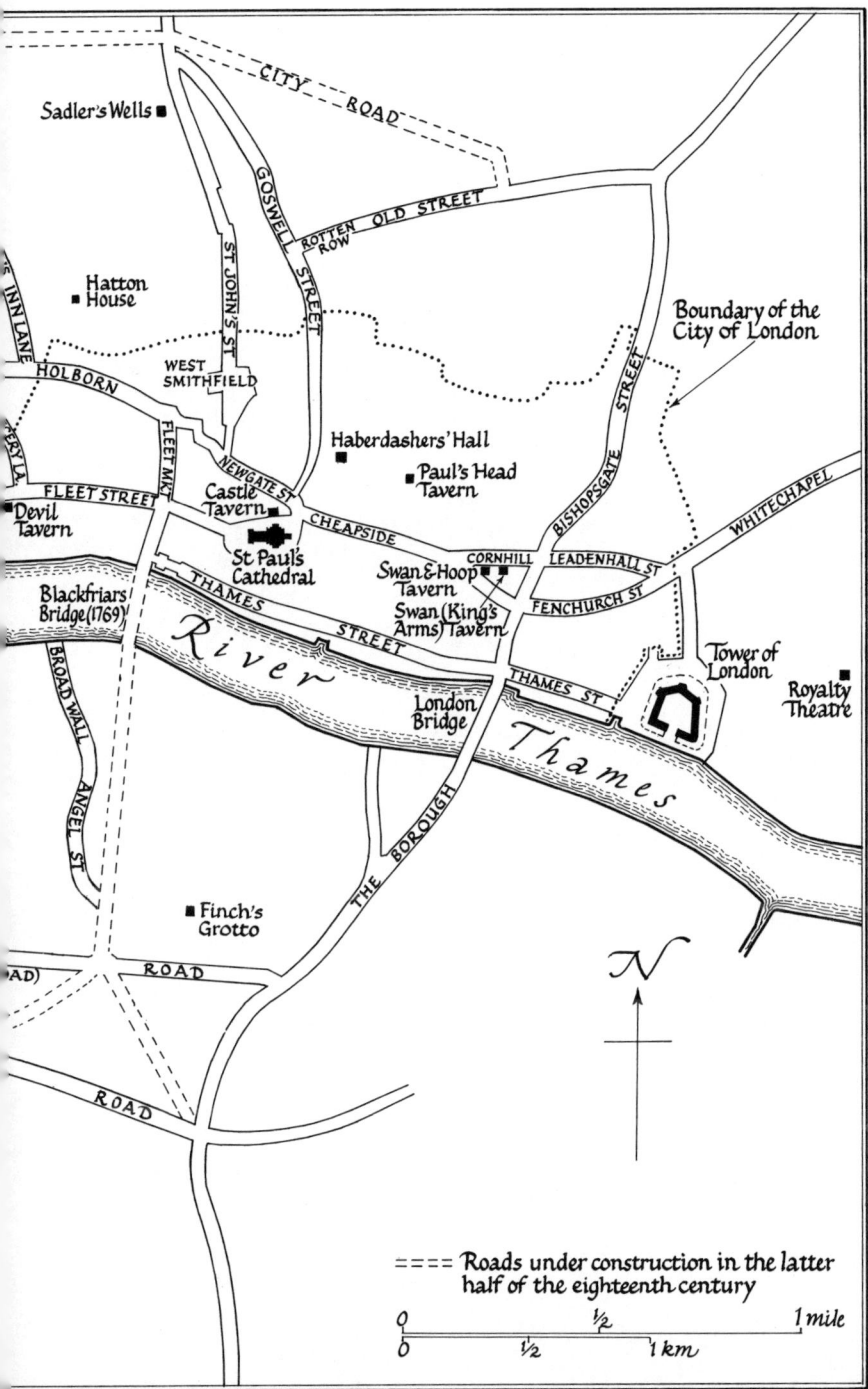

Sadler's Wells ■

CITY ---- ROAD

GOSWELL STREET

ROTTEN ROW OLD STREET

ST JOHN'S ST

■ Hatton House

'S INN LANE

HOLBORN

WEST SMITHFIELD

RBY LA

FLEET MKT

Boundary of the City of London

Haberdashers' Hall ■

■ Paul's Head Tavern

BISHOPSGATE STREET

WHITECHAPEL

FLEET STREET

NEWGATE ST

Castle Tavern ■

CHEAPSIDE

CORNHILL   LEADENHALL ST

■ Devil Tavern

St Paul's Cathedral

Swan & Hoop ■ Tavern

FENCHURCH ST

THAMES STREET

Swan (King's Arms) Tavern

Blackfriars Bridge (1769)

River Thames

London Bridge

THAMES ST

Tower of London

■ Royalty Theatre

BROAD WALL

ANGEL ST

THE BOROUGH

■ Finch's Grotto

AD)   ROAD

N

ROAD

==== Roads under construction in the latter half of the eighteenth century

0 ———— ½ ———— 1 mile
0 ——— ½ ——— 1 km

Prologue

The rage for music

Around 1790 London was in the grip of an unprecedented fervour for musical entertainment, ritually described as the current 'rage for music'. The number and variety of musical entertainments, the publicity they attracted and the extent of public enthusiasm were prodigious. Although music continued to play a major role in the theatre (at the Italian Opera and the two main playhouses), the phrase was primarily applied to concert life. Often it was used defensively against imaginary foreign taunts: 'The present rage is music. – The Professional Concert, the [Concert of] Ancient Music, the Oratorios in Tottenham Court-Road, and Salomon's Concerts – Four such meetings cannot be paralleled in any part of Europe.'[1] The fashionable vogue was frequently satirised. For Vauxhall Gardens in 1788 James Hook set the following verse in his comic dialogue *The Musical Courtship*:

> All the Modish World appear
> Fond of nothing Else my dear.
> Folks of Fashion eager seek
> Sixteen Concerts in a Week.

In reality the craze was not limited to the upper reaches of society. As one journalist put it, 'the present encreasing rage for Musick, is a contradiction of the character given by Foreigners of John Bull ... There are concerts in every part of the town, and the lower sort of people have their musical clubs, to which they nightly resort.'[2] A letter sent to a German magazine mocked London's universal 'epidemic of Melomania', noting that concerts were so popular at all levels of society that the nation itself was in danger of collapse.[3]

Newspapers before each season contain endless speculation about new performers and forthcoming repertoire. Often they published a scheme of regular musical events for the new season, and even weekly updates, as in the following example of *The Morning Chronicle*'s 'Mirror of Fashion' in 1792:[4]

1

MONDAY.	Her Royal Highness the Duchess of YORK's Concert.
	The Professional Concert.
TUESDAY.	The QUEEN's Concert, Buckingham-house.
	The Pasticcio, Hanover-square [Gallini].
WEDNESDAY.	Their MAJESTIES and PRINCESSES, will attend the Concert of Ancient Music, Tottenham-street.
	Mrs. VANNECK's Concert.
THURSDAY.	The QUEEN's Concert and Card Party, Buckingham-House.
	[Academy of] Ancient Music, Free Mason's Tavern.
FRIDAY.	The Duchess of GLOUCESTER's Concert.
	SALOMON's Concert.
SATURDAY.	The Pasticcio, Hanover-square.
	Catch and Glee Concert.
SUNDAY.	Duchess of GLOUCESTER's Concert.
	Lady HAMPDEN's Concert [Nobility Concert].
	Mrs. STURT's Concert.
	General TOWNSHEND's Concert.
	Mrs. R. WALPOLE's Concert.

Even if the press coverage was partly whipped up by concert managers, London concert life was undoubtedly going through one of its most brilliant and vital phases. Foreign visitors, perhaps expecting a *Land ohne Musik*, were constantly surprised by the important role played by music in London's social life. Memoirs and letters bear witness to the intense interest that concerts attracted, as in the graphic reaction of Miss Iremonger to Salomon's concerts of 1791:

The Reviewers remark that 'At the Concerts in Hanover Square, where [Haydn] has presided, his presence seems to have awakened such a degree of enthusiasm in the audience as almost amounts to frenzy!' You have my thanks for procuring me the opportunity, which I did not lose, of being one of the Infected.[5]

London now supported a well-established season of public concerts, organised on more-or-less commercial lines with fully professional performers. Such events occupied a central place in the social calendar. Yet both the widespread enthusiasm and the modes of concert organisation were comparatively new phenomena, as a glimpse at London music in 1690 and in 1740 will illustrate.

Changes in London's concert life during the eighteenth century

London played a pioneering role in the development of the concert. Indeed Europe's first major public concerts were those organised in 1672 by John Banister at his Whitefriars music-school, an initiative quickly followed up by others at the York Buildings room and at the Vendu in Charles Street. From

1678 to 1714 Thomas Britton, the 'musical small-coal man', put on his celebrated concerts in a loft above his Clerkenwell shop; despite the eccentric venue and low price (rising to only 10/- a year), Britton's concerts were patronised by a surprisingly high-class clientele. Nevertheless a glance at London newspapers for 1690 reveals as yet only a handful of public-concert advertisements. Though attended by the quality, concerts at the York Buildings room had an informal, even haphazard nature, reminiscent more of a house music-party:

> Here was consorts, fuges, solos, lutes, Hautbois, trumpets, kettledrums, and what Not but all disjoynted and incoherent for while ye masters were shuffling out & in of places to take their parts there was a totall cessation, and None knew what would come next; all this was utterly against the true Model of an entertainment, which [for] want of unity is allway spoiled.[6]

Fifty years later music played a much greater role in the life of the town. Italian opera had achieved a certain security, and musical productions were heard at the English playhouses of Covent Garden and Drury Lane. London's concert life had also grown in extent and organisation. A major subscription series was offered at Hickford's Room in Brewer Street, London's foremost concert venue: twenty concerts took place from January to May for a subscription of 6 guineas (single tickets at 5/-). The individually advertised programmes featured large-scale vocal works by John Christopher Smith and included solos by London's premier violinist, Michael Christian Festing. Meanwhile, at Lincoln's Inn Fields Theatre, Handel promoted an oratorio season, as he had done in most years since 1733; he himself contributed an organ concerto each night. The performance on 28 March was devoted to the 'Fund established for the Support of Decayed Musicians and their Families', administered by the Society of Musicians. Some half-dozen other benefit concerts were also advertised, either oratorios or concerts 'of Vocal and Instrumental Musick'. During the summer high-quality instrumental music was on offer nightly at Vauxhall, Marybone and Cuper's Gardens.

In addition to these fully publicised concerts, mostly in the West End, the City supported three well-established musical societies, whose meetings were not advertised. The Academy of Ancient Music met fortnightly at the Crown and Anchor Tavern. Founded in 1726 as the Academy of Vocal Musick, the society's original purpose was for members of the choral foundations to sing older polyphonic music, but it soon expanded in membership and repertoire, with Handel oratorios taking their place alongside motets and madrigals. The two other societies, also founded in the 1720s, met at the Swan Tavern in Cornhill and at the Castle Tavern in Paternoster Row. But like the Academy of Ancient Music, these were essentially gentlemen's clubs, designed for the wealthier bourgeois of the City (according to Hawkins, the Swan concerts were set up by 'a great number of merchants and opulent citizens').[7] Regulations published by the Castle Society in 1751 reveal that it was run as a non-profit-

making exercise by an elected committee; strict rules were applied and fines
levied for infringements. Membership was available to both performers and
auditors, but the performers retained clear control over the proceedings, with
the right to fix the repertoire and nominate new members. Hawkins mentions
that aspiring 'young persons of professions and trades' attended, but certain
categories were statutorily excluded: vintners, victuallers, keepers of coffee-
houses, tailors, peruke-makers and barbers, as well as journeymen and
apprentices. Two important features of such organisations set them apart from
public concerts in the modern sense. First, the performers were drawn from the
membership, apart from some professional stiffening (in the 1740s John Stanley
'despotically reigned' at both the Castle and the Swan).[8] And, second, ladies
were not allowed to subscribe, though ladies' tickets might be made available
to members on a limited basis.

Looking back later, Charles Burney summed up London's concert life in the
1740s as follows:

The only subscription concert at the west end of the town at this time, was at Hickford's
room or dancing-school, in Brewers-street; and in the city, the Swan and Castle
concerts, at which the best performers of the Italian opera were generally employed, as
well as the favourite English singers.[9]

Concerts had begun to be promoted on a more regular basis and with a clearer
sense of programme-planning. The foundations had been laid for later
expansion. But several of the principal institutions were City mens' clubs
designed for amateur performance. The series at Hickford's Room in the West
End was a foretaste of what was to come, but after a similar venture the
following year the idea was abandoned, indicating that the subscription series
was far from an essential feature of the season. It is also noteworthy that
concert programmes of 1740 were typically based around larger vocal works,
with only the briefest mention of any instrumental items.

By 1790 London's musical life had been transformed. The 'rage for music'
was at its height, and both the number and the variety of musical entertainments
far outstrip those of 1740. Table 1 presents a summary of the musical events of
the season, but even this constitutes only a selection: it excludes numerous
private concerts and lesser societies, as well as such informal events as band
concerts in St James's Park.

Out of all this varied musical activity, public interest in music outside the
theatre was largely focussed on the fashionable West End subscription
concerts: 'THE PANTHEON, it is said, means to have a vigorous conflict
with the PROFESSIONAL CONCERT, and to try which will be most
successful in gaining the patronage of the higher circles.'[10] These organisations
were quite different from the men's clubs that Burney identified as at the centre
of London's concert life in the 1740s. Both were run as essentially commercial
exercises, designed to make profits for the organisers – the Pantheon shareholders on the one hand, the orchestral musicians themselves on the other.

Table 1. *Music in London in the 1789–1790 season: the principal organisations*

Theatre	Italian Opera, temporarily removed from the King's Theatre to the Theatre Royal, Haymarket (later Covent Garden Theatre), generally twice a week from 7 January to 17 July (including benefits)
	Plays and English Opera at Covent Garden and Drury Lane Theatres, nightly from 12 September to 16 June; at the Theatre Royal, Haymarket from 14 June to 15 September (including benefits)
	Dibdin's *The Oddities* at the Lyceum, four times a week from 7 December
Modern concert series	Professional Concert: 12 concerts at Hanover Square Rooms from 15 February to 17 May
	Pantheon Grand Concert: 12 concerts from 28 January to 29 April, additional concert on 6 May
Oratorios	Covent Garden Theatre: 11 performances from 19 February to 26 March
	Drury Lane Theatre: 11 performances likewise
Ancient music	Concert of Ancient Music: 12 concerts at Tottenham Street Rooms from 27 January to 5 May
	Academy of Ancient Music: 8 concerts at Freemasons' Hall from 17 December to 8 April
	Handel Festival: 4 morning concerts at Westminster Abbey from 26 May to 3 June, profits to the Royal Society of Musicians, the Sons of the Clergy, Middlesex Hospital
Other societies	Anacreontic Society
	Noblemen and Gentlemen's Catch Club, Madrigal Society, Glee Club
	Handelian Society, Cecilian Society
Benefits	26 concerts (including 9 April for the New Musical Fund with 250 performers, and 18 May Charles Clagget's promotion of newly invented instruments)
Mid-day concerts	Summer performances on the musical glasses by Sormany (from 27 July)
	Organ recitals at the Tottenham Street Rooms and the Pantheon by Vogler (from 1 May), and subsequent demonstrations at Longman and Broderip's factory in Tottenham Court Road
Private concerts	Nobility Concert, Ladies Concert
Court	New Year and Birthday Ode performances at St James's Palace
	Queen's Concerts, sacred concerts at Buckingham House
Church	Feast of the Sons of the Clergy charity at St Paul's Cathedral (rehearsal on 18 May, service on 20 May)
	Anniversary Meeting of the Charity Children at St Paul's Cathedral on 10 June
Gardens	Ranelagh: three evenings a week from 5 April
	Vauxhall: nightly except Sundays from 18 May (gala)

Fully professional orchestras put on programmes based around major symphonic works, and a high public profile was maintained by regular advertisements and copious reviews in the daily press. Attendance was open to any who could afford the 5 guinea subscription, including ladies; the Professional Concert attracted its maximum of 500 subscribers, enabling them to hire singers of international reputation. Thus over the previous half century London musicians had succeeded in creating a market for expensive and high-budget concerts, to which they attempted to lure the public with ever-changing repertoire and personalities. Only two features prevent such major subscription concerts from being regarded as pure unfettered enterprise. First, there were several ways of engineering a suitably select audience; and second, influential patrons such as the Prince of Wales and the Duke of Cumberland played a more-or-less direct part in the formation of artistic policy.

It should not be thought, therefore, that commercial modes of organisation (concerts open to a ticket-buying public, the advertising of enticing novelties) implied a bourgeois cultural leadership. Indeed, the extent of middle-class attendance at West End concerts remains a matter for debate, as will be seen. Furthermore, the City itself maintained a certain artistic independence. Only later did it begin to adapt its institutions in emulation of the West End. The Academy of Ancient Music, for example, had changed by 1790 from a gentlemen's performing club with a missionary zeal for old music into a major subscription series; audiences were now in the hundreds, with ladies allowed to subscribe and entirely professional performers. But this was imitation, not innovation. Modern musical taste was undoubtedly formed by aristocratic patrons in the fashionable end of town. It is therefore dangerous to attempt to explain changes of style in terms of bourgeois taste, citing sensationalist effects, colourful orchestration, catchy folk-tunes and the like. Even élite audiences varied widely in their degree of musical sophistication, and the nobility was quite susceptible to so-called 'bourgeois props', as their reception of Haydn symphonies clearly showed.

A critical factor in the rise of public concerts during this period was not the ability to attract large bourgeois audiences but the establishment of subscription concerts within the fashionable week. The subscription was much more than a convenient method of financial planning, for the expense defined prestige and effected social screening. It was a concept that accorded closely with the ostentatious extravagance of the 1760s and 1770s. Already by 1774 the foremost concert series were well on the way towards a position of social pre-eminence, as a high-society schedule published by *The Public Advertiser* on 4 February makes clear: 'On Monday the Pantheon [Concert], Tuesday the Opera [Italian Opera at the King's Theatre], Wednesday Bach and Abel's Concert, Thursday Almack's [Assembly], and Saturday the Opera again.' In both *Evelina* (1778) and *Cecilia* (1782) Fanny Burney put subscription concerts high on the social agenda of her young heroines. Cecilia's zealously fashionable hostess gave a clear idea of her own priorities in the 1782 season:

Lord, I have done nothing for you yet, and you never put me in mind. There's the ancient music, and Abel's concert; – as to the opera, we may have a box between us; – but there's the ladies concert we must try for; and there's – O Lord, fifty other places we must think of!

Even Bach and Abel could scarcely rival the Italian Opera, but certainly by the 1780s the Professional and Pantheon Concerts ran the Opera a very close second (a position strengthened by legal disputes and by the burning down of the King's Theatre in 1789).

The early 1780s represents something of a watershed in this study. Interest in modern symphonic music was strongly fuelled by the arrival of Haydn's symphonies, scarcely known in London until 1782. The public showed a voracious appetite for new works during the later 1780s, an enthusiasm fanned by Haydn's arrival himself in 1791. It is no coincidence that the 'rage for music' coincided with the very decade up to his departure in 1795. Music came to unprecedented public prominence through widespread reporting in the daily press. The modern orchestral repertoire undoubtedly began to reach a much wider clientele, and the social range of audiences at subscription concerts may even have begun to broaden. The aristocracy responded to these developments in two quite different ways. The first was, paradoxically, to withdraw from the public concert life they had helped to create, in favour of their own select private soirées. Some of these were organised on the grandest scale, with full professional orchestras and top soloists. The second departure was still more radical, involving the creation of a new aristocratic musical culture, as William Weber has shown. In 1776 the Concert of Ancient Music was founded as a serious-minded alternative to modern concerts, with the declared aim of perpetuating musical 'classics' of earlier eras. The resurrection of older music was not in itself new: its study led to the well-known histories of Hawkins and Burney, while the Academy of Ancient Music, the Madrigal Society and the Catch Club were already reviving Renaissance vocal music. But the Concert of Ancient Music had a new function. It contributed to the current redefinition of the aristocracy as responsible guardians of the nation, in a potent statement of artistic leadership. The favoured composer was Handel, and his supposed centenary in 1784 provided an excuse for an elaborate Commemoration on a massive scale, which gave public expression to this leadership. The support of the King, an enthusiast for Handel's music and a consistent opponent of the modern repertoire, added a special cachet. Indeed in the mid 1780s the ancient movement represented a kind of artistic stability, comparable to the establishment of Pitt's government after years of political turmoil; it also accorded with a general social trend towards simplicity of manners and away from the frivolous extravagance widely associated with the upper classes. Thus it was by no means a disadvantage to the instigators that the Commemoration sparked off a popular bout of Handel-mania which contributed as much to the 'rage for music' as Haydn's symphonies over the next decade.

For the musician, London's musical life was dominated by two focal points: the theatres on the one hand, modern and ancient concert organisations on the other. In many ways concerts were not so much an end in themselves as a key to further advancement. The series was only the public face of a complex commercial web in which many interests interlocked. The leading performers usually took an annual benefit concert, at which profits could be so considerable that benefit terms often formed part of a contract. The same performers were in constant demand for the private concerts of the élite, and less prestigious artists sometimes advertised their availability to play at private houses on demand. There was also a strong relationship between concerts and teaching. Some musicians even regarded attracting students as the prime function of public concerts, while conversely scholars themselves formed audiences: the appeal to well-born singing pupils was said to account for the unexpected success of the Vocal Concert in the 1790s. At a lesser level, music-teachers occasionally advertised a subscription concert as part of a combined package. Thus in 1780 the proprietor of a music-school in High Holborn, with several 'Eminent Professors, Foreigners', offered lessons at 1 guinea per month, with (for an extra half a guinea) a private concert every week for pupils and friends.[11] Another major commercial connection involved music-publishing. Typically manuscript music obtained by an impresario would be sold at the end of the season to a publisher who could then advertise it 'as performed at Mr. Salomon's Concert' or the like. Finally, concert promoters sometimes advertised new instruments: Charles Clagget's benefit mentioned in table 1 was unashamedly directed at showing off his inventions.

One consequence of these developments was a sharpening of the distinction between professional and amateur music-making. It is difficult to imagine Viotti in the 1790s leading the largely amateur orchestra of a music club at a City tavern, as Giardini did in the early 1750s. London's concert life became more clearly polarised between professional concerts of the highest quality and purely amateur gentlemen's clubs meeting 'for their own practice or amusement'. It is significant that this period also saw a proliferation of glee clubs, allowing gentlemen of some musical ability the opportunity to join in convivial musical ensembles, perhaps with some professional assistance. One of the most popular societies of the period, the bourgeois Anacreontic Society, actually juxtaposed the two modes – a first-class professional concert to begin the evening, with (after dinner) songs and glees in which members of the society joined. Thus the orchestral concert series, developed by the amateur City club and taken over by professionals for West End society, returned to the City in a new guise emulating aristocratic practice. At both ends of town an essentially passive concert culture had been created, based around professional performance of a new orchestral repertoire and of ancient vocal music. In the latter area a canon of unassailable masterworks was beginning to be recognised. The pattern of London's concert life, if not the detail, was looking increasingly towards future developments.

The social role of
the concert

'An exclusive principle': subscription and ancient concerts

Exclusivity and emulation

Music had long been a way of advertising social status: it had the advantage of involving both conspicuous spending and pretension to good taste. These characteristics led directly to a conscious social grading within London's musical life. Perhaps the distinctions were more overt in the stage sphere, with its clear divisions between Italian Opera and English playhouse, and between boxes, pit and galleries. But a hierarchy was perceived also within concert life, as the following crude assessment in *The Morning Post* for 21 January 1789 indicates: 'The HANOVER-SQUARE [Professional Concert] – QUALITY. The TOTTENHAM-STREET [Concert of Ancient Music] – GENTRY. The FREEMASONS'-HALL [Academy of Ancient Music] – PEOPLE. And the ANACREONTIC [Society] – FOLKS.'

The distinction of audience levels in any case requires great caution, since it impinges on many complex issues of class definition and perception. Social historians have in recent years refined the notion of eighteenth-century society as an hierarchical ladder of infinite mobility in favour of a more broadly structured model. This book will be mainly concerned with the upper reaches of polite society, a broad élite consisting of a number of strands. Of course it included the landed nobility and gentry ('the quality'), but it also incorporated a range of professionals, clergy and men of letters; indeed anyone who could pass himself off as a well-educated gentleman of good bearing. In addition, money opened doors without too many questions, and increasingly London's wealthy urban bourgeois joined this heterogeneous élite. This latter point is critical to a number of features of London's concert life as it is generally perceived, but the complex interrelationships between bourgeois and landed classes are still the object of controversy. Even an élite of broadly shared interest was subject to endless gradations. In particular it remains unclear how far the richest middle classes participated in the social life of the West End; to quote Donna Andrew, 'it is less certain how often the male offspring of the big bourgeoisie, unlike their wealthy heiress relatives, were invited to attend its functions'.[1] Even if top bankers and overseas merchants attended Hanover Square concerts, the reins of taste were firmly in the hands of the higher aristocracy. This applies as much to their unobtrusive influence on modern concerts as it does to the more overt statement of artistic principles embodied in the Concert of Ancient Music. It was a period when the relatively closed ranks of the nobility were attempting to reassert their position in society, with (for example) active involvement in the commercial world. Music they cultivated not so much for its commercial potential as for its role in defining a less tangible cultural status and leadership.

Certainly the principal concerts were aimed at the *bon ton*, and the entire system, to William Jackson's regret, was built on an *'exclusive principle'*.[2] Exclusivity could be engineered in a number of ways. The subscription system in itself was essentially designed for this purpose. More generally, prices could be maintained at an artificially high level, as at the Pantheon, where the half-guinea entrance fee was specifically designed to exclude 'the *Bourgeois'*.[3] Unashamedly explicit restrictions were operated by Mrs Cornelys, who in 1770 celebrated the Queen's birthday with a concert and gala only for peers and peeresses, foreign ministers, subscribers to her assemblies or friends presenting a written order. Less tangible barriers were provided by the expense of transport and fine clothing; even at Ranelagh Gardens Carl Moritz 'saw no one in all that throng who did not wear silk stockings'.[4]

Exclusivity could also be enhanced by restrictions on the availability of the product. Thus in 1791 the 'public at large' was quite unable to see Haydn outside Salomon's high-priced subscription series, until his subsequent appearance at the King's Theatre. Principal performers, often well-known opera singers, might have such restrictions built into their contracts: in 1790 Pacchierotti was not allowed to sing outside the Pantheon at any theatre or other concerts, public or private. Besides making a series more attractive, this practice served to reconfirm the social standing of the select audience. Even private concerts could exploit a similar situation. Harriet Fox Lane (Lady Bingley) patronised the violinist Felice Giardini, who rarely performed in public during the 1760s, and the singer Regina Mingotti: 'With two such performers, the concerts she gave to her choice friends were subjects of envy and obloquy to all those who were unable to obtain admission.'[5] The perpetual search for novelty was an inevitable consequence of the 'exclusive principle': it represented not just a thirst for new sensations but also emphasised status, since the latest foreign arrivals could generally be heard only at the most prestigious venues. Exclusivity had to be carefully nurtured.

Inherent in such a system was the assumption that the high-class product was desirable to those lower down the social scale, and that those outside the 'quality' would try to emulate their superiors in extravagance and taste. Such a process must have applied to London's concert life to some extent, as Thomas Robertson's comments in 1784 suggest: 'In England, not only the higher, but the middle ranks are rich; and riches begetting caprice, call for variety:

foreigners are courted, and old foreigners must give place to new. The lower people have come to have little time for Music.'[6] Numerous barbed satires mock middle-class pretensions to musical taste, especially the archetypal daughter's piano lessons. There is certainly evidence of the widespread appeal of polite culture, with symphonies by composers from Abel to Haydn achieving popularity at Vauxhall. But some cross-currents obscure this mirror. Ambivalence towards the values of fashionable modern concerts and Italian opera resulted in a certain independence of taste even among the higher reaches of the middle classes. In particular they showed a continuing commitment to Handel, resulting in a strange alliance of interest. On the one hand were aristocratic connoisseurs, deliberately adopting the high artistic ground at the Concert of Ancient Music; on the other were the sober-minded middle classes of the Academy of Ancient Music, less conscious of their role, but naturally conservative and admiring of the frugal virtues of Baroque music. Of course some emulation was involved here too, but the Handel vogue of the last two decades took off partly because it tapped into an existing wide base of middle-class support.

A simple model – of musical progress supported by the élite and emulation by the broad middle classes – cannot therefore be sustained. Aristocratic taste itself fragmented into two streams, and at the same time those lower down the scale remained suspicious of certain aspects of upper-class culture.

West End subscription-concert series

The most prestigious concerts, leaving aside ancient music, were the fashionable West End subscription series. These were held mainly within the main winter season (during George III's reign from the Queen's official birthday on 18 January to the King's birthday on 4 June); concerts took place weekly, with a recess around Easter when many of the quality left town. In practice only four days of the week were available, since public concerts could not be held on Sundays and the Italian Opera took up Tuesdays and Saturdays. The number of concerts for a typical 5 guinea subscription varied during the period, but a general reduction can be perceived from twenty around 1750 to twelve by the 1780s. All the series under consideration were widely advertised in the press; indeed this is one of their distinguishing features by comparison with musical societies. Of course, the performers here were fully professional – no true gentleman would exhibit his (usually meagre) instrumental abilities in such a public forum.

The weekly concert series was known in London as early as 1689, and series were promoted sporadically throughout the first half of the century. In 1731, for example, Geminiani advertised a series of weekly concerts at Hickford's old room; and shortly after Hickford moved to Brewer Street in 1738 there was renewed enterprise in a similar vein (one such series has been mentioned above). But the concept was given a considerable boost by the collapse of the

Italian Opera after the 1749–50 season, and by the arrival in 1751 of Felice Giardini, whose modern virtuosity and dynamic leadership transformed musical standards in the 1750s. A number of high-prestige, fully advertised series took place during the early 1750s, notably those at Ogle's room in Dean Street. The most important of these took place on the normal opera nights. The year 1753 saw three rival series: one on Saturdays promoted by Ogle's widow, another on Tuesdays organised by Giardini and the English oboist Thomas Vincent, and a third, less important, on Thursdays. Significantly, subscribers to the main series had been consulted about the regulations to be followed as early as March of the previous season. There was a widespread perception that public entertainments suddenly blossomed at this period; and a French visitor was clearly impressed by London's musical life in the early 1750s: 'In the winter season they have a great many good concerts in London, which are generally supported by subscription.'[7] With the restoration of the Opera in November 1753, however, the idea soon languished. Only one significant series took place between 1756 and 1763: the notorious concerts promoted in 1760 by Ann Ford in defiance of her father's blockade around the theatre.[8] Audiences, perhaps more attracted by the scandal than by her music, were both sizeable and fashionable. But this venture was quite outside the mainstream, and it took a new approach to resurrect the subscription series proper.

A crucial role was played by the colourful figure of Mrs Teresa Cornelys, opera-singer turned society-queen. Having acquired an elegant mansion named Carlisle House in Soho Square, she single-mindedly set about making it the centre of London's fashionable life. Her select group of subscribers, termed 'The Society', met for the first time on 27 November 1760: twelve assemblies took place this season, and similar enticements were offered in succeeding years. Music dominated the first part of the evening: 'The vocal and instrumental music, by an orchestra at the end of the room, begins at seven o'clock and lasts until nine; dancing afterwards goes on until one or two.'[9] A later writer attributed directly to Mrs Cornelys's concerts the transformation of London entertainments – as he saw it, a decline from rational elegance to opulent luxury.[10] He did not fail to point out that she was a foreigner (though one himself), mirroring the view that masquerades were a decadent import from the continent. Mrs Cornelys operated a system that guaranteed exclusivity even more strongly than price: subscribers were required to apply to one of various aristocratic ladies who kept lists for the purpose. When in 1764 she separated off the concerts from Society meetings, this system was retained. Such exclusivity by its very nature diminished the public nature of the concerts (neither performers nor programmes were advertised). Mrs Cornelys's concerts were essentially large-scale soirées.

In 1764 the concerts were directed by Gioacchino Cocchi, but in 1765 there began a famous collaboration between John Christian Bach and Carl Friedrich Abel.[11] The series established the pattern for many years to come – weekly concerts on Wednesdays directed by Bach and Abel in alternation, at a subscription of 5 guineas. It appears that Mrs Cornelys was the promoter of the so-called Bach–Abel concerts for the first three seasons. In 1768, however, the musicians took over the management. They began to advertise the concerts themselves and Bach opened an account at Drummond's Bank; and they transferred the concerts to Almack's new room in King Street, a room already made fashionable by the select assemblies held there. In 1774 the concerts were back in Soho Square, following Mrs Cornelys's precipitous decline from favour, but the following year they moved to a new venue. Bach and Abel had joined in partnership with Giovanni (Sir John) Gallini to build a handsome new room in Hanover Square. Here Gallini promoted assemblies known as 'festinos', somewhat on the lines of The Society, while Bach and Abel continued their concerts much as before, with ladies' lists apparently still in operation.[12] Mrs Harris enthused about the new setting for the concerts: ''Tis a great stroke of Bach's to entertain the town so very elegantly.'[13] At their height the concerts were certainly both socially prestigious and at the forefront of musical development:

As their own compositions were new and excellent, and the best performers of all kinds which our capital could supply, enlisted under their banners, this concert was better patronised and longer supported than perhaps any one had ever been in this country; having continued for full twenty years with uninterrupted prosperity.[14]

But even Burney hints that the programmes lacked variety, and public interest in the concerts dwindled towards their close. One factor in this decline was the rise of successful competition.

In 1774 Bach and Abel were seriously challenged for the first time on their own ground, with the opening of a major series at the magnificent new Pantheon in Oxford Street. There had been other rivals before, but none so ambitious or with such a strong public profile. Under the direction of Mattia Vento and Samuel Arnold, the new series adopted a blatantly anti-German stance by featuring Italian and English music. While the restriction was not maintained in further seasons, the Pantheon concerts retained an Italianate bias. Lucrezia Agujari was twice engaged at great cost to sing Italian songs and in 1780 the series was known as the 'Italian Concert'. At their height the Pantheon concerts were the most fashionable entertainment in London, the Italian Opera always excepted. Evidently the high-risk strategy was successful: Mrs Harris went to the Pantheon just to hear Agujari, noting that 'the best company goes off soon after the concert is over'.[15] For several seasons further competition was provided by a third major series, with the singer-impresario Venanzio Rauzzini playing an important part; and a new kind of opposition emerged with the foundation in 1776 of the Concert of Ancient Music.

Such intense rivalries persisted for much of the rest of the century. After Bach's death the Hanover Square concerts were continued by Abel in 1782 and by the Earl of Abingdon for two further seasons. Abingdon was well known for his radical politics, yet he made the most of his noble rank in an attempt to

Plate 1 The Hanover Square Rooms: engraving from the *Illustrated London News*, 1843 (after alterations and the addition of an organ)

set the concerts at the centre of fashion. Not only did he retain at first the system of ladies' lists, but he also appointed a committee of ten gentlemen subscribers to act as treasurers and to oversee the management of the concerts. This unique venture, a series promoted and financed directly by a nobleman, may well have been a conscious attempt to counteract the aristocratic revivalism of the Concert of Ancient Music; Abingdon went out of his way to obtain and publicise the most modern music (Haydn symphonies) and significantly the principal patron was the Prince of Wales. The musical establishment was surely the most brilliant yet heard in London; Sylas Neville described the orchestra as 'a band of the most distinguished excellence'.[16] Despite unprecedented publicity, however, the public response was only lukewarm; in the summer of 1784 Abingdon resigned the management, blaming the ingratitude and illiberality of the public and £1,600 the worse for his pains. A more radical reorganisation was the setting up in 1785 of the Professional Concert, a co-operative headed by Wilhelm Cramer. After a slow start the organisation had by 1787 achieved fashionable and musical recognition surpassing even the Bach–Abel concerts. William Parke wrote that in 1788 the concerts 'were allowed to be of the most perfect and gratifying kind, the band being composed of performers of the first talent in the kingdom, and the company of the most elegant description'.[17] Dominating musical speculation in this decade was the prospect of Haydn being lured to London, a promise first made by Abingdon in 1782. Even if the promise was not to be realised by the Professionals, their celebrated orchestra based its reputation on the performance of Haydn's symphonies, some of which they received in manuscript from the composer himself.

Opposition to these Hanover Square enterprises was at first muted. In the early 1780s fashion turned away from the Pantheon; Burney (one of the shareholders) thought the proprietors showed lamentable caution.[18] An attempted series at the Freemasons' Hall in 1783 was directly thwarted by Abingdon, who refused to allow his players to participate. Even the engagement of Gertrud Mara for a short series at the Pantheon in 1784 failed to raise enthusiasm: this time Burney blamed the general election. The increasing prestige of the Professional Concert was, however, matched by later alternatives at the height of the 'rage for music' – notably the Pantheon series of 1788 and 1790. These concerts could not match the instrumental brilliance of the Professional Concert, but they boasted singers of outstanding calibre, including Mara herself and Gasparo Pacchierotti.

On several occasions the leader of these alternative series was Johann Peter Salomon. During the 1780s he himself promoted only one short series in 1786, but late in 1790 he pulled off the coup of persuading Haydn to visit London, initiating the most intense rivalry of the period. Like the Professionals, Salomon held his concerts at the Hanover Square Rooms, with Haydn's new symphonies proud centrepieces of the programmes. The Professionals, having failed to entice Haydn away from Salomon with monetary promises, engaged his pupil Pleyel in 1792. But the English public quickly saw through the pretender, and after an unfortunate final season in 1793 the Professional Concert folded. Curiously, Salomon received only moderate support in his first two seasons, but in 1793 (ironically the year between Haydn's two visits) he was dominant: 'We were happy to find, in the number, the fashion, and the elegance of the company who honoured SALOMON's Concert on Thursday, that his indefatigable attention and exertions to secure the favour and patronage of the public, are likely at last to meet with their proper reward.'[19] Salomon's success was obviously based on the presence of Haydn and on his exclusive rights to the new symphonies. His series flourished up to 1794 in spite of a new threat, a completely new kind of subscription concert. In 1792 the English singers Samuel Harrison and Charles Knyvett opened their Vocal Concert, devoted primarily to songs and glees of the English school. Somewhat surprisingly, perhaps, it attracted the same fashionable patronage as the orchestral concerts.[20] Publicly this success was attributed to the number of their singing pupils among the subscribers, but it may be that an English concert reflected the nationalistic mood of the 1790s (even the Opera Concert of 1795 was described by Salomon as a 'National School of Music', meaning a kind of national monument similar to the Royal Academy of Arts).

Contemporaries certainly viewed their own musical life in terms of all these rivalries, which were seen as encouraging healthy enterprise. A 'spirit of opposition' between the Professional Concert and the Pantheon in the 1790 season was deemed beneficial for the exertion it encouraged.[21] More rancorous was the direct confrontation between Haydn and Pleyel, but even this was artistically productive. The Concert of Ancient Music and the Professional Concert were also regarded as competitors for the same subscribers, despite their different aims; while the Vocal Concert provided 'an agreeable contrast' to the instrumental repertoire of other concerts. Similarities with the British system of confrontational politics were not lost on contemporary observers, one of whom likened Salomon to the Opposition party.[22]

Only with the tapering of London's musical life towards the end of the century did the various factions coalesce and overt competition decline. For reasons that will be discussed in chapter 4, London was unable to sustain the same intensity of concert life up to the end of the century. In 1795 a coalition took place, resulting in a single high-prestige series known as the Opera Concert, based at a new room attached to the rebuilt King's Theatre. This united elements from the Opera, the Professionals and Salomon's Concert (choruses too were initially advertised, presumably to be selected from Handel, but these were in fact hived off separately). In 1796 Salomon revived his concert for one season, but otherwise only a single major orchestral series took place each season up to 1800. That in 1799 was a last-minute attempt by Cramer to resuscitate the Professional Concert, but the idea had lost its vitality; and even the Vocal Concert closed after the 1795 season.

One important factor in so competitive an environment was the ticketing system. The ideal had always been a single and expensive subscription with no single tickets available – in order (as one impresario expressed it) 'to continue these Meetings very Select'.[23] Bach and Abel strengthened exclusivity further by the system of ladies' lists. But the whole concept was continually under threat. Almost all promoters allowed subscribers to lend tickets to friends of the same sex, and it was possible to obtain single tickets through newspaper advertisements or from the bookseller Thomas Hookham, who kept a register of customers' requirements. Impresarios railed against these abuses: in 1781 Antonio Sacchini claimed that Hookham made a profit of 1/6 on each ticket and tried to foil him by writing subscribers' names on the tickets.[24] When subscriptions did not match up to expectation, the impresarios themselves made concessions, sometimes offering partial subscriptions as the season progressed; in 1793 Salomon even allowed subscribers to buy single tickets for their friends, thereby filling the Hanover Square room.

There were also more radical departures. The Pantheon proprietors were prepared to maintain exclusivity by price alone. In 1774 they required subscribers to pay 6 guineas for twelve tickets, which could be used on any night: but later in the season single tickets were being sold at 10/6, the only stipulations being that two had to be bought and that they had to be obtained in advance (even these limitations were waived in some later years). Such an experiment was perceived as a risky lowering of social barriers. At one Pantheon concert in 1788, when the audience included more single-ticket holders than subscribers, one observer was relieved to find that 'the etiquette of dress is much attended to there'.[25] A reviewer in 1785 was less circumspect, noting that after a partial subscription was introduced the concerts were 'infinitely more resorted to than before, without any diminution as to the quality of the visitors'.[26] One puff observed still more baldly that the price of half-a-guinea 'prohibits bad company'.[27]

Modern concert series were evidently directed straight at the cream of fashionable society. Advertisements were ritually addressed to 'the nobility and gentry', which is unambiguous enough even allowing for flexibility in the concept of gentry. Who actually attended in practice is a more complex issue. Since subscription lists do not survive, it is impossible to analyse audiences precisely, but newspapers and memoirs do contain sufficient pointers to enable some general observations to be made.

In 1788 Mara's concerts at the Pantheon were 'so crouded with visitors of the higher sort, that it was difficult to procure a seat', while even those lacking titles 'were of the *first class*'.[28] The Professionals were similarly patronised this season, their subscription list being headed by four members of the royal family (the King's brothers, the Dukes of Cumberland and Gloucester and his sons, the Prince of Wales and Duke of York); the organisers did not fail to get this an early mention in the press, since the presence of royalty was both a powerful social magnet and a certificate of quality. No substantial audience lists have been found for 1788, but reviews in 1783 and 1784 give a clear idea of the high society attendance at Hanover Square concerts. These rosters are dominated by peers and their families, alongside a few other titled persons and foreign ambassadors. The latter were an important concert clientele: the support of the *corps diplomatique* was regarded as an attraction for Mara's 1788 series, worthy of advance publicity. Lower down the scale, the less cultured gentry visiting London for the season were mocked in a supercilious review of the 1790 Pantheon concerts ('two airs were very properly translated for the country gentlemen').[29] The Harris family from Salisbury, loyal supporters of the Bach–Abel concerts, might appear to be in this class, except that James Harris was a far-from-philistine member of the squirearchy: nephew of the third Earl of Shaftesbury and M.P. for Christchurch, he was the author of a well-known philosophical study of music.

Many aristocratic patrons were regarded as musical cognoscenti and they played a major role in the formulation of artistic policy, even apart from Abingdon's direct intervention. Private concerts functioned as a preliminary trial. During the 1780s newly arrived foreigners were often heard at the Duke of Queensberry's house. According to Michael Kelly, the Duke was passionately fond of music, 'but his being very blind and very deaf, was certainly somewhat against him';[30] of course the Prince of Wales and other guests did not suffer the same disadvantages. The Prince was undoubtedly the most influential arbiter: he was, for example, widely credited with appreciating Mara's talent before anyone else. New music was tried out in a similar way. Haydn's 'Paris' symphonies were first heard in London at the Prince's Carlton House; he was also responsible for channelling music received from Pleyel to the Professional Concert four years before the composer's arrival. From the composer's point-of-view this process clearly functioned as a kind of market research, as well as a source of advertising. *The Morning Herald* for 13 February 1792 noted that Pleyel had some new symphonies approved 'in the private circles' in order to protect his high reputation. Influence was even exerted at the level of orchestral personnel: William Parke was appointed to the Professional Concert under the auspices of the Duke of Cumberland, according to his own entry in Sainsbury's *Dictionary* of 1824.

Thus to a large extent aristocratic patronage remained both socially and artistically central to the success of subscription concerts. But the social make-up of audiences as a whole remains a matter of speculation. A typical subscription from the 1760s to the early 1790s was 500; an attendance of between 300 and 500 was perhaps normal, though there are reports of audiences of 600 and even higher. The new King's Theatre Room, opened in 1794, was designed to hold 800 people and in 1798 'eight or nine hundred persons of the first rank (all subscribers)' attended the first Opera Concert.[31] This comment cannot be interpreted literally to mean titled or even landed classes, and probably a wide range of the leisured wealthy attended such concerts. But the extent of bourgeois attendance at major subscription concerts remains a matter for debate. The traditional view has held that the rise in public concerts can be attributed to a social broadening of audiences which were based around 'solid (in those days not stolid)' middle classes.[32] This view is in need of qualification. In the first place, one should probably limit consideration to the 'big bourgeoisie', such as Haydn's friend the banker Nathaniel Brassey, and to wealthy professionals. It is by no means clear that the less-aspiring middle classes frequented the Hanover Square Rooms, even when they could afford to do so. Furthermore, the City supported its own musical institutions, which maintained some independence from West End values. Not until 1818 was a City subscription series founded (the City Concerts), and this was regarded as a new departure: 'We could never be brought to understand why the solid opulence of trade should not admit the same opportunities for intellectual cultivation.' The mercantile classes were described as 'an almost entirely new class of protectors of music'.[33] It would be fair to conclude that those bourgeois who regarded themselves as members of polite society might attend subscription concerts, but that for others attendance at such venues would have been anathema. Certainly the growth of public concerts does not necessarily represent as significant a shift in patronage as it might appear at first sight. It would be quite wrong to anticipate nineteenth-century developments by arguing that public symphony concerts developed in response to a new middle-class musical culture.

A slight modification of this picture may be needed, however, in connection with the later years of the century, when some change in tone can be perceived. Indeed the foundation of formal private concerts at aristocratic houses, and even that of the Concert of Ancient Music, suggests a certain dissatisfaction with the audiences and advertising associated with public concerts. Two witnesses hinted at a broadening of the social range in the last two decades:

[The Professional Concerts] were started upon the failure of those of which Bach and Abel were the proprietors, and which had been hitherto supported by lovers of music and the old nobility... They soon found that the subscribers, even by introducing friends for the night, could not support the intention, so they were obliged to admit the gentry.

Pleyel also established Concerts [the Professional 1792] in Opposition to those of Salomon, which were patronized by the Nobility.[34]

The first of these statements, by the notoriously unreliable Mrs Papendiek, is simply misleading: perhaps she recalled Abingdon's abandoning the ladies' list system, or perhaps she was referring to Salomon's decision to admit subscribers' friends in 1793. This apart, both writers clearly perceived some liberalisation of audience-levels. But it is important to stress that neither implies that this was an object in itself. Even Salomon's concerts were directed at the most fashionable clientele, who patronised him in abundance in 1794. He was certainly not responding to middle-class energies, nor was artistic policy

21

directed at satisfying bourgeois tastes, except in so far as such tastes were universally shared. If Salomon's audiences were more broadly based, this was a by-product caused by commercial necessity.

The Concert of Ancient Music and the Handel festivals

As prestigious as the subscription concerts, but in a different way, was the Concert of Ancient Music. The society was founded in 1776 at the instigation of the Earl of Sandwich with an aggressively conservative premise – the promotion of music more than twenty years old. Some organisational features were adopted from the Academy of Ancient Music in the City. Explicitly amateur control was vested in the hands of a board of directors, many of them peers, who presided in turn and selected the programmes. The concerts were not advertised, and membership required intercession with one of the directors (only limited transfer of tickets was permitted). At first some amateur instrumentalists may have taken part, and Sandwich is reputed to have played the timpani. The musical director until 1793 was Joah Bates, Sandwich's protegé and a civil servant, who was celebrated as a gentleman performer of high accomplishment (even if both attributes were questionable). Yet this was in reality no mere musical club. In the first place the Concert was in effect run by the directors as a high-prestige subscription series, without reference to the membership. Ladies were permitted to subscribe. The cost was high (at first 5 guineas, later 8 guineas), and the concerts naturally took place in West End concert halls: the Tottenham Street Rooms, the King's Theatre Room (from 1794), the Hanover Square Rooms (from 1804). Finally, by the late 1780s all the performers were well-known professionals, including some of the most celebrated prima donnas of the day.

More fundamental cultural and social issues were also involved, as William Weber demonstrates in his recent book *The Rise of Musical Classics in Eighteenth-Century England*.[35] The founders undoubtedly saw themselves as protectors of the national taste, their unequivocal aim to sustain or revive traditional musical values; these values were represented mainly by later Baroque music, especially that of Handel. Since true appreciation of these qualities required understanding of the science of music, the Concert cultivated an intellectual cachet that it sought to deny to modern concerts. More generally it represented a conscious campaign against secularity and frivolous pleasure-seeking in favour of an artistic and moral high ground. There were also strong if undeclared social aims during a period of aristocratic resurgence and redefinition. The Concert was associated at an early stage with high social position: a reviewer in *The Public Advertiser* for 14 April 1783 regarded supporters of ancient music as synonymous with the nobility, of both old and new creations. In reality subscribers came from a somewhat broader social spectrum (Weber has shown that only 39 per cent in 1782 came from titled families), and the newspaper paragraph quoted on p. 11 put the social level below that of the Professional

Plate 2   An Interior View of Westminster Abbey on the Commemoration of Handel's Centenary, Taken from the Manager's Box, painting by Edward Edwards (*c.* 1793)

Concert. Nevertheless the organisation was evidently intended to perpetuate traditional values and to provide a focal point for the cohesion of the aristocracy, in a deliberate and self-conscious closing of ranks. More subtly it attempted to link taste for great music of the past with the social élite, creating what Weber calls the 'powerful social myth' of the congruence of class and taste. It is significant that whereas ladies controlled admittance at the Bach–Abel concerts men of learning took this role at the Concert. Another factor that deserves to be stressed is the considerable proportion of English music heard here, especially if one includes Handel oratorio extracts: while Italian music was not excluded, this was a clear assertion of principle at a time when most modern concerts did not even hint at the English repertoire.

It would be a mistake, however, to assume that audiences at the Concert and at modern concerts were entirely separate, different as the two ideologies may have been. In 1785, when the King began to attend the Concert, there was a sharp rise in the number of subscribers from 258 to 373, with 'most of the fashionable world' subscribing also to the Professional Concert.[36] Even some of the directors attended modern concerts: three of the eight, including the ardent Handelian Sir Watkin Williams Wynn, heard Mozart and Haydn symphonies at the first Professional Concert of 1788.[37] In the same year the Prince of Wales subscribed to both organisations. In fact the King's patronage incorporated the Concert into the court calendar, with all that that entailed in terms of formal ceremony and a sense of aristocratic duty. The King also insisted on seeing programmes in advance and he exerted influence on the appointment of performers.[38] Though diarists sometimes complained that the evenings were long and heavy, the attraction of the King's presence maintained the society's popularity to the end of the century and beyond: by 1800 the number of subscribers had risen to 572.

The Concert of Ancient Music was the inspiration behind the famous Handel Commemoration of 1784 and its successors in 1785–7 and 1790–1. Each season ended with festivals of four gargantuan midday performances at Westminster Abbey, with programmes of oratorio selections, *Israel in Egypt* and *Messiah*; in 1784 a secular evening concert at the Pantheon was added. This year at Westminster Abbey there were 525 performers, both professional and amateur; by 1791, when Haydn attended, numbers had reached 1067 (among them William Gardiner, the Leicester manufacturer, who hired a violin at a London shop).[39] Each year the massive profits were split between various charities, with the largest share reaching the (Royal) Society of Musicians. The first festival, attended by the entire royal family, was greeted with a universal enthusiasm that London's musical life had never remotely witnessed before. Newspapers and magazines were awash with lively anticipation before the event and fulsome reviews after it. Numerous diarists and letter-writers recorded their impressions of these festivals; indeed the set-piece description became almost a test of literary elegance. Anna Seward, visiting from Lichfield in 1786, provided a typical example:

The single airs have perhaps been heard to greater advantage in smaller rooms, but the sublimity of the harmonies in overture, concerto, symphony and chorus, exhibiting all those splendid effects which their great author conceived, but which the then but emerging state of general musical knowledge made it impossible he should hear with his mortal ears, – the exclusion of everything harsh and disagreeably noisy, by the care taken that, in an orchestra consisting of 750 performers, no order of instruments or voices should preponderate: the exquisite softness with which the single songs, duets and trios, were accompanied by a few selected instruments of perfect skill – the picturesque effect of several of the choruses, which caused the ear to perform the office of all the other senses – the brilliant appearance of an audience, consisting of more than 3,000 well-dressed ladies and gentlemen – the presence of the Monarch, surrounded by his lovely family, while 'at his left hand stood the Queen in a vesture of needlework' – the grave bishops in their black robes, extending in a sable line on each side the royal pair, and encircled by the flower of the English nobility, – these things combined equalled all the demands of my imagination, which had been busy and bold with the subject.[40]

Most observers mention the rapt silence in the Abbey, and the musical impact of these vast performances undoubtedly defied the sceptics. There still remained one or two doubters: in *The Task* (1785) William Cowper voiced a passionate disapproval of the use of Westminster Abbey to venerate a composer. But almost all who recorded their impressions of the Handel festivals were profoundly moved by the experience.

More fundamentally, as Weber has demonstrated, these festivals took on the function of a national ritual. At one and the same time, they provided a focus matched only by a coronation for a confirmation of establishment values, based around a conservative political consensus, the Anglican church and (by extension) an appeal to British patriotism. After traumatic years of political instability and the loss of the American colonies, such demonstrations of national loyalty became ever more relevant as the ruling classes abroad came increasingly under threat. The ceremonial aspect tended to reinforce an established social order hallowed by tradition, an implication that the King was quick to appreciate. While the Commemoration was directly inspired by three Handelians at the Ancient Concerts and organised by the Society of Musicians, George III proved a more than acquiescent patron in all this. Though Weber's view that 'there is little evidence that the King had much special interest in Handel prior to the Commemoration' is an exaggeration,[41] his penchant moved now from a private hobby to a public affirmation. Indeed the festivals were the most conspicuous example of propagandist royal pageantry in the 1780s, counterpointing the deliberate simplicity of George III's private life-style.[42] Significantly, it was the King who wanted to maintain the festival when the directors sought to discontinue it in 1792. In the end, instead of insisting on an Abbey performance he decided to support the Royal Society of Musicians directly at a single Handelian benefit at St Margaret's, Westminster.[43] Similar performances took place at various venues until the end of the century.

The purely musical results of the Handel festivals were immeasurable. There was an immediate impact on London concert programmes and on the size of performing forces. More lasting was the confirmation of Handel's music in the canon of classical masterworks, at a time when his reputation was just beginning to fade. Provincial festivals, on which the Commemoration had partly been modelled, were in turn revitalised and musical life in the

Plate 3   An Inside View of the Pantheon exhibiting their Majesties Box &c. as fitted up under the direction of Mr. James Wyatt, for the Commemoration of Handel, engraving by William Angus after John Dixon (1784)

nineteenth century was profoundly affected. Even at the time concern was expressed about the possible petrifying effect of the Commemoration: William Jackson suggested in 1791 that other composers might be represented, and there was talk of an Arne festival.[44] But by this stage the pattern was set.

Other types of concert

In terms of social cachet, the various subscription series, and later in the century the Concert of Ancient Music, were undoubtedly London's principal concert organisations; and to a large extent they also set the musical agenda. But all sorts of other concerts were promoted at a range of different venues in London, some attended by the *haut ton*, others distinctly below the salt. These include oratorio series following the tradition established by Handel, concerts at City musical societies and at the pleasure gardens, and innumerable benefits put on by individual musicians at each level of London's concert life. In addition, private concerts of every degree of elaboration were organised by the wealthy, with the royal family proving among the most active patrons.

Oratorio series

More ambiguous in social standing than either subscription concerts or the Concert of Ancient Music were the oratorio series at the playhouses, presented usually on Wednesdays and Fridays during Lent.[1] The standard range of prices – from 10/6 down to 3/6 – allowed a much wider audience-range than any of the concerts so far considered (even though these prices were around double those of a normal play). Handel's oratorio seasons had threatened to fall between two poles, appealing neither to aristocratic devotees of sensual Italian opera, nor to those of puritanical inclination who objected to sacred topics in the theatre.[2] But the hybrid genre was enthusiastically accepted by a more middle-class audience, following the abandonment of the subscription concept in 1747 and the jingoistic association of *Judas Maccabaeus* with the defeat of the Young Pretender. The momentum was maintained through the 1750s, and after Handel's death the torch passed to John Christopher Smith, John Stanley and later Thomas Linley. Against all precedents, however, Handel's works proved indestructible, with new oratorios seldom lasting more than a single season.

To some extent the oratorio series may be regarded as the preserve of the middle classes. It is tempting to suggest that the oratorio concept itself suggests moderation: the blend of entertainment with moderate evangelicalism, of modest vocal virtuosity with solid choral tradition, of foreign musical sophistication with homespun English qualities. The price-levels also represent an intermediate social position: varied enough to attract a broader clientele, yet 'too exorbitant to be afforded by the generality of the Frequenters of Play-houses'.[3] Indeed the two English theatres, situated between West End and City, were always regarded as a meeting-ground for social diversity. On the other hand, cognoscenti apart, the modish upper reaches of society viewed the genre with some disdain. In 1771 Mrs Harris remarked with some sarcasm on a rare visit by her daughter to the oratorio, 'a great condescension for so Italianised a lady'; four years later her daughters were 'too refined' for Handel.[4] Only in 1773 was this general pattern broken, when the enchanting voice and personal charms of Elizabeth Linley attracted all to Drury Lane:

> One of those whims by which the public are continually influenced, has made it the *ton* to resort to this theatre to hear and see Miss Linley, the syren of Bath. This young lady who is greatly indebted to nature for the *éclat* with which she is followed, and not a little to the fortuitous concurrence of remarkable incidents in her life has drawn crowded houses incessantly; and this success has been insured by the constant attendance of his Majesty and the Royal family at this theatre.[5]

Thirteen years later this series was still being recalled as the most successful ever.[6]

Two additional factors influenced audiences at the oratorios. The first was competition. Several English oratorio composers put on rival series, including Thomas Arne (even during Handel's lifetime) and Samuel Arnold. From 1768 to 1778 two series operated on identical nights, and in 1773 there was a third. By contrast with subscription concerts, opposition oratorio series usually undercut with lower prices. When in 1768 Arnold first introduced playhouse prices (5/- to 1/-) such crowds were attracted that the money-takers were unable to keep control.[7] Despite such measures, however, these alternative schemes rarely attracted success. Arne's oratorios were 'so unfortunate, that he was always a loser whenever they were performed'.[8] Even Arnold was unable to compete successfully because of high expenses and the 'opposition of Court interest'.[9] Nevertheless the fact that so many series were attempted must indicate a still-vital oratorio culture at this time.

A second factor was the appearance of the King. Although George II had by 1750 stopped attending Handel's oratorio seasons, George III was a keen patron of Handel's successors up until 1785. His support of Smith and Stanley may have originated as a reward for a trivial service,[10] but it undoubtedly matched his artistic preferences. Royal command performances were always advertised in the press and many are the references to their drawing-power. When in 1775 the King transferred his patronage to an alternative Handel series put on by Bach and Abel, Stanley played to poor houses except on the single evening when the King reverted to Drury Lane.[11] The King's attendance alone was not,

Plate 4 An oratorio performance at Covent Garden Theatre, drawing by A. van Assen (late eighteenth century)

however, sufficient to ensure success. Five years earlier Bach had taken the unusual step of promoting Italian oratorios at the King's Theatre. The King attended at the instigation of his wife, but the English public shunned the combination, resulting in an oft-repeated anecdote ('I have no wish to intrude on his Majesty's privacy').[12] It is indeed possible that Londoners were delivering a mild rebuke to the monarch for his desertion of the home-grown product.

For all the continuing appeal of Handel's music, public taste was not immutable. In the twenty-five years after his death, certain works became established favourites while others disappeared from the repertoire entirely (there were no performances at all of *Belshazzar*). *Messiah* had already gained a special status and the vogue for the war-mongering *Judas Maccabaeus* persisted. But in general the tide was against Handel's biblical oratorios, even if *Samson* and other Old Testament dramas were never completely forgotten. Instead the lighter secular works (*Alexander's Feast, L'Allegro, Acis and Galatea*) were clearly favoured. A reviewer in 1782 thought the latter Handel's most popular work, while deeming all three 'equally acceptable to the Man of Music and the miscellaneous Man'.[13] He also approved the series' schedule which started with such works and moved 'in due Gradations' through *Solomon* and *Samson* to close with *Messiah*. Increased prominence was also accorded to instrumental concertos between the acts – not only organ concertos in the Handelian tradition, but often virtuoso showpieces performed by imported soloists. A more ominous development was the practice of making selections from the oratorios. Admittedly Handel had initiated the concept with his *Occasional Oratorio* (1746), but this had had a special purpose. When in 1763 John Brown selected music from Handel and others to fit his libretto *The Cure of Saul*, the ostensible object was to exemplify the author's theory of the narrative ode, yet a subsidiary aim was to obviate complaints about the unevenness of Handel's works. Several new libretti were fitted out with Handel selections in ensuing decades; even the Concert of Ancient Music unambiguously put on miscellaneous programmes.

Despite all these experiments, support for public oratorios was waning by the early 1780s. Writing in 1807, John Marsh recalled 'the languor, with which the oratorios of Handel were carried on in Lent a little more than twenty years ago'.[14] Attendance had declined drastically: on 24 March 1784 when *Acis and Galatea* was performed at Drury Lane, 'the House, to the Disgrace of our idle People, was very indifferent indeed'.[15] It seems likely that the oratorio season would have died altogether had it not been for the Handel Commemoration. Even this did not inspire an immediate revival, since it invited unwelcome comparisons, but an astute move enabled Arnold to capitalise on the latest enthusiasm. For his 1786 series he adapted music from the Commemoration programmes to a new libretto entitled *Redemption*; it was an immediate success, and complete oratorios were declared out of fashion. The way was paved for the miscellaneous selections that dominated the series of the 1790s, both those promoted by Linley and Arnold and those of Samuel Harrison and John

Ashley. Meanwhile prices settled at or near the playhouse level, and oratorio series inescapably took on a populist tone far removed from their original conception, especially as arias and ballads began to be included. In 1786 the Concert of Ancient Music endeavoured to return the genie to the bottle by promoting public performances of complete Handel oratorios, including the great biblical dramas – but at full price which 'cannot be afforded by that class of people, who usually frequented the galleries',[16] the venture did not survive beyond 1788. *Messiah* apart, hardly a single complete biblical oratorio by Handel could be heard at the playhouses during the 1790s. Even the choral masterpiece *Israel in Egypt* did not benefit from its revival at the Handel festivals: a single performance on 13 April 1791 unusually incorporated amateur singers from the Handelian and Cecilian Societies, but this anticipation of the oratorio's future role was not followed up.

Bourgeois concerts: the City

George Rudé has observed that 'it would be misleading to suggest that London's intellectual and cultural life, or even its fashions, its sports and entertainment, were solely dictated by the nobility and gentry or by "the polite end of the town"'.[17] Bourgeois society did indeed support a flourishing musical culture, centred on the City. This culture maintained a profile distinct in many ways from that associated with fashionable society. The principal concerts here began essentially as gentlemen's societies, with members participating in the performance. Newspapers of the 1750s and 1760s contain numerous invitations to membership of such societies, which usually met at City taverns; a few met in the West End, probably reflecting the significant bourgeoisie involved in servicing the upper classes rather than the latter themselves.[18] The grandest City organisation was the Castle Society described in chapter 1: it continued until at least 1775, with various changes of venue and a reduction to twelve concerts.[19] Other important societies were the King's Arms Concert (the former Swan Concert, last advertised under a different name in 1763); and the St Caecilian Society, in existence at least from 1753 to 1759. These last three all employed some professionals, but they could not (nor did they wish to) rival the international profile of the West End subscription concerts. Indeed, it would be a mistake to confuse the aspirations of the two types of concert. The City maintained a strong sense of its own identity and it eschewed what it regarded as the extravagant frivolity of the West End. One foreign visitor noted that there was 'a kind of hatred between the inhabitants of each'; another attended a ball at Haberdashers' Hall where the subscribers were all 'City men, as nobody from the Westminster side is admitted'.[20] Significantly it was local opposition that forced Mrs Cornelys to abandon a plan for a City assembly room in 1766.[21] The more sober virtues of City music included careful fiscal management by committees (who tended to mistrust expensive foreign musicians) and a less ostentatious repertoire stressing British values (in 1756 under the direction of Arne the St Caecilian Society was designated 'for English Musick'). Nor were modernity and novelty worshipped here as in the West End: all these societies seem to have mixed tried-and-tested favourites with newer music where they could obtain it. This antisensual moderation, tinged with a certain innate conservatism, naturally contributed to the continued vogue for Handel oratorios. City men may have aped the pretensions of the nobility in many respects, but they maintained some independence when it came to musical taste.

The City was not entirely immune to change, however, and from the 1770s the style of the West End did begin to impinge on musical life there. The popular Anacreontic Society, run 'by a set of bankers and merchants', provides a striking example.[22] It had been founded in 1766, as a small dining-club meeting at the London Coffee House on Ludgate Hill; songs and glees were provided by the members, as well as some instrumental music. But by the 1780s the organisation had grown out of all recognition, and a modern symphonic concert had been added, as William Parke described:

The meetings were held in the great ball-room of the Crown and Anchor Tavern in the Strand, once a fortnight during the season, and the entertainments of the evening consisted of a grand concert, in which all the flower of the musical profession assisted as honorary members. After the concert an elegant supper was served up; and when the cloth was removed, the constitutional song, beginning, 'To Anacreon in Heaven,' was sung by the chairman or his deputy. This was followed by songs in all the varied styles, by theatrical singers and the members; and catches and glees were given by some of the first vocalists in the kingdom.

R. J. S. Stevens recalled that after midnight the proceedings declined to 'Improper Songs, and other vicious compositions'; nevertheless the earlier part of the evening showed a marked similarity to West End concerts. Indeed the concert was performed by London's very best instrumentalists, and both repertoire and musicians were tried out here before exposure to 'more fashionable *amateurs*' at the Professional Concert.[23] Clearly the Anacreontic Society was becoming more of a subscription concert (audiences of 400 are recorded in the late 1780s). This impression is confirmed by the admittance of ladies to the first part of the evening. But a reviewer in 1789 hinted that they overstayed their welcome by not leaving after the concert, and there were similar complaints in later years. This factor eventually caused the dissolution of the society in 1794, when the presence of the Duchess of Devonshire (albeit concealed on a platform) acted as an unwelcome restraint on the after-dinner singing.

A similar transformation from gentlemen's amateur club to professional concert series overtook the Academy of Ancient Music. The society was also directed largely at the monied middle classes: the subscribers were also 'chiefly bankers and merchants from the city', 'the Mercantile Interest'.[24] Already in 1749 auditors were admitted, but an attempt soon afterwards to engage first-class performers failed, through 'the great increase of late years in the number of places of public diversion, and the consequent increase in the demands of eminent performers'.[25] Radical change had to wait until the 1780s. Most significant was the admittance of ladies, first in 1780 as guests, then in 1788 as subscribers (this year the subscription was set at 280, each paying 5 guineas); at one concert in 1792 there were ten ladies to each gentleman.[26] In 1784 the society moved to the more commodious Freemasons' Hall, and certainly by the later 1780s the performers were entirely professional. Indeed the Academy began to resemble the Concert of Ancient Music in many ways, and in the late 1780s the Marquis of Carmarthen (subsequently the Duke of Leeds) was a director at both societies. But these grandiose aspirations only resulted in financial straits and disagreements among the management. In part the crisis reflected a financial inability to achieve the very best performance standards, a situation exacerbated by the lack of proper rehearsal. A chorus of press complaints during 1789 resulted in the replacement of the long-serving Benjamin Cooke by Samuel Arnold and the appointment of Salomon as leader; and standards do seem to have improved in the 1790s. But more fundamentally the society had lost its sense of mission. No longer featuring serious Renaissance music, the programmes mirrored the late Baroque focus of the Concert, but with a more permissive streak (Haydn symphonies were introduced by 1787). Ultimately the Academy failed to match the West End concerts that it increasingly imitated, and in 1796 it reverted to its 'original plan' with a limited number of subscribers meeting at the Crown and Anchor once more; no reference has been found after 1797.[27]

Professionalism was clearly spreading from the West End. Revealingly, and uniquely for such an eminent performer, Wilhelm Cramer promoted two benefits in the City in 1786 and 1788: both were specifically directed at 'his Musical Friends and Patrons in the City', the second attracting his numerous 'friends of the Anacreontic Society'. One reviewer saw this as a valuable new initiative, pontificating that 'the *Sons of Commerce*' would surely be inspired in the future 'to patronize what must necessarily tend to the credit of themselves'.[28] Also in 1788, John Hindmarsh directed an oratorio series at the ill-fated Royalty Theatre in the East End. Yet the general picture of bourgeois musical activity is an ambiguous one. Some commentators in the 1780s perceived a general tide of emulation flowing eastwards, with the concerts just considered merely at the top of a pyramid:

Music is every where the rage – it has spread from the West to the East, and a very elegant concert was given a few evenings ago at a butcher's near Leadenhall-market... *Three-penny* Concerts in a Hay-loft, and *Six-penny* Sunday Concerts, at a common Public-house, are proofs that the rage for Music is extending from the higher to the *lowest* classes of society.[29]

In 1783 John Marsh recorded in his diary a visit to just such a club, where glees and songs were performed alongside overtures and the like through a fog of pipe-smoke. Yet if one were to judge from newspaper advertisements there was a significant decline in the number of City musical societies during the last quarter of the century (the Castle Society is not known after 1775). This may reflect a demand for more professional standards on the one hand and for purely amateur enjoyment on the other. Most of the clubs listed in Doane's *Musical Directory* of 1794 were devoted to amateur performance of ancient and English vocal music. Besides the continuing Madrigal Society, these included the Glee Club (started in 1783 as a bourgeois imitation of the Catch Club, and constituted in 1787), and several amateur choral societies. This was a new concept of the 1780s, mirroring current fashion in an attempt to satisfy 'a taste for the sublime Choruses by Handel and other composers'. The Handelian Society and the Cecilian Society were the most prominent, but other societies in outlying districts of Marybone and Southwark are also listed.

An impression of the decline in the traditional type of gentlemen's club is reinforced by Henry Angelo's comments, published in 1828:

About this period [*c*. 1780] there were several musical societies and concerts, held at certain taverns on the east of Temple-bar. I remember one, at the Old Queen's-Arms tavern, situated on the north side of Newgate-street, to which, on Thursday nights, admission was obtained by tickets at two shillings each. The performers at this time were in part professional, and others were amateurs... Latterly, the society sunk into second and third-rate performers, and I believe the concerts ceased about thirty years ago... Up to within the last half century, there were, perhaps, ten or a dozen musical meetings, private and public, held weekly 'within the sound of Bow-bells'.[30]

Angelo looked back on these days as a golden age of conviviality and high musical standards: we should perhaps be wary of taking his nostalgic memories as an objective assessment. But the 1827 edition of Thomas Busby's *Dictionary of Music* also refers to the 'Amateur Concert' for non-professionals and their friends as a thing of the past.

Benefit concerts

Each season numerous individual benefit concerts were held, with as many as thirty advertised in the 1792 winter season. Frequently these benefits were the offspring of the regular organisations, and accordingly audiences closely mirrored those discussed above. Clearly at the top were high-prestige benefits, usually closely related to the principal modern series. Apart from slight differences in programme emphasis, these concerts were largely indistinguishable from those of the parent organisation. Similarly highly priced at half a guinea a ticket, they were aimed at an identical market:

The concerts in London are allowed to be very grand, and the English in general prefer them to the music of the opera-house; but as the price of a ticket is half-a-guinea, none but the higher ranks can receive any gratification from them.[31]

The benefit was traditionally regarded as a public reward for long service, to be promoted with seemly reluctance. Benefitees were expected to hawk round tickets to patrons' private houses, thus attracting an audience largely known to them; a card which William Lee presented on such occasions is preserved in the Banks Collection. Generous patrons might add a substantial gratuity, as at Giardini's last benefit in 1792 when the Dukes of Gloucester and Dorset each presented the violinist with £100. But as the century progressed the relationship changed somewhat in tone, if not in essence. A report in 1792 suggested that whereas performers formerly used to wait on patrons and entreat their protection, now they condescended to announce a benefit solely to oblige their friends.[32] Indeed the benefit system began to be regarded as a 'tax on the nobility', with many of the top performers taking a benefit each year as if by right.

As ancient music entered the fashionable calendar (especially from 1785) and English vocal music followed suit in 1792, benefit promoters needed to keep an eye on various constituencies. Often they were themselves involved in the different musical spheres, and programmes then presented a more variegated mixture of modern, ancient and English music. In 1788, for example, Mrs Billington was praised for her mix of ancient and modern items, as much for the broadening of the audience as for the variety of the programme.[33] Such a blend is particularly clear in the 1790s programmes of Wilhelm Cramer, leader at the Italian Opera, the Professional Concert and the Concert of Ancient Music. A link between ancient and English music was made evident at Charles Knyvett's benefit on 9 May 1794, the programme advertising pieces from both the Concert of Ancient Music and the Vocal Concert; Knyvett is indeed a striking example of a minor English singer achieving a high-profile benefit in a way that would have been inconceivable twenty years earlier.

Benefits were put on for a wide variety of other causes, besides London's principal performers. Prodigies' names could be used to attract attention, even if (as with the Mozarts) the proceeds went towards family expenses. Some prestigious benefits were overtly charitable. They might be promoted by individuals appealing for sympathy: the singer Tenducci imprisoned for debt, or the Colla brothers 'lately relieved from Slavery in Algiers'; victims of fires and other misfortunes; aristocrats fallen on hard times. Among the latter was the well-born French emigrée Madame de Sisley, whose plight in having actually to sing herself was regarded as the height of misfortune – though sympathy was mixed with a certain Francophobic amusement. Other recipients were deserving groups, ranging from victims of a hurricane in the West Indies to unpaid singers and dancers at the Opera. Sylas Neville found not a seat to be obtained at the latter concert, but the following day a benefit for the Westminster Lying-In Hospital was less successful: 'Pity their great exertions this evening did not draw a greater crowd as they were for a Charity, but with too many of the rich & powerful that is a reason for staying away upon such occasions.'[34]

In addition there were several regular opportunities for musical philanthropy, in an age when conspicuous support for charities co-existed with
manifold social injustice. The Society of Musicians promoted a grand annual
concert from 1739 to 1784 in aid of its musicians' benefit fund. Most of these
concerts took place at the King's Theatre, with a three-part programme
performed by the Italian Opera singers and orchestra; some years between 1759
and 1769 an English oratorio was offered instead, no doubt responding to
pressure from members such as Arne and Arnold. In 1785 the society was
allowed to style itself Royal, at the same time as the annual concert was
subsumed into the Handel festivals discussed above. In 1786 a rival organisation
(the New Musical Fund) was founded by Philip Hayes of Oxford and Edward
Miller of Doncaster, nominally to cater for provincial musicians, but also
reflecting some dissatisfaction with the Society.[35] It proved a rival in other
respects also, effectively taking over the annual benefit with a largely modern
repertoire.

The close alliance between church and music in the cause of charity can be
traced back at least to 1655, when St Paul's Cathedral began to host fund-
raising services in aid of the Corporation of the Sons of the Clergy. The service
soon became an annual festival with elaborate music, orchestrally accompanied.
By 1760 the music of Purcell had been displaced by that of Handel and Boyce;
the programme thereafter changed very little to the end of the century, but both
the event itself and the public rehearsal two days earlier were akin to a public
concert. It was a type of fund-raising particularly favoured by London
hospitals, some of which expanded the idea in the second half of the century to
encompass oratorios or sacred selections (matching the development of
provincial cathedral festivals). Most famous were the midday performances of
Messiah at the Foundling Hospital.[36] During Handel's lifetime audiences often
numbered well over 1,000; indeed so many people were sold tickets for the first
performance in 1750 that they could not all be accommodated, and a repeat had
to be organised. After Handel's death, Smith and others took over the
management, but audience-numbers went into decline; and after a brief revival
when the Linley sisters were engaged in 1773 the tradition petered out in 1777.
Similarly long-lived were concerts in aid of the Lock Hospital, a venereal
hospital with a strong Methodist background. Handel was also involved in the
early 1750s, but the guiding light here was Giardini, whose oratorio *Ruth* (on
an appropriate story of female industry rewarded) formed the Lock's answer to
Messiah. John Wesley attended the performance in 1765, finding the sense
admirable, the poetry 'not contemptible' and the music 'exquisite'.[37] By this
date oratorio had already become established as the medium for charitable
rather than personal benefits; another oratorio specially written was John
Abraham Fisher's *Providence*, first performed in aid of the Middlesex Hospital in
1777.

At an intermediate level were those benefits given in the West End or at the
theatres with tickets at 5/- or so. Often these were promoted by British

musicians, such as the Welsh harpist Evans, who organised a mid-price benefit most years from 1753 to 1787. In 1767 Thomas Arne unveiled a new kind of concert programme, directly emulating the Catch Club by selecting catches and glees from their collection: his first concert took place at Ranelagh, but in later years they were given at theatres with prices around the playhouse level. Less prestigious in general were City benefits held at livery company halls or tavern rooms. Often these must have been put on by performers at societies as yet unidentified: the British musician John Hindmarsh, for example, took several benefits in the City during the 1780s, leading the orchestra though a mere viola-player at West End concerts. Typical of the 5/- City benefit was one given by the minor organist Thomas Curtis at the Paul's Head Tavern in 1783; the programme was enlivened with his imitations of the horn and bassoon, sung to his own harpsichord accompaniment. But musicians evidently avoided giving concerts in the City if something better turned up. The prodigy Miss Casson, for example, announced that she had cancelled her City concert as she had too many private concerts to attend.[38] Consistent information on benefit concerts at a lower level is hard to procure. A few were advertised at 3/- and below, but there can be no doubt that all kinds of miscellaneous concerts took place in the City and in London's suburbs of which we shall for ever remain ignorant. For what purpose, for example, was a symphony by John Wall Callcott played at the General Post Office, Lombard Street?[39]

Miscellaneous and garden concerts

The events so far considered have been mostly formal evening concerts. Other types of musical entertainment were more relaxed and they attracted less clearly defined social groups. One such type mixed the spoken word with music. Some of these entertainments – Christopher Smart's bizarre 'Old Woman's Oratory', mixing satire and burlesque musical items; Charles Dibdin's one-man shows with songs at the piano – can scarcely be considered concerts at all.[40] But the 'Attic Evening's Entertainment', promoted in 1769 by Thomas Sheridan, was a serious attempt to intermingle oratory with musical items; he even went some way towards relating the two, though since the beneficiary was an academy for the teaching of English the music was clearly there to sugar the pill. One observer considered the idea a model of rational entertainment, by contrast with Mrs Cornelys's Society,[41] and clearly Sheridan hoped to attract some of the educated classes to the Haymarket Theatre. Others followed his initiative in the 1770s, but during the 1780s promoters such as Lacy and Trew abandoned any intellectual pretensions in favour of a more populist tone: both the choice of items and the style of advertising reveal that they were now aiming at a middle-brow audience.

Formal concerts during the daytime required the special permission of the Lord Chamberlain. Most daytime concerts were therefore quite different in nature, being marketed as exhibitions and appealing to audiences of all classes as such events customarily did. In much the same way as curiosities such as 'the Learned Pig' or a mechanical chess-player, the young Mozart was in 1765 put on display, carrying out keyboard tricks, playing the harpsichord with a handkerchief over his hands, and so on. The performances took place initially at the Mozarts' Soho lodgings, later at the decidedly down-market Swan and Hoop Tavern in Cornhill. Mozart was in fact contributing to a spate of daytime concerts in the early 1760s, coinciding with a fashion for the musical glasses; thus in 1761 one Drybutter could be heard at his house every day from noon until two o'clock, playing ten tunes to each set of company for 1/-. The glasses were one of the instruments of Ann Ford, who (contrary to some reports) reappeared at the Spring Garden Room giving half-a-crown daytime appearances from 15 October 1761 onwards. Another prominent daytime performer during this decade was Marianne Davies, who featured Benjamin Franklin's new waterless musical glasses; an additional incentive on one occasion in 1762 was the presence of three Cherokee chiefs, who were hawked round numerous venues this summer. There is every indication that some of these daytime performances attracted a certain percentage of the *ton*; in *The Vicar of Wakefield* (1766) Goldsmith introduced the musical glasses as a topic of fashionable conversation. But the vogue for such displays soon waned, and only occasional curiosities were featured in later decades: exhibitions of the prodigy William Crotch in 1779 and 1785, and the extraordinarily flamboyant secular organ recitals pioneered by Georg Joseph Vogler at the Pantheon in 1790.

Social boundaries were also blurred at the summer garden concerts. Indeed this feature was often remarked with surprise by foreign visitors: even at Ranelagh 'contrary to the custom which generally prevails in England, no distinction is made between the several classes'.[42] Certainly it was here that good-quality music was most readily available to a wide cross-section of the London public. Many of London's best-known singers and instrumentalists could be heard at the gardens, if not the very top stars, and entrance was cheap.

Many gardens in and around London – spas and tea-gardens such as Bagnigge Wells and White Conduit House – had long rooms where an organist entertained the crowds; but these were essentially daytime resorts, popular on Sundays. The best music was promoted by the evening gardens. Vauxhall opened in its modern form in 1732 and three years later the famous open-air 'orchestra' was built; the music wafted over the crowds standing nearby or sitting at supper-tables (in poor weather a Long Room was opened). Both Cuper's Gardens and Marybone were soon imitating the idea: in 1738 the Marybone proprietor engaged an orchestra to play every evening from six until ten 'Eighteen of the most celebrated Concerto's, Ouvertures, and Airs'. Curiously, vocal music was a later addition at these venues, perhaps through concern for tradition and acoustics: only in 1744 were songs introduced at Marybone 'to please those who are fond of vocal music', to be followed a year later by Vauxhall. Music at Ranelagh started rather differently. Here the focus was the enormous rotunda, with the orchestra initially placed in the centre,

Plate 5   The rotunda at Ranelagh Gardens, painting by Canaletto (1754)

later moved to the side. According to Burney, music began here with morning concerts featuring oratorio choruses, until a complaint that 'the young merchants and city apprentices were frequently seduced from their counting-houses and shops by these morning amusements'.[43] The breakfast concerts ended in 1752, by which time evening performances had already been initiated.

In fact 1752 saw a general tightening-up of London's entertainments. On 1 December the provisions of 25 Geo.II, c.36, came into force, requiring the licensing of all places of public entertainment within twenty miles of the City or Westminster. Cuper's Gardens was refused a music-licence for the 1753 season, and despite ruses involving 'private' subscriptions it became merely a tea-garden. The three main gardens achieved a virtual monopoly, and for many years summer music was presented on six evenings a week at Vauxhall and Marybone, on three evenings at Ranelagh.[44] Concerts at Ranelagh, taking place indoors, began as early as April (overlapping with the end of the winter season); the other two gardens generally opened in May. The season closed around the end of August, often with benefits for soloists and servants before the main playhouses re-opened. Of course the relatively formal concerts here were just one of the attractions on offer: bands of horns and clarinets, for example, added to the enchantment of the Chinese Temple at Ranelagh.

The social mix at the gardens was a subject of endless fascination. A reviewer described the company at the expensive Vauxhall Jubilee of 1786:

There were last night above 6000 persons present, and among them some of the first people in the kingdom, but as is always the case at Vauxhall, it was a *melange*; the cit and the courtier jostled each other with the usual familiarity; the half guinea was no repellant to the middling order; John Bull loves to shoulder his superiors in rank, his betters he'll not allow them to be; and where he pays as much for admission, he never considers them to be more than his equals.[45]

This was somewhat parodied by Henry Angelo, who thought Vauxhall in 1776 'more like a bear garden than a rational place of resort, and most particularly on the Sunday mornings. It was then crowded from four to six with gentry, girls of the town, apprentices, shop-boys, &c. &c. Crowds of citizens were to be seen trudging home with their wives and children.'[46] The standard admittance was only 1/- and annual passes could be obtained quite cheaply (Marybone charged 1½ guineas for two persons in 1768). Some social problems resulted. Cuper's suffered particularly from a reputation for immorality, despite pleas that subscription tickets not be passed on to 'people of ill-repute'. Even Vauxhall was subject to hooliganism on the last night of the season. In 1780 around 8,000 attended, 'the generality of which, however, were of the middling, and inferior classes'. It was regarded as a success that there was no riot until 3 a.m. when 'between thirty and forty lamps were broken by three blades, two of whom were a hair-dresser and an attorney's clerk'.[47] Indeed the final night became so notorious for rowdy behaviour that in 1783 the proprietors stopped advertising it. On many other occasions, however, the

Plate 6   A concert at Vauxhall Gardens, watercolour by Thomas Rowlandson (*c.* 1784)

most fashionable company attended the principal gardens; the Prince of Wales and the Duchess of Devonshire frequented Vauxhall with no particular ceremony and in 1768 the King of Denmark was entertained there in the company of the highest nobility. The gardens also figure repeatedly in the social round depicted in current novels. While the reviewer quoted above suggests a belligerent independence on the part of the middling ranks, one of the main objects of visiting the gardens was in fact to relish social distinctions, emphasising the ambiguous British attitude towards class.

The gardens were perceived in a clear hierarchy. Ranelagh, charging 2/6 rather than 1/-, was the most exclusive, followed by Vauxhall and (across the fields) Marybone. To a considerable extent these levels were reflected in the clientele, though Sylas Neville qualified this view rather sourly: 'At 6 went to Marybone Gardens, a place of the kind of Ranelagh – but not so elegant nor frequented by such good company – indeed much indifferent company resort to both.'[48]

In some ways the musical programme of Marybone is the most interesting. The succession of proprietors included several musicians (Thomas Lowe, Thomas Pinto, Samuel Arnold), but they faced a constant struggle against financial adversity and strenuous efforts were necessary to attract a public. Certainly the entertainments were more widely advertised and more varied than those elsewhere. Burlettas (Italian comic operas in translation) were a particular speciality, being staged there at a separate small theatre in 1758–60 and 1770–4. Marybone also maintained some masonic connection, for on 28 June 1763 a masonic song was sung by 'Brother Lowe', with brethren from the audience invited to take part in the chorus. Yet despite ever more elaborate enticements in the early 1770s (especially Torre's pyrotechnic exhibitions), Marybone rapidly fell out of fashion: no regular concerts were given in 1775 and after one more miscellaneous season the gardens closed.

Though most prestigious, or possibly because of this, Ranelagh had a more chequered career than Vauxhall in the latter part of the century. Admiration for the magnificent rotunda was often tempered with suggestions that the endless perambulation of the beau monde was dull by comparison with the lively outdoor atmosphere and enchanting illusion of Vauxhall's lamplit avenues. The Pantheon, opened in 1772 as a 'winter Ranelagh', provided direct competition during the spring and Ranelagh itself went into serious decline in the 1780s: one night there were only seven paying customers, and it was suggested that if the Pantheon reduced its admission from 3/6 to 2/6, it must 'give the finishing stroke' to Ranelagh.[49] In 1788 Ranelagh's musical establishment was reduced, with singers being replaced by an additional wind band, reflecting an inability to match the high standards of London's principal concerts.[50] Ranelagh survived these setbacks and the full musical programme was restored, but the gardens lasted only three years into the next century.

Vauxhall, on the other hand, maintained a steady course throughout the half-century: evidently it achieved the delicate balance of social and economic

43

Plate 7   George, 3rd Earl Cowper, with the Family of Charles Gore, painting by Johann Zoffany
(*c.* 1775)

factors that eluded its two main competitors. It maintained a subtle mix of
gentility with a hint of freedom, of popular entertainment with elegance and
class, of reality with a magical dream-world. Only in the last decade of the
century did the character begin to change. The price was raised in 1792 to 2/-,
to Boswell's disapproval: 'The company may be more select, but a number of
honest commonalty are, I fear, excluded from sharing in elegant and innocent
entertainment.'[51] Yet it was these last two characteristics that were most under
threat. Already in the later 1790s newspapers paid much less attention to the
music and in the new century emphasis was laid on spectacular populist turns
such as tightrope-walking and sword-swallowing; meanwhile Vauxhall's moral
reputation was becoming increasingly dubious. The gardens struggled on until
1859, but by the 1820s Parke noted a decline in the music at that 'once elegant
and fashionable place of resort'.[52] Vauxhall represents a quintessentially
eighteenth-century form of refined but not precious amusement.

Private concerts

Mid eighteenth-century London supported no residential musical establishments of the kind that James Brydges (later the Duke of Chandos) had
maintained in the 1710s and that were still to be found on the continent. Some

vestige of the system remained in the employment of minor musicians as servants: William Tebbett told the Society of Musicians that he 'performes on the Violin Tenor at several private concerts, lives with His Grace the Duke of Malbrough as private Musician'. Sir Thomas Robinson offered R. J. S. Stevens £30 per annum to be his private organist, playing on Sundays, at dinner and after he had retired for the night.[53] But most concerts in private houses were even less attached to traditional modes of patronage. Typically they were informal morning or evening gatherings with a few dilettante or celebrity performers.

Foreign travellers were struck by the amount of music to be heard in the English home. Wendeborn was amazed that in private companies 'even of the better sort' a song might be performed by a gentleman or lady after dinner.[54] Kielmansegge attended several more formal private concerts, where he was impressed by the singing and harpsichord music of the ladies. On 12 March 1762, for example, he attended a 'very pleasant little concert' at Mrs Bladon's house. The two Misses Bladon sang, and an Italian violinist played 'a few nice solos very well, which, together with some of the songs, Lady Diana Clavering accompanied equally well on the piano'.[55] Some idea of the flurry of excitement in organising such private concerts is given by the lively correspondence of Mrs Harris.[56] In 1764 she writes: 'We are now very busy in preparing for our concert Wednesday morning, and I am greatly afraid there will be too great a crowd; however, it will be of good company.' On 9 March 1775, their friend Sacchini rehearsed a *Miserere* at their house for performance a week later, the young Louisa Harris singing alongside the best opera singers. In her early diary Fanny Burney described one of the concerts in March 1778: 'On Thursday morning, we went to a delightful Concert at Mr. Harris's. The sweet Rauzini was there, and sung four Duets with Miss Louisa Harris ... La Motte, Cervetto, ... played several Quartettos divinely, and the morning afforded me the greatest entertainment.' Amateur ladies showed off their accomplishments, while professional string-players added musical sophistication.

Quite rare are references to gentlemen performing on such occasions. London society included some well-known gentlemen violinists, cellists and flautists, who ignored Lord Chesterfield's celebrated advice against 'neither piping nor fiddling'.[57] But while many ladies approached a professional standard on the keyboard very few gentlemen had the application or the inclination to achieve anything comparable: it was far more suitable for them to signal music's role as a trivial ladies' pastime by acceptance of an incidental role in accompanying sonatas. Accordingly, references to amateur chamber-music are scarce. In 1784 Mary Hamilton (Sir William's niece) went to a concert given by Mrs Delany, the much-loved Handel enthusiast: while Borghi, Cervetto and Sir William played Handel songs arranged for string trio, 'the tears were trickling down her venerable cheeks'.[58] The same year Mrs Thrale recorded an amateur string quartet party: '& the Desks were set about 8 o'clock, when Giardini's Quartettes were very sweetly performed'.[59] But the evidence suggests that while accomplished gentlemen might meet in the morning to play through string quartets they would rarely be called on to perform them, especially after a heavy dinner. The principal musical accomplishment of gentlemen undoubtedly resided in the singing of glees, which provided exactly this after-dinner function, whether at home over port or in the male dining-clubs popular with the aristocracy and bourgeois alike.[60]

Professionals carried out two main musical functions at small private concerts: to perform themselves and to supplement amateur participation. Their own contributions seem often to have been quite informal, such as Geminiani improvising for two or three hours, Giuseppe Viganoni singing to his own accompaniment on the Spanish guitar.[61] String chamber music was a favoured repertoire. The private concerts of William Sharp, surgeon and member of a musical family, were famed for professional string quartet performance. One musician looked back from 1845:

Despite of the advance of art, chamber instrumental music, in the days of George III, was more in vogue than at present. The patriarch Dragonetti had his two-guinea subscription concerts at the houses of the nobility. Salomon, and the leading men of his time, were nightly engaged in similar entertainments; and where there is now no territory sacred to the promulgation of this species of music in the mansions of our modern wealthy amateurs, there were at least a dozen in the period alluded to.[62]

Payment on such occasions might take the form of a dinner (Parke called these 'bread-and-butter parties', confirming that they were a speciality of Salomon).[63] But others disdained mere prestige and the prospect of further patronage: an anecdote about the oboist Johann Christian Fischer ended with the unwise retort 'My Lord, my oboe never sups.' Fees were in fact often paid for private performances; Giardini was credited with regulating these to obviate haggling. The second function of the professional is clearly demonstrated in Stevens's *Recollections*. He made a speciality of directing songs and glees from the harpsichord, at venues ranging from Lambeth Palace to the miserly Mr Blencowe's crowded room over a shop (where 'the discord, yell, and grumbling, in this exhibition could never be exceeded'). In 1799 Stevens increased his fee for such services by promising to include in the programme six manuscript glees of his own.

While small private concerts took place throughout the period, a new development was the rise of grander and more formal private concerts as an alternative to public entertainments. Burney regarded Mrs Fox Lane, patron of Giardini, as a forerunner in this regard: he noted that large-scale private concerts were a rarity in the middle of the century, but that by 1789 elegant concerts were 'frequently given by the nobility and gentry at their own houses'.[64] To some extent private concerts filled a gap when public concerts were not available, for example during Easter week. And sometimes they provided the only opportunity to hear a celebrated performer. Elizabeth Linley, renouncing public appearance after her marriage to Sheridan in 1773, could only be heard at her own house concerts, to which entrance was ardently sought. But a much more significant factor was a turning away from public concerts.

The upsurge in private concerts exactly matched the explosion in high-prestige public concerts in the late 1770s and especially the 1780s. To some extent this trend reflects general interest in music at all levels. But it also represents a reaction against public entertainments, partly because of the discomforts attending crowded venues, but more significantly for their decline of exclusivity. It matches a vogue among the nobility for private theatricals, and a rejection of once-fashionable masquerades. According to a newspaper report of 1783 most 'Ladies of Character and Rank' avoided public entertainments; instead 'private Houses are opened for the Ladies, and the more elevated and accomplished among the Gentlemen'.[65] In 1791, the year of Haydn's first concerts in London, Lady Stafford summed up the current ambiguous mood of the aristocracy: 'Your Sisters go by turns to publick Places, and they, I believe, like it; I suppose Susan does, but she does not express much pleasure.'[66]

Concerts were regarded in exactly this light, to judge from one review of a 1783 subscription concert: 'The company was select not numerous. The fashion of domestic concerts, among people of fashion, have, in a great degree, crushed public exhibitions, and the high price does not bring them within general reach.'[67] It was a conspicuous example of aristocratic retrenchment, forming a parallel to the Concert of Ancient Music. Not only was there an explicit social dimension, but the trend also allowed connoisseurs to exert the most direct control over the selection of performers and repertoire. Public concerts were not in fact abandoned by the quality, but private parties with major stars and even complete orchestras undoubtedly provided an alternative. The 'Mirror of Fashion' in *The Morning Chronicle* for 1791 often lists concerts week after week at the same distinguished households. Lady Yonge, for example, put on six, in alternation with the Academy of Ancient Music since Salomon was leader at both. A review of one of her concerts from an earlier season lists a complete symphonic programme, virtually indistinguishable from those of the public arena.[68] Other promoters included well-known cognoscenti such as the Earl of Exeter and Sir Watkin Williams Wynn, both directors of the Ancient Concerts and subscribers to Hanover Square. Their two series carried such weight that Mara was given special dispensation to sing there by the 1785 Pantheon management.[69] From a quite different background came a 'blue-stocking concert', held in 1787 at the house of Mrs Montagu herself; presumably it was a serious-minded soirée, but whether the music was ancient or modern is not revealed.[70]

Most conspicuous in rivalry to the public subscription concerts were two 'private' series. No single patron would afford a full orchestra on a regular basis, and this hybrid system provided the aristocracy with all the benefits of the public subscription system with none of the disadvantages. Thus in 1782

the select subscribers to the 'Grand Private Subscription Concerts' paid 10
guineas for twelve Sunday evening concerts at various houses, with performers
of the very highest quality.[71] The series was also known as the 'Sunday
Concerts' or the 'Nobility Concert'. In 1787, according to Parke, it was
attended by 400 of the 'flower of the nobility and gentry'; the orchestra was the
Professional with the addition of royal patrons. There were some questions
about the propriety and legality of a Sunday concert, but the series lasted at
least until 1793. The second subscription series was known as the Ladies
Concert. It is not clear exactly when this was founded. References in 1782 seem
to refer to the Sunday concerts above (Burney called these the 'Concert des
dames' in a letter of 24 February). But certainly by 1791 there were two separate
organisations, with the Ladies Concert meeting on Fridays in direct competition with Salomon.

A special type of private concert was that promoted by prominent
musicians themselves. Charles Burney's well-known house-concerts were
good-humoured occasions for a small invited audience; a few professionals
participated alongside amateurs, but no programme was fixed.[72] The concert
on 4 May 1772 typically linked Eligio Celestino and Sir William Hamilton on
the violin, Joseph Tacet and William Beckford on the flute; Burney's nephew
Charles Rousseau Burney was the professional keyboard-player. A more
elaborate concert took place in May 1775 in honour of the Danish Ambassador
and his wife, with a dozen or so guests from the gentry and professional classes.
Songs and keyboard music were contributed by the ladies and by C. R. Burney,
with some variety provided by Edward Jones, the Welsh harpist. Less well
considered was Burney's celebrated attempt to mix people from quite diverse
walks of life – his patrons the Grevilles, the brewing family the Thrales, Dr
Johnson and the singer Gabriele Piozzi. The evening ended in the stony silence
of mutual disdain.

More formal were the subscription concerts organised by Charles Wesley
(brother of John) at his Chesterfield Street home from 1779 to 1785.[73] Seven
concerts were given each season, the object clearly being to further the careers
of Charles's two sons as well as to make a profit. The number of subscribers,
each paying 3 guineas, varied between 28 in 1779 and 52 in 1781; among them
were directors of the Ancient concerts and prominent evangelicals and
Methodists. The principal attraction was the performances of Charles junior on
the organ and Samuel on the violin, but some singers and a minimal orchestra
were also engaged; the programmes explicitly mixed ancient and modern,
including the Wesleys' own compositions. Another interesting attempt to
exploit the ancient vogue was made by the organist John Worgan in 1787, at
the very end of a long career; a selection from his own sacred compositions was
attended by 'most of the Directors of the Concert of Ancient Music'.[74]

Musicians' concerts served a variety of functions, quite apart from personal
entertainment. Most importantly they formed an opportunity to foster contacts
within the profession and to forge and maintain links with patrons. Parke

described how Baumgarten 'occasionally gave music parties on Sunday evenings, at which his friends attended to hear his masterly compositions', these friends being identified as Alderman Kirkman, Sir Thomas Cave, Linley and Sheridan.[75] Parke himself first made an impression as an oboist at one of these concerts in 1779. More experimentally, the musician and publisher William Napier tried to harness West End amateur music-making into something resembling a City society. In the late 1770s he founded a morning concert at the Thatched House Tavern in St James's Street. The performers were gentlemen amateurs with some professional assistance, and the concerts were well patronised by nobility (but not ladies) on their way to court. This was not pure altruism on Napier's part, however. When it was proposed to revive the idea in 1792, a newspaper feature acknowledged dual aims: to improve the taste and science of the amateur and to introduce professional merit to the highest patronage.[76]

Others used private concerts to entertain their students and to show off their success as teachers: 'After he had been here a few years, [Giardini] formed a morning *academia*, or concert, at his house, composed chiefly of his scholars, vocal and instrumental, who bore a part in the performance.'[77] The performers listed were well-known lady amateurs of the time. In 1789 Stevens organised a concert for his young lady students, attended only by their parents and a few friends; though he constantly railed against the nervous exhaustion they caused him, similar concerts followed in later years. Some teachers included concerts as part of their package to entice new students. The elder George Smart revealed an even more practical purpose behind his subscription concert of 1784: performers had free use of instruments and music from his music warehouse, but only for use at the concert.[78]

Music at court

It has already become clear that court music did not occupy a central place in London's cultural life. In practice most of the royal family were active supporters of modern music, exerting considerable influence at private musical gatherings and by attendance at public concerts. As early as 1763 Queen Charlotte engaged J. C. Bach, one of the leaders of the new movement; though she did not go to subscription concerts she certainly took an interest in the latest developments, sending Fanny Burney to appraise a new singer at the Pantheon in 1790.[79] But such activities tended to reinforce current trends rather than transform London's concert life; most royal musical activities indeed appear largely indistinguishable from the broad run of aristocratic music in the period. Only George III's penchant for Handel's music forms a significant exception to this pattern, since it played a major role in the public Handel revival of the 1780s.

Throughout his reign the King encouraged music as part of court life. Already in 1761 there were informal music parties: 'The Queen has a Concert every Wednesday, at wch. the Pss. of Wales and all her children are present. The Queen and Lady Augusta play on the Harpsichord & sing, the Duke of York plays on the Violoncello, & P. William on the German Flute; the King never plays in Concert, but when they are alone he sometimes accompanys her on the German Flute.'[80] Diaries and memoirs contain abundant references to concerts – domestic and formal, ancient and modern – at St James's Palace and the various royal residences: Buckingham House in winter, Richmond Lodge, Kew House, the Queen's Lodge or Windsor Castle in summer.[81] In the absence of detailed court records, however, ambiguities remain about the precise nature of these concerts and of the musicians involved.

Three instrumental groups need to be considered. The official court orchestra remained the King's Band, founded by Charles II and still nominally numbering twenty-four musicians. But since foreigners were excluded the Band did not represent the cream of London's music and some of its members were not even professionals, as will be seen. Shortly after George III's marriage in 1761, a private orchestra was founded, known as the Queen's Band but as yet 'all Natives of England';[82] in 1770 there were nine members, all British professional musicians. In addition a select Queen's Chamber Band was formed around Bach, Abel, Cramer and Fischer, reflecting the Queen's preference both for modern music and for German musicians.[83] In 1783 the full Queen's Band was augmented by the deliberate importation of twelve Germans, 'to put the natives of poor Old England out of countenance as much as possible', as one of the aggrieved put it.[84] Perhaps a certain unease resulted in a public relations ploy: the official lists published in the *Court and City Register* include none of the new players and imply that both Bands were allowed to run down as posts fell vacant.

The King's Band was a formal ceremonial unit, its principal function being to join Chapel Royal singers for the New Year and Birthday odes set by the Master of the King's Musick. The odes were generally performed during the midday drawing-room at St James's Palace. On New Year's Day 1762 Kielmansegge found the room very full and the ode, less than half an hour long, 'not badly done'.[85] *The Morning Chronicle* on 2 January 1784 revealed that the singers were placed in a passage adjoining the Council Chamber, with the orchestra out of sight in another room. Naturally these official occasions were attended by all the royal family and the cream of the nobility, with whom the King conversed during the performance.[86] Sometimes a rehearsal was reviewed in the press, but everyone recognised that these old-fashioned formalities were peripheral to London's essential musical concerns. Much the same could be said of other court odes, even if they were sometimes promoted on a lavish scale. In 1763 Queen Charlotte celebrated the King's birthday with a secretly organised outdoor performance of a Boyce ode, the garden of Buckingham House transformed by the most elaborate architectural and decorative effects.

Less well documented are unofficial concerts at court, the royal equivalent of the private concerts considered above. Mrs Papendiek, one of the Queen's attendants, states that there were evening parties on Tuesdays and Thursdays, lasting from eight o'clock until ten, 'when between two and three hundred were invited to cards and music. The concert consisted of the private band, with the addition of other talented performers.'[87] These must be one and the same as the Queen's Concerts at Buckingham House, frequently mentioned in the press during the 'rage for music'; there were also concerts of sacred music on Sundays during the season. When the King was in residence at Windsor, music was performed every night. Mrs Delany was frequently invited to concerts at the Queen's Lodge there; she noted that the orchestra played in a side-room, and that 'the King generally directs them what pieces of music to play, chiefly Handel'.[88] These Handelian evenings were of great importance to George III, to judge from his insistence on a concert the very evening of an attempt on his life.[89] For courtiers, on the other hand, attendance was evidently something of a chore. A concert at Windsor in 1789 was heard by over a hundred of 'the first Officers of State and their wives, the Queen's family, several of the King's Lords and their wives, and some particular favourites', but clearly the main interest was in George III's restoration to health.[90] The orchestra at these royal concerts is variously identified with the King's and the Queen's Band: the latter is surely correct (Mrs Papendiek's 'private band'), an impression confirmed by a report that the musicians spoke more German than English.[91]

Contemporary music was also heard at court through the influence of the Queen. At evenings of modern chamber music the Chamber Band played a leading role. Mrs Papendiek states that this ensemble gave 'private quartett parties' twice a week, except in the summer when they took place only once a fortnight.[92] Such a concert was described by Mrs Delany in 1779: 'I had two hours most delightful entertainment; the musick, tho' modern, was excellent in *its kind* and well performed; particularly the first fiddle by Cramer, Abel on the *Viol de Gambo* (tho' I don't like the instrument) and a new hautboy, just come from Germany.'[93] George III did not specifically audition new performers as his grandfather had done. Sometimes musicians performed at court at his request (the Linleys received £100 after a five-hour concert in 1773),[94] but more usually such appearances formed part of a carefully planned entrée into musical society by foreign visitors and young performers. Leopold Mozart's informative description of his son's appearance on 19 May 1764 will bear repetition:

The King placed before him not only works of Wagenseil, but those of Bach, Abel and Handel, and he played off everything *prima vista*. He played so splendidly on the King's organ that they all value his organ-playing more highly than his clavier-playing. Then he accompanied the Queen in an aria which she sang, and also a flautist who played a solo. Finally he took the bass part of some airs of Handel (which happened to be lying there) and played the most beautiful melody on it and in such a manner that everyone was amazed.[95]

Leopold was even more pleased to receive 24 guineas in cash, rather than an addition to his collection of snuff-boxes.

Many other members of the royal family held their own small private concerts. The Dukes of Gloucester and Cumberland both maintained small musical establishments, at least from 1775; the latter held concerts both at his Windsor lodge and in London twice a week during the winter.[96] More ostentatious in their support for new music were the Prince of Wales and his brother the Duke of York. No doubt for the Prince this was a deliberate gesture of defiance towards his father, and it certainly gave ample opportunity for his notorious extravagance. Nevertheless, he undoubtedly developed a cultivated taste and he provided a focus for the patronage of new music, mirroring the King's preference for Handel. Even before he came of age in August 1783 he organised musical entertainments, which Giardini directed: 'After the Queen's parties were over, the Prince's began, and two or three times a week he would have a quartett party, and sometimes quite a grand concert.'[97] Birthday celebrations in 1782 and 1783 included especially elaborate concerts. The following year he moved into the stylishly refurbished Carlton House; but, curiously perhaps, 'there were not the same grand concerts or gala nights as heretofore'. The Prince's preference was for small morning chamber concerts, in which he himself played the cello alongside the cream of London's instrumentalists. Unusually these were private occasions, as 'he is too great an amateur to suffer the buz of conversation to interrupt the harmony of his concerts'; string quartets were the favoured repertoire.[98] Even the more elaborate evening concerts were still of a chamber character, as we learn from a report of 1791:

Yesterday his Royal Highness had a Concert at Carlton House, at which were Haydn, Salomon, Jarnowick [Giornovichi], David, and the principal performers, vocal and instrumental. – Such a band for a Chamber Concert it would be difficult for any other metropolis to select. – Detached morsels of the most exquisite modern compositions, Quartetts, Catches and Glees, made up the Miscellany of the Musical Feast.[99]

On such occasions, however, the musicians were merely servants providing background music: Haydn noted that 'the orchestra often had to wait for several hours until the Prince rose from table'. One of the Prince's concerts, held at the Duke of York's house on 1 February 1795, was attended, unusually, by the entire royal family; the programme of Haydn's music was evidently a serious attempt by the Prince to win over the King. The composer himself recalled the reconciliation with some pride: 'The King, who hitherto could or would only hear Handel's music, was attentive; he chatted with me, and introduced me to the Queen, who said many complimentary things to me.' Yet he also noted laconically that only the Duchess of York came to his final benefit concert.

The concert in London life

Expanding demand

London's concert life clearly flourished in this period as never before, and no European capital (not even Paris) could rival the scale and variety of entertainments on offer. This growth appears to reflect closely Britain's economic boom in the 1760s, but two questions immediately arise. How far can the vogue be attributed to the product itself and how far to its conspicuous capacity to demonstrate wealth and leisure? Interrelationships between taste and money are impenetrably complex, especially in the absence of precise information on attendance or on individual life-styles; no definitive answers can therefore be proffered. But it is clear that musicians and entrepreneurs proved adept at manipulating both a musical and a social demand for their product. On the social side they engineered a much higher profile for concerts within the fashionable calendar, even as they adopted increasingly commercial styles of promotion. On the musical side they made the most of stylistic changes by means of aggressive marketing – of the new German symphonies in the 1760s, of Haydn and Handel in the 1780s, of glees in the 1790s.

A second question concerns the bourgeoisie. It is a platitude of music history to equate the expansion of public concerts with the rise of the middle classes. It is commonly pointed out that the population of London rose from some 575,000 in 1700 to 900,000 in 1801, and that London's increasing wealth was also spread more widely than ever before. But the development cannot be viewed so simply. As we have seen, modern concert life was not a bourgeois creation, and concert life only expanded into the City in later emulation, in the same way as the bourgeois bought gentility in the form of pianos and daughters' lessons. While some of the new wealthy bourgeois may have swelled the ranks of the élite, extension of the market through widespread emulation required an established aristocratic culture. A secure élite concert life simply did not exist in the 1740s, and from a musician's point-of-view its establishment was a first requirement. Only then could a market be expanded from polite society downwards, as Josiah Wedgwood was able to do with pottery.[1]

As already suggested, the most vibrant regular concerts of the early eighteenth century were City clubs and Handel's playhouse-oratorios. There were sporadic attempts at West End series before 1750, but it was not until the temporary collapse of the Italian Opera and the arrival in 1751 of the modernist prophet Giardini that subscription series began to take off. Fashionable status for the new music was aided by the domineering support of Mrs Fox Lane. The process accelerated markedly during the extravagant 1760s and 1770s, spurred on by Mrs Cornelys, the 'presiding genius in the polite vices' in Paul Langford's memorable phrase.[2] Her palace of pleasure, regarded by many as the focus of aristocratic immorality or, at best, of the marriage market, was the fount of modern concert life. Mrs Cornelys astutely saw the potential for concerts within the context of fashionable assemblies. Though in reality a commercial undertaking, her 'Society' took place at an elegant mansion and was socially screened. The Bach–Abel concerts developed directly out of such society events, and indeed promoters may have deliberately sought to confuse the two concepts (when the public-concert idea was transferred back into the salon the differences were scarcely marked). By the 1770s the subscription concert was firmly established within the fashionable week.

The new concerts were also given a clear identity through their focus on symphonic music, a process that quickened dramatically in the 1780s as musicians used every technique of press coverage to encourage a public craze for orchestral concerts and for Haydn symphonies in particular. New papers such as *The Morning Post* (founded in 1772) had begun to incorporate gossip in a way unknown to the old advertisers. While gossip about musicians was not always flattering, it raised their public profile considerably; more positively, newspapers of the 1780s began to include lengthy concert reviews and informative arts columns as part of their fashionable social coverage. All this publicity made a very significant contribution to the 'rage for music'.

The concept of the public-concert series fitted easily into the endless search for entertainment during the London season, a search which often appeared frenetic and wilful. This rampaging consumerism was largely perpetrated by a leisured minority, 'most of whom took their responsibility to be rich and idle with the utmost seriousness'.[3] London society was ever self-conscious about its own entertainments. Not only do newspapers list events of the coming week in great detail, but the social round forms a sub-plot to many novels of the period. In *Cecilia* Fanny Burney wrote that 'among fashionable people, public places seemed a never-failing source of conversation and entertainment'. Sometimes the fashionable world was split by many competing attractions, as on 14 April 1785 when Mrs Siddons performed at Drury Lane before the King, Mrs Abington was at Covent Garden, Le Picq danced at the Italian Opera and Madame Mara sang at the Pantheon.[4] Memoirs and letters confirm the pace of the social life of the lady of fashion. A vivid account of the musical calendar is provided by the letters of Mrs Harris: in 1775, for example, the family attended the Opera and oratorio, the Bach–Abel concerts at Hanover Square, the

Pantheon concerts, and numerous private concerts. The ever-enthusiastic Miss Iremonger attended in 1793 both Professional and Salomon's Concerts (by bartering tickets with Hookham), in addition to the Opera and Covent Garden oratorios.[5] In some respects concert life even began to overshadow the Opera. Certainly the Opera's artistic and financial problems (not to speak of the King's Theatre fire in 1789) diminished its position in London's musical life in the last two decades of the century. It could not match the enthusiasm for Haydn's arrival in 1791 – and it was not Haydn's proposed opera that was the source of the fervour.

Ladies were particularly dependent on social engagements for amusement, denied the stimulus of business activities and the conviviality of gentlemen's clubs and dinners. Usually it was ladies who organised house-concerts, to the annoyance of their philistine husbands according to the entertaining parody in the *Connoisseur* for 1756:

If my wife could be satisfied, like other musical ladies, with attending public performances, and now and then thrumming on her harpsichord the tunes she hears there; I should be content. But she has also a concert of her own constantly once a week. Here she is in still greater raptures than at the opera, as all the music is chosen and appointed by herself. The expence of this whim is monstrous, for not one of these people will open their mouths, or rosin a single string, without being very well paid for it. Then she must have all the best hands and voices, and has almost as large a set of performers in pay as the manager of the opera. It puts me quite out of patience to see these fellows strutting about my house drest up like lords and gentlemen. Not a single fiddler or singer but what appears in lace or embroidery, and I once mistook my wife's chief musician for a foreign ambassador.[6]

It is significant that women were allowed to attend public concerts on their own (often to the surprise of foreign visitors): 'In *Great-Britain* the ladies are as free as the gentlemen; and we have no diversions, or public amusements, in which the one may not appear, without any offence, as frankly as the other.'[7] Indeed concerts were generally more attractive to ladies than to gentlemen, who had other pressing engagements. Around 1760 dinner was taken at three o'clock, after which ladies retired for tea while gentlemen passed round the port: 'This naturally makes a run on the Public places; as the women has little amusement at home.' The men followed later, but often arrived in an unfit state.[8] In 1788 a more worthy excuse was provided by the length of debates in the House of Lords.[9]

Other evidence also indicates that modern concerts played a less prominent part in the lives of gentlemen. This does not mean that they did not attend, for advertisements often specify equal numbers of tickets for men and women; and men, including connoisseurs, figure in the surviving lists of prominent audience-members. But few male diarists or letter-writers make more than cursory reference to concerts, indicating the small place music played in their lives. A significant exception is provided by Sylas Neville, whose diary for 1767 records impressions of the oratorio and all three gardens. In 1782, now a qualified doctor, he visited London as a gentleman of science: the diary tells not of balls and masquerades but of trips to see a dromedary and Sir Ashton Lever's Museum. He nevertheless attended a wide range of operas, plays and concerts, this year and the next, before finally renouncing 'the great theatre of human folly'. Ancient music presented a rather different case. Its connotations of erudition and its role in aristocratic definition meant that its leadership was dominated by men, from the King downwards (as we have seen, men controlled entry to the Concert of Ancient Music, ladies entry to the Bach–Abel concerts). The Handel festivals of the 1780s were quite different in tone from normal society events: even Neville returned for the 1784 Commemoration, of which he left a particularly full account.

The vogue for concerts thus developed for a number of different reasons. Above all, it fulfilled the increasing demands of the leisured and the wealthy for high-quality exclusive entertainment, formerly provided only by the Italian Opera. Further expansion resulted from artistic fissure, when ancient music became a cause in itself, centred around the male nobility. The available audience was swelled by some broadening of the ranks of the élite, and to a certain extent new markets opened up through bourgeois emulation. But differing social demands and musical tastes imposed a limitation on market-extension; and problems arose with cheaper imitations, as the Academy of Ancient Music discovered. Ultimately, musicians themselves were more concerned with establishing the concert ideal and with keeping their own place in the West End culture than with actively attempting to spread it into the City.

Halls and refreshments

An important factor in the social role of concerts was provided by the halls themselves. Few venues were designed specifically with concerts in mind, and accordingly their social status tended to derive from their other functions. They included theatres (King's, the three main playhouses), churches and chapels, fashionable assembly-rooms (Carlisle House in Soho Square, Almack's, the Pantheon), general-purpose halls used for dancing-schools and auctions (Hickford's Room, Dean Street Room, Spring Garden Room), livery company halls (especially Haberdashers' Hall), Freemasons' Hall, long rooms attached to taverns (the Crown and Anchor in the Strand). Just two major halls were built with public concerts in mind. In 1775 the Hanover Square Rooms were opened to host both Gallini's 'festinos' and the Bach–Abel concerts (later Gallini bought up the musicians' share); a second large concert-room was opened in 1794, alongside the new King's Theatre in the Haymarket. The Concert of Ancient Music met at first at Francis Pasquali's Tottenham Street Rooms, about which little is known except that in 1785 they were enlarged and lavishly fitted up to receive the King and his retinue. Following the 1752 Act, all London concert venues had to be licensed. Surviving information indicates

Table 2. *Concert-room sizes*

Room	Length (feet)	Width (feet)	Source
Hickford's, Brewer Street	49	29	*Survey of London*, vol. XXXI, p. 124
Spring Garden	62	52	*Survey of London*, vol. XX, p. 68
Almack's/Willis's	90	40	*PA* 1 December 1764 (*OR* 26 February 1794: 82 × 40)
Hanover Square	79	32	*OR* 26 February 1794
Freemasons' Hall	90	43	Adam Carse, *The Orchestra from Beethoven to Berlioz* (Cambridge, 1948), p. 162
Crown and Anchor Tavern	81	36	*OR* 26 February 1794 (see also *WO* 17 April 1787)
King's Theatre Room	97	48	*OR* 26 February 1794
Ranelagh rotunda	155		Diameter: unidentified cutting, BL, 840.m.28
Vauxhall rotunda	70		Diameter: *A Description of Vaux-Hall Gardens* (London, 1762), p. 20

that (pleasure gardens apart) Justices of the Peace renewed licences without much ado; but at least one benefit at an unlicensed tavern was interrupted by the long arm of the law.[10]

Some churches and theatres could accommodate large audiences: the new Drury Lane of 1794 seated 3,611. But most of these halls were of modest size, as can be seen from table 2. By way of comparison, the Hanover Square Room was only slightly longer than Oxford's Holywell Music Room (65 ft × 32 ft), regarded now as a small chamber-room; the Wigmore Hall is very much larger. The Hanover Square Room was intended to seat 500 (the normal subscription there), the King's Theatre Room 800. If reports of audience size are to be believed, even larger numbers sometimes attended.[11] Even though the entire audience was not necessarily in the concert-room at the same time, it is hardly surprising that a constant complaint against public concerts was that they were crowded and hot. In direct response, an attempt was made in 1783 to enlarge the Hanover Square Room with an invention by Joseph Merlin, an orchestra platform that could be raised or lowered at will; needless to say, this curious contraption was never heard of again. The Concert of Ancient Music ran a more select subscription policy; but, since Pasquali's enlarged room could only hold 300 comfortably,[12] it too became suffocatingly crowded as the number of subscribers rose towards 400 in the early 1790s. Much the largest hall was the Pantheon, whose cruciform shape could easily accommodate well over 1,000 people.

The fashionable appeal of a hall was judged not only by its programme, but also by its comfort and décor. In many ways even a public concert retained aspects of the aristocratic drawing-room (this was the recollection of Henry C. Lunn writing in *The Musical Times* on the demise of the Hanover Square Rooms in 1874). Reviews and even advertisements draw attention to ample fires and luxurious carpets. Seating usually included some settees: thus at Hanover

Square there were three rows of sofas at the sides with benches covered with cloth in the middle.[13] The room had a beautifully painted half-domed ceiling, with reliefs in all the piers, and it was adorned at various times by a statue of Apollo, by ten lighted transparencies and by Gainsborough's portrait of Abel. One report of 1791 described the room as magnificent if old-fashioned in its decoration, with large mirrors separated by golden ornament '*en baroque*'.

A striking earlier venue was Mrs Cornelys's mansion in Soho Square (Carlisle House), which received favourable comment in 1761: 'The rooms in which they play, as well as the large ballroom, are very fine and beautifully lighted, and exceedingly well furnished.'[14] By 1774, however, Mrs Harris thought 'the furniture, like Madame Cornely' in decline. Both Carlisle House and Almack's equally splendid ball-room were undoubtedly eclipsed by the one London hall that was regarded as an architectural wonder. James Wyatt's magnificent Pantheon opened in 1772 to almost universal admiration. The great room made a breathtaking spectacle with its impressive dome and columns, its green and purple lamps, and its gilt decoration. Mary 'Perdita' Robinson, visiting the Pantheon concert for the first time, gave a typical reaction: 'As soon as I entered the Pantheon Rotunda, I never shall forget the impression which my mind received: the splendour of the scene, the dome illuminated with variegated lamps, the music, and the beauty of the women, seemed to present a circle of enchantment.'[15] Some felt that the rotunda at Ranelagh offered a more striking *coup de spectacle* and there was an occasional gripe about the crowded side-rooms and staircases; but during the 1770s the splendour of the Pantheon was certainly an attraction in itself. Early in the next decade, however, fashion suddenly turned away. The building was declared moribund and one wag suggested that it would be better turned into a church.[16] As far as concerts were concerned, the Pantheon shared with Ranelagh the problem of an over-resonant acoustic. A false ceiling was tried during the 1770s and in 1788 the idea was revived with considerable success. A further inducement in 1790 was the construction of boxes around the sides, from which the *ton* could look down on the remainder of the audience on sofas and benches below. These strenuous efforts did succeed in rehabilitating the Pantheon briefly, but in vain, for the building was demolished by fire in 1792.

A significant factor in a hall's reputation was ease of transport. Arrival was rarely a problem, since it was not usual for everyone to turn up at the beginning (only the Abbey Commemoration caused a crush of people at nine o'clock in the morning, three hours before the performance). Leaving a concert was never as easy. Arrangements were usually made so that traffic went in one direction ('Horses Heads towards Grosvenor-square'), but extreme congestion could still result. After one concert at the Pantheon attended by some 1,600 people, there was such heavy rain that some waited for carriages from eleven o'clock at night until three in the morning.[17] The return from Vauxhall and Marybone was notoriously treacherous because of the risk of highwaymen. On 25 May 1767 Sylas Neville, having listened to music at Vauxhall from seven o'clock

Plate 8 A ticket for Giardini's benefit, 1780, engraved by Francesco Bartolozzi after Giovanni Battista Cipriani

until ten, tried in vain to get a coach; deeming the usual river-route dangerous, he decided to walk and arrived home at 1.30 a.m. Well might he confide to his diary: 'The music at Vauxhall is agreeable if one could easily get home as soon as it is over.' Marybone tried to entice a higher class of clientele by obligingly providing an attended parking-lot for those with their own carriages.[18]

Concerts were sometimes accompanied by additional enticements, even outside the pleasure gardens. It was customary for the organiser to provide light refreshments (with tea and coffee) in a side-room. At minor venues a concert was often followed by a ball. At the Pantheon too there was dancing and card-playing in adjoining rooms, a combination that linked a public concert still further to a society assembly. As a final bonus, concert tickets were sometimes specially engraved; those designed by Cipriani and engraved by Bartolozzi for Giardini's benefits were regarded as minor art-works.

Audience attitudes and behaviour

One consequence of incorporation into the social week was the need to follow its mores. Many indications would seem to suggest that serious attention to the music was a rarity. For one thing, concerts failed to keep track with fashionable later hours. Even as starting times moved on during the period from seven o'clock to eight, it was certainly not good form to arrive at the beginning of a concert. The Prince of Wales missed the entire first half of one of Salomon's concerts, and Fanny Burney thought nothing of having Cecilia arrive during the second half of a Pantheon concert. Haydn, seeing late-comers drifting in during the first half, requested that his new symphonies be performed after the interval. His biographer Dies implied that such late-comers were often gentlemen arriving from post-prandial port who were 'so gripped by the magic of the music that they went fast to sleep'. There is other evidence that prestigious performers were kept for the second half: at an Opera Concert in 1796 annoyance greeted an interchange of items as 'a great part of the Audience were not in time' to enjoy Giornovichi's concerto, moved to the first part.[19] Even at the gardens late hours were kept. In 1777 Horace Walpole observed that it was fashionable to arrive at Ranelagh at midnight, two hours after the music finished.[20]

It scarcely needs mentioning that a concert was an opportunity to see and to be seen, with all the inevitable consequences for ostentatious finery and social intrigue. Fanny Burney's novels make it abundantly clear that the concert-hall was a principal venue for conversation and assignations. It is rather depressing to find that even the novelist herself came to regard the concert in much the same light, to judge from a letter of 1792, which shows no trace of her former irony:

Last Night, for the first Time, I ventured to a public place. I went to salomon's Concert, & was quite enchanted by sweet sounds, long strangers to my Ears. It was *My First Appearance in Public* for many Years. – Yet there was no particular applause upon my entrance! – For which reason, finding it so little answer, I do not purpose repeating the same abstinence for quite as long a period in haste.[21]

Both Carlisle House and the Pantheon were well-known places for young ladies to look out for a good match, while other women had less respectable aims. Having gone to the Pantheon to hear Agujari sing, Thomas Campbell was not at all surprised to see courtesans arrayed in peacock-feathers among the lords and ladies.[22]

Furthermore, fashionable audiences never sat through an entire concert in reverential silence. Burney complained that even 'the best Operas and Concerts

are accompanied with a buz and murmur of conversation'; instrumental music
in particular was only rarely 'attentively regarded' in fashionable circles (John
Marsh found much the same at Vauxhall in 1770).[23] In both *Evelina* and *Cecilia*
Fanny Burney censured audiences at the Pantheon concerts:

There was an exceeding good concert, but too much talking to hear it well. Indeed I am
quite astonished to find how little music is attended to in silence; for though every body
seems to admire, hardly any body listens.

They entered the great room during the second act of the Concert, to which as no one
of the party but herself had any desire to listen, no sort of attention was paid; the ladies
entertaining themselves as if no Orchestra was in the room, and the gentlemen, with an
equal disregard to it, struggling for a place by the fire.

Cecilia opined sarcastically that music inspired conversation: 'I think every
body talks more during the performance than between the acts.' Occasionally
a reviewer admonished members of the audience for their behaviour at the
theatres, but only when obviously taken to excess:

Some stupid young men in the Front Boxes were extremely troublesome during the
[oratorio] performance: anxious to shew their wit, they rendered their folly conspicuous,
and exposed themselves ultimately to the contempt and indignation of all around them.
Talking loud, and lolling in the laps of loose women, during the performance of *Sacred
Music*, is a species of indecorum that calls for the severest reprobation.[24]

It was perfectly normal for audiences to walk around during concerts. When
Haydn appeared, cognoscenti crowded forward towards the front of the room;
but when a minor singer like Marie Chanu was performing the audience was
completely indifferent and wandered around the hall.[25] Private concerts
attracted similar complaints. Attending a private rout, Cecilia could scarcely
hear the concert for other ladies talking about forthcoming dances, though 'not
one of them failed, from time to time, to exclaim with great rapture "*What sweet
music!*"'. Even the King conversed with the company during the performance
of court odes, and at the Duke of Queensberry's concerts cards 'proved a
powerful rival to the music'.[26] It is hardly surprising that for serious chamber-
music the Prince of Wales insisted on dedicated morning concerts without
conversation.

Doubts were inevitably cast on British taste. Goldsmith in *The Citizen of the
World* (1762) observed that the English nobility were 'not fond of thinking'
and supported music merely to 'indulge an happy vacancy' while retaining
cultural pretensions. A later writer observed, with some justification, that the
English tire of 'mere Music' at a concert, requiring the extra entertainment
provided by the playhouse or the pleasure garden.[27] Some even questioned
whether lavish public patronage of concerts was based on any genuine feeling
for music. The following is characteristic of plaints in newspapers around 1790:
'And thus we see that the incomparable talents of HAYDN meet with
becoming respect from a nation, which, though smitten with the *rage* of Music,
is not really musical.'[28] William Jackson was particularly scathing about

London's concert audiences and he thought their enthusiasms insincere, suggesting that the music least understood received the most applause, since no-one wished to betray a lack of refined taste.[29]

Yet it would be a mistake to write off all London audiences as philistine and unresponsive, and Fanny Burney may well have exaggerated for satirical effect. Dedicated societies seem to have maintained more decorum: the Castle Society met at seven o'clock for a two-part programme with a twenty-minute interval, and fines were levied on anyone walking around or talking aloud during the music. Whether audiences at the Concert of Ancient Music were similarly riveted it is hard to say. But this society by its very nature encouraged a lofty attitude towards the concert, focussing attention on musical values rather than on performers. The role of learned connoisseur was scarcely compatible with casual manners, especially in the presence of the King. Certainly the 1784 Commemoration was honoured with rapt attention.

Even at modern concerts certain performers and composers do seem to have inspired genuine appreciation. When Mara first appeared, for example, there was 'perfect silence', and similar anticipation greeted Haydn's new symphonies at Salomon's concerts: according to Mrs Papendiek, at the first concert of 1791 'the company rose to a person and stood through the whole of the first movement'.[30] If such courtesies were a rarity here, audiences did demonstrate their reactions with striking lack of inhibition. Songs were often encored, as were single movements of Haydn symphonies. Even at the Professional Concert, a scena sung by Mrs Billington drew 'rapturous plaudits from an audience too polished to be generally boisterous'.[31] Applause might break out during a performance at any kind of concert. At an oratorio concert in 1784, 'the audience could not suppress their feelings till the pieces were finished, but clapped at the end of every part'.[32] A report of Haydn symphony performances in 1794 defined acceptable limits to public expressions of delight:

Passages often occur which render it impossible to listen to them without becoming excited. We are altogether carried away by admiration, and forced to applaud with hand and mouth. This is especially the case with Frenchmen, of whom we have so many here that all public places are filled with them. You know that they have great sensibility, and cannot restrain their transports, so that in the midst of the finest passages in soft adagios they clap their hands in loud applause and thus mar the effect. In every symphony of Haydn the adagio or andante is sure to be repeated each time, after the most vehement encores.[33]

Perhaps this was a relatively new phenomenon. *The Public Advertiser* on 20 March 1789 recalled the old-fashioned civility of Handel's day:

At the conclusion of each Oratorio, the audience gave their approbation or not at their pleasure of the piece performed. Secondly, the principal singers paid their respects, and were generally honoured with approbation or not at pleasure. And immediately after Mr. Handel himself came forward and paid his respects, and never failed to receive marks of general approbation from the generous public.

Yet, either way, these quotations do suggest critical discrimination on the part of audiences.

A further sign of audience interest resides in advertising and programmes. In the early 1750s and from the late 1770s onwards most concert advertisements listed forthcoming programmes in some detail, suggesting some discernment on the part of audiences. Still sporadic is precise identification of works, requiring knowledge of an existing repertoire. 'Symphony, Double Orchestra, Bach' was always felt sufficient, but favourite songs could be named and individual Haydn symphonies highlighted by characteristic features ('with the Military Movement'). At ancient concerts pieces were naturally identified quite exactly, since it was an essential feature of the movement to pander to the (real or pretended) discrimination of the audience. The amount of information provided at the concerts themselves varied considerably. At Vauxhall a programme-order was simply posted at the bar. Following operatic practice, oratorio libretti could be bought for 1/-, and both ancient societies provided printed programmes. How far modern concerts followed suit is difficult to determine, since so few programmes have survived. A number of advertisements (as late as Abel's 1782 series) promise lists of the performance, suggesting this was not yet the norm. But this appears to have changed during the 1780s: there are references to programmes at the Pantheon (Cecilia consulted hers) and a programme for Haydn's 1795 benefit survives with pungent annotations.

The link with publication also reinforces this view. The tag 'as performed at the Professional Concert' was more than a general advertising ploy, for some letters refer directly to patrons obtaining prints of concert music. The piano repertoire heard at public concerts to some extent inspired the vogue for ladies' accomplishment on the instrument: some aristocratic ladies were soon able to play the most difficult of Clementi's sonatas.[34] Furthermore, the major concert repertoire was published in keyboard arrangement, from Corelli concertos and Handel overtures to symphonies by Bach and Haydn. This argument should not be pushed too far, but many certainly did attend concerts of all kinds simply because they enjoyed music. The German visitor Wendeborn felt it necessary to reassure his countrymen that 'the Britons love music'; even Thomas Robertson, while criticising the capriciousness of English taste, acknowledged that they have some 'passion for Music'.[35] At Ranelagh in 1782, Moritz noticed a group of music-lovers who 'had gathered to delight their ears in front of the orchestra'. Writing to Burney from his Essex vicarage, Thomas Twining argued the relative merits of modern composers just as much as the interpretation of ancient Greek music; and in May 1791 Burney arranged for Twining to meet Haydn by organising 'an excellent Concert for real judges of good Music, unmixed and unannoyed by loquacity'. Modern music had by this date become a worthy pursuit for the cultured classes, and had even begun to achieve some of the intellectual respectability of the ancient repertoire. As E. D. Mackerness has observed, any sophisticated audience included a substantial proportion of genuine connoisseurs, 'an enlightened patronage, not merely an indulgent one'.[36]

For and against London's concert life

The value of music for the individual and for the nation as a whole was a question that was repeatedly aired. Some held unequivocally that the 'rage for music' was in itself admirable and something to be approved. The sheer number of concerts was seen as general proof of the nation's good taste or culture, usually expressed as a defence against imaginary foreign jibes. While any notion of music as cultural responsibility rather than entertainment was still unformed, music was beginning to be admitted into the gentleman's intellectual armoury (and not only ancient music). Haydn's symphonies played a crucial role in this development. It was recognised at an early date that they required some application on the part of the listener; John Marsh, for example, observed in 1796 that they needed to be heard more than once for true appreciation.[37] This trend closely matched a current of improvement and instruction throughout the entertainment industry.

Many British aestheticians felt that music could have a directly beneficial effect on the individual listener, by allaying sorrow and infusing tranquillity.[38] This idea was clearly linked with the concept of the beautiful in music (to be discussed in chapter 8): wild and irregular music, with its tendency towards an imbalance of the passions, had a quite different effect. The concept of personal stability could also be extended more broadly to society as a whole; it was therefore widely held that musical harmony could contribute directly to social harmony. A rather different line was taken by those stressing music's capacity for moral and spiritual elevation, since this approach tended to emphasise the religious sublime. Certainly many of evangelical or Methodist leanings approved sacred music in the cause of religious contemplation and Christian life-style. Jonas Hanway, for example, published in 1765 his *Thoughts on the Use and Advantages of Music* in which he laid out an idealised concert plan, apparently to harness the current fashion for concerts. He did not object to ladies of leisure studying music as an intellectual pursuit: it 'not only enlarges their ideas, but furnishes an employment for the mind ... It also serves, in some instances, to keep *evil spirits* the more at arms-length.' But he strongly advocated private over public concerts as more conducive to moderation and pious reflection. His detailed plan accordingly set out two kinds of private concert – one for a small invited audience, giving preference to settings of psalms and scriptures; the other for the family, interleaving serious readings with a little sacred music. The latter, he wrote, would give more solid satisfaction than 'all the pompous, tedious, elaborate musical entertainments' of the day.

Oratorios were also regarded as morally improving by those who did not reject their theatrical background. Thus Catherine Talbot wrote in 1756 of a

Messiah performance: 'I think it impossible for the most trifling not to be the better for it. I was wishing all the Jews, Heathens, and Infidels in the world (a pretty full house you'll say) to be present.'[39] When John Wesley heard *Ruth* at the Methodist Lock Hospital Chapel in 1765, he concluded that it 'might possibly make an impression even upon rich and honourable sinners'.[40] The connections of oratorio with philanthropy (often itself associated with evangelicalism) naturally intensified this attitude. The Concert of Ancient Music attracted many of similar inclination: more generally, as we have seen, the society stood out for moral respectability against frivolity and dissipation. Even the Handel Commemoration was thought to provide a worthy contrast to the 'sauntering follies of the Metropolis', being beneficial for trade, for national musical taste, and even for 'the national character in morals'.[41] Rather less clear was the position of instrumental music. Richard Eastcott defended music in general by arguing that it was intrinsically enriching and uplifting, but in 1769 Daniel Webb was a lone figure in claiming that instrumental music could match the exalted qualities of vocal music.[42]

Ranged against these apologists for London's concert life, however, were many contrary voices, and their arguments were often expressed more articulately. It was commonly said that London simply supported too many entertainments: the 'multiplicity of publick amusements' spoiled them all.[43] Even Leopold Mozart eventually found the endless pursuit of pleasure wearisome. Least impressed by London's season were educated gentlemen from the country. Thomas Gray from Cambridge railed against 'that tiresome dull place! where all people under thirty find so much amusement'.[44] Visiting London in 1783 and again in 1790, the Cornwall vicar William Johnston Temple attended a number of concerts; but his diary is a catalogue of complaints against London and its amusements: 'No pleasure here. Nothing but noise and madness... No satisfaction in this kind of Life: nothing but bustle and hurry.'[45] Others pointed out that meeting the same people everywhere led to an 'ennui of idleness'. Ladies too sometimes affected a world-weary disdain for the fashionable round: Annamarguerita Porter went so far as to confess to her diary her revulsion at London's vacuous pleasures, a revulsion that she could scarcely admit publicly.[46] Music was sometimes singled out in such plaints, especially during the 1780s when many thought it had become an infatuation. In 1786, for example, a newspaper paragraph suggested that London was 'sated with concerts – spiritual and temporal – and fatigued with orchestras'.[47] This kind of affected indifference was directly targeted by Fanny Burney in *Cecilia*. Her Mr Meadows, having berated the dull round of public places, complains: 'I believe that solo will never be over! I hate a solo; it sinks, it depresses me intolerably.' He is still more dismissive of orchestral and vocal music, and concludes: 'All my amazement is that these people think it worth while to give Concerts at all; one is sick to death of music.'

More fundamentally, serious objections were raised against the very idea of public concerts. At the lowest level they could be directly associated with vice. James Malcolm tells of illegal gatherings in 1759, so-called charity concerts where young men and apprentices were confronted instead by 'notorious Procuresses' of the town. Later, despite frequent police raids, both the Dog and Duck spa and the Apollo Gardens remained 'obstinate places of vicious amusement' under the guise of concert venues.[48] More generally, some saw all public amusements as symbols of folly and dissipation, especially when their pursuit became the sole end of life. Many tracts attacked the abundance of luxury for its corrupting effect on individual and national morals. The object of their attack was not so much the poor as the upper ranks, especially the *nouveau riche* middle classes; for while commercialism was not in itself condemned, it could easily lead to misplaced extravagance. Concerts were regarded as a prime example of the vice of luxury, and the grounds for complaint were numerous. There were some of puritanical inclination who frankly disapproved of the enjoyment of music as the worship of a false god. More common was the view that music (even secular music) had its place, but that if mishandled it could damage the individual's moral fibre. Superficiality and frivolity were encouraged by modern music's seductive charm and brilliance, with voluptuous Italianate music particularly corrupting.[49] Others were concerned about music's ability to transport its listeners out of themselves – the effect of the sublime – when its object was not religious veneration; this represented a potentially threatening loss of control, comparable with that enshrined in the masquerade.[50] Another complaint was that modern music no longer attempted to inspire repose and calm contemplation but instead mirrored life's tumults and meaningless activity. A few writers chose not to distinguish between the possible effects of the music itself and associations with the life-styles of its protagonists, in the same way that rock music is sometimes condemned today: thus the Suffolk rector Charles Davy deemed modern instrumental music as just the first step on the road towards debauchery and licentiousness.[51]

Also of concern were the practical effects of concerts on individual lives and on society. Not only could they be seen as a waste of time and money in themselves, but they tended to foster idleness and excess.[52] A closely associated accusation was that music was effeminate and enervating – in short, dangerous for the national character. Excessive cultivation of music could damage England's intrinsic valour: to the contemporaries of Gibbon it appeared a symbol of the decline of a great nation. As early as 1754 a writer in *The London Magazine* argued that music was a pleasing amusement, but not 'the labour, principal attention, or great business of a people. Yet, how far, how scandalously it has of late prevailed, as such, in our country, let the shameful number of concerts now subscribed for in this kingdom, declare.' The issue was explicitly confronted in 1786, when the earnings of musicians were contrasted with the meagre lot of the common soldier, reduced to half-pay: and there were perfectly serious calls during the 1780s for a tax on concert-tickets and musical instruments.[53] Scheming foreigners were often blamed for seducing Londoners into this life of degenerate luxury, contaminating their natural contentment with extravagant desires. It is significant that two of London's principal musical impresarios during the century (Heidegger and Mrs Cornelys) were not only foreign but also promoters of masquerades, emblems of dangerous liberty.

In addition some more specific worries were raised about the detrimental social effects of public amusements. John Andrews thought that bringing together strangers in the pursuit of pleasure was itself a recipe for wantonness. This is really a veiled attack on the mix of social classes (the 'promiscuous mixture of all kind of company').[54] Also disruptive to the social order was the licence given to women to go unescorted to masquerades and concerts: this freedom may have been strictly circumscribed but it did represent some concession to women's independence. Hanway went further in suggesting that crowds at public places were inimical to the institution of marriage; indeed 'Perdita' Robinson, the Prince of Wales's mistress, actually blamed the Pantheon for introducing her to the corruptions of society.[55] Others expressed reservations about mixing with professional musicians, 'wretched minstrels' in Davy's opinion. No sooner were public performers invited to dine in fashionable society than *The Times* thundered that 'debauchery among the great, was the origin of Rome's downfall'.[56]

For several writers cited in this section the primary aim of music was religious. But few opposed concerts as such: rather, like Hanway, they proposed the adaptation of existing institutions to less secular ends. In two areas, however, music and Christianity came into conflict. One was the oratorio, which had always been an ambiguous genre. Increasingly the Lenten oratorio seasons focussed on Handel's secular works, and even Brown's ode *The Cure of Saul* was advertised in 1768 as 'an Entertainment of Sacred Music'. Complaints about the secularisation of Lenten oratorio series increased during the 1790s, even if in law there was no strict requirement for the music to be sacred. *The Monthly Mirror* ran an article in March 1796 on 'the prostitution of Lent', calling on the Bishop of London to speak out against the performance of Handel's secular works, as well as the introduction of Arne songs and the like into sacred programmes. A second area of controversy concerned Sunday concerts. Strictly these were forbidden, but the private Nobility Concerts of the 1780s were held on Sundays by the ruse of including some oratorio extracts. Not everybody was persuaded, however, especially when those less well off were prosecuted for the same offence. In 1788 the Handelian Society was fined £50 for holding sixpenny concerts on Sunday evenings.[57]

The decline towards 1800

The last years of the century saw a marked decline in the vitality of London's concert life. After a high-point in the period 1790 to 1793 the flood subsided considerably. With the exception of 1796, each season from 1794 to 1800 supported only one major orchestral series; and from 1795 there was only a single Lenten oratorio series. The number of benefit concerts held each year also diminished dramatically (in 1792 thirty were advertised, in 1798 only eleven). Other aspects of London's concert life tell a similar story: after 1791 the Handel festivals were reduced to a single concert, the two surviving pleasure gardens were on the wane, the Academy of Ancient Music collapsed. Even the Prince of Wales abandoned music soon after his marriage in 1795. William Parke was aware of these changes, observing that in 1800 concerts 'were not so numerous perhaps as in former seasons'; by 1808 James Malcolm thought 'the amusements of the present day ... very confined', by comparison with their earlier glories.[58]

Several factors contributed to this decline. Most obvious were economic constraints associated with poor harvests and exacerbated by war with France from 1793 onwards (Parke wrote bluntly that the art of music was 'superseded by the art of war'). Certainly turmoil abroad directly impeded the import of foreign stars, as Salomon claimed when he abandoned his 1795 series. But this cannot be the whole story. Even if provincial festivals were temporarily abandoned through a decline in manufacturing,[59] London society was quite capable of maintaining the same level of concert activity if it wished: indeed the press frequently expressed surprise that in general leisure continued to be pursued as assiduously as before. In May 1797 *The Monthly Mirror* observed: 'Notwithstanding the disjointed state of the times, and the general scarcity of cash, public amusements have not been so numerous, and where they have been conducted with spirit, better attended for many years.'

Evidently money could still be found to patronise the old pleasures; and there was even a wartime determination to maintain amusements come what may. But it is possible also to detect an underlying change in social attitudes, which had begun to show itself in the 1780s. The founding of the Proclamation Society in 1787 embodied this reaction against the moral excesses and extravagance of the 1770s; its activities were directed as much against the frivolous life-style of the upper classes as against common loose living.[60] Less overt was a redefinition of the public image of the threatened aristocracy, from profligate pleasure-seekers to responsible servants of the country (something George III had already achieved through domestic frugality and moral propriety). Respectability, marked by seriousness of purpose and simplicity of taste, became the fashion. In 1792, for example, we read that 'OECONOMY seems now the prevailing rage among the Nobility – Fêtes, Assemblies, Dinners, &c. are heard of no longer'.[61] Henry Angelo observed in 1828:

In no period of our domestic history has so universal a change in the manners and habits of the people generally, taken place, as within the last half-century. Even up to the period of which I am now speaking, about the year 1790, there were clubs and societies of humourists, of a cast and character so dissimilar to modern habits, that, with reference to their frequency then, we may be said to be no longer the same people.[62]

The reformation-of-manners movement had religious, moral, social and political threads running through it: indeed many of its targets were identical with the criticisms levelled against modern concerts. Concerts may well have fallen victim to moderation in the conspicuous display of luxury; certainly the decline of aristocratic patronage in the later 1790s was not matched by a rise in a new middle-class clientele. It is very significant that during the 1780s the ancient-music movement laid claim to the moral and artistic high-ground, matching precisely the aims of the Proclamation Society (with which some of the Directors of the Concert of Ancient Music were involved). The Ancient Concerts provided at one and the same time a worthy form of musical diversion, and a focus for responsible aristocratic leadership.

There were also other more purely musical reasons for the decline. After the long anticipation of Haydn throughout the 1780s and the crowning success of his twelve symphonies, the departure of Haydn in 1795 undoubtedly burst the bubble of the 'rage for music'.[63] No new symphonist of stature emerged; and no other composer was able to kindle the public imagination, as Mozart or Beethoven might have done had plans for them to come to London materialised. A natural cycle had come to an end. In 1799 no subscription series would have been organised at all without Cramer's last-minute revival of the Professional Concert; and despite a brilliant line-up this received only desultory attention. Some blamed the ascent of vocal music, symbolised by the success of the Vocal Concert; for in the longer term London's public concert life had to be dependent on a major symphonic repertoire. It was not until the founding of the Philharmonic Society in 1813 that London saw a self-conscious return to instrumental music, with a 'combination of excellence such as no other concert (since the dissolution of the professional concert) could boast'.[64] Looking back from the 1830s, Samuel Wesley judged the state of music in England by its public symphonic concerts: he was undecided as to whether it flourished most in the time of Bach, Abel and Giardini, or in that of Salomon and Haydn.[65]

Attracting an audience

The musical product: novelty and familiarity

The burgeoning of London's concert life during the later eighteenth century resulted, therefore, as much from social as from musical factors. Concerts achieved a social cachet quite independent of their intrinsic worth through appeals to exclusivity and emulation. Certain venues drew audiences through their own aura and associations, while some concerts became closely identified with well-known charities. At the same time the structure of London's concert life was becoming more clearly stratified, in terms of both audience and music, so that certain norms became established. Thus by the 1760s everyone knew quite precisely what to expect of the Covent Garden oratorio series under Handel's successors: temporarily at least they monopolised an established demand. There was no longer a need for the very idea of a concert to be sold to the public.

But this stabilisation of concert life by no means guaranteed success to promoters themselves. They were often subject to the most intense competition from other attractions of the town, from other concert-types and from direct rivals. Many seasons supported two subscription series, two oratorio series and two pleasure gardens (and often, some way behind, a third in each case). There were even two ancient-music societies and two royal orchestras. Individual musicians competed to attract audiences to their benefits during the crowded months of April and May. The press intensified such rivalries by establishing a whole series of critical dualities (Giardini against Cramer, Mara against Billington, Haydn against Pleyel and so on); in this respect London's musical scene resembled that of Paris, even if it lacked the same sense of intellectual partisanship.

Advertising

This chapter and the next are concerned with 'external' ways of making the musical product appeal to its target. While this target may have been essentially London's affluent élite, they were still susceptible to commercial marketing techniques. Concerts were advertised in several different ways. Handbills were

NEW MUSICAL FUND.

Under the PATRONAGE of their
Royal Highneſſes the PRINCE of WALES & DUKE of YORK.

At the King's Theatre, Pantheon,

On THURSDAY, FEBRUARY 24th, 1791,

WILL BE PERFORMED

A GRAND MISCELLANEOUS

CONCERT

O F

Vocal and Inſtrumental MUSIC,

FOR THE BENEFIT OF THE

New Muſical Fund,

ESTABLISHED FOR THE RELIEF OF

Decayed MUSICIANS, their WIDOWS, and ORPHANS, reſiding
in England.

Leader of the Band, Mr. CRAMER;
Conductors, Dr. HAYES and Dr. MILLER.

The BAND will conſiſt of near THREE HUNDRED PERFORMERS, for which an Orcheſtra will
be erected on the Stage. Among the Performers are—many of the Gentlemen of the OPERA BAND
and PROFESSIONAL CONCERT, the Young Gentlemen of His MAJESTY'S CHAPEL ROYAL, and the
Choir of WESTMINSTER ABBEY.

ACT I.	ACT II.
GRAND SYMPHONY — HAYDN.	CONCERTO VIOLIN, Maſter *Clement.*
CHORUS, " Gird on thy Sword." HANDEL.	SONG, Mr. *Neild.*
CONCERTO Grand Forte-piano, Mr. *Cramer*, Jun.	GLEE, " Awake, Æolian Lyre," for four Voices, DANBY.
SONG, Mr. *Bartleman.*	TRIO Two Violins & Violoncello, Mad. *Gautherot,* Mr. *Griesbach,* and Signor *Speratti* VIOTTI.
QUARTETTO, Meſſ. *Salomon, Mountain, Hindmarſh, & Menell* — HAYDN, M.S.	SONG, Signora *Storace.*
SONG, Signor *Paccheretti.*	SOLO VIOLIN, Mr. *Barthelemon,* } CORELLI. (by particular Deſire) —
CHORUS, " He gave them Hailſtones." HANDEL.	RECITATIVE and CHORUS, " Sing ye to the Lord." — — — HANDEL.

☞ PIT and BOXES TEN SHILLINGS and SIXPENCE;
And GALLERY, or GREEN BOXES, FIVE SHILLINGS.

⁎ The Doors will be opened at Half-paſt SIX o'Clock, and the Performance begin at Half-paſt Seven.

Subſcriptions are received, and Tickets delivered at Sir HERBERT MACKWORTH and Co.'s, Bankers, New Bond Street;
Meſſrs. HAMMERSLEY & Co.'s, Bankers, Pall-Mall; Meſſrs. LONGMAN and Co.'s Muſic Warehouſes, Cheapſide and
Haymarket; Meſſrs. THOMPSON's, St. Paul's Churchyard; Mr. FENTUM's, No. 78, Strand; Mr. FORSTER's, No. 348,
ditto; Mr. PRESTON's, ditto; Mr. BUCKINGER's, ditto; Mr. BLAND's, Holborn; Mr. BIRCHALL's, New Bond Street;
Mr. ANDREWS, ditto; Meſſrs. BETZ's, Royal Exchange; the Secretary's, Mr. H. KING, No. 358, near the Pantheon,
Oxford Street; the Office of the Pantheon; the Bar of the Crown and Anchor, Strand; and of the Society's Treaſurer,
Mr. SMART, at his Muſic Warehouſe, Corner of Argyll Street, Oxford Street.

VIVANT REX & REGINA.

N. B. A Subſcriber paying ONE GUINEA, will have TWO TICKETS; each of which will admit One Perſon to any Part of
the Houſe.

Such LADIES and GENTLEMEN as may be deſirous of encouraging the Society, by ſubſcribing to the Annual Performance,
are reſpectfully informed, that Tickets (emblematical of the Inſtitution, and which may be retained by Subſcribers) are
ready for Delivery at the above-mentioned Places.

BOOKS of the PERFORMANCE, with a LIST of the SUBSCRIBERS, both honorary and profeſſional, (ſold for the BENEFIT of the
FUND,) to be had at the PANTHEON only, Price One Shilling.

N. B. The Company are reſpectfully requeſted to order their Coachmen to ſet down and take up with their Horſes' Heads
towards Hyde-Park: The Door in Blenheim-Meuſe for Chairs only.

Plate 9 A handbill for the New Musical Fund benefit, 1791

posted around the town and features were occasionally run in the monthly magazines (in 1785 *The London Magazine* printed Burney's translation of an effusive German poem lauding the blind Maria Theresia Paradis). But the most conspicuous promotion was to be found in the daily press – in advertisements, puffs and reviews.

London promoters used newspaper-advertising from the very start of public concert life (unlike their counterparts in Vienna). Indeed public concerts can virtually be defined as those advertised in the daily press, since hardly any others have come to light from other sources. Press advertising was used for more than just basic information: it served to reassert the product's fashionable status as well as to keep promoters' names in the public eye. While repeated and over-emphatic advertisement could be a sign of increasing desperation, major series continued to advertise each individual concert in detail even when the subscription had been filled. It is difficult to document advertising practices and many questions cannot yet be satisfactorily answered. Newspapers undoubtedly had different types of readership: *The Public Advertiser* was a general advertiser originally directed at business interests, *The World* was a high-society paper emphasising fashionable amusements, *The Morning Chronicle* was a prominent Opposition paper in the 1790s, and so on. But the extent of their music coverage changes unpredictably from year to year. Certainly concert promoters do not seem to have targeted specific readerships; instead they scattered advertisements across the various titles in order to achieve a broad spread.[1]

The amount of information given varied considerably. For the first half of the period it was generally thought sufficient to provide a few performers' names to establish a concert's credentials. From the 1770s more detail is often given, in the shape of outline programmes that focus more on the compositions themselves; sometimes a badge of approval is added, such as direction by Bach and Abel or patronage by the Concert of Ancient Music. By the 1790s few advertisements fail to cite a complete programme, often itemising songs and glees by title. Even instrumental pieces could be identified in a rudimentary way ('the New Overture, as performed last Friday'); the Professionals emphasised quality by listing their complete orchestra. These trends reflect the rise of symphonic programmes, in which the nature of the instrumental music and the precision of its performance both played a vital role.

Such increasingly sophisticated packaging was not without its problems, however, since audiences enjoyed taking exception to last-minute changes. At the less refined venues, there were near-riots if an advertised performer failed to appear, resulting in grovelling apologies and accusations against malingering singers. A particular difficulty arose for subscription-series promoters. The system was designed to allow them to engage performers according to the number of subscribers. But prospective customers began to want more information before committing themselves: in 1785 Mara was chided for her 'admirable *deception*' in advertising a series with no details at all, and the Concert of Ancient Music was similarly criticised for selling a '*pig in a poke*'.[2]

The Professionals caused disquiet in 1790 when they announced that their main singers would only be arriving in the middle of the series; no doubt they were particularly sensitive to criticism since the previous season they had been let down by Mrs Billington only days before the first concert.

A less straightforward form of promotion took place in the daily news columns. Unashamedly partial promotional puffs such as the following undoubtedly required payment:

Miss Madden, the young Lady who is engaged to sing at the Hanover-square Concert, is the sister of Mrs. Cramer, and she promises to be a great acquisition to the musical world – She has never yet sung in public, but she is said to possess a very pleasing voice, with a considerable degree of sensibility and taste. Tenducci is her master, and he derives much honour from the proficiency of his scholar.[3]

Few readers can have been deceived by this surreptitious advertising. But the founding of *The Morning Post* in 1772 changed the tone with its emphasis on enticing news-scoops and personal gossip. A positive aspect of this transformation was increasing coverage of the performing arts, often now in columns headed 'Musical Intelligence' and the like. Some of this coverage was simply information or traditional puffing. But there was also a fair measure of malicious scandal amongst it. How far all this was news designed to sell newspapers and how far it was influenced behind the scenes it is impossible to discover. One revealing example of manipulation is the saga of Mara's disgrace and rehabilitation in 1785. She was persistently harangued in the press for her behaviour at the Abbey *Messiah*, in laughing insolently during the rehearsal and not staying to the end of the performance. Gleeful outrage greeted her refusal of an engagement at the Professional Concert to promote her own series. Particularly vituperative were *The Morning Post* and *The Daily Universal Register*, until the latter experienced a mysterious conversion, expressed in conciliatory paragraphs and a public apology from Mara. All these would certainly have been paid for; they were apparently written on her behalf by the author John Taylor. The campaign was completely successful, for within a year all the papers were agreed that Mara had been grossly mistreated.[4]

Concert reviews also played a major role in establishing reputations and promoting causes, especially after headed articles became common in the early 1780s. These anonymous reviews vary from useless panegyrics to substantial and well-informed critiques of individual pieces; sometimes they also include long lists of aristocratic and knowledgeable audience-members. But all is not as it seems. Reviews could be paid for, or strongly influenced, by concert managers. The minutes of the Lock Hospital Committee for 1 May 1766 record without any embarrassment its own concert review, to be inserted in *The Public Advertiser*. Reviews in the same newspaper in 1784 suggest that Abingdon's concerts were crowded with fashionable company, yet at the end of the series he resigned the management blaming the illiberality of the public. Sometimes newspapers were evidently persuaded to take a party-line. In 1790 *The World*

Che 🏵 Morld.

FRIDAY, MARCH 11, 1791.

At PLAY-HOUSE PRICES.
At the THEATRE ROYAL, DRURY-LANE,
THIS EVENING, MARCH 11th, 1791,
will be performed
A GRAND SELECTION,
From the Works of HANDEL.
The Principal Vocal Parts by
Mr. SPENCE, (being his first appearance in public)
Miss BROADHURST, (being her first appearance in Oratorios)
Miss HAGLEY, Mr. DIGNUM,
Mr. BELLAMY, Jun. (being his first appearance)
And Miss CECILIA DAVIS detta Inglesina,
(Being her first appearance in Oratorios)
Conductor, Mr. LINLEY.
First Violin by Mr. SHAW.
PART I.
Overture—Ariadne. Chorus, He smote all the first-born of Egypt.
Song—Mr. Bellamy, Honour and Arms—Samson.
Song—Miss Hagley, No more shall Edom's Sons. Chorus, Hear us O Lord.—Judas Mac.
Song—Miss Broadhurst, O magnify the Lord.
Song—Mr. Spence, Total Eclipse.—Samson. Chorus, O first Created Beam.—Samson.
Song—Miss Cecilia Davis, Let the bright Seraphims.
Coronation Anthem—Zadock the Priest.
PART II.
Introduction and Chorus, Ye sons of Israel—Joshua.
Song—Mr. Bellamy, Tears such as tender fathers shed.
Song—Miss Broadhurst, O had I Jubal's Lyre—Joshua.
Song—Mr. Dignum, There beneath a lowly shade.
Concerto on the Violin, by Master Clement, (being his 1st appearance at this Theatre.)
Chorus, Fallen is the foe—Judas Mac.
Song—Mr. Spence, Why does the God of Israel sleep?
Song—Miss Cecilia Davis, O Liberty!—Judas Mac.— Accompanied by Mr. Mason, on the Violoncello.
Chorus, The many rend the skies—Alexander's Feast.
PART III.
Grand Concerto, 5th—Handel.
Recit. I. not the King most mighty?
Song—Miss Hagley, On the charmer fondly gazing.
Chorus, For unto us a child is born—Messiah.
Song—Miss Broadhurst, Every day will I give thanks.
Song—Mr. Bellamy, Jehovah crown'd—Esther.
Chorus, He comes—Esther.
Song—Miss Cecilia Davis, Prophetic raptures—Joseph.
Song—Mr. Spence, O come let us worship.
Grand Chorus, Hallelujah, for the Lord God Omnipotent reigneth—Messiah.
No Money to be returned.—Books of the Performance to be had at the Theatre.
Places for the Boxes to be taken of Mr. Fosbrook, at the Theatre.
Boxes 5s.—Pit 3s.—First Gallery 2s.—Second Gallery 1s.
The Doors to be opened at Half past Five, and to begin at Half past Six o'Clock.   Vivant Rex et Regina!

AT PLAYHOUSE PRICES.
At the THEATRE-ROYAL, COVENT-GARDEN.
THIS Present Evening, March 11, A Grand SELECTION of
SACRED MUSIC,
From the Works of HANDEL,

READINGS,
LISLE-STREET, LEICESTER-FIELDS.
THIS EVENING will be Read, by Special and particular Desire, the favourite Comedy of Moliere, called
M. DE POURCEAUGNAC.
In Three Acts.
On Monday, the 14th instant, will be read, an entire new Comedy, which has been sanctioned in France with the greatest success, and called
LE PRESAGE VAINCU.
In Three Acts.
Subscription, as usual, One Guinea for four Readings, or four persons coming together.
Half a Guinea Subscriptions, for one person on two nights, but positively not for two persons coming together.
The Readings begin precisely at Eight o'Clock.
Subscription Tickets delivered in Lisle-street.

HANOVER-SQUARE.
MR. SALOMON most respectfully acquaints the Nobility and Gentry, that his Concerts will commence, without any further delay, This Evening, and continue every succeeding Friday.
PART the FIRST.
Overture—ROSETTI.
Song, Signor TAJANA.
Concerto (Oboe) Mr. HARRINGTON.
Song, Signora STORACE.
Concerto (Violin) Madame GAUTHEROT.
Recitativo e Aria, Signor DAVID.
PART the SECOND.
New Grand Overture, HAYDN.
Recitativo e Aria, Signora STORACE.
Concertante for (Pedal Harp and Piano Forte) Madame KRUMPHOLTZ, and Mr. DUSSECK;
Composed by Mr. DUSSECK.
Rondo, Signor DAVID.
Full Piece—KOZELUCH.
Mr. HAYDN will be at the Harpsichord.
Leader of the Band, Mr. SALOMON.
Subscriptions, at Five Guineas for the Twelve Concerts, to be received, and Tickets delivered, at Messrs. Lockharts, Bankers, No. 36, Pall Mall.
Tickets transferable—Ladies to Ladies, and Gentlemen to Gentlemen only.
The Ladies' Tickets green, and Gentlemens' Black.
☞ The Subscribers are intreated to give particular orders to their Coachmen, to set down and take up at the side door in the street, with the horses heads towards the square. The door in the square, is for Chairs only.

The following is the ANSWER of MR. HIPPISLEY, to Colonel MACLEOD's Communication of his intended MOTION in the House of Commons on Wednesday:
Grosvenor-street, March 9, 1791.
SIR,
I Am extremely obliged to you for the candour of your communication; and am to regret that I am still unable to attend my duty in the House, where I might have had an opportunity of replying to any observations you might make on the Statement read by Mr. Taylor at

THE CO
and Co
notice, That a
journment, on
furenoon, on spe

THATCHE

THE Se
will be
Th
Co
N. B. Suc
to send their
that it may b

King-str
WILL
qu
that the first
17th instant.
N.B. Pla
delivered at t
St. James's-s
☞ WILL
such of the N
quests they v
before the co
will be admit
are past.

Revised and
a N
LESSO
This first
elementary p
the best inte
be unmask
effect in Eng
In Englan
factions, and
has sold five
in the distrib
or any Arist
were publis
through Eur
The Publi
ness with w
putation of
known; the
revision; an
had for 6d. b
In order to
drawn from
House, and
colours:

Plate 10   Advertisements for Haydn's first London concert and for a Handel selection, 1791

consistently fêted the Pantheon concerts, ignoring the Professional Concert until a curtly dismissive review of their seventh concert: 'There was neither gaiety nor grief; more noise than work; and therefore the less that is said about it the better.'[5] The Professionals in their turn are supposed to have planted similar smears against Haydn in 1791. Occasionally an 'impartial critic' responded to such an attack: in the *Public Advertiser* of 18 March 1783 VERITAS defended Harrison, saying that neither puffs nor malice could touch him.

One way to curry favour with newspaper-editors was by the placing of advertisements. Though advertising did not guarantee review space, nevertheless there was a clear link between the two. Thus in 1789 the Professionals cut their advertising down from some seven newspapers to only three as the series progressed, and these were virtually the only papers to continue with reviews. Similarly when Salomon in 1786 persisted with advertisements in the minor *General Advertiser*, after the Professionals had stopped using it, he was rewarded with laudatory reviews. Conversely when the Professionals withdrew their advertising from the *World* its readers were informed of its 'poor, dull, heavy performance' attended only by 'a few straggling visitors', in contradiction of all available evidence.[6] Reviews could evidently be manipulated in the same way as puffs and they must often be regarded in the same light.

Not all promoters adopted the blandishments of high publicity. Bach and Abel seem to have disdained such an obviously commercial approach, advertising neither performers nor programmes. They relied instead on the social standing and musical reputation of their concerts; indeed they may consciously have sought to preserve the quasi-salon ambience as a prestige factor. Most organisers, however, actively sought to engage the attention of the public. Enticements pulled in two contradictory directions, stressing novelty on the one hand and familiarity on the other. When a complete concert programme was advertised, it had exactly this dual function: to emphasise the tried-and-trusted and to herald something new. Programmes for concerts at Marybone Gardens habitually highlighted songs as either new or favourite. Symphonies could even be advertised as 'the new favourite', an extreme example of eighteenth-century 'hype' which indicates how quickly a new symphony could attain a high profile.

Undoubtedly novelty was the more persuasive of the two. It would be an over-simplification to suggest that concert programming closely mirrored the inbuilt obsolescence of current consumerism, in the way that sales of piano music clearly did. London appreciated both familiar performers and recurrent repertoire. Yet the attraction of novelty was as potent here as in any other area of London's entertainment. A reviewer in 1788 described Giovanni Punto's horn concerto as 'new and astonishing', comparing it without irony to the current marvel 'the famous Stone-eater'.[7] Sometimes reviews focus only on 'the novelties of the night'. One consequence of a primarily contemporaneous musical culture, as William Weber has argued, was that it encouraged a unity of a broad public, whose taste did not need to defer to the authority of musical connoisseurs ('training was appreciated but not demanded').[8]

Thomas Robertson's analysis of the capricious taste of the British public, quoted on p. 12, might appear to suggest that the middle classes were themselves responsible for the emphasis on novelty. But genuine novelty was a powerful symbol of wealth and status, since it was not available at lesser concerts; it also reflected a progressive outlook, much in tune with the times. Novelty, though allied to aggressive commercialism, was therefore used to define the most fashionable concerts; others could attempt to emulate it as they wished. Foreigners regarded the unquenchable thirst for novelty as a British malady, and it undoubtedly resulted in shallow whims of caprice. Early in the period Mrs Delany described G. B. Marella cynically as 'our new, and *therefore* favourite performer'.[9] When Elizabeth Linley appeared at the Drury Lane oratorios in 1773 this of itself was enough to sweep them into fashion: 'The whole Town seem distracted about her. Every other Diversion is forsaken – Miss Linley Alone engrosses all Eyes, Ears, Hearts.'[10] Ten years later novelty was used as a principal marketing ploy for an attempted series at Freemasons' Hall, a review in *The Gazetteer* for 12 March noting that there would not be a permanent roster but 'all the variety that can be procured'.

It is impossible to escape the impression that performers and composers were subject to the same crazes as other entertainers. The career of Maddalena Sirmen provides a striking example. The dominant violinist of the 1771 season, she was eclipsed in 1772 by the horn-player Punto, and she returned disastrously as an opera-singer in 1773. Even the Mozart family found a second season much less encouraging than the first. A reviewer of the 1788 Professional Concert remarked rather caustically that 'it is not always that excellence receives the *stamp* of *fashion*'.[11] Yet the influence of novelty and fashion was not entirely negative. Anticipation of Haydn's arrival was fuelled by vigorous press coverage in the 1780s, his reception heightened rather than diminished by delays. While some felt that the capitalist exuberance of London's musical life was bound to lead to vulgarisation, others argued that this very abundance improved quality because of intense competition. As well as manipulating patronage and price, entrepreneurs sought both the distinctively new and the manifestly excellent, something Salomon conspicuously achieved with his engagement of Haydn as 'Europe's greatest composer'. Neil McKendrick has argued that fashion in general came increasingly under the control of the producers rather than the consumers towards the end of the century.[12] Though the transitory nature of the musical product makes it rather different, impresarios could at least nurture, if not dictate, quite radical changes in musical fashion, such as the vogues for Handel, Haydn and English vocal music in the last two decades of the century.

Personnel

The primary means of advertising a concert was through personnel. For much of the period it was thought sufficient simply to name the principal singers and instrumental soloists, whose names served alone as a signal of concert status: the product was defined, set within certain norms. This slant tended to emphasise stability and familiarity by calling upon established reputations. But at the same time promoters constantly sought new ways to attract attention by highlighting the exceptional and the sensational. Their efforts concentrated on three main areas: (1) previously unknown performers; (2) transfers across generally perceived boundaries of concert level; (3) novelties such as child prodigies, women instrumentalists or the handicapped.

The most conspicuous draw, usually heavily advertised, was a newly arrived performer. A début preceded by a continental reputation and by successful private appearances was always a major event of the season. Mrs Papendiek's account of London music is dominated by reports of débuts, and though careless in many details she recaptures much of the breathless anticipation of these occasions. Her account includes lengthy descriptions of the débuts of Salomon, Dussek and Haydn; and the following, of Mara, specifically engaged for the Pantheon concerts in 1784:

When Salomon brought this wonderful woman forward, there was perfect silence ... She tried her voice in a sort of prelude, a new idea among us. Then the *tutti* or symphony of the air commenced, and led up in *crescendo* to a high note, upon which Mara began. She held it for a few bars, then brought it to a long shake, and from it ran down an octave or more in notes as clear as bells. When she had finished her song the excitement was intense. The people almost screamed. The Prince [of Wales] came down and spoke to her as she descended the steps of the orchestra, and said how greatly he admired her.[13]

Elsewhere she mentions that concerts promoted by the Society of Musicians took place early in the season specifically in order to introduce new foreigners.[14] Sometimes these débuts gave the appearance of gladiatorial or territorial contests, for all Mrs Papendiek's girlish enthusiasm. Performers were constantly held up to comparison with present incumbents. The distinguished cellist Jean-Louis Duport, for example, played 'in a very finished stile', but could not rival John Crosdill or James Cervetto; he was said to be their equal in the upper and middle range, but deficient in the lower.[15] Even performances of specific works were venerated: at her trial in 1787 Miss Mahon was thought unwise to have attempted a Sacchini air popularised by Franziska Lebrun.[16] Charles Burney left a vivid account of his own début as a replacement for Stanley at the King's Arms concerts:

[This] I undertook with fear and trembling, being always extremely timid in public playing; but more now than ever, as I was sure that however well I may acquit myself professionally, all Stanley's friends w^d be my enemies, & very unwilling to be pleased. Luckily the first night I did not chance to play a Concerto of Handel, or of Felton, wch Stanley had ever played, & in which *l'esprit de comparaison* w^d certainly not have been in my favour ... I fortunately composed a concerto for the occasion, in wch I had not forgotten the sweetness of the Hautbois stop in the Adagio, wch by means of the swell happened to please.[17]

Such public scrutiny placed great pressure on new performers. Reviewers often describe the 'embarrassment' of a new soprano, and even Punto suffered acutely from pre-concert nerves.[18] Furthermore, the London audience liked to flaunt its independence. It was not always inclined to be sympathetic, especially towards those most extolled in advance: thus, for reasons that will be seen, the international star Luigi Marchesi met with lukewarm or even hostile reactions.

A successful début, however, was a guarantee of success for one season or beyond. Giardini first played at a private concert, where he 'threw into the utmost astonishment the whole company, who had never been accustomed to hear better performers than *Festing, Brown*, and *Collet*' and his public début received applause 'so loud, long, and furious, as nothing but that bestowed on Garrick had ever equalled'.[19] His reputation was made immediately, resulting quickly in concert appearances and a large number of aristocratic students. Viotti, too, was immediately acclaimed in this competitive environment: 'He combines the spirit and energy of CRAMER, with the elegance and expression of JARNOVICK [Giornovichi], and he sometimes surpasses both.'[20] Given the comparatively limited number of concerts and the vagaries of fashion it was quite possible for one performer per instrument to dominate a season, especially before the influx of foreigners in the 1790s. Thus in 1769 all other oboists were put into the shade by Fischer, and the popularity of Punto in 1772 was such that almost all important concerts contained a horn concerto (he performed at the two main oratorio series on alternate nights).

Foreigners were, of course, most fêted as novelties. Italian singers were in demand for concert appearances throughout the period. At first Italian instrumentalists were also dominant, but increasingly they gave way to those from German-speaking countries – the 'Teutonic interest and Germanic body' of Burney's description. Many reasons can be offered for this shift: connections made during the Seven Years' War, dispersal of German courts after it, new openings after the death of Handel, the preference of the Queen, musical style-changes. Certainly musicians thought it worthwhile to stress their Germanic origins. Thus at his benefit in 1758 Koerbitz advertised himself as musician to a current ally, the King of Prussia: the programme included music by the King himself and by Richter, 'Cabinet Composer to his Highness the Elector Palatine, who lately arrived from Germany'.[21] The situation in France after 1789 resulted in a new influx of foreign musicians, seldom French themselves but often connected with the royal court: 'Nothing less than the demolition of one Monarchy, and the general derangement of all the rest, could have poured into England and settled such a mass of talents as we have now to boast.'[22]

Concert promoters sought actively to attract such novelties from abroad. The Pantheon proprietors entered into the same market as the Opera by engaging singers such as Agujari, who was single-handedly able to fill the large hall.[23] Bach and Abel enticed instrumental soloists 'at a very great expence from Paris, Manheim, &c.', notably Cramer and Fischer.[24] To maintain novelty and exclusivity as long as possible promoters tried to negotiate contracts restricting performance elsewhere; sometimes advertisements stress this aspect by noting not only a first appearance, but a second and a third. In consequence it became necessary to ensure that all the newest novelties were on show, so that in 1785 the Professional Concert promised to engage 'all eminent performers who are, or may arrive in England'. This put considerable pressure on promoters: with Mara's quickly escalating success, the public came to expect her to be among the performers, even if she demanded £50 for a single aria.[25]

The bias towards foreigners, matching the upper-class predilection for Italian opera, did result in an unrivalled assemblage of outstanding performers, and for the most part Britain was sufficiently confident to accept the European influx. Even an English oboist, Redmond Simpson, had to admit to the superior talents of Fischer.[26] But the penchant was also frequently satirised. The *Connoisseur* article already cited mocked private concerts where (Catholic) Italian fiddlers and singers strutted around in lace or embroidery:

She is as busy in promoting their benefits as if she was to have the receipts of the house; and quarrels with all her acquaintance, who will not permit her to load them with tickets. Every fidler in town makes it his business to scrape an acquaintance with her, and an *Italian* is no sooner imported than she becomes a part of my wife's band of performers.

Foote and Sheridan included similar parodies in their plays. More direct was the xenophobic 1785 press campaign against Mara's proposed concerts, one of the grounds for complaint being that she intended employing only foreigners: *The Morning Post* during November took pains to remind her that British generosity to foreign singers was dependent on gratitude in return. The stance of public and promoters alike reflected a considerable vein of prejudice against British performers of real talent. It was suggested that the violinist Hindmarsh would enjoy a 'distinguished reputation' were he an Italian.[27] In 1790 the singer Thomas Curtis rather forlornly advertised that he hoped his being an Englishman would 'be no impediment to his being heard'. Inevitably, too, it was difficult to market British performers as novelties: by way of substitute, an advertisement in 1782 drew attention to Eliza Wheeler's recent return from Italy.

Even the most celebrated foreigner faced the danger of over-familiarity as his career progressed. By 1788 Fischer himself was all too well established, and a review followed a standard line: 'though the novelty is gone, the excellence remains unimpaired'.[28] Such items may have formed part of a deliberate marketing strategy. One newspaper printed a panegyric of the violinist Cramer ('it is nothing less than ludicrous, when *John Bull*, with ideot Wonder, runs after every new Pretender'): only for another to hint that this had been planted by Cramer himself, as an oblique attack on Louisa Gautherot. Two years later London was informed that the same violinist 'can easily put out of countenance the obtrusive *novelties* of the day'.[29] Another ruse was the come-back performance: Cecilia Arne returning after twenty years in 1774, Caterina Galli after sixteen years in 1773. Most sensationally, if ill-advisedly, the septuagenarian Galli was back again in 1797, singing Handel's 'He was despised' and claiming it had been written for her. The end of a London career also had some marketing value. Sometimes a last performance took the form of a sentimental farewell benefit: Giardini took his leave after forty-one years with a performance of *Ruth* at Ranelagh Gardens, attended by an unprecedented 'assemblage of professors and esteemed connoisseurs', who added financial reward to their appreciation. Such occasions could, however, be rather desperate objects of charity. Having already taken two benefits in 1751, the ageing Francesca Cuzzoni gave a final concert on 23 May out of 'extreme Necessity' to pay her creditors.

Another significant if temporary marketing ploy was the breaking-down of established norms. Especially later in the century, performers became stratified according to the various layers of London's concert life, with nationality playing a significant role. This phenomenon will be investigated in more detail in chapter 11. In summary, however, the main subscription concerts were dominated by Italian opera singers and foreign instrumentalists; the principals at the top English concerts, including oratorios and gardens, were mostly British singers and instrumentalists from the playhouses, or organists and singers from the best choral foundations; while at the lower reaches of London's concert life were inferior British performers on the fringes of theatrical and church activities. Musicians from the different layers did not often mix, as evidenced by a remark in 1786 that the Anacreontic Society was 'the only place where the performers of the English stage join with the orchestra performers of the concerts'. In the same year Cramer declined the offer of leadership at Vauxhall Gardens, and it was a matter for regret that 'Maras and Billingtons' could not be heard there.[30] Impresarios were therefore quick to seize upon exceptions to these normal patterns.

Upwardly mobile movement was comparatively rare. Most conspicuously it involved the infiltration of British singers into the top stratum. Both Harrison and Mrs Billington achieved early recognition at the Hanover Square concerts in the 1780s, Harrison's success confounding the assertion 'that foreigners are preferred to English professors, regardless of their comparative merits'.[31] Almost invariably, however, they sang Italian songs on these occasions, Mrs Billington modelling her style on that of Allegranti. More notable for publicity purposes were excursions of the top performers downwards. In 1768 the Covent Garden oratorio-promoters broke with their normal practice by advertising the famous opera-singer Tommaso Guarducci. It was also at such series that the widest audiences could hear top instrumentalists play concertos, and the attraction of these is attested by complaints in 1766 when the number of concertos was reduced. Towards the end of the century concertos were often performed by guest artists not otherwise involved: Dussek, for example, played piano concertos at many Covent Garden oratorios in the 1790s.

Ancient music represented something of a special case after royal patronage of the Concert of Ancient Music catapulted it to the highest status. English oratorio singers were here joined by top international artists such as Mara and Banti; Cramer took over the role of top Handelian leader. Not everyone was convinced by the engagement of foreign singers in Handel, and mutterings about faulty pronunciation recalled the 1730s. But audiences at the Concert became accustomed to the very best singers of the day. This served only to exaggerate the sensation of Mara's appearance at the 1787 Drury Lane oratorios, where she even joined the management with Linley and Arnold. The Academy of Ancient Music likewise sought to enhance its more fashionable tone by engaging singers from a higher bracket. The leadership of the Academy neatly encapsulates this change – escalating from an amateur gentleman, through David Richards and Barthelemon, to Salomon in 1789.

Appeals to the curious were made by parading minorities of all kinds (ethnic, young and old, non-Christian, handicapped); even women might be regarded in a similar light. In almost all cases success was measured by how closely these performers measured up to the achievements of the European male aged twenty to fifty. Thus the young mulatto violinist George Polgreen Bridgetower was marketed as the 'son of the African Prince', his father dressed in extravagant Turkish robes. Yet he had been trained at the Esterházy court and he performed standard Giornovichi and Viotti concertos. Following his father's disgrace, he was groomed to appear as a young English gentleman, following in the footsteps of the black violinist the Chevalier de Saint-Georges. Though it would never have been advertised, the Jewishness of the Abrams sisters was thought by George Selwyn worthy of comment:[32] but they were prominent performers of Christian sacred music at the Ancient Concerts and elsewhere.

Perhaps the only nation to maintain a distinctive voice was Wales. London audiences heard a number of Welsh harpers, notably John Parry (who retained the traditional triple harp) and Edward Jones. Their product was both unusual and fashionable. Celtic songs were already popular from the theatre, but their untainted beauty – evocative but not uncomfortably foreign – could be emphasised in concert performance. Harpists thus advertised Welsh airs at the centrepiece of their programmes. There must have been some Welsh expatriate market (Parry was employed by Wynn, prominent member of the Society of Ancient Britons), and Evans gave one concert in 1757 'for the Encouragement of the Welch Harp'. But it seems likely that such concerts had a wider middle-prestige appeal. No comparable Scottish endeavour has been identified: James Oswald's 'Society of the Temple of Apollo' was only a club of musicians associated with Scotland, not a concert organisation.

Some handicapped performers drew attention to their disability, again aspiring to be judged against 'normal' standards. Blind performers treated their blindness in different ways. Some like Stanley and Parry made no mention of it, some traded on it as a charitable cause, others made it an attraction similar to shows in town. Thus Friedrich Ludwig Dülon was advertised as a blind flautist, and he let it be known that he had memorised over 500 concertos; similarly the young blind pianist Miss Paradis became, through the full glare of London publicity, an object of considerable curiosity. All of these performers aspired to present a picture of normality. So too in a different way did the Polish dwarf 'Count' Boruwlaski. Though he performed at his benefit on 13 June 1783 on the English guittar (an undemanding lady's instrument) and appeared at first in national dress, he changed during the interval into the garb of an English gentleman, and his real act was to be regarded as a man of breeding and culture.[33]

Most performers neglected to draw attention to their advancing age (Cervetto the elder was still a concert cellist at the age of eighty-three). Unusually, Gaetano Besozzi on his arrival in London in 1793 gave his age as nearly eighty (in reality sixty-six, which was still remarkable for an oboist). Young performers, on the other hand, were a constant theme: girls as singers and keyboard-players, boys likewise (but favouring the organ over the harpsichord) and as violinists. To be worthy of note, the age had to be below fourteen, and typically it was reduced by a year or more, as in the case of Mozart. Many of these prodigies were exploited by musical parents at benefit concerts – annually in the case of the Davies family in the 1750s or the Weichsells in the 1770s. Mrs Weichsell was careful not to flood the market, advertising that Charles and Elizabeth (later Mrs Billington) would perform only once in 1776. An apprentice might also be thrust into the public gaze, with the name of his teacher advertised to give credibility to the performer and publicity to the master. Arne's name was often prominently displayed in this way, and Clementi ensured that his name was associated with his talented young apprentice Field. It was also useful if some further credentials could be advertised, such as the name of a patron, an appearance before royalty, or training abroad: Joseph Agus was able to describe himself in 1773 as a 'Scholar of Sig. Nardini, lately arrived from Italy'.

Even more attractive was a concert of two prodigies, such as the memorable concert given on 2 June 1790 by the young violinists Franz Clement and George Polgreen Bridgetower (both well known from their subsequent Beethoven performances). Uniquely a whole concert on 23 April 1760 featured young performers, all aged supposedly between nine and thirteen: Hugh Barron, violin (later a prominent artist); Burney's daughter Esther, harpsichord; James Cervetto, the famous cellist; Gertrud Schmeling, violin (Madame Mara). The Wesley family preferred not to subject Charles and Samuel to this demeaning public scrutiny; they did not however neglect to charge admission to their private concerts, and concertos by the young performers featured strongly.

Again there was counterpoint between presentation and performance. Though as a boy Charles Weichsell might stand on a stool, he was expected to play a violin concerto by one of the masters of the day. Prodigies aspired to be regarded as fully fledged concert artists, and criticisms are almost always addressed to this very issue: Clement was judged 'a mere child in age, but a veteran in ability'.[34] Indeed the only concession made to youths was that they were not required to play their own concertos – it was worthy of note that

Clement did – and they might choose less demanding genres such as the sonata. Mrs Thrale added a touch of cynicism to the same line: 'Little Bridgetower – a Boy not quite ten Years old plays on the violin like a 1st rate performer – and as the best proof of his Merit, – is paid like one.'[35] But there were also more cautious, perhaps more honest assessments: Miss Paradis performed 'better than could have been expected', Robert Lindley played a cello concerto 'in a very fine style for his years'.[36] Some young sopranos were gently recommended to take some tuition or visit Italy, and one critic wrote much more acerbically:

Miss Paradis, with various abatements, how many prodigies in the musical world have appeared – allowing this and that deficience, how wonderful. So it has been with every infantine exertion of late – the Mozart, the Thomasino [Linley], little [Maria Hester] Parke, &c, – But what is all this to positive excellence? To Charles [Rousseau] Burney, Miss Guest, and yet more to Clemente? – Very well it may be for a poor blind girl – But – why is the auditor at an half-guinea concert to be fobb'd off with buts?[37]

There was also awareness of the danger that a child prodigy might not fulfil his promise: '[Clement] is one of those Musical Prodigies which should be seen when *young*, as their Value generally decreases when their talents may be expected to ripen.'[38] In fact all the prodigies so far mentioned did 'ripen' into established performers, though Thomas Linley's career was tragically cut short by a boating accident. But many others did indeed simply disappear from public view, and it was certainly an important step in the career of a prodigy to shed the label at some point. J. B. Cramer, for example, toured the continent from 1788 to 1790, before returning as a fully fledged artist. Back from training in Italy, Weichsell (or the Pantheon proprietors) took the precaution of inserting a puff in *The Morning Post* for 31 October 1789: 'It is not for the sake of novelty that this young man is preferred to the veteran performers now in this country; but because no veteran performer is to be considered as his superior, so that he brings with equal talents all the fire of juvenile enthusiasm.'

As far as attracting an audience is concerned, women must be regarded as a special case. Women singers (usually with a stage connection) took part regularly in concerts and presented no particular novelty, though no concert could be without one, and reviewers regarded looks and manner as part of the product on offer. Women instrumentalists attracted more comment. They were now transferring into the concert hall not the theatre but the private salon, with strong social implications; and by taking music seriously enough to be able to perform in public, they represented an implied threat to the social order.[39] The sense of transfer was emphasised by the fact that they were inevitably 'separate', not being part of the orchestra. Most women performed on fashionable ladies' instruments – harpsichord or piano, musical glasses, English guittar in the early 1760s, harp from 1774. While all these instruments were designed for solitary amusement or demonstrations of accomplishment, most could also take the solo part in concertos: indeed some women professionals were undoubtedly first-rate artistes, especially foreigners such as the harpist Anne-Marie Krumpholtz.

More radical was performance on 'male' instruments – the flute by Marianne Davies, the viola da gamba by Ann Ford, the violin by Maddalena Sirmen and Louisa Gautherot. The violinists were regarded as a particular curiosity (Mrs Delany called Sirmen 'the *fiddling woman*'). They were subject to two main criticisms. In the first place the violin was regarded as intrinsically unsuitable for ladies, challenging social norms still further: not only was it a traditional gentlemen's instrument, but as the instrument of the leader it was a symbol of dominance (women did not play in orchestras, let alone direct them).[40] London ladies managed to persuade Miss Schmeling (Mara) to develop her voice instead of the violin, and even Sirmen toyed with the harpsichord and singing. As Mrs Thrale commented pithily in 1789: 'How the Women do shine of late! ... Madame Krumpholtz' Tasteful Performance on the Harp, Madame Gautherot's wonderful Execution on the Fiddle; – but say the Critics a Violin is not an Instrument for *Ladies* to manage, very likely!'[41] A critic was moved to write that he had 'no objection to the efforts of the sex on the Violin' *per se*, but he then voiced the second recurrent gripe, 'that it requires the more muscular tone of a man, than the delicacy of female nerves to accomplish the instrument'.[42] For all these criticisms, however, both Sirmen and Gautherot achieved genuine celebrity for their performances of the most demanding violin concertos of the day.

Instruments and techniques

One way to attract attention was through new or improved instruments, or through unusual instrumental techniques. This area was particularly susceptible to whim, and there were the usual adverse comments, such as the following in *The Morning Chronicle* of 8 March 1791: '[The harp] is an instrument that *caprice* has for a few years made fashionable, but which *true taste* will speedily dismiss.' Yet meaningless stunts, such as Castrucci's '24 notes with one bow' advertised in 1731, were distinctly uncommon in the more sophisticated later years of the century, and they would have been regarded as embarrassingly gauche at major concert series. More notable were changes that involved mechanical improvements – facilitating chromatic-playing, expanding the expressive range for the new music, seeking more brilliance and volume for the concert-hall concerto. Such improvements could be stressed both for their novelty value and as emblems of progressive modernity, as if advanced mechanical invention was also a sign of artistic worth.

Solo instruments carried over from the 1740s included the violin, cello, flute, oboe, bassoon, harpsichord and organ. All of these underwent considerable alteration during the next half-century, with some changes originating at home and some imported from Europe. The violin bow saw major experiment, partly independent from French developments (one transitional bow was even associated with Cramer). Fischer introduced a new design of oboe from Germany, and the range of the flute was increased. The London harpsichord-makers Shudi and Kirckman led the way in the 1760s with their powerful, opulent models and new forms of dynamic control such as the Venetian swell. England retained a special partiality for the organ (in 1764 Mozart played an organ concerto at a Ranelagh charity benefit, 'the act of an English patriot'); but the pedal-board was virtually unknown, until in 1790 Vogler demonstrated alterations he made to the Pantheon organ.[43] The 1790s also saw a change in attitude towards male singers. Castrati had always taken a major role at fashionable concerts (culminating in the rival appearances of Marchesi and Pacchierotti at rival series in 1790), but the following decade witnessed their rapid decline from favour. It is surely significant that (in Davide and Fischer) Salomon engaged a tenor and a bass of international reputation.

Major though all of these changes were for the sound of the music, they were nevertheless rarely remarked directly. Of much more immediate appeal to audiences were new solo instruments. Some of these were destined for oblivion, some were occasional oddities, a few eventually settled into permanence. Among the latter were hitherto lowly orchestral instruments that now firmly achieved the status of solo instrument. Viola concertos were played by several violinists, and a real specialist emerged in Carl Stamitz (whose violin playing was 'very inferior'). The viola was still regarded, however, as a lesser kind of violin, so that when in 1789 Borghi could not play second violin in Cramer's quartet Blake moved up from viola to take his place. The double bass became an acknowledged solo instrument in the hands of Joseph Kaempfer in 1784 and Domenico Dragonetti in the 1790s. Both used a virtuoso solo-tuning: Kaempfer retained the German five-stringed bass, while Dragonetti preferred a three-stringed instrument, on which he achieved a tone 'infinitely more pleasant than was ever before thought possible'.[44]

The horn already had a prominent role in orchestral music. During the 1750s advertised programmes commonly add the phrase 'with horns' to concertos (presumably implying symphonies and suites such as the *Water Music*); four horns were promised at a benefit in 1758. But the players remain unidentified until the rise of modern concertos around 1770. The travelling virtuosi Rodolphe and Punto did much to establish the instrument. Nevertheless the horn retained a strong curiosity value, with not everyone relishing its charms:

To those who love trick, and unexpected discovery of what an instrument can perform, Pieltain's horn is a great treat: the French horn is by him made so soft, so voluble, and minute in its modulations, that it might accompany a female voice in a room ... The Horn Concerto of PIELTAIN was surprizing for such an instrument and was as pleasing as it is possible to render sounds that, singly considered, have so little alliance with what is understood by the term *Music*.[45]

Three chromatic French horns appeared for the first time at the 1776 Covent Garden oratorios, though it is unclear what is meant by this; it was similarly remarked that Palsa and Türrschmidt could modulate through different keys without changing crooks.[46] Like horns, orchestral trumpets were accorded special mention during the 1750s, but concerto performances were rare. At Vauxhall around 1790 even London's principal trumpeter James Sarjant preferred to play an arrangement of Handel's 'Se l'arco'. Not until 1799 did the trumpet concerto re-emerge when John Hyde introduced his chromatic slide trumpet. The timpani achieved a transient solo role in the preambles for four kettle-drums played by Joseph Woodbridge in 1752; but an unexpected mantle followed the construction of outsize 'double kettle-drums' for the 1784 Commemoration, so that the timpanist in ancient music advertisements might even be highlighted in preference to others.

Some more peripheral instruments came to greater prominence after 1750. The viola da gamba had never established a permanent place at London's public concerts, but Abel continued to play solos on it until the year of his death (1787); even if 'every one disliked' the querulous tone of the instrument, the reputation and influence of Abel's playing were immeasurable.[47] The harp had been demanded by Handel in special circumstances (it was David's instrument in *Saul*); in *Judith* (1761) Arne responded to the text 'Wake, my harp' with a conspicuously galant aria featuring the instrument. Presumably these pieces were intended for the Welsh triple harp, which figured in concert advertisements well into the second half of the century. By 1769 the single action harp had reached England, and in 1775 Edward Jones felt it necessary to advertise performance on the 'Improved Welch or Pedal Harp', to which he had been converted on a trip to Paris.[48] Further development of the harp, together with its adoption as a domestic instrument, gave it a new status in concerts, and during the 1790s Anne-Marie Krumpholtz performed major concertos by Dussek. The harp was also used to accompany songs, notably the simple but affecting 'Ah che nel petto io sento' (or 'Hope told a flatt'ring tale'), popularised in 1791 by Mara and the young harpist Meyer. This vogue capitalised on the fashion for the harp among young ladies, while also carrying Gothic overtones of the lone Celtic harper.

The clarinet had appeared in London concerts as early as 1726, but it only slowly gained acceptance. Its primary function was in military bands and in small wind groups at the gardens. In the concert hall it was popularised by Charles Barbandt, who in 1755 advertised a concerto grosso with clarinets, horns and kettle-drums. During the next decade Arne introduced the clarinet idiomatically into his English operas, while J. C. Bach soon showed his understanding of its mellifluous potential in both Italian operas and symphonies. But as a solo instrument it came to prominence only from 1773 in the hands of John Mahon, and one reviewer clearly still disliked the instrument ('Mahon's Clarinet is as well as a Clarinet can be').[49] Bach himself wrote little solo clarinet music, and the instrument maintained only a peripheral place in concert orchestras until 1792. Even then Haydn did not employ clarinets throughout his last six symphonies and he showed conspicuous caution in his limited allocation of solos.

The piano was unknown in England until the 1750s. Often described but still a matter of some debate are London's rapid achievements in piano-manufacture, encouraged by the arrival of Germans such as Zumpe.[50] The early square pianos were small instruments, cheaper than full-size harpsichords, but highly fashionable as domestic instruments from the late 1760s onwards. The piano's first recorded public appearance was in 1767 (Dibdin accompanying a song at Covent Garden on 16 May); Hook followed with a piano concerto on 7 April 1768 and J. C. Bach with a solo on 2 June. It is difficult to imagine, however, that Bach had not already introduced a piano at his subscription concerts to play the Op. 5 sonatas, published in 1766. These early performances may have used a Zumpe square, but towards 1770 Backers developed his new grand piano design; it is surely significant that Bach's first piano concertos (Op. 7) were published in that very year. The grand became well established in concerts during the 1770s, though as yet the harpsichord refused to die, and the two instruments were even combined by Merlin in 1774. But by the next decade the piano was clearly in the ascendancy. Clementi was credited by Samuel Wesley with raising its esteem; another writer traced the source of the modern piano school to Clementi's brilliantly pianistic Op. 2 sonatas of 1779.[51] In 1785 Paradis was censured for retaining the harpsichord for a concerto. Piano design was still changing rapidly, and during the 1780s Broadwood's large grands overcame earlier technical deficiencies and limited dynamic capabilities. Dussek twice persuaded Broadwood to add to the range of the instrument, and like other London soloists of the 1790s he made distinctive use of the sustaining pedal in softly syncopated passages. Later he went into the piano business himself, adding further 'refinements' such as the triangle and tambourine.[52] Meanwhile the piano achieved the highest profile as a solo instrument, at last rivalling the violin. Whereas the harpsichord and early piano had often been played by women and children, in the 1790s London heard many performers of international repute, including Clementi, J. B. Cramer, Dussek, Steibelt and Field.

Other instruments must be mentioned more briefly. All of these by virtue of their rarity received special mention in the press, including the piccolo; the tenor oboe, oboe d'amore and cor anglais; a pair of basset horns; musical bells ('tintinnabula'). After over forty years of quiescence orchestral trombones were revived at the 1784 Commemoration; a single trombone was widely used to reinforce the bass-line in symphonies from 1792 onwards, reflecting the relative weakness of the bass area in the Classical orchestra. Turning to stringed instruments, several violinists introduced the viola d'amore and such variants as the viola partout, 'lain by unattempted for 130 Years' until 1768; while during the 1770s Andreas Lidl made a speciality of the baryton. A number of mandolinists appeared in London, and the 276-stringed pantaleon was only one of many unusual plucked instruments heard there. Even concert performances of the bagpipes and Indian instruments are recorded. Some obscure performers plainly specialised in obscure instruments – thus Merchi played the Spanish guitar, calascioncino and his own liutino moderno; Gonetti the mandolin, English guittar, psaltery and musical glasses. Even Abel advertised his 1763 benefit only as a concert featuring new instruments, one of which was perhaps Sir Edward Walpole's pentachord.

Two instruments unique to this period enjoyed a brief vogue as ladies' instruments before the establishment of the piano. Possibly both reflected the search for a solo instrument more 'expressive' than the harpsichord. The English guittar (a type of cittern) was an undemanding domestic instrument in fashion briefly from about 1757; in 1760 it made some rather lowly public appearances. The following year musical glasses came into fashion in London's concerts, either in their original form or in Benjamin Franklin's waterless version (introduced as the 'armonica' by Marianne Davies in 1762). The years 1761 to 1764 saw a spate of daily exhibition performances given by young ladies and by self-publicising teachers. Though the fashion proved short-lived, the instrument was revived from time to time throughout the period. In 1794 the blind Marianne Kirchgessner played Mozart's quintet K. 617 at a Salomon concert, while in 1800 John Cartwright leavened his scientific demonstrations at the Lyceum with performances on the glasses.

New instruments were sometimes described in some detail and advertisements were not necessarily restricted to the performance itself. Thus in 1763 Davies made sure to point out that she had an armonica for sale, and William Crotch advertised in 1785 that he would play on a portable organ by Holland. The inventor Charles Clagget used the concert platform unashamedly to promote his new instruments. On 18 May 1790, for example, he featured his teliochordon (a piano with improved tuning), a chromatic double-horn and a metallic organ (a form of celeste). The concert was co-ordinated with advertisements for the collection of instruments he called his 'Musical Museum'. During another concert in 1793 he read out an address on instrument design, including a testimonial from Haydn.

Some instrumentalists made a special point of particular effects. Ashe advertised that he would play double notes on the flute; Weichsell performed Ferrari's violin solo 'with the Harmonic Stops'; the oboist Fischer showed off his ability to swell a very long note from pianissimo to forte and back again. Extending an instrument's standard range was always worthy of comment, not only violinists 'fiddling away in alt' but also the oboist William Parke attempting a top G as if it were an Olympic record. Ludwig Fischer was commended for his extraordinary vocal range from a deep bass to countertenor 'without the slightest break in the voice', when most men went into falsetto above E.[53]

Noteworthy changes took place in orchestras and choirs, as will be seen in chapter 12. For much of the half-century, orchestras remained around thirty to forty in strength, and choirs around twenty-five to thirty-five; but exceptional features could form a special attraction. Thus in the 1750s attention was drawn to the presence of horns, trumpets or clarinets, and Niccolo Pasquali added brass instruments to one of Corelli's string concertos. Later J. C. Bach's symphonies for double orchestra were frequently advertised. More sensationally Carl Stamitz in 1778 promised a second orchestra as an invisible echo, and something similar was tried at Vauxhall in 1781. A choir was in itself worthy of comment, since they were rarely used outside 'ancient' venues. Thus Tenducci rather naively promised 'a good Choir' at Ranelagh Gardens in 1762. At Covent Garden on 26 February 1773 an important transformation took place: at a performance of Arne's *Judith* women were first introduced into a London choir.

Unusual numbers of performers were always worthy of advertisement: near 60 at Arne's benefit in 1776, over 100 at a charity benefit in December 1779, perhaps as many as 240 at the 1775 Ranelagh regatta festivities. The 1784 Handel Commemoration with its 525 performers of course inspired a more general increase in numbers. As the festival reached gargantuan levels in 1791 (the 1,067 performers were at last too unwieldy, according to one review), oratorio series had to move some way along this road. Ashley employed over 200 at Covent Garden in 1795, and the rival King's Theatre series could raise nearly as many. The following year the New Musical Fund advertised a band of 400 for its benefit. Though these were quite exceptional events, the trend had some influence on ordinary symphonic concerts. In 1792 the Professional Concert drew attention to its extra instrumentalists, an attraction that Salomon felt obliged to match; while three years later the Opera Concert raised orchestral numbers to sixty. Even for a benefit, Harrison engaged 100 performers in 1794 in order to perform Handel choruses.

A quite new kind of concert outfit was the military band, which first came to public notice on parade in St James's Park. When in 1783 an octet was succeeded by the Duke of York's 24-piece German band large crowds were attracted.[54] In 1790 the same band appeared on important nights at Vauxhall, playing selections of martial music; the practice continued during the 1790s, as war became an ever more pressing topic.

Repertoire: novelty and familiarity

The marketing of concert repertoire shared many features with that of personnel. Again novelty was a major factor, one that became increasingly important as competition increased in the 1780s. In order to highlight specific works, rather than just the composer, they were often advertised as new or manuscript; in 1797 Dussek announced that he would play a new piano concerto 'for the only time this season'. Again exclusivity and prestige attached to an impresario that could command such events. Certainly it was not easy to assure exclusivity of repertoire, because of the ever-present possibility of pirating and the temptation to publish soon after performance. On the other hand, composers themselves, producing a stream of new works, did not go out of fashion as quickly as did performers. Furthermore, some works were already becoming part of an established repertoire, works whose very familiarity was itself a selling point.

The minority composer was a much less marketable commodity than the performer. The element of exhibition was lacking and few such musicians had received sufficient training. Solo repertoire apart, prodigy composers are hardly ever advertised (Mozart's symphonies in 1765 thus provide a striking exception). Still rarer was performance of music by women composers. Songs or keyboard music were occasionally heard, such as Mrs Billington's sonata on 7 May 1792. But these were scarcely major contributions. Two concerts must therefore be regarded as quite remarkable: one promoted by Elisabetta Chazal (née Gambarini) in 1764, at which two of her own odes were given; and a performance in 1792 of the oratorio *Comala* by Harriet Wainwright, 'a young Lady, not professionally educated'.[55]

As with personnel, norms of repertoire were clearly perceived. Principal concerts were dominated by music from the continental traditions – Italian for vocal music, Italian and Austro-German for orchestral music. This was either provided by resident foreigners or imported in manuscript and foreign editions. English concerts on the other hand (including those at the gardens) were based round songs, odes and overtures by British composers. In 1756 the St Caecilian Society announced its devotion to the cause of English music under the direction of Arne. Fashionable prejudice against English programmes was reflected in a review of Samuel Webbe's 1785 benefit, complaining of the unattractive selection of eight out of fifteen items by the English school.[56] English composers hit back with parodies of Italian vocal music, such as Hook's dialogue *The Musical Courtship*, greeted with roars of laughter at Vauxhall in 1788, and Dibdin's amusing 'You must begin pomposo'.[57] In his 'Comparison' of 1796 John Marsh wrote with real regret of this divide between foreign and British musical cultures, especially that between Italian and English vocal music. Evidently the division was deeply felt.

Promoters of fashionable West End concerts were even less inclined to risk crossing these boundaries by introducing British music than they were by employing local soloists. During the 1750s English songs by Stanley and Greene did find their way into the Dean Street and Decayed Musicians' concerts. But British vocal music was seldom heard at the most prestigious concerts thereafter: even Storace's topical 'Captivity ... supposed to be sung by Marie Antoinette' was not well received at the Professional Concert in 1793. The stand taken at the 1774 Pantheon Concert, which combined Italian and English interests, was short-lived: the English element was soon dropped, so that when in 1780 Elizabeth Harper sang an Arnold song 'in a different stile of musick from the rest of the concert' this received special comment.[58] It was almost impossible for an English composer to get his instrumental works performed in such company, despite press comments that there were neglected composers in London. An unusual exception was the brief promotion of the young Thomas Rawlings by the Professionals in 1791–2; but a much better known composer among their violinists, William Shield, received not a single performance there. Only the radical departure provided by the Vocal Concert in 1792 raised the English vocal school to the fashionable level; even the Professional Concert included glees in its 1793 programme and top benefits began to include some English vocal music.

English concerts, by contrast, were much more willing to feature foreign music than foreign performers. This reflects not only its general availability and a recognition of its qualities but also some appeal to novelty and fashion. Only occasionally were arias sung in Italian: the inclusion of several arias in Michael Arne's 1751 benefit was a rarity, even if aspiring sopranos continued to be fond of Italian showpieces and Harrison occasionally included them at the Vocal Concert. More typically Italian music was taken over into the English repertoire in translation, either via the playhouses or directly, as with some of Bach's Vauxhall songs. At Marybone the burlettas of Pergolesi and Galuppi were naturally performed in English. Still more striking was the transfer of foreign symphonic repertoire, which after initial resistance took hold in the later 1760s with the general acceptance of the new German symphonies. Sometimes this repertoire itself originated in the playhouse (in 1762 Abel contributed the overture to *Love in a Village*), but usually it must have come from subscription concerts via printed editions. Haydn's symphonies were introduced at Vauxhall in 1783,[59] and modern Austro-German symphonies were soon dominant here, alongside though not ousting English theatrical overtures.

Prestigious concerts were able to ensure novelty in their repertoire through European connections. Some attempts to publicise unusual sources were made early in the period. In 1750 Geminiani put on a concert of sacred music collected in Italy, while four years later Giuseppe Passerini brought back music from the Prussian court; in 1764 Jommelli's *La passione* was lent by a gentleman. New music was certainly arriving all the time from Europe, both through the lively enterprise of publishers and in manuscripts brought by travelling musicians. Thus Richter introduced his unfamiliar Mannheim symphonies in 1758, while in 1773 Punto put on a Haydn symphony (the first known performance in London). But there was not as yet a concerted attempt on the part of London promoters to obtain foreign music as a selling-point. This all began to change in the late 1770s with the opening up of a more European awareness. In some ways this was a direct response to current dissatisfaction, as Burney realised:

The same concert now subsists in a still more flourishing way than ever, under the denomination of the PROFESSIONAL CONCERT, with the advantage of a greater variety of composition than during the regency of Bach and Abel, to whose sole productions the whole performance of each winter was chiefly confined.[60]

In fact Bach and Abel had already begun to respond, with the latter promising in 1782 music by Haydn, Boccherini, Dittersdorf, Cambini and Stamitz. The death of Bach on New Year's Day 1782 raised the stakes.

There followed strenuous attempts to obtain new music from abroad. Ideally promoters wanted foreign composers to appear in person (following practice at the Opera), but manuscript music was a very acceptable second-best. It was a trend accentuated by a change in concert management towards committee systems or impresarios who were not themselves symphonists. Indeed during the 1780s there was an acute awareness that London lacked composers of major stature. Only Clementi had pretensions in this regard, and as a composer his relationship with London's musical establishment was always precarious. Another development was the acceptance of composers who were not themselves virtuoso executants: indeed many of the main figures of the 1780s and 1790s were required only to take a directing role.

During the 1780s Graf was engaged by Abingdon and Gresnick by Mara, but everyone recognised that these were minor figures. The main news-story of the decade was the attempt by Abingdon and the Professional Concert to secure the services of Haydn, whose reputation had soared over just a few years:[61]

The *musical world* are rather alarmed, lest the celebrated *Haydn* should decline visiting England. His stay is so much courted by persons of the first fashion and eminence on the continent, so engaged is he in his studious avocations and domestic concerns, that Lord Abingdon, who is at the head of the new *Festino* concert, has yet received no positive assurances that he will come over.

HAYDN is not to be in London this winter, as was expected, for the purpose of composing for the Professional Concert; as long however as he continues to supply them, it will be of little consequence.

The prestige of the various Hanover Square concert series was much enhanced by the novelty of Haydn's symphonies, even if it is now apparent that Haydn wrote little or no music specifically for them. Other possible composers, including Paisiello and Mozart, were the subject of much speculation. Mozart might indeed have come to London if Thomas Attwood could have obtained a contract with the Opera or a subscription concert:[62] but already manuscript works sent by Pleyel were more popular at the Professional Concert than any music by Mozart. In the end only one composer of international reputation arrived to take part in concerts during this decade. The Prussian composer Reichardt was put through a trial of fire at the Pantheon in 1785, but his music was compared unfavourably with that of Handel.[63]

Haydn of course dominated the 1790s. Outside a doomed operatic project, his main brief was to provide Salomon with new instrumental works, though he did resort to some vocal music and some recycling. In 1792 the Professional Concert announced aggressively that Pleyel would produce a new instrumental work at every concert and Haydn was put under very great pressure to match this:

My labours have been augmented by the arrival of my pupil Pleyel, whom the Professional Concert have brought here. He arrived here with a lot of new compositions, but they had been composed long ago; he therefore promised to present a new work every evening. As soon as I saw this, I realized at once that a lot of people were dead set against me, and so I announced publicly that I would likewise produce 12 different new pieces. In order to keep my word, and to support poor Salomon, I must be the victim and work the whole time. But I really do feel it. My eyes suffer the most, and I have many sleepless nights, though with God's help I shall overcome it all. [64]

Overcome he did: one of the works was vocal (*The Storm*), but it was both substantial and self-evidently new. Both organisations tried to retain novelty and exclusivity as long as they could by deliberate under-exposure and tight control over their repertoire. Salomon bought from Haydn the British rights to the 'London' symphonies; he limited British publication at first to piano and chamber arrangements, not only reducing opportunities for pirate publication but also hindering unauthorised performances. Similarly the three symphonies that Pleyel wrote for the Professional Concert were infrequently lent out, and only one reached publication a decade later. Other foreign symphonists had also arrived in London and the intense competition resulted in a veritable explosion of new music, but none could remotely match Haydn and after his departure in 1795 symphonic music languished. Only a new work by Haydn in 1800 revived a similar level of interest, which was fanned by a dispute. Both Ashley and Salomon claimed the authentic score of *The Creation*, so Salomon had to content himself with advertising authentic performance, based on 'particular Directions [from Haydn] on the style and manner in which it ought to be executed'.

To be advertised as new, music only had to be unfamiliar in the London concert repertoire, however long ago it might have been composed. The label 'Manuscript' was a magic key, but even recent publications could qualify, and Haydn's 'La Chasse' symphony, imported from Vienna by January 1784, was still regarded as new in London in 1785. Furthermore, publication in Europe, even in Paris, did not bring instant recognition in London's concert halls; the 'Farewell' symphony was unknown in London until 1785, though published in Paris as early as 1775. Once known, however, a work could only be marketed as a novelty for a single season, perhaps for only a few performances. After this it quickly became 'the favourite', or for a brief halcyon period 'the new favourite'.

It is a common mistake to underestimate the durability of repertoire in this period. During a single season a piece that caught the public imagination could be heard again and again. In 1753 Handel's 'Return, O God' was performed by

Gaetano Guadagni at least six times in three months – twice at each of two subscription series, twice at benefits. Dussek played his Military Concerto at six concerts between 23 February and 28 March 1798, and Thomas Milligan has suggested that one new concerto was sufficient for a whole season;[65] certainly the very identification of such a work by its title is sufficient to indicate its continued popularity. Pieces also became associated with particular performers: thus in 1788 a Pleyel quartet was so linked with Salomon that Cramer was advised not to attempt it.[66] At the nightly gardens' concerts, songs stayed in the repertoire until audiences tired of them. Hardly a benefit concert at Marybone in 1767 lacked a rendering of Arne's glee 'Which is the properest day to drink', which Sylas Neville went specially to hear on 23 June. Similarly the Vauxhall 'lists' of 1791 reveal that Peter Duffey sang Hook's drinking song 'Let philosophers prate' in fifty-nine of the seventy-seven programmes.

Some reviewers approved this constant repetition. In 1785, one writer looked forward to frequent performances by Tenducci of Bach's 'Vo cercando'; another said that he would attend both 1778 oratorio series in alternation to hear Mrs Wrighten and Mrs Farrell sing particular songs.[67] Others were highly critical:

> By those who are in a habit of frequenting many Concerts, the want of novelty is an evil not a little to be complained of.
>
> On the present occasion a remark of this kind chiefly applies to Mahon, and indeed to Harrison also, who ... made bad worse by an irksome *da capo* of an air we have heard him [sing] more than a dozen times this winter, viz. 'Time and truth', &c. [68]

William Gardiner commented too on Harrison's limited repertoire: 'Such was the paucity of concert-music at that time, that [Webbe's 'A rose'] was hacked about at all the music-meetings for more than twenty years.'[69]

The survival of musical works across several seasons is a more complex issue. Much music from the earlier part of the century simply stayed in the repertoire. This clearly applies to larger Handel vocal pieces such as *Messiah*, *Samson*, *Judas Maccabaeus*, *Acis and Galatea*, *Alexander's Feast* and the Coronation Anthems: each of these was performed virtually every year at the oratorio seasons until selections took over in the 1780s. The Sons of the Clergy festivals maintained a largely fixed Handelian repertoire based on the overture to *Esther*, the Dettingen *Te Deum*, the Hallelujah Chorus and *Zadok the Priest*. The playhouses themselves perpetuated older music, both in their own repertoire (Arne's *Comus* music was still being performed there up to the end of the century) and in interval music such as concerti grossi. Concert performances of such works should be regarded in this light: certainly the minuet from Handel's overture to *Ariadne* (really *Arianna in Creta*) was regarded as common property and referred to as such in Sheridan's *The Critic* (1779).[70] The gardens also played a part in the perpetuation of such repertoire. Handel's English music remained popular long after his death; at Marybone in 1765, for example, there was a vogue for extracts from *L'Allegro*. At Vauxhall five years later John

Marsh found Handel's music 'then chiefly performed there', and only in 1781 did Ranelagh introduce modern symphonies: 'The Orchestra in other respects is the same as last year, except in the introduction of modern instrumental music, which blended with the heavy grandeur of the ancients, promises an entertainment, more adapted to the present taste, than what has hitherto been given.'[71] Burney implied that Handel concertos were the staple fare of organists at the gardens throughout the first half of the period.[72] Probably all of these sources exaggerate. The few surviving programmes from the 1760s suggest that the gardens blended ancient and modern repertoire: thus Marybone audiences on 7 September 1768 heard orchestral pieces by Bach, Abel, Arne and Handel. Indeed this liberal mix remained an attractive and unique feature of the gardens. At Vauxhall in 1786 overtures from the 1760s were still being played, alongside ancient music and the latest symphonies of Haydn.

Examination of the explicit revival of ancient music is outside the range of this study.[73] It involved not only perpetuation but also the active accumulation of earlier music, whether late Renaissance polyphony, Purcell theatre scores, Hasse arias or even lapsed music by Handel. To a certain extent the Ancient Concerts simply established their own repertoire based around Handel, pieces which were brought out year after year. Yet at the same time there was a serious attempt to add unknown earlier pieces, which themselves had some novelty value: indeed William Weber has suggested that the directors may have deliberately avoided the most popular works of Handel. Clearly only part of the music heard here could be counted as familiar repertoire that had never left circulation.

One of the consequences of the 1784 Commemoration was the establishment of a core of Handelian extracts – some widely known before, some not – which were continually repeated in subsequent festivals. Burney had his doubts about this, which he endeavoured to conceal. On the very first day of the Commemoration he wrote to Sir Joseph Banks of the public's unswerving loyalty to Handel oratorios, 'though they have heard them so long, that they are heartily tired of them'.[74] Some weariness undoubtedly did follow: in 1791 Burney thought that neither the wealthy nor enthusiasts would want to attend 'such an expensive performance year after year, merely to hear the same pieces repeated'.[75] Advertisements for this very year make a particular point of identifying pieces new to the Abbey performances. Nevertheless, many of the same pieces survived throughout the 1790s.

The Commemoration also spurred a revival of ancient items in modern concerts. In 1785, the year when the King first patronised the Ancient Concerts, both subscription series programmed ancient songs or concertos. Admittedly this practice dwindled rapidly (neither Salomon nor the Opera Concert subscribed to it) but ancient music did sometimes figure in major benefit programmes designed to appeal to a wide musical clientele. Similarly, at the minor Pantheon concerts of 1786–7 Barthelemon mixed ancient and modern items specifically to please both 'the patrons of Freemason's Tavern [the Academy of Ancient Music], and Hanover Square'. Some ancient instrumental works became associated with particular instrumentalists. François Hippolyte Barthelemon, one of London's foremost virtuosi, established a reputation for his performance of Corelli's violin sonatas, which he often included in public concerts during the 1790s. More sensationally, Dragonetti performed in 1799 a Corelli sonata on the double bass to Lindley's cello accompaniment.

At the modern end, international singers maintained a repertoire of favourite songs, songs with which they were closely identified over several decades. Mara was renowned for her rendering of 'Son regina' by Sacchini, Pacchierotti for 'Non temer' by Bertoni and so on. Only a bold singer dared attack on the same ground. Thus it was thought injudicious of Marie Chanu to introduce 'Non temer' in her first London season, while Sophia Dussek was firmly advised to abandon a taxing Gresnick aria popularised by Mara.[76] Instrumentalists also performed the same works for several years: Giornovichi featured a concerto with Russian variations (No. 14) for at least three seasons up to 1793.[77] Sometimes over-repetition was caused by sheer laziness. Burney reported that Abraham Brown brought from Italy a solo of Tartini, 'with which alone he figured at all concerts, for at least six or seven years, without ever entering into Tartini's true style of playing it'.[78] Perhaps audiences did not always notice or care. But Clementi was curtly rebuked for his piano sonata at the first Professional Concert of 1788: 'From so voluminous a writer, and so fertile a genius, we expected something new.'[79] John Marsh used over-repetition in general as an argument for mixing the various styles in subscription-concert programmes, observing that individual items would not become so hackneyed.[80]

Some orchestral and chamber music also survived over many seasons. Bach's symphonies for double orchestra were played from at least 1772 to 1796 and a few sinfonie concertanti and chamber works were given repeated performances. Tenducci billed his 1786 benefit as a Commemoration of Bach, including several of the most esteemed works on the programme. Publications of Bach's music continued to be advertised long after his death; in 1789 Bremner announced reprints of concertos by Bach and Abel, describing them as 'Classical Works'.[81] The performance history of Haydn's symphonies is impossible to determine, given the lack of identification, but we know that 'La Chasse' was given frequently from 1785 to 1791, and several of the 'London' symphonies passed immediately into the repertoire. It is difficult to say whether any of these instances constitute canonic status as yet, but these works were certainly performed repeatedly in preference to newer ones.

No new large-scale vocal work achieved anything like a secure foothold in the repertoire. Arne revived his oratorios *The Death of Abel* and *Judith* from time to time, but only one oratorio not by Handel was graced with annual performance. This was Giardini's *Ruth*, the Lock Hospital's answer to the

Foundling Hospital's *Messiah*. Glees, on the other hand, had a special status through their widespread familiarity among men and women alike. Some were newly composed, but to judge from advertised programmes concert audiences usually wanted to hear old favourites, often Catch Club prize winners by the likes of Webbe or Stevens.

The musical product: programming

Programme-planning

Concerts around 1700 had been somewhat chaotic in their presentation, 'without designe or order' to judge from the comments of Roger North.[1] But during the early part of the century more regularity was imposed, and by 1751 subscription concerts had established a standardised two-part programme-format of some ten to twelve items, alternating instrumental and vocal items. Even the Concert of Ancient Music followed a similar pattern, selecting vocal items from Handel oratorios just as modern concerts extracted Italian opera arias, and a move towards uniformity can also be seen in programmes at the gardens. The solo or chamber recital was still in the future. Apart from short midday exhibitions, only one example of a solo recital has been found – a low-profile evening concert by a French lady who both sang and played the piano at a tavern room.[2]

The standard design of a programme was a convenient way of imposing some kind of order on an essentially disparate medley of items. It imposed rigid demands on the composer, and it tended to emphasise the succession of varied genres above all else.[3] Yet, despite major changes in musical style during the period, the format remained extraordinarily static. As symphonies and concertos increased markedly in scale there were constant complaints about their length, and also about the tilting of the balance away from songs.[4] Inevitably concerts themselves became longer. A total of three hours was regarded as ideal: Salomon was mildly criticised when his concerts lasted until midnight, having started at eight. Only once was a concert deemed 'rather *deficient in Quantity*', indeed not quite value for money.[5]

There were a few attempts to introduce a variety of structure or presentation. One was the sacred concert or concerto spirituale, used for several charitable concerts during the 1750s. This formed a bridge between concert and oratorio – and indeed when the latter gave way to selections the two became indistinguishable. Others drew attention to a special repertoire, such as the Anglican anthems around which the Society of Sacred Music (1776–7) structured their programmes. A further variant was the inclusion of longer works that took up much of one part of a concert. Both the ancient organisations programmed multi-movement choral anthems and Latin liturgical works, as well as lengthy Purcell theatrical scenes. But in modern concerts vocal works sustained on this scale were hardly ever heard, nor were extended instrumental works popular. Geminiani's ballet score *The Enchanted Forest* received only a single performance in 1761 and in the 1790s Haydn's *Seven Last Words* had to be split into two.

Some promoters attempted to blend music with other entertainments. Concerts alternating readings with music have been discussed in chapter 3, and occasionally dancing was introduced: attending a benefit for unpaid opera singers and dancers on 27 May 1783, Sylas Neville found the combination a novel and enjoyable experience. More radical were attempts to transform the concert into dramatic presentations. In 1782 Daniel Arrowsmith presented a Purcell mad song at a tavern concert dressed in 'a tattered blanket, with a straw sceptre and crown, and rattling his chains, to the extreme terror of the ladies';[6] while in 1798 Sampieri presented a concert 'upon an entire new plan' with transparencies accompanying representational music. But such extravagances seem to have had little attraction for fashionable audiences. When in 1772 Mrs Cornelys marked the death of the King's mother with a threnody performed around a black-canopied tomb, Mrs Harris described it as a 'most odd entertainment ... a most ridiculous whim'.[7] Eight years later Le Texier went so far as to present an entire concert in costume – a venture rewarded only with 'bad Success'.

Most concerts therefore retained the regular format, within which a number of programme-planning trends can be perceived. There were elusive shifts in the balance between vocal and instrumental music. The fame of the Bach–Abel concerts rested heavily on the reputations of the two composers, and both the Professional Concert and Salomon's concerts stressed orchestral excellence and repertoire. Symphonic music was coming into its own, both as a popular draw and in aesthetic acceptance. Concerts at the Pantheon, on the other hand, were famed for their singers: Agujari in the 1770s, Mara in the 1780s, Pacchierotti in 1790. Both the inauguration of the Vocal Concert in 1792 and the emphasis of the Opera Concert from 1795 contributed to a perception that during the 1790s vocal music was in the ascendancy, for all Haydn's achievements.

We have already seen that English concerts, especially at the gardens, maintained a mix of musical styles. But not until the 1780s did major benefits introduce ancient music to reflect its new status, with English vocal music following in the 1790s. Benefit programmes began to include Handel choruses, formerly unusual in this context, in an attempt to satisfy the taste encouraged by the Handel festivals. Perhaps this trend partially placated John Marsh, who advocated in his 1796 'Comparison' the mixture of ancient and modern music on three grounds: to obviate complaints about long unvaried programmes, to prevent pieces becoming hackneyed so quickly and to bring unexpected pleasure to musical bigots. But his advice was not followed at either modern subscription series or the Ancient concerts, and decades later Samuel Wesley was still arguing for programmes to set modern symphonies and solos beside older choruses and madrigals in a carefully regulated aesthetic whole.[8]

Genres

The development of the professional public concert, attended by sizeable audiences in proper halls, coincided with major musical changes. Indeed several of these changes can be regarded as direct consequences of the new concert milieu. In many areas an essentially chamber character was replaced by a markedly public manner during the second half of the century. This is a complex issue, since some cross-currents can be detected; but, broadly speaking, as the period progressed public concert-music became more assertive and brilliant, more spacious in conception and more vivid in contrasts and scoring. This trend can be allied directly to the replacement of the concerto grosso by the modern symphony and to the development of new genres such as the string quartet. But existing genres were also deeply affected. In the concerto, for example, the development of ever more extravagant virtuosity resulted in a steadily widening gulf between professional concert repertoire and music for amateur relaxation. The present section is concerned with general trends affecting concert genres; more detailed stylistic examination will be left to later chapters.

The older instrumental genres (concerto grosso and French overture) were still frequently heard during the 1750s, even at the Dean Street subscription concerts; while Boyce's trio sonatas, presumably played orchestrally, were popular at Vauxhall Gardens. But at fashionable concerts these genres went rapidly into decline. Outside ancient venues, only the gardens retained some allegiance to concerti grossi and Handel overtures, although in response to the 1784 Commemoration such works made a limited return at winter concerts and oratorios. In the modern sphere, though, the older genres were replaced directly by the dynamic new symphony (sometimes still called 'overture'). Burney gave a loose but revealing description of the changing repertoire, of which only the first part seems to refer to the playhouses:

[Purcell's airs] were played as overtures and act-tunes in my own memory, till they were superceded by Handel's hautbois concertos, and those, by his overtures, while Boyce's sonatas, and Arne's compositions, served as act-tunes. In process of time these were supplanted by [San] Martini's concertos and sonatas, which were thrown aside for the symphonies of Van Maldere, and sonatas [orchestral trios?] of the elder Stamitz. About this time, the trios of Campioni, Zanetti, and Abel, came into play, and then the symphonies of Stamitz, Canabich, Holtzbauer, and other Germans, with those of Bach, Abel, and Giardini; which, having done their duty many years very pleasantly 'slept with their fathers'; and at present give way to Vanhall, Boccherini, Haydn and Pleyel.[9]

The symphony expanded not only in length but also in stature, so that by the 1790s programmes were built round orchestral works: at Salomon's concerts Haydn symphonies were deliberately placed at the beginning of the second half. Programmes typically lightened towards the end, so that in the 1790s they often ended with a single-movement 'full piece' or finale. Never, though, was a symphony split up into different parts of a single programme, as occurred in Vienna.

Instrumental soloists were expected to write their own display pieces, retained for their exclusive use: it was a matter for shame that Cramer may have been helped in his compositional trials by Bach. Only prodigies and women were exempt from this requirement, though there was some relaxation in the 1790s. Two genres were available: the concerto and the solo (the English name for the sonata with continuo). The solo remained an important vehicle for virtuosic display well into the period, and the published repertoire consists almost entirely of professional concert music. This should not be regarded as a conservative British stance, since it closely mirrored continental practice: as late as 1785 the violinist Antonio Lolli hardly played anything but solos, perhaps selected from his astonishingly difficult Op. 9. Already during the 1770s, however, the solo had begun its decline, partly because the texture was out of accord with the musical language, partly because the genre lacked the brilliance and public projection of the concerto. One reviewer wrote in *The Public Advertiser* for 13 March 1783: 'We cannot but recommend Concertos instead of Solos'; and it soon became rare for an instrument other than the cello or viola da gamba (with their intrinsic balance problems) to play a solo.

Perhaps the balance question encouraged some pianists in the 1770s and 1780s to prefer the sonata to the concerto. Almost always they preferred the solo sonata without violin or cello. The accompanied sonata was essentially an amateur domestic medium, designed for lady pianists of moderate skill and gentlemen string-players of yet more slender accomplishment. Thus Clementi's Op. 2 sonatas (1779) make a clear distinction between three brilliantly virtuosic solo sonatas and three accompanied sonatas of limited technical and musical demands. The bravura character and orchestral scale of many solo sonatas by London's major pianists give them an unmistakable aura of professional concert repertoire – even if the composers often attempted to disguise the fact by opening a publication with the least taxing work and even by adding optional violin accompaniments. The accompanied format was obviously demeaning for professional string-players. Very unusually, in 1793 Dussek and Felix Yaniewicz played a sonata from the pianist's Op. 20 (C. 54–6), in which the violin receives unusual prominence; but no composer followed this lead towards the concert violin sonata. In any case, with the establishment of Broadwood's large grands, the piano concerto prevailed and after 1793 major pianists hardly ever performed sonatas in public concerts.

The solo was superseded not only by the concerto but also in the 1770s by a new genre – chamber music, which more closely reflected the spirit and textural potential of the new musical idiom. The first recorded string quartet performance is of one by Kammell in 1769, perhaps from his melodious but texturally dull Op. 4. From 1774 onwards, chamber works were a regular feature of London's public-concert programmes, in striking contrast to Viennese practice, and every major combination could be heard. These included all the standard string genres from the duo for violin and viola to the string quintet (but rarely the trio sonata or violin duet, which had amateur connotations). Sometimes flute or oboe were added, and Bach made a speciality of chamber music with piano, probably conceived for the Queen's chamber concerts. It is important to recognise that this was not simple domestic repertoire, but concert music designed for professional soloists, their names advertised in concert programmes. Quartets and quintets were habitually included in publishers' catalogues under the same heading as symphonies: 'For Concerts'. The London chamber repertoire could be extremely virtuosic (see, for example, Gyrowetz's concerto-like quartet Op. 13 No. 1, dedicated to the Prince of Wales).[10] Often concertante textures were used in a highly soloistic way, with brilliant breaks or high melodies for all the instruments; and even where these are lacking there is a strongly concert-orientated projection.

This style was not unique to London, but it is at variance with Haydn's more intimate conversational argument. Indeed much the most popular chamber composer in London in the 1780s and early 1790s was not Haydn but Pleyel. Almost all of Pleyel's string chamber music was speedily published there. It varies considerably in its technical demands, but the quartets B. 331–42 and 353–8, as well as the quintets B. 274–6, are written in a grand and brilliant style, with arresting soloistic writing and driving orchestral sonorities. The quartets Haydn wrote for Salomon's 1794 concerts (Opp. 71 and 74) should certainly be viewed against this background.[11] Clearly Haydn was well aware of London's rather lukewarm reception of his previous sets, and the new quartets differ markedly in tone. While he eschews solos for the lower instruments in the ostentatious concertante manner, he writes brilliant parts for Salomon and (more importantly) he uses the quartet itself as a virtuosic concert instrument, with an extrovert exchange of motives and a whole panoply of striking orchestral contrasts and effects.

Apart from appearances by military and wind bands at the gardens, wind chamber music was scarcely a concert genre: only a single reference in 1800 has been found to a 'Harmony for wind Instruments'. In the years around 1790, however, London was introduced to the lighter Viennese genres, variously entitled serenata (Pleyel), divertimento or notturno (Haydn). These multi-movement works were scored for large chamber groups featuring most of the orchestral instruments. Even if those of Haydn were rescored from other pieces, such works were clearly designed to show off orchestral principals in an undemanding musical context. A broadly similar idiom is also adopted in Pleyel's first and third concertantes (B. 111 and 113), heard in London in 1788 and 1792; the latter uses a full complement of seven soloists.

Special circumstances were generally responsible for performances of works for more than one keyboard player, such as the young Mozarts' harpsichord duet in 1765, and a duet for two pianos played by the prodigy J. B. Cramer with Clementi in 1784. Indeed the four-hands duet quickly became a domestic medium after Burney's sonata publication of 1777. But there were occasional exceptions. Clementi's brilliant Op. 6 duet was heard in concerts from 1779, and Dussek's impressively symphonic Grand Overture (C. 144) was performed by the composer with his wife in 1796. Several performances are recorded of another virtuosic duet by Dussek, written for harp and piano; the London version (C. 102) incorporated the finale from a piano concerto.

A new genre was introduced in the 1770s at the same time as modern chamber music. The sinfonia concertante took on some of the role of both concerto and symphony, and though Parisian in origin the genre was developed with alacrity in London by all the major symphonists. Here the colourful concertante chamber-music idiom is elevated to the scale of the concerto. The genre also symbolised the co-operation of soloists of equal status in organisations like the Professional Concert; sometimes the slow movement even featured a different soloist from the outer movements. Barry Brook has suggested that the genre was directly intended to appeal to a wider audience; no specific evidence has been found in London sources to confirm this, though it is noticeable that even William Jackson grudgingly accepted the merits of the concertante, as more melodic and less inclined towards empty display.[12] Concertantes show much less uniformity of scoring than chamber music, perhaps because problems of integrating the texture were partially solved by the structure itself. Some works were written for string soloists, especially violin and viola, but the most popular works balanced strings and woodwind, especially the oboe. Bach's most celebrated concertante was scored for flute, oboe, violin and cello, while all Abel's known works are scored for oboe, violin and cello. Pleyel went further with a concertante for flute, oboe, bassoon and string quartet (B. 113); but really eccentric combinations were also used to attract attention: piano, horn, violin and viola; or organ, oboe and viola. Graf, however, was criticised for his attempt to combine disparate forces.[13]

With the death of Handel, the field of oratorio composition was opened up to all comers. Works like Smith's *Paradise Lost* (1760), Stanley's *Zimri* (1760) and *The Fall of Egypt* (1774) perpetuated the concept of oratorio based on Old Testament stories. A moralising tone begins to be felt in *Zimri*, an unenticing tale of the 'guilty joys' of unwise love. Much stronger dramatically is Arne's *Judith* (1761), based round a valiant heroine in Handelian tradition; no doubt for this reason the oratorio was performed at the Lock Hospital in 1764. On this occasion, however, the song 'Haste to the gardens of delight', relishing the sensual pleasures of the Assyrians, was tactfully omitted in favour of an adaptation of the 'Hymn of Eve' from *The Death of Abel*. Italian oratorios introduced at the King's Theatre included works by Jommelli, especially his well-known *La passione*. Such works follow the Italian preference for reflective plots, articulated in expressive operatic idioms with minimal use of chorus. Bach himself broadly followed this line in his *Gioas, rè di Guida* (1770), though he was careful to include numerous choruses (mostly adapted from his earlier music). In 1795 Guglielmi's popular *Debora e Sisara*, a sacred opera in mature Classical style, was imported for oratorio performance. Quite unlike anything ever heard in London was the dramatic opening scene, in which the bellicose Deborah exhorts in heroic coloratura a piteous chorus of Israelites.

But hardly any of these works survived more than a handful of performances. Instead – and this can hardly have been foreseen by anyone in 1760 – Handel's oratorios proved indestructible. Changes in taste resulted in some changes in format. The secular works were generally in two parts only (*L'Allegro* was normally performed without Part 3), requiring a third miscellaneous act on the lines of the theatrical afterpiece; usually this consisted of a selection, or perhaps the four Coronation Anthems. Another development was the whole evening of selections, as we have seen in chapter 3. The most successful compilations to new libretti were *Omnipotence* (1774) and *Redemption* (1786). The latter, selected by Arnold from music heard at the 1784 Commemoration, was a variable musical feast, but it retained a broad dramatic framework: an epic survey of the main themes of both Old and New Testaments. The trend, however, was towards more miscellaneous selections, following the practice of the Concert of Ancient Music. Some series clung to Handel's sacred music, but others broadened the repertoire considerably: Arnold's *The Triumph of Truth* (1789) included music by a variety of composers from Purcell to Haydn. Many abhorred the practice of selections in principle, especially when secular songs such as Purcell's 'Mad Bess' and Arne's 'The soldier tir'd' were added to the mix. While the practice of selections did enable a wider appreciation of Handel's music, this was gained at undoubted artistic cost. One loss was a complete collapse in British oratorio composition during the 1780s. Stanley wrote bitterly that 'there is little reason to suppose that any other than Mr Handels musick would succeed'.[14] As Handel-mania declined towards the end of the century the ambitious Thomas Busby re-entered the field; but only with the triumphant blend of styles in Haydn's *Creation* (first London performance in 1800) was the Handel tradition both revitalised and projected into the next century.

Longer secular works by other English composers were rarely heard in London. The Concert of Ancient Music kept alive some Purcell odes and theatrical music; some of this repertoire found its way into public oratorio series, especially the quasi-nationalistic music for *Bonduca*. The only other such work to retain popularity after 1750 was Boyce's sensual idyll *Solomon* (1742); its erotic tone could hardly allow acceptance as a surrogate oratorio, but it was given several performances at the gardens and elsewhere up until 1767. This was not a fertile period for new secular odes, despite the need for occasional pieces for the court, for celebrations of royal birthdays at the gardens, for formal inaugurations and the like. Most of these odes are now lost; even Boyce and J. C. Bach were not inspired by sycophantic court texts to write works of more than ephemeral interest. Furthermore Handel's music, including the Coronation Anthems, was still available for many of these functions. The genre had an old-fashioned feel to it, and earlier styles were perpetuated in some new odes, such as the impressive *Ode on the Spirits of Shakespeare* by Thomas Linley the younger, performed at Drury Lane in 1776. Much more novel in its conception was Philidor's *Carmen Seculare*, introduced to London in 1779. The text was selected by Baretti from Horace, most popular of the Latin poets in eighteenth-century England. But the combination of Latin words and French choral idiom must have perplexed London audiences: Philidor advertised that he had modified the work before a later performance the same year.

The solo vocal repertoire at the principal concerts of the 1750s mixed Italian opera arias with Handel oratorio airs and English songs. But after Handel's death the subscription-concert repertoire was largely restricted to modern Italian arias: singers contrasted bravura and cantabile arias from serious operas by Italian or German composers. They seem to have maintained their own supply, and there is no evidence that songs currently in repertoire at the Italian Opera were transferred to the concert hall. Three arias chosen by Pacchierotti for the Pantheon concert of 11 February 1790 are illustrative: 'Non dubitar, verro' (from Sarti's *Giulio Sabino* of 1781, performed in London in 1788), 'Bene adorato, addio' (from J. C. Bach's *Orione*, London, 1763) and 'Lungi dal caro bene' (performed in *Giulio Sabino* in its London version). The first is a large-scale musical complex – an accompanied recitative and an aria in three sections of increasing tempo – displaying both vigorously heroic Italian melody and coloratura of the most bravura kind. The Bach aria, by contrast, is a charming, rather old-fashioned Andantino in minuet style; while the final song is an engagingly simple cavatina on the smallest scale. During the last two decades of the century some singers introduced opera buffa songs, such as Guglielmi's 'Se mi vedi a far l'amore', but the distinction was never advertised.

In 1789 John Brown criticised the introduction of violently emotional arias, unacted and out of context.[15] He was perhaps reflecting a trend towards the selection of longer and more dramatic operatic scenes. Tenducci had already popularised J. C. Bach's longer scenas in London's concerts. A typical example is 'Infelice in van mi lagno', in which an aria breaks off for a recitative-arioso section before a pleasant love-song in rondo form. Sarti's 'Non dubitar' is an even more extended aria-complex. During the 1790s it became common to advertise such longer works as scenas; Haydn showed his mastery of the genre in 'Miseri noi, misera patria', an aria on the grandest scale which he revised for London. Separate works were known as cantatas, usually consisting of two recitatives and two arias; Burney thought such a 'drama entire' particularly appropriate for concerts.[16] It was a trend that another critic embraced enthusiastically: 'We rejoice to see the Cantata rising into fashion. It is so tasteful a composition, and so well adapted to a musical chamber.'[17] Haydn's *Arianna a Naxos*, sung by Pacchierotti in 1791, was particularly successful in

London. It is an intensely emotional but not vocally overpowering piece, and with its piano accompaniment it was probably restricted to private concerts.[18] A much more theatrical public response to a similar scene of desertion was provided by Haydn's orchestral *Scena di Berenice*, written for Brigida Banti in 1795. In this light it is significant that two of Purcell's most popular pieces at this time were 'Mad Bess' and 'From rosy bow'rs', mad scenes presenting a kaleidoscope of changing moods – irrationality contained within a rational framework.

The vocal repertoire at English concerts and the gardens was sometimes new, sometimes borrowed from the playhouses. There were two main types of English song: the strophic ballad and the more complex through-composed aria type. The distinction is not entirely clear-cut, however, and the term ballad had no narrative implication. Characteristic were sentimental songs of love gained or love lost (often in an Arcadian or Scots setting), songs of rural innocence or the pleasures of the hunt, drinking songs and patriotic trumpet and sea songs. Lively comic or burlesque items mocked the ways of the rich and fashionable. In common with the general trend, the most ambitious English songs adopted a fully public manner, with colourful orchestral accompaniments and the most brilliant Italianate bravura; indeed some of the music Arne wrote for Charlotte Brent and Shield for Elizabeth Billington is of Fiordiligian technical difficulty. Early in the period orchestrally accompanied solo cantatas were still popular at the gardens, and Arne's *Cymon and Iphigenia* retained a place at English concerts into the 1770s. Around this time cantatas like Arnold's *The Milkmaid* (Marybone, 1772) exchanged Arcadia for a rustic setting, but the genre was already well into decline. Lesser concerts, by contrast with the genteel gardens, often displayed a much less refined taste. A benefit given by James Mathews in 1789 at the Crown and Anchor Tavern featured only the lightest songs by Dibdin, Arnold and others; while a series of Readings and Music at Freemasons' Hall in 1795 unashamedly stressed folk-ballads such as 'Sally in our alley' and the saucy below-stairs dialect songs of William Reeve.

Vocal ensemble works were a special feature of the gardens. The simplest of these were strophic dialogues and closing 'odes' in which all the singers joined. More ambitious were orchestrally accompanied catches and glees, some of which set varied groups of men and women in lively exchange (as, for example, Hook's comic catch 'The scornful maids', of 1785). Hook went further by developing at Vauxhall short twenty-minute dramas performed with minimal gestures.[19] These serenatas are really debased comic masques with a pastoral background, usually involving a Judgment-of-Paris choice. Thus in *The Cryer* (1784) each of three sopranos (representing the courtier, the lover-hunter and the sensitive heart) puts forward her claim as a potential wife. The idea was adapted the same year for an entertaining musical parody of the current election, *The Poll Booth*. A sub-text to all of these works is 'Vauxhall as paradise', designed to emphasise the pleasurable make-believe of the gardens and to close each evening's entertainment with a rather forced jollity.

Works for more than one singer were comparatively rare at the major concerts early in the period. But during the 1770s there were numerous performances of multi-singer Italian cantatas, specially composed by London's opera composers. Ensemble numbers from operas were also introduced: a quartet by J. C. Bach from *Astarto* (presumably 'Deh torna') was performed at the Fund concert on 8 February 1771. By the 1780s Italian vocal trios and quartets figured quite frequently in fashionable programmes. These works formed the vocal equivalent of soloistic chamber music and concertante. The connection is made explicit in Haydn's trio 'Pietà di me', sung at the Professional Concerts in 1791; in effect this is a concertante for three vocal and three instrumental soloists. Furthermore, like the cantata the multi-section ensemble gave scope for more extended drama. Some comic ensembles were introduced, but even seria ensembles were written in the same flexible idiom; Bianchi's 'Ah padre ascolta', sung at an Opera Concert in 1797, is a typical lovers-against-father trio in buffa manner.

In 1767 Arne promoted at Ranelagh a selection of catches and glees from the Catch Club collection, performed with orchestral accompaniment; the following year he transferred it to Drury Lane Theatre, the first of many similar concerts. In succeeding decades glees played an increasing role at English public concerts – a striking change of social function – and in the 1790s this repertoire even invaded the fashionable sphere. The genre mixed several social strands: a popular bawdy tradition, gentlemen's post-prandial entertainment, ancient antiquarianism. Increasingly, too, it contributed to ladies' domestic amusement, as in such publications as *The Ladies' Collection* (1787–90) or *Apollonian Harmony* (c. 1795–8, 'The Words consistent with Female Delicacy'). Evidently Harrison and Knyvett's Vocal Concert in 1792 was aimed at the latter market, and their fashionable success was such that 'the taste for glees superseded that for instrumental music';[20] the Professional Concert felt compelled to compete directly in 1793. The very idea of unaccompanied vocal music at concerts was regarded as novel (glees were sung 'sotto voce' with minimal instrumental backing).[21] Yet its success was such that even songs were turned into glees; for his wife's benefit in 1795, Dussek went so far as to include a glee version of the 'Grand March' from Gluck's *Alceste*.

The glee repertoire selected or written for public concerts was undoubtedly of the more genteel and artistic type (rejecting entirely the more risqué type of catch). It reflects a similar range of subject matter and musical expression to the English songs discussed above; an added sub-genre included glees about music itself, as a symbol of convivial friendship. The settings vary markedly in length and complexity of texture, from the simplest chordal setting (Stevens's 'Sigh no more ladies') to elaborate multi-sectioned glees with madrigalian textures and a dramatic response to the text. Some found the glees selected for concerts 'doleful' and too reminiscent of 'the cathedral style';[22] perhaps this reflected a more serious approach to the genre than listeners normally associated with it, though no marked difference in style can be detected in those glees specially written for the Vocal Concert.

Choruses outside ancient concerts were a rarity for both practical and stylistic reasons; sacred choruses caused a particular problem, as Tenducci found when he proposed introducing them into his Ranelagh benefit in 1764. All this changed, however, after the Handel Commemoration. At Ranelagh in 1785 choruses were introduced as a novelty, in direct response to the royal patronage of Handel's music.[23] Larger mixed-style benefits of the 1790s drew attention to choral numbers, often the grandest Handel double choruses. But hardly any examples of specially composed choruses have been found. Even Haydn did not follow up his successful *Storm*, the English quartet and chorus which did a great deal to endear him to the London public in 1792. The composer blamed difficulties in engaging boy choristers, but it was not an experiment to which he felt the need to return in 1794.

Topical and programmatic references

One way to attract an audience was with external references of one kind or another – to events of topical interest or to non-musical sources. Topical alignments were comparatively rare at subscription series. The rather crude jingoism of many such pieces would have jarred here, and in any case neither English words nor choruses were customary. Thus topical works were mainly heard at English concerts, such as Elisabetta Chazal's 1764 benefit with her own odes 'On the Occasion of Peace' and 'On the Accession to the Throne'. Such pieces were most naturally at home at the gardens, where the direct appeal and full sonority of the patriotic ode were best appreciated. Vauxhall in particular made a speciality of royal birthday galas, with suitably patriotic songs and odes; Ranelagh countered in the 1760s and again in 1789 with fireworks to the accompaniment of Handel's music. George III's vicissitudes were also opportunities for money-spinning celebration. His escape from assassination in 1786 was celebrated at Vauxhall with a loyal song by Hook and an organ concerto with variations on 'God save the King'. When his first serious illness ended in 1789 the Drury Lane oratorio-promoters introduced a 'Prelude on the Happy Recovery of his Majesty'; and each concert closed with 'God save Great George our King', compelling Covent Garden to come up with a rival version 'harmonised by Greatorex'. Communal performance was evidently a new idea, but at Drury Lane on 18 March the anthem was 'repeated by the whole audience of both sexes'.[24] During the war-torn 1790s the anthem was frequently introduced at oratorio series, in part as patriotic gesture, in part as loyalist support for the King in his self-cultivated role as benevolent father of his people.

Handel's four Coronation Anthems were especially popular at the gardens around George III's birthday (4 June), though they were at first regarded more as a celebration of national pride than of the Hanoverian succession or of the monarch himself. Sometimes just 'God save the King' was extracted from *Zadok the Priest*. The Coronation Anthems were also heard at Mrs Cornelys's royal festivals from 1769 onwards and at charitable benefits of all kinds, playing on a sense of philanthropic well-being. None could hope to rival Handel on this high royal and patriotic ground. But royal events were often commemorated with new music: the death of Frederick, Prince of Wales, with a dirge by Worgan; George III's marriage with Arne's *Beauty and Virtue*; and so on. Most unusually Arnold included an ode in honour of the Queen's birthday at the first Pantheon concert in 1774. At the other end of the political spectrum the name of John Wilkes was kept alive with a birthday ode on 31 October 1769, the advertisers being careful not to reveal other details of the performers. Meanwhile royalty were also susceptible to gentle satire in music, as in the gloss on the Prince of Wales's private life in Hook's Vauxhall song 'The lass of Richmond hill'.

Musicians also played the patriotic card in all kinds of other ways, especially in time of war. Some stage works performed in concert appealed to nationalistic sentiment. Arne's opera *Eliza* (1754), a rather vapid if colourful evocation of pastoral life and naval success under Queen Elizabeth, was revived by his son for the 1784 oratorio series, now with choruses added from Arne's other works. More ambiguous was Purcell's music to *Bonduca*, included frequently in public oratorio series in the early 1780s; as Curtis Price has shown, Purcell's music is far from a straightforward patriotic celebration, despite the brilliant C major style of 'To arms' and 'Britons strike home'.[25] New gardens' songs frequently made reference to current military engagements in similar propagandist style, exhorting valour or celebrating success.[26] The Vauxhall performances of martial music by the Duke of York's band during the 1790s were seen in the same context: 'nothing could be more consonant to the present warlike spirit that universally prevails'.[27] British naval prowess was especially lauded. Arne's 'When Britain' (including 'Rule, Britannia') was surprisingly rarely heard, but when it was introduced at the Vocal Concert in 1794 it was advertised as a naval ode. Even foreign visitors joined the parade. Rather unexpectedly Carl Stamitz wrote a chorus celebrating Admiral Rodney's triumphs in 1780; even Haydn began to set a celebration of Britannia's dominion over the seas, perhaps in response to Howe's famous naval victory of 1 June 1794. In rather different circumstances, Barthelemon's *Victory* capitalised on popular celebrations of Admiral Keppel's court-martial acquittal in 1779. No comparable celebrations of the land victories of Clive and Wolfe have been found, perhaps reflecting traditional British distrust of the army. A more sober reflection on war was provided by Arne's 'New Funeral Dirge, in Honour of the Heroes who die in Service of their Country', appended to his patriotic *Alfred the Great* in 1753: the performance was ironically in aid of a new maternity hospital. Other national heroes were drawn from the artistic world. Arne's charming if rather slight *Ode upon Dedicating a Building to Shakespeare* (written for the 1769 Jubilee at Stratford) reached London later that year; and

Reichardt's *Ode in Praise of Handel* was introduced, with no great subtlety, at Salomon's 1787 benefit.

Foreign visitors and allies could also be honoured with odes. The very final concert at Cuper's Gardens on 30 August 1759 included an ode for those 'inspired with Prussian Glory'. More obliquely Passerini brought over from Berlin a pastoral named *Charlottenburg festeggiante*, composed by the King of Prussia and composers of his court. Passerini's successive adaptations of this attribution are interesting: in 1755 the additional composers are named, the next year they are 'others' and in 1760 they are omitted altogether. In 1793 sympathy for Marie Antoinette was engaged with settings by both Storace and Percy of 'Captivity', another song of the abandoned-woman type that turned up frequently in concerts around this time. In the same year Haydn's 'La Reine' symphony was advertised, as was the inevitable funeral march and dirge for Louis XVI.

More intrinsic musical associations, still open to direct marketing, were provided by folk-song and by pictorial or programmatic representations. These traits, too, were often associated with the repertoire at English concerts; some perceived them as vulgar and it can be argued that they were props deliberately inserted to make music more accessible to a middle-class public. Certainly they increased markedly in number towards the end of the period, matching a similar explosion in domestic piano music. Yet at the same time all of these features can be found in art-music at the principal modern concerts.

National songs, especially Scottish songs, were in vogue in London from the late seventeenth century via *The Beggar's Opera* (1728) right up to the period around 1800 (when the Haydn and Beethoven harmonisations were published). Such songs were essentially the province of English concerts, especially those at the gardens. But there are rather few references to their public performance, and probably more popular were imitation Scots songs by Arne and Hook. A more genuine folk tradition was transmitted by Welsh harpists such as John Parry and Edward Jones, with their public renderings of Celtic airs (Jones was a prominent figure in the revival of Welsh culture). Only rarely were such songs performed at the fashionable concerts. The castrato Tenducci unexpectedly made a feature of Scots songs: having sung two in *Artaxerxes* in Edinburgh in 1769, he introduced them to London concerts in galant arrangements by J. C. Bach.[28] On 10 May 1779, for example, he sang Bach's setting of 'The braes of Ballenden', accompanied by several instrumentalists of top calibre.

Even the most sophisticated concert audiences, however, regularly heard folk-songs and similar tunes in concertos, especially in sets of variations or in rondos. This practice started at least as early as J. C. Bach's Op. 1 No. 6 (1763) with its facile variations on the National Anthem. Other tunes used in concertos include English, Scots and Irish airs ('Come, haste to the wedding', 'The yellow-hair'd laddie', 'Gramachree Molly'); imitations (William Leeves's 'Auld Robin Gray', Shield's 'The ploughboy'); popular melodies such as Arne's 'The wanton god'; a current dance ('Hillisberg's Favorite Pas Seul');

Russian and Polish tunes. All of these were thought worthy of advertisement in some form or another. As late as 1799, Field introduced Hook's Scots song 'Within a mile of Edinburgh town' into a piano concerto.

Folk-song impinged on art-music through a number of interlocking causes: a nationalistic preference for British sources; an attempt to appeal to a 'popular' taste; a more general search for pre-romantic exoticism; a desire for simplicity and pathos, often allied to an evocation of pastoral innocence. The last of these will be considered in chapter 8 in the context of a more general discussion.

The nationalistic aspect appears very limited. In the 1790s 'Rule, Britannia' was introduced into concertos, but British songs were not exploited overtly in the nineteenth-century sense. Even Shield's opera *Robin Hood*, which uses many such airs, is only one of a series of works in every conceivable national setting. More importantly, British songs were perceived as a way of appealing to a certain audience taste:

Mr. C. ASHLEY's Violoncello Concerto [was] admirably calculated to command the feelings of an English audience; the first part shewed wonderful execution; in the second, the slow air of *Auld Robin Gray* had a very good effect, and was a happy introduction to the tune of *When I was an Oxford Scholar*, converted into a Rondeau.[29]

Whether this taste was laudable was a matter for debate. Some felt it displayed vulgarity: 'Parke's Hautboy Concerto was very neat in the Execution – but why not a little better in the Composition? – Why give us nothing new? – Why two Movements made up of common Ballads?'[30] In the *Morning Chronicle* for 11 April 1785 Pieltain was castigated for introducing into a concerto 'a vile street walker's air'. The very use in concertos of the same tunes as English operas turned them into a metaphor for the idealised village, a practice discordant with some audiences for the playhouse association and the implicit glorification of social inferiors. When Giardini introduced 'Come, haste to the wedding' into a concerto, William Gardiner thought that public delight showed a lamentable lack of taste.[31] On the other hand, Dibdin saw it as a vindication of national melodies in the face of meaningless virtuosity:

The *dexterity* was *wonderful*, but for heaven's sake where was the *pleasure*? This is a solid fact – and to prove it, let me ask how came GIARDINI and BARTHELEMON constantly to call in *Lango Lee*, *The Dargle*, &c. to help out their concertos.[32]

One critic saw both sides, perhaps suggesting a measure of hypocrisy on the part of sophisticated audiences: he deemed Salomon's introduction of the ballad 'Colin stole my heart away' vulgar, but thought it appealed to the heart as Adagios seldom do.[33]

Folk material also contributed to a vein of pre-romantic exoticism, expressed in picturesque foreign colouring. In this it recalled the widespread vogue for chinoiserie in the 1750s, and the evocative foreign settings of many English operas later in the period. So-called Turkish instruments (bass drum, cymbals, tambourine, triangle and 'jingling johnny') came to prominence when played by black band-musicians during the 1780s. The idiom did not have the same influence that it did in Vienna, but it received a distant transformation in the 'Military' Symphony. There are also resonances of exoticism in many other London works. Russian melodies were introduced in the 1790s by Dussek and Giornovichi (straight from Moscow), at the same time as the 3/4 polacca of the Parisian violin concerto provided a novel finale rhythm. In one concerto Viotti used the Swiss 'Ranz des Vaches', combining in one blow the exotic with strong associative qualities and nostalgia for a pastoral idyll of lost contentment:

VIOTTI performed a most beautiful Concerto, in which he introduced the movement, whose effects arouse that *Amor Patriae* in the SWISS, which makes them sicken after the blessings of a distant home. In truth, there is such a divine simplicity in the strain, it corresponds so well with our impressions from the country, and its most happy inhabitants, that to hear it without emotion is impossible.[34]

A most surprising venture in this direction, and a much more genuine exploration of a foreign culture, was a concert in 1800 featuring Hindustani music with Indian instruments – though still accompanied by 'a full Band'.[35]

Even the perennial enthusiasm for Celtic airs, a sentimental mystique of an ancient, pure and noble culture, can be viewed in this 'exotic' light: in Gothic literature the Welsh harper was a symbol of this mystique. Surviving material could be adapted to sound more antique, as we find in Jones's 1784 collection (compare the heightened sensibility of James Macpherson's *Poems of Ossian*).[36] But for London concerts this could not be taken too far. The more distinctively Gothic material (Welsh laments, Scottish pibroch) was passed over in favour of more Classical-sounding (often more recent) airs. For all the exaggeration of superficially exotic characteristics, to emphasise their departure from the norm, the tunes were fundamentally tamed and civilised within an eighteenth-century vocabulary.

Another form of external reference was to pictorial or programmatic ideas. The role of representational music within musical imitation (mimesis) had long been a favourite topic of aesthetic literature. It was customary to distinguish descriptive imitation from the imitation of ideas or affections (the expression of the passions). British musical writers around the middle of the century began to sharpen the distinction by redefinition of terms such that imitation was restricted to this descriptive aspect, whereas the true aim of music was expression. Thus the direct representation of natural sounds was frequently denounced as puerile or inexpressive, following Avison's vociferous lead in 1752.

For much of the half century London's concert programmes seem to be in tune with this attitude. The orchestral description in Handel oratorio choruses was a special case, since it served to reinforce the sentiments of the text. It was instrumental music like Vivaldi's 'Spring' concerto, performed in London in 1755, that aroused Avison's particular ire. But not until the 1780s did descriptive orchestral music make a significant impact. In 1783 Johann Friedrich Klöffler put on a battle between two orchestras, to be followed two years later by Ignazio Raimondi's 'Battle' symphony, with its clichéd depictions of preparations, a battle scene, cries of the wounded and a victory celebration. To judge from its repeated performances it must have been a great success, but not all commentators approved Raimondi's primitive devices. The following is a review of his 'Telemachus' symphony:

Not even the presence of his Royal Highness could enliven this paliquinade, or attract a tolerable audience, to witness the mummery of a collection of musicians run mad, attempting the description of a love scene, by a duetto on the flute, the raging of the sea by a bassoon, and the motion of an elephant by a few *andante* passages on the violencello.[37]

Haydn's 'Farewell' symphony also came in for criticism in 1785 for its '*frippery* of invention very unworthy that master'.[38]

The last decade of the century saw a veritable vogue for pictorialism in music; if this appears to follow a continental musical trend, it was at the same time closely in accord with a general artistic pattern in Britain. The two principal themes were manifestations of nature and military representations. The traditional pastoral view of nature was not jettisoned. Indeed, folk-tunes with their resonance of rustic simplicity are pastoral in tone, as is the hunting finale of Haydn's oft-repeated 'La Chasse' symphony. Even Haydn's most infamous musical effect was interpreted in pastoral terms: 'The surprise might not be unaptly likened to the situation of a beautiful Shepherdess who, lulled to slumber by the murmur of a distant Water-fall, starts alarmed by the unexpected firing of a fowling-piece.'[39] But much more novel, and more remarked by contemporaries, were representations of the wild side of nature. Certainly Handel had written memorable raging seascapes, but the full variety of the modern orchestra was able to bring a new dimension of raw terror to such depictions. In 1789 Raimondi followed up his earlier success with a symphony depicting a storm at sea and the following year Vogler transferred the idea to the organ, illustrating a pastoral scene interrupted by a storm. The finale of Steibelt's 'Storm' concerto of 1798 repeated this same idea, anticipating Beethoven by ten years. A rustic dance is first interrupted by a threatening rumble of thunder; then a torrential storm breaks out with rushing scales, tremolando diminished sevenths, pianistic flashes of lightning and sudden contrasts. Calm is restored (much too early) with a dominant pedal, and smooth woodwind lines lead back to the dance-rondo. Haydn also contributed to the genre, with his short vocal *Storm* ('Hark! the wild uproar of the winds'), written for Salomon's 1792 concerts:

This piece is an exquisite specimen of imitative harmony, adapted to English words; the horrors of a tempest, contrasted with the gradual serenity of a calm, were finely represented, and highly admired... The *Storm* harrowed up all our feelings, and the invocation for calmness and serenity... was truly affecting.[40]

Haydn uses similar gestures to those of Steibelt, but he achieves a powerful cathartic effect by following the storm with a prayer for salvation; the entire process is then repeated, before calm is eventually gained.

Clearly such works played on the current fashion for the romantic sublime, the terrifying aspects of unfettered nature. Many of London's operas and exhibitions at the time featured storms, tempests and shipwrecks, and this was also the heyday of the sensationalist Gothic novel. Only a few such subjects were suitable for musical treatment, since music was not allowed to be in itself unpleasant, and composers retained conventional means for representing standard topics. Furthermore traditional associations were not easily overthrown: while the melancholy strains of the harp or the plaintive sounds of the oboe were potent literary symbols, neither instrument shed its pastoral image in concert music.[41] Nor did unrelieved Gothic scenes always find favour with the London public. When a concerto performed by Madame Krumpholtz in 1792 imitated '*Tom Tom Gongs*, and other funereal Instruments', she was evidently admonished, for the movement was dropped at the second performance.

The storm motif, however, was a recurrent theme in music of the 1790s, even where not so identified; and awesome natural catastrophe acquired additional associations. Thus Haydn's *Seven Last Words*, with its representation of an earthquake, was allied to events in Europe:

The PASSION, to our minds, presents

> 'Nothing liketh Image of *the time*,
> The *horror* of it.'[42]

This last quotation clearly allies the sublimity of horror with political comment. The fate of the French royal family, and the Terror of 1793–4, lent a certain frisson to London life, as long as these events did not threaten British stability. But the ever-present danger of French invasion brought the reality of war much closer to the popular imagination than it had been in previous conflicts. War-like trumpet songs in patriotic vein had long been a stock-in-trade; now composers began to catch the military mood with more immediacy. Banal representations of military engagements were open to accusations of vulgarity: Mazzinghi's *The Siege of Bangalore*, performed at the Professional Concert in 1793, was regarded by one reviewer as 'a hazardous subject'. In some major works, however, military images were subsumed into serious musical structures – most famously in Haydn's highly successful Symphony No. 100 (1794), but also in concertos by Dussek and others. Though the military aspect in such works may appear to us purely patriotic and even over-glorified, it had a different effect on one observer:

The reason of the great effect [the cymbals] produce in the military movement is that they mark and tell the story: they inform us that the army is marching to battle, and, calling up all the ideas of the terror of such a scene, give it reality. Discordant sounds are then sublime; for what can be more horribly discordant to the heart than thousands of men meeting to murder each other.[43]

The mere emblems of war – marching music – are sufficient to summon up ideas of the terrible sublime. Only at the end of the movement does Haydn even hint at the horror the listener experienced (the A-flat outburst that follows the trumpet call). He was to deepen this response on his return to Eszterháza in the threatening trumpets and drums of the Benedictus to the *Missa in Angustiis*.

Haydn also returned to picturesque music in *The Creation*. Here the English tradition was specifically honoured by the English origin of the text and by a certain debt to Handel. Yet Haydn may also have recalled the English penchant for colourful representation, which he had himself helped to develop. The ferocity of nature is evoked in memorable storm and sea scenes associated with sin or godlessness, and the concept is remarkably transformed into the aimless horror of the opening 'Chaos'. Haydn consistently contrasts these scenes of darkness with idyllic pastoral nature-scenes, culminating in the radiant depiction of 'morning, young and fair' as a symbol of human innocence.

Taste and national idioms

Many references of the time indicate that a distinct 'English taste' could be perceived and cultivated. Already in 1753 Passerini promised that a subscription series would provide 'Musick agreeable to the Taste of the English Nation', while Philidor was prepared to alter his *Carmen Seculare* in response to adverse reaction by the English audience.[1] Haydn was undoubtedly sensitive to this factor, planning alterations to his Symphony No. 91 ('for I have to change many things for the English public') and re-orchestrating a cantata and perhaps Symphony No. 54.[2] As we shall see, it is possible to suggest some ways in which he did indeed modify his style to suit London audiences. Charles Burney viewed the continuing appeal of Handel's music in terms of the national character: 'The English, a manly, military race, were instantly captivated by the grave, bold, and nervous style of Handel, which is congenial with their manners and sentiments.'[3]

There are, however, fundamental difficulties in addressing the issue of a national taste. To begin with, the term reflects a very wide constituency, ranging over diverse audiences, venues and social functions. Furthermore, assessment can only ever be based on incomplete evidence. No writer, whether aesthetician, letter-writer, diarist or newspaper hack, ever pretended to impartiality, and frequently there were axes to be ground. There is scarcely a single issue on which opposing interests were not ranged. Still more problematical is the evaluation of musical evidence. A complete repertoire can seldom even be defined, since programme information survives for only a few organisations (there is none at all for the Bach–Abel concerts); and rarely do we have detailed information on the reception of a particular work. Even where such a picture can be built up there still remains the problem of a work's significance: can it be used to define taste-criteria, since it reflected current attitudes closely, or did it manipulate a change in audience taste? The relationship between composer and audience is always in a constant state of flux. It seems clear, for example, that Haydn initially went some way towards matching London norms, before guiding his audience along more sophisticated and experimental paths on his second visit. But specific features of London's

119

taste can be isolated only by applying the most stringent controls: comparison with other London repertoire, with earlier and later works by the same composer, with contemporary repertoire elsewhere. Analyses of Haydn's London quartets by László Somfai and of the London symphonies by David Schroeder begin to develop such methods,[4] but only rarely will it be possible to isolate features which unequivocally have their origin in English taste. We will therefore take a broad view of the repertoire in London concerts, based on a wide-ranging study of music known to have been performed there and focussing on those issues most remarked by contemporary British writers.

National idioms

The music heard at London's concerts in many ways reflects continental stylistic trends, but it also displays some distinctive features. These arose both from indigenous idioms and from British attitudes towards continental styles. The present section will first examine foreign styles in London and then move on to the reactions of English composers.

It has already become apparent that the most prestigious concerts were dominated by music by foreign composers throughout the period. The predominant idiom around 1750 was the Italian. London had been somewhat slow in embracing the latest modern idioms from Italy, but the view that England never knew a transitional post-Baroque period requires some qualification. Operas by Hasse and Galuppi performed in the early 1740s already show a lighter style, while Lampugnani and Ciampi later in the decade were clearly writing in an early galant manner (their arias dominated Dean Street programmes in the early 1750s). Comic Italian operas were introduced to London in 1748. Some opera overtures in a set published in the same year show signs of the modern manner: three movements including bustling Allegros and affettuoso Andantes, modern use of oboes and horns. But a decisive change in instrumental style was engendered by Felice Giardini, whose arrival in 1751 opened 'a memorable aera in the instrumental Music of this kingdom'. Burney elaborated:

We went on in the tranquil enjoyment of the productions of Corelli, Geminiani, and Handel, at our national theatres, concerts and public gardens, till the arrival of Giardini, Bach, and Abel; who soon created schisms, and at length, with the assistance of Fischer, brought about a total revolution in our musical taste.[5]

Giardini's overtures rely unashamedly on graceful melodic appeal, with simple homophonic textures and elementary harmonic schemes. Giardini was also responsible for introducing the rather more subtle music of Giovanni Battista Sammartini ('of Milan') during the 1750s, and by the early 1760s London was very familiar with the tuneful Italian overture style. Many overtures were published separately, including that to Piccinni's popular opera buffa *La buona figliuola*. The unshakeable appeal of Italian opera and the new influx of instrumental music led one French observer to write unequivocally in 1755: 'The Italian music is that which is most esteemed in England, where it is in some measure naturalized.'[6] The principal characteristics of Giardini's music – elegantly shaped lyricism coupled with an energetic Allegro idiom, but without violent surprise or complex texture – continued to be regarded as a touchstone of the Italian idiom throughout the half century, for all the considerable sophistications it underwent.

A striking new development was the arrival in the late 1750s of modern German music, concert symphonies from Mannheim in which the orchestral effects of the Italian overture were exaggerated to ends in themselves. This arrival was also somewhat belated (a symphony by Johann Stamitz had been heard in Paris in 1751, to be followed by the composer himself in 1754). The new style was introduced by either Richter or Thomas Alexander Erskine (the Earl of Kelly).[7] Symphonies by Richter were performed in London on 25 May 1758: two years later John Walsh published a set as Op. 2. Meanwhile Kelly had in 1756 returned from his studies in Mannheim with Stamitz, and a set of unashamedly pastiche symphonies was published by Robert Bremner in Edinburgh five years later. The earliest recorded London performance of Stamitz's own music was not until the same year, though when Bremner (now in London) began his famous series of Periodical Overtures in 1763, six symphonies out of the first twelve were composed by Stamitz. German symphonic dominance was sealed by the arrival of Abel (Op. 4, 1762) and of J. C. Bach (Op. 3, 'as they were performed at the Wednesday Subscription Concert', 1765). Bach and Abel were the first major London composers whose reputation was founded on concert activity and symphonic music.

Not all were delighted by these new departures. As early as 1764 Charles Avison (in the introduction to his Op. 8 sonatas) railed against 'the innumerable foreign Overtures, now pouring in upon us every Season, which are all involved in the same Confusion of Stile'. Two years later John Gregory noted the present fashion for the 'wild luxuriancy' of the new German style, though he predicted that it had too little 'elegance and pathetic expression' to stand the test of time.[8] Others soon realised that the unfamiliar idiom was more than a passing curiosity. In a letter of 1776 Charles Burney praised the inventive and unpredictable German idiom over the comfortable style of an Italian composer ('on sçait par coeur all Ventos music'),[9] and indeed the *History* makes it clear that he saw instrumental music during the period in terms of a shift from Italian to German.

It would be a mistake, however, to over-exaggerate regional differences in the decades after 1760. Ever-increasing interaction between diverse musical cultures, encouraged by travel and publishing, led towards a common cosmopolitan language in the 1760s and 1770s, local idiosyncracies notwithstanding. J. C. Bach, after training in Berlin and journeyman years in Italy, remained in constant contact with Italian opera musicians and he also visited Paris and Mannheim. Even Abel (who never set foot in Italy) was widely regarded as an Italianate composer, somewhat to his annoyance.[10] The broadly Italianate style of Bach and Abel, tinged with the early Mannheim orchestral idiom and a certain Germanic solidity of structure, represents a lingua franca of the early Classical style. It was shared by most instrumentalists at London's major concerts in these decades, composers from a variety of musical backgrounds: Giardini, Borghi, Barthelemon, Kammell, Fischer, Schroeter, Wilhelm Cramer, Carl Stamitz. This was also the idiom of Mozart's early London symphonies (indeed one of Abel's symphonies was long known as Mozart's K. 18). Similar too are Italian arias selected for London's concerts, whether by local composers Bach and Sacchini, or by Piccinni and Paisiello (both represented in *Six Favorite Italian Songs* 'performed at Mr. Bach's Concert' by Tenducci). If some solos with figured bass retained a relatively old-fashioned idiom, comparison of two sets of cello solos by James Cervetto (Op. 1, 1768 and Op. 3, 1777) shows that the bold leap into a modern Classical world was possible here also. This lingua franca survived in London into the 1780s and beyond, in imported arias by Sarti, Salieri and Cimarosa; in Borghi's symphonies Op. 6, performed at the 1787 Professional Concert; in Giorno-vichi's violin concertos of the 1790s. For many the elegant sensuousness and undemanding brilliance of the Italian style was central to modern concert music. But in some ways the style had reached a natural maturity. London in the 1780s was ready for the new inspiration of two major developments. One was the revitalisation of ancient music in London's concert programmes. The other was the arrival of Viennese music, which meant a new style shift in London.

The first 'Viennese' composer to make a major impact there was the Bohemian symphonist Vanhall. Burney recalled that his symphonies paved the way for those of Haydn, an assertion borne out by programmes of the Pantheon concerts in the late 1770s;[11] and Bremner published eight symphonies by Vanhall between 1774 and 1782. By comparison with J. C. Bach's leisurely style, Vanhall's music was at once more urgent and incisive, with sharply etched motivic themes taken through the dramatic and harmonic twists of symphonic argument. Yet the prophet was largely forgotten once Haydn's own four-movement symphonies took over. They were not completely unknown in the 1770s, but it was not until the astonishing success of No. 53 in 1781 that Haydn leapt to prominence. The floodgates were immediately opened: at the 1783 Hanover Square Concerts ten out of twelve programmes included a Haydn symphony (the official composer Graf restricted himself to con-certantes), as did most subscription concerts over the next decade and beyond. Meanwhile London publishers hurried to obtain the latest works of the master and to catch up with older symphonies. Novelty of invention and arresting fiery drama were the characteristics that seized critical attention. Reviewers often remarked the unpredictable quirkiness of idiom, quite unlike the bland lingua franca, yet they also recognised the force of Haydn's symphonic intent. Already in 1783 one critic noted that a new symphony was not only boldly original but also '*loaded* with *meaning*'.[12] For all the exaggeratedly catchy tunes and rustic idiom of the so-called 'popular style', the symphonic argument was carried out in a serious and grand manner that sometimes touched the elevated and profound. It was music with a sense of stature that resolutely avoided shallowness: in this Haydn's essentially anti-galant stance contrasted markedly with that of his predecessors in London.

Most London composers of the 1780s and 1790s were in Haydn's shadow, with even Italians such as Viotti under his influence; certainly an Austro-German hegemony in instrumental music can be argued from this date. The essentially derivative music of Pleyel, Gyrowetz and Kozeluch followed Haydn to temporary success in London in the late 1780s and early 1790s. Clementi's symphonies Op. 18 (1787) also clearly respond to Haydn's style and symphonic form, with their four movements and the slow introduction to No. 2. Indeed the case of Clementi well illustrates the problems faced by composers in competition with Haydn. He was often set up as Haydn's main concert rival and his symphonies were constantly held up for comparison; yet as early as 1787 he was warned against trying to copy Haydn's style too closely.[13]

Only outside the symphony and quartet did Clementi and other London composers find an individual voice, and indeed a distinctive contribution emerged at the hands of a group of soloists during the 1780s and 1790s. Foremost among these are the so-called London pianoforte school (Clementi, Dussek, J. B. Cramer, Steibelt, Field) and the violinist Viotti. All were more or less influenced by Haydn, as well as by the grandeur and melodic limpidity of Mozart's version of the lingua franca. A decisive change in Clementi's music towards a more expressive intensity has been assigned to 1780, following a revelatory experience of Bach's '48'.[14] It is also significant that during the 1780s several others were in Paris, home of the extrovert display concerto, but also the source of a more grandiose and impassioned orchestral style. The music of the London group already shows 'romantic' leanings well before 1800, with a mix of grand nobility, idiomatic bravura, sentimental naiveté, minor-key intensity, and striking dramatic effects. Some of these features can be linked with developments of piano manufacturing in London (in Viotti's case with the Parisian violin bow); but it is also clear that these composers wished to bring to the solo repertoire the same stature and expressive variety they discerned in current symphonic and operatic repertoire. In this their influence extended well beyond London.

All the music considered so far was associated with the top prestigious modern concerts. The question now arises as to the interaction of this repertoire with English concerts, and the influence of the various styles on native composers. As has been suggested in chapter 5, English concerts maintained at first a certain distance from modern developments, and the music of Handel never lost its foothold here; but after 1760 the new continental repertoire increasingly infiltrated, and local composers found themselves under its spell.

Around 1750 English idioms were quite distinct from the modern Italian. Oratorios by Handel and others show continuing allegiance to high-Baroque idioms (see the coloratura arias that Arne added to *Alfred* in 1753). Yet from the late 1730s onwards the songs and cantatas of Arne, Boyce, Greene and Stanley tend away from the elaborate da capo aria in favour of appealing melodies in binary dance forms. This revitalised English style may have been a deliberate national gesture, especially in the wake of the defeat of the Young Pretender in 1746: even some of Handel's music shows a similar trend. Burney recognised these distinctive qualities:

Indeed, the melody of Arne at this time, and of his Vauxhall songs afterwards, forms an aera in English Music; it was so easy, natural and agreeable to the whole kingdom, that it had an effect upon our national taste; and till a more modern Italian style was introduced ... it was the standard of all perfection at our theatres and public gardens.[15]

English instrumental music between 1740 and 1760 is likewise distant from the contemporary sinfonia. On the one hand it was haunted by the twin Baroque ghosts of the Corelli–Geminiani concerto grosso and the French overture, even if both are handled with individuality and a light touch: concertos and overtures by Handel, Stanley, Greene, Arne and Giuseppe Sammartini contain numerous fugal movements, as do Boyce's popular trio sonatas. On the other hand English composers developed their own brand of mid-century style, a spirited homophonic idiom with a solid bass line that is usually found in opening binary Allegros. Nos. 3 and 5 of Arne's *Eight Overtures* begin thus, and it is significant that both of these were advertised for a benefit on 5 February 1751. Boyce also adopts this tuneful late-Baroque English manner in several of his *Eight Symphonys* (published in 1760 but taken from earlier vocal works). Yet for all its relative modernity, this style scarcely approaches the early galant of Giardini's overtures.

Before 1760, therefore, foreign and English tracks had run in parallel or even diverged: the Italian towards the modern galant, the English faithful to the high-Baroque or sturdily independent. Now, however, the distinctive English voice was gradually lost as foreign music was accepted into English venues and local composers imitated the new styles without individuality. The arrival of Italian comic operas at Marybone in 1758, the increasing popularity during the 1760s of Italian songs in translation, the spreading vogue for foreign symphonies culminating in Haydn's domination – all these represented a potent threat to local creativity. A stylistic crisis faced English composers with Handel's death in 1759 and a new influx of foreigners. Stylistic uncertainty can be seen clearly in the new oratorios of 1760, Smith's *Paradise Lost* and Stanley's *Zimri*.[16] Both bring together a variety of idioms. Solidly Baroque are French overtures, choruses and striking arias such as Smith's descriptive *furioso* in C minor 'See thro' yon clouds' or Stanley's virtuosic 'Fly' for Arne's pupil Charlotte Brent. Less interesting are songs in a lighter 'English' style of four-bar phrasing. But quite exceptional in style is the aria for Adam, 'He who rules in heav'n', set by Smith in pure galant simplicity to represent unquestioning innocence. Despite some modernist leanings, however, both composers came to be regarded as guardians of English solidity. Perhaps remembering his *The Fall of Egypt* (1774), an article of 1784 praised Stanley's 'good sense' in the face of 'what is called *Taste*' in others.[17]

Arne continued to maintain a more progressive stance, though he rarely sacrificed a certain originality. In the early 1760s he made an ambitious modernist pitch, writing in quick succession the comic opera *Thomas and Sally* (1760), the oratorio *Judith* (1761), the serious English opera *Artaxerxes* (1762) and the opera seria *L'olimpiade* (1765, lost). The overtures give an English slant to modern idioms. In the three-movement overture to *Artaxerxes*, a popular concert item, Arne selected the sprightly English gavotte for the finale; while the opening 'Con Spirito' of *Judith* subtly transforms the new Mannheim style into an English vein. Indeed, *Judith* as a whole represents a remarkably successful blend of idioms. Many arias come close to the Italian galant; but Arne's characteristic English style is not forgotten and the Baroque is retained for special moments (Judith's 'Sleep' aria, the imposing chorus 'Who can Jehovah's wrath abide').[18] In parts of *Artaxerxes* he matched J. C. Bach in the most modern Italian operatic style (the aria 'Fly', also for Miss Brent, is in striking contrast to that of Stanley). This popular score provided items for English concerts for many years, especially the virtuosic military song 'The soldier tir'd of war's alarms', the galant-folk 'If o'er the cruel tyrant love' and the English minuet 'Water parted from the sea'.

The galant idiom invaded the pleasure gardens during the 1760s and 1770s. A marked change can be seen in Arne's fourteenth collection of gardens' songs (1764), and the younger generation of Arnold and Hook followed the same route. Their published collections include numerous elegantly turned minuets and rondos, as well as full-scale modern coloratura arias; such pieces are barely distinguishable from the popular gardens' songs of the Italian opera composer Tommaso Giordani. A collection of songs sung by Tenducci at the Castle Society (composed by Arnold and others) shows clearly how the graceful Italian affettuoso had infiltrated the British song style.[19] Even Webbe's perennial glee 'You gave me your heart' (1776) adopts the sentimental galant minuet idiom.

English instrumental music also began to imitate new styles, although composers showed a continual willingness to modify continental practice: by including characteristic movements such as the march, jig or gavotte; by incorporating melodies in Scots or English idiom; by exploiting colourful instrumental timbres. There is genuine individuality in Arne's overtures (*The Guardian Outwitted* and a set of 1767), while Fisher's overture to *The Syrens* (1776) unusually grafts minor-mode suspensions and a chromatic bass-line on to the lingua franca. But most orchestral music of the period is all too clearly indebted to idioms derived from Mannheim or Bach symphonies. This applies equally to symphonies for the gardens by John Collett and William Smethergell, as to widely played operatic overtures of the 1760s and 1770s such as Rush's *The Royal Shepherd*, Kelly's *The Maid of the Mill* and Hook's *The Lady of the Manor*. A similar path was followed by Fisher's staggeringly difficult violin concertos and Hook's more mundane keyboard concertos. Even Stanley touched on the modern idiom in his curious organ concertos Op. 10 (1775), although, for all the simplified textures, these rarely actually sound like galant pieces. Samuel Wesley's youthful violin concertos were clearly influenced by those of Giardini and his contemporaries, and his symphonies are effective imitations of J. C. Bach's mature style. Well might the French visitor Pierre Grosley comment that though 'the English flatter themselves that they have a national music', it was in fact a dialect of German music, itself derived from the Italian.[20] This was the environment in which Boyce's attractive but old-fashioned *Twelve Overtures* so conspicuously failed to attract interest in 1770.

The general enthusiasm for Haydn's symphonies quickly spread to English concerts. But the overwhelming success and authority of Haydn had a similar effect to that of Handel on oratorio: English pretensions to symphonic composition were virtually extinguished. Local composers received less encouragement than ever before, and even that fertile source of English concert music, the playhouse overture, seems virtually to have dried up. Only a few facile overtures of the 1780s by Hook and Arnold maintained a place at Vauxhall; no instrumental music by Shield, Storace or Attwood passed into the English concert repertoire. Some attempted to imitate Haydn. Callcott studied instrumental composition with him, and even proudly announced the fruits in a single performance of a quartet on 12 April 1791, an ambitious gesture that was never followed up. Dilute traces of Haydn's influence can be perceived in the later Vauxhall music of the magpie Hook (see the finales in his concertos Op. 55 of *c*. 1790); but he was largely content to maintain an insipid lingua franca.

This chapter may appropriately be closed with a consideration of composers whose music failed to find popularity in London. The most significant group here must be the Franco-Belgian school. When in 1783 Noverre and others promoted a Concert François including unstaged extracts from Grétry's *opéras comiques*, this proved an isolated experiment, even if a similar repertoire was already well known in translation at the playhouses. Concerts by French refugees in the early 1790s attracted only a marginal interest, which waned as hostilities intensified. Likewise very few performances of Parisian orchestral music have been discovered (just a few symphonies by Gossec and Leduc). It appears that the broad-brush French orchestral idiom, lacking Italianate melodic sensuousness, was of only passing attraction. Three overtures from French operas achieved some popularity in London around 1790: J. P. A. Martini's grandly regal *Henri IV* (a gesture of sympathy for Louis XVI?), the stormy *Démophon* by Vogel and Cherubini's *Lodoïska*, with its dramatic introduction. But none of these composers was himself French and only Barthelemon settled in London, at the very start of his career. In spite of

London's musical links with Paris, only a single major French composer made any impression there – Philidor, who already had a large following as a chess-master. Indeed, to describe music as French in style was tantamount to an insult, a synonym for shallow charm and empty virtuosity. Early in the period Mrs Delany abused Marella for playing the violin in the French taste (*'froth and nonsense'*), and even Viotti was criticised by Burney for degenerating into 'the levity and frivolity' of the modern French school in his concerto finales.[21]

Similarly unsuccessful in London was North German music. Burney's comments on the music of C. P. E. Bach are revealing. He held that the experience of writing for the public in a major European capital would have led Bach to simplify his style, and that less 'fantastical and *recherché*' music would have been more generally intelligible: for Burney this would have made him one of the greatest musicians of the century.[22] Reichardt, *Kapellmeister* at the Berlin court, actually visited London in 1785 but his reception there was anything but favourable. One critic thought that the Prussian school as a whole showed an excess of 'gravity, self-importance [and] pedantry'; he approved only Graun, whose *Te Deum* indeed found a peripheral place in London's concert programmes.[23]

But most problematical is the reception of Mozart's music. Haydn himself testified that by 1792 London had not been won round: 'I only regret that before his death he could not convince the English, who walk in darkness in this respect, of his greatness – a subject about which I have been sermonizing to them every single day.'[24] During the 1780s there was a surge of interest, partly inspired by the return in 1787 of the English Mozartians Attwood and Storace. Mozart symphonies were heard several times at Hanover Square in 1784, and occasional public performances of symphonies and concertos followed in later seasons. When in 1787 the press carried speculation linking Mozart and London, the coverage reflected widespread awareness of his achievements since 1765. But Mozart's music was much more frequently heard at the semi-private Anacreontic Society, where piano concertos and chamber music were introduced between 1786 and 1788 by J. B. Cramer, Clementi and Attwood. This seems to suggest a rare discontinuity between professional aspirations and public taste. Certainly after 1788 Mozart's music largely dropped from public view. A new manuscript symphony heard at the Anacreontic Society late in 1788 does not seem to have reached public concerts, and at the same time the modest stream of Mozart publications began to ebb.

London's neglect of Mozart's music cannot be attributed solely to lack of repertoire. The quartets dedicated to Haydn were imported in 1787, and the last three concertante quartets and the quintets K. 515–16 followed some five years later; but not one public performance of Mozart chamber music has been identified in this period. Only two piano concertos were heard after 1788, both performances in May 1792 by musicians formerly connected with the composer (Hummel and Hässler). Reviews of symphony performances range from a startling indifference ('if not the best composition we have heard from the same quarter, [it] is not altogether the worst') to outright hostility:

The Overture by Mozart, owed its success rather to the excellence of the band, than the merit of the composition. Sterne was an original writer, – Haydn is an original musician. It may be said of the imitators of the latter, as of the former, they catch a few oddities, as dashes – sudden pauses – and occasional prolixity, but scarcely a particle of feeling or sentiment.[25]

Even Burney was reluctant to embrace the Mozartian cause and the view prevailed that Mozart's music was strange and difficult, that it exceeded Haydn in discontinuity and harmonic abandon.[26] This may appear curious now, since Mozart's music seems to embody a deepening of J. C. Bach's classically balanced style: we might regard him as a natural successor to Bach. But it was not until 1800 that London's concert programmes showed a marked revival of interest. At Sophia Dussek's benefit on 23 April 1800, the programme unprecedentedly contained two symphonies and five vocal items, including two choruses from *La clemenza di Tito*. The singer Viganoni felt it worth advertising for his benefit on 2 June 'several of the most celebrated Pieces of Mozart's Music, for the first time in this Country'.

Musical style: 'music intended to reach the heart'

For all the importance attached at the time to distinctions of national style, many features of London's concert repertoire clearly cut across any such boundaries. This chapter and the next will address the more general issues of musical taste raised by British critical writing. Much of this criticism was set up in terms of dichotomies: virtuosity against pathos, melody against science and so on. Since so many of these dichotomies interlink, it will be clearest to take the various critical concepts singly, at the cost of some repetition, in an attempt to match the repertoire with perceived English taste.

Simplicity and pathos

Two interconnected themes run through much British writing of the period: the classical notion of simplicity as an artistic goal and the desirability of 'music reaching to the heart'. Neither of these concepts was new in itself, but the dawning of the age of sensibility in the third quarter of the century brought a heightened awareness of the power of human feelings. The most famous exponent of the new philosophy was Rousseau, whose writings were well known in England and whose opera *Le Devin du village* (1752) reached London in Burney's translation in 1766. Rousseau overtly set natural simplicity against artistic contrivance, summoning melodic directness in the cause of subjective feeling and contrasting pastoral rural innocence with the corruption of the town. Similar ideas run through much mid-century thought, and British writers were in full agreement that simplicity was a fundamental condition for expression and pathos, that is for 'music from (or to) the heart'. Thus Avison writes in 1753:

a pompous Display of Art will destroy its own Intentions: on which Account, one of the best general Rules, perhaps, that can be given for musical Expression, is that which gives Rise to the Pathetic in every other Art, *an unaffected Strain of Nature and Simplicity*.[1]

John Gregory stated unambiguously that 'SIMPLICITY in melody is very necessary in all Music intended to reach the heart, or even greatly to delight the ear.'[2] The argument is extended further by James Beattie, in his 'Essay on Poetry and Music, as They Affect the Mind', written in 1762. Having stated that 'Pathos, or Expression, is the chief excellence of music', he goes on to investigate where these qualities are to be found:

A great part of our fashionable music seems intended rather to tickle and astonish the hearers, than to inspire them with any permanent emotions. And if that be the end of the art, then, to be sure, this fashionable music is just what it should be, and the simpler strains of former ages are good for nothing... Simplicity makes music, as well as language, intelligible and expressive. It is in every work of art a recommendatory quality. In music it is indispensable; for we are never pleased with that music which we cannot understand, or which seems to have no meaning. Of the ancient music little more is known, than that it was very affecting and very simple. All popular and favourite airs; all that remains of the old national music in every country; all military marches, church-tunes, and other compositions that are more immediately addressed to the heart, and intended to please the general taste... are remarkable for simplicity.[3]

Such attitudes are replicated in newspaper criticisms throughout the period, but they gathered force during the 1780s. One should be wary of making exaggerated deductions, as this was the very decade when regular reviewing became established. Nevertheless, the emphasis on such values would be in line with a general trend away from conspicuous elaboration and luxury.

Beattie's reference to ancient Greek music is ritual intellectual ballast. Yet this was also the period of rediscovery of the 'noble simplicity' of Greek sculpture, which had considerable influence on the fine arts. In the absence of actual Greek music, that of the Renaissance and the Baroque had to do duty as symbols of an ancient simplicity. This connection is made explicit in Cooke's essentially neo-classical setting of Collins's *Ode on the Passions*. Published in 1784 with a dedication to the directors of the Handel Commemoration, the music is written largely in the Baroque manner. Yet the score includes a part for the ancient double-pipe ('tibiae pares'), and it ends with a fervent exhortation in unadorned C major: 'O bid our vain endeavours cease, Revive the just designs of Greece, Return in all thy simple state! Confirm the tales her sons relate!' Philidor's *Carmen Seculare* (1779), a more modern setting of Horace's hymn for the Roman centenary games, also evokes in part an antique devotional simplicity.

Rousseau's ideas could readily be transferred to literature and to the stage, but their realisation in purely musical terms was more problematical, since a deeper musical subjectivity seemed incompatible with the naive charms of artless melody. The English also prided themselves on their taste in championing simplicity, but seldom is it carefully defined. Indeed the notion can be purely theoretical, enabling rhetorical attacks on virtually any artistic device, such as modern melody, harmony or modulation, counterpoint, orchestral effects, virtuosity. In practice all but the most extreme commentators took a moderate line, as articulated by Burney's blandly reasonable call for a balance between the extremes of dull rusticity and wanton innovation, 'under the guidance of Judgment and Science'.[4]

Simplicity and pathos were frequently brought into discussions of national styles. Dibdin was a vehement advocate of the English styles of Purcell and Arne, praising the 'natural ease and irresistable grace' of Purcell's melodies over the complexities of Handel or the tricks of Haydn; the latter he compared to a rope-dancer who 'frisks and jumps about, [but] keeps you in a constant state of terror and anxiety for fear he should break his neck'.[5] Others cited the expressive elegance and clarity of the Italian cantabile in attacks on the German idiom. Indeed Austro-German symphonies were regarded by many, and not just by Dibdin, as perversely difficult and fantastical. Even a supporter of Haydn wrote in 1784 that his music could be wild and extravagant, 'bordering upon madness'.[6] Thomas Twining mentioned in several letters of the early 1780s his general preference for the expression and pathos of Boccherini's music, though he began to relent after Burney responded with a list of 'pathetic' passages by Haydn.[7]

Such rather undisciplined discussions partly reflect and partly intersect with four mainstream aesthetic topics: the sublime and the beautiful, expression, the pathetic, and the primacy of vocal music.[8] Ever since Joseph Addison's 'Essay on the Pleasures of the Imagination' (1712), a clear division had been perceived between the sublime and the beautiful, a division that could be applied more or less directly to music. Sublime music, to be discussed below, was grand and elevating, its effects primarily achieved by harmonic and contrapuntal means; the term was usually applied to large-scale choruses that inspired a strongly emotional response. While sublime music could also be commended for its simplicity, this was a quality usually associated with the beautiful. Beauty could refer generally to symmetry and proportion, but it also acquired a more specific connotation of calm serenity and gentle elegance, leading to emotions of tenderness and love. In musical terms this meant an absence of abrupt transitions and an emphasis on mellifluous melody. William Crotch wrote that in beautiful music 'the melody is vocal and flowing, the measure symmetrical, the harmony simple and intelligible, and the style of the whole soft, delicate, and sweet'.[9] It was music that delighted rather than transported, typically solo airs rather than choruses: Handel's biographer John Mainwaring made a direct contrast between the sensibility of Italian melody and 'the great and sublime' in Handel's oratorios.[10]

Both the beautiful and the sublime could only be communicated through expression, the mainstay of the British aesthetic stance. British writers had generally followed tradition in equating musical expression with the raising of the affections or passions. Alexander Gerard's essay 'Of the Taste of Harmony' (1759) typically describes how music affected the listener:

But still the chief excellence of music lies in its *expression*... It infuses into the breast passions correspondent; settles into calm security, melts into tenderness or pity, sinks into sorrow, sooths into melancholy, agitates with terror, elevates with joy, excites to courage, or enraptures with devotion; and thus inexpressibly delights the soul.[11]

Yet the term expression was now beginning to take on a somewhat different meaning – not just to describe the process of communication, but also to suggest an emotional response in itself. Both Avison and Beattie, in the quotations given above, tie expression directly to pathos and simplicity.

The pathetic, associated with intense emotions of grief, sorrow and pity, occupied a problematical position in the aesthetic scheme. Traditionally it had been regarded as part of the sublime, but in 1747 John Baillie recognised that the agitated passions aroused by the pathetic were inconsistent with the solemnity of the sublime.[12] Avison in his 1752 essay elevated the pathetic to a third category, on the same level as the sublime and the beautiful; such music was characterised by the minor mode, and by chromatic or dissonant harmony. The separate category was not universally accepted, however, and in practice a third view generally prevailed, wherein the pathetic was broadly incorporated within the beautiful. This view recognised that the pathetic was more consistent with the gentle passions than with the lofty emotions of the sublime; but again it was not formally adopted.

The fourth important issue for aestheticians of the period was the traditional primacy of vocal music in the engaging of the affections, and therefore in the entire theory of musical imitation or mimesis. The most well-known discussion of the relationship of poetry and music was the 1763 *Dissertation* by John 'Estimate' Brown. He illustrated his ideas with an ode entitled *The Cure of Saul*, but as all the music was selected from the works of dead composers this was scarcely an innovative collaboration. Indeed, the stance of many such writers remained largely theoretical. Instrumental music had achieved an unprecedented artistic prominence well before Adam Smith in 1795 intimated a theory of absolute music outside the mimetic tradition.

Drawing these diverse and often contradictory strands together in a study of London's concert repertoire is no easy matter. Though concepts of the beautiful and the sublime persisted in aesthetic literature beyond the end of the century, the development of the Classical style introduced new factors; and eventually a separate aesthetic category ('the picturesque') had to be introduced. A further difficulty is that not all writers follow accepted aesthetic divisions, with the term pathos proving particularly problematical. In practice the term normally referred not to an element of the sublime or even to Avison's special category, but to the gently affecting melody of the beautiful. Already in 1755 a French writer noted: '[The English] generally prefer such compositions as are tender, languishing, and pathetic; and are not near so fond of those which are lighter, and more expressive of gaiety.'[13] Certainly the terms expression and pathos may suggest to a modern reader more emotional intensity than they were intended to convey. In this period both are of restrained application, suggesting the delicate emotional sensitivity of the 'sentimental' novel of the

1740s to 1770s: music of a tender sensibility rather than deep anguish, perhaps a major-key vocal rondo or a soft folk-tune in minuet time. An example of the pathetic given in William Jones's *Treatise on the Art of Music* (1784), example 151, is a surprisingly graceful major-key Andante from a symphony by van Maldere, quite unlike the grief-laden examples of Avison.

The following three sections are directly concerned with issues arising out of the notions of simplicity, pathos and expression.

Melody and national airs

One of the primary requisites for simplicity and expression, and a constant theme with critics, was intelligibility of melody. Typically such discussions refer to some notion of primitive or archetypal national unaccompanied airs. Numerous writers applauded Scots music for its easy, natural simplicity. A review of a concert given by the Welsh harpist Edward Jones combined many of these ideas:

Not departing from the sweet simplicity of nature, ... the music of the Welsh bards is more expressive of the '*native wood-note wild*,' and more issuing, whilst, as it varies, it excites a consonant variety of emotions, *from* and *to* the heart, than many of the laboured, and, of course, too cold productions of the present period.[14]

There was some theoretical debate about novelty in melody, but only an extremist such as Dibdin suggested that melodies of the national type might prevail. Gregory felt that a cultivated taste 'begins by degrees to relish [other melodies], besides those which are national', and that melodic simplicity palls without the assistance of harmony.[15] Different views were expressed, however, on where simple and affecting melody was to be found in art music. Many writers, perhaps with reference to ancient Greek music, brought Renaissance and Baroque music into the equation, with broad attacks on all modern music for its lack of 'air' or melody, while others allied the modern Italian style with clarity and expressiveness. Thomas Robertson, on the other hand, after proclaiming the virtues of Scottish, Irish and Welsh melodies ('in tenderness and in passion' excelling all others), praised the music of Haydn for his union of melody and harmony.[16]

Since most music of the eighteenth century, whether Baroque or Classical in idiom, is predicated on the idea of melody as the carrier of expression, it is hardly surprising that commentators tended to find melody in the music they supported, and there is a danger of meaningless generalisation. But a topic of such universal comment requires examination. The following discussion will focus on the English taste for tuneful or affecting melody within a variety of styles.

Of the genuine folk-songs heard in London the most popular seem to have been sentimental Scots strophic ballads of disappointed or lost love, usually in 3/4 or 4/4. Tenducci sang these songs in a slow and melancholy manner, which listeners found deeply moving.[17] Some melodies, such as 'Tweedside', retained an irregular phrasing, but in general rhythmic oddities and distinctive modal twists were smoothed over in modern tonal settings. Externals such as the drone bass and Scots snap were retained to signify the idiom, but the latter may not even have been an original feature. In John Parry's collection of airs with variations for the harp (published in 1761), the treatment afforded to 'Thro' the wood, laddie' and to Handel minuets is strikingly similar. Some settings of these beautiful tunes were published in galant orchestrations. Shield and Samuel Wesley were therefore quite exceptional in their respect for the distinctive modality of such tunes.[18]

Many English composers from Arne and Boyce onwards explicitly imitated this style, in ballads for the gardens as well as the theatre. Not everyone approved this Celtic fakery – a letter in *The Public Advertiser* of 7 August 1767 derided the 'Scotchified Namby Pamby' at Vauxhall – but it was remarkably adaptable to radical style-changes around it. Hook in particular cultivated a sanitised late-eighteenth-century version of the Scots song. 'Typical' Scots snaps and fermatas on climactic notes are retained but Hook imposed a galant framework based on regular phrases, simple tonal harmony and minuet clichés. He similarly redefined the lively 2/4 English song, by concentrating on springing quaver rhythms and bright major-key harmony. By the 1780s he had evolved a standard design for ballads, ultimately owing more to binary dance-forms typical of the middle of the century than to genuine folk song:

8 bars	4–8 bars contrast	4–8 bars, sometimes forming a reprise; often extended to a high pause before the final cadence
Perhaps to V	Perhaps touching II or VI	I

'The lass of Richmond hill' epitomises Hook's coyly charming manner, and it has been mistaken for a genuine folksong ever since. Music at Vauxhall depicted a specially invented bucolic world, as remote from its urbanised listeners then as it is now.

A compromise with this unabashed folk-idiom was the inclusion of folk melodies in modern instrumental art music. As we have seen in chapter 6, many regarded this practice as vulgar, and it also caused artistic problems. It was musically discordant with both opera arias and sacred oratorio airs. Furthermore, it encouraged only the simplest sectional construction, such as the rondo form. Anna Seward was scathing about audiences' delight at the return of 'Malbrook' or 'Come, haste to the wedding', after their indifference to 'the most elegant embroidery that florid and inventive fancy' could produce.[19] Sometimes, as in Dussek's 'Ploughboy' Harp Concerto (C. 53), the tune even recurred during the episodes. Yet at the same time the practice had an unimpeachable intellectual pedigree through its preservation of noble simplicity and a supposed link with antiquity; it could suggest all the major aesthetic categories (the sublime, the beautiful, the pathetic, the picturesque). Burney was clearly aware of the problems raised by this dichotomy, which he resolved into a position of characteristic moderation. As implied above, he regarded folk music as uncouth and barbaric, while at the other extreme he opposed excessive contrivance, preferring to set an ideal elegant simplicity somewhere between the two.

The problem of the incorporation of folk-like material was central to Haydn's later music. During the 1770s and 1780s he developed the so-called 'popular style' in symphonies that were immediately successful in London.[20] Here he assimilates all kinds of diverse elements: disarming Allegretto variation melodies, lively rondo tunes reminiscent of the contredanse or jig, rustic minuets with trios in ländler style. A striking new feature was a jaunty kind of regular secondary theme, marked by tonic and dominant harmonies, broken-chord accompaniments and pizzicato bass. All of these elements constitute a strongly pastoral folk-imagery, whether genuine or not. In particular, regular tunes are used to signify a folk-style, which may be reinforced by such features as drones and slides, exotic chromatic inflexions and orchestration featuring oboes and horn-calls.

Many of these images were in some form already familiar in London, especially through the English repertoire. Pastoral signifiers including drones and slides were well-known from Handel's music (the pifa in *Messiah*, the third number of *My Heart is Inditing*, the musette in Op. 6 No. 6). The *chasse* image was promulgated through innumerable hunting songs, of which Boyce's 'With horns and with hounds' was the most enduring. Furthermore, Haydn's folk-type tunes accorded with the well-established use of British melodies, and the pert innocence of his rondos is not far from Hook's Vauxhall style. It is significant that the process could be easily reversed. The Andante from Symphony No. 53 achieved widespread popularity as the song 'Jemmy and Jenny's farewell' (the prelude to 'Auld Robin Gray') and a pastoral tune from a Pleyel symphony (B. 137) was universally known as 'Henry's cottage maid'.[21]

Haydn's symphonies thus did not enter totally new ground in London, even if the exaggeratedly popular style in which these ideas masqueraded was an outrageous departure. By the time of his arrival there, audiences were fully reconciled to the combination and Haydn could manipulate such materials in all manner of subtle ways – in the extraordinary orchestration of the trio section in No. 97, in the combination of horn-call and melodic tag in the finale of No. 103, in the subtle transfer of finale material to several of the opening movements. Often the use of a musical topic itself becomes the essence of the musical discourse, focussing the listener on the compositional process. Thus the light 'rondo-theme' in the first Allegro of No. 103 only becomes truly comprehensible when its relationship to the slow introduction is explained as the movement progresses. Similarly, the drone D in the finale of the 'London' Symphony achieves a dramatic compositional significance when it is ap-proached by a pedal on C sharp at the moment of recapitulation. Many of the London symphonies parade a gentle vein of self-parody. In the 'Surprise' and the 'Clock' movements the *innocente* Andante is taken to an absurd naivety, while in the finale of No. 98 Haydn repeatedly guys his own trick reprises of trivial melody (and a slower reminiscence turns out instead to be the start of a whirlwind coda).

Haydn's followers in London copied the pastoral signs from Haydn until they became clichés. Often the most complex movements include passages of ingenuous simplicity. The ambitious finale of J. B. Cramer's First Piano Concerto, for example, interleaves an Allegretto drone theme and a self-consciously *semplice* second idea with sections of stormy intensity and bravura. But no-one dared Haydn's extremes of naivety and sophistication. Only Viotti made a successful commentary on the drone: in the finale of Concerto No. 23 the orchestra begins with a drone-type theme, but this turns out to be merely an accompaniment to the main melody in the violin.

Some features observed in folk-settings and imitations can be detected throughout the period in the English concert repertoire, some of it transferred from the playhouses, in music from the lightest glees and strophic ballads to oratorio airs and orchestral music. One can hardly attribute these features directly to the folk tradition, given the complex interaction between genres. But almost every modern commentator has observed a vein of outdoor tunefulness in English music dating back at least to Purcell: the 'mixture of English vigour and freshness' that Julian Herbage remarked in an early study of Arne's songs.[22] This is easier to sense than to define, but typical features include sturdy major-key diatonicism, rhythmic vitality, regular repeated phrases and limited use of sequence and melisma; the accompaniment is often a strong and mobile bass line. Such melodies may have lacked the graceful decorative elegance of Italian music, but neither were they effeminately seductive or 'Popish'. Indeed the 'John Bull' type of English song, dating from before 1700, lives on in Arne's *Alfred* and *Eliza*. It is still detectable in patriotic music of the 1790s, such as Hook's pomposo song 'The good ship Britannia' and Callcott's sea-shanty glee 'You gentlemen of England'. Another distinctively English idiom was the buoyant gavotte style, for all its French origin. It appears in Boyce's overtures and also in more modern contexts, such as Arne's *Artaxerxes* overture and a bass aria in *Judith*. Abel took care to introduce a gavotte finale in his overture for *Love in a Village*; as late as 1790 a gavotte closes one of Hook's organ concertos Op. 55. Other recognisably English types include the charming pastoral, the affecting minuet and the lively patter song, although all of these were susceptible to absorption in the general galant manner.

Many of these 'English' characteristics seem to transcend conventional definitions of Baroque and Classical style. While English songs of the 1740s and 1750s remained indebted to Baroque idioms, they often display dance-like regularity of phrasing and an endearing tunefulness. This comment applies not only to forthright gardens' songs, but also to Arne's more ambitious works and to Boyce's *Solomon*. Even instrumental music of English composers tends to break the lively Allegro of the late-Baroque 'concerto style' into regular phrases without sequential extension. Conversely, even as English composers turned to the galant idiom, they frequently moderated its effect by retaining the solid underpinning of the active Baroque bass-line. In consequence, much English music of the central third of the century stubbornly resists traditional classification. A modern analysis of airs from Smith's *Paradise Lost* (1760) suggesting that they 'illustrate a blend of late-Baroque and early Classical tendencies' is accurate so far as it goes, but it imposes a quasi-historical judgment on an idiom that simply developed an unusual relationship between texture and phrasing.[23]

It is in this light that we should view the longevity of Arne's early songs and overtures in English concert programmes (many of them still in the theatre repertoire). 'Sweet echo' and 'The wanton god' from *Comus* (1738) and the charming cantata *Cymon and Iphigenia* (1753) were still not regarded as old-fashioned in the 1770s, to judge from their continued popularity in concert programmes. The preference for Handel's secular works at the oratorio seasons must also be connected. Several popular songs from *L'Allegro* suggest a delightful 'English' idiom, and even *Jephtha* provided the light bourrée 'The smiling dawn' to oratorio selections. The one lively Italian aria to achieve widespread currency, 'Nasce al bosco', is characterised by a tuneful regularity.[24] This was one of the airs that Burney most approved at the Commemoration, in line with his general preference for those Handel pieces that foreshadowed modern idioms. It may also be significant that the five concerti grossi most often heard later in the century – Handel's Op. 3 Nos. 2 and 4, Op. 6 Nos. 1 and 5, Geminiani's Op. 3 No. 1 – all include strikingly tuneful movements in the major key. Much the same could be said of those older madrigals to achieve popular success, such as Morley's ballett 'Now is the month of maying' and Michael East's 'How merrily'.

At the most fashionable concerts, British music occupied only a marginal role and here there was some ambivalence towards the use of folk-sounding material in symphonies or concertos. Until the craze for Haydn's symphonies in the 1780s, the principal melodic idiom at such concerts was the Italian cantabile, elegantly phrased and decorated, but underpinned by simplicity of line, harmony and texture. Italian arias heard in London in the early 1750s lacked genuine melodic appeal, for all their limited texture and harmony. The rather vapid extracts selected from operas by Ciampi and Lampugnani are typical of their period in their patchwork of short irregular fragments and their mannered sighing figures and triplets. The only aria from this repertoire to achieve lasting fame was 'Vo sol cando' from Vinci's *Artaserse* (later a regular item at the Concert of Ancient Music): this starts arrestingly but soon lapses into empty coloratura writing in an additive construction. Many of the same criticisms could be levelled at the early instrumental music of Giardini, although three catchy rondo finales in his Op. 1 solos reveal a surprising melodic piquancy. But as the Italian galant style matured it developed a more recognisably melodic language, based on rounded regular tunes. The elegantly suave music of J. C. Bach epitomises this trend. His music from the early 1760s remains somewhat short-breathed, but by the 1770s he was writing expansively arched eight-bar melodies, confidently allied to a slow harmonic background. Long expressive appoggiaturas and sensitive chromatic inflexions are hallmarks of Bach's idiom. This development was certainly not unique to England (indeed Bach's 'Mozartian' melodic style typifies the cosmopolitan lingua franca). But it was certainly limpid melody that appealed most to fashionable London audiences.

Italian opera arias heard at London concerts began to differ markedly in structure from those of the early 1750s. The old da capo concept was subject to constant variation and truncation.[25] It remained popular for full-scale heroic arias. As the A-section reached massive proportions, it increasingly resembled a concerto movement, complete with full orchestral ritornello and dramatised solo entry (see, for example, Paisiello's 'Cara fiamma' sung at the Bach–Abel concerts by Tenducci). Often the second and third sections were dropped entirely, as in Sacchini's coloratura showpiece 'Son regina' popularised by Mara. These sonata-like proportions allowed more variety of contrasting material, with broad cantabile melodies being incorporated within the bold bravura idiom. This trend was emphasised by the linking together of two or more arias in varying melodic styles into large dramatic scenas. On the other hand, many of the most well-known Italian songs were written in a more ingratiating style. It was possible to mould the affecting Italian minuet idiom to the da capo form, as Bach showed in some of his most enduring arias from the 1760s. But, increasingly, simple sectional and repetitive forms came to dominate. A common type was the charming 2/4 *romance*, with two upbeats and a delicately sensuous accompaniment. Such arias vary greatly in scale, but they rely almost entirely on engaging melody in duple Andante metre – sometimes sophisticated in phrasing and texture, but always limited in range and rhythmic variety. The ternary 'Lungi dal caro bene' with its serenade accompaniment is merely the slightest cavatina; but concert items were more commonly rondos, usually with two episodes offering brief contrast and perhaps a breathless hint of minor mode. The form was, however, capable of more complexity and some dramatic contrast, a useful attribute for concert arias. Frequently a closing section was added as a stirring cabaletta; this section might itself be in rondo form or it might reintroduce a version of the first melody. Sarti's delightful 'Ah non sai', sung by Sophia Corri at Salomon's concerts in 1792, shows the composer making the most of his melodic invention in just such a double-rondo.

Instrumental music followed similar trends. Memorable rounded melodies were the mainstay of symphonic movements in the lingua franca: opening 'singing Allegros' (Bach often writes eight-bar cantabile second themes), lyrical Andantes, graceful minuet finales. Sectional thematic forms came into prominence here too. The rondo finale achieved early popularity in London, and British enthusiasm may have contributed to its universal acceptance.[26] The 'eternal rondeau' was well established by 1776, when Twining derided it as 'a snake with its tail in its mouth'.[27] Later the simple ternary *romance* with its innocent four-bar phrases was imported for concerto slow movements. English audiences also showed a particular penchant for the orchestral chaconne, no longer tied to a recurrent harmonic framework, but an extended structure in four-bar phrases with both local repetitions and rondo elements. The model here was a well-known movement from a symphony in E flat by Jommelli, which spawned several imitations, of which the overture to Guglielmi's *Le pazzie d'Orlando* (1771) achieved widespread popularity.

English concert music began to imitate the Italianate lingua franca in the 1760s, in both instrumental and vocal genres. English gardens' songs mirror the affecting and (less often) the heroic idioms of Italianate arias, with an occasional glance at the buffa 6/8 patter song. Some English composers maintained their individuality while acknowledging the new style. Arne continued to write memorable songs, such as 'Vain is beauty's gaudy flow'r', and both Webbe and Stevens were able to adapt the galant idiom successfully to the glee. But often the imitation resulted in a rather facile uniformity, as English composers seized on Italianate melodic clichés to enervating effect. The simplified English galant can come remarkably close to the earlier English melodic style and even to the Scots idiom; but it rarely recaptured the former originality as pastoral charm lapsed into the sentimental. We might contrast three songs sung at the Vocal Concert in 1795: Rauzzini's delicately expressive and sophisticated 'Cynthia' as against Callcott's plainly predictable 'Breathe soft ye flutes' and Attwood's maudlin 'The convent bell'. An extreme case of debased English galant must be Thomas Billington's extended cantatas, including the banal and sentimental *Children in the Wood*, frequently performed in 1786; while the only interest in his misguided setting of Gray's *Elegy* lies in his attempts to reconcile ten-syllable lines with four-bar phrases.

Even Viennese instrumental music was susceptible to melodic influence from the Italianate lingua franca, increasingly so as composers began to aim at an international market in the 1780s. This is particularly evident in the inclusion of rounded cantabile melodies as secondary themes. Already London's alternative overture-finale to Haydn's Symphony No. 53 introduces the characteristic texture of lyrical melody accompanied by Alberti-type inner parts and pizzicato bass. Such themes crop up in several symphonies of Pleyel and Haydn that were known in London in the years around 1790. Viennese composers arriving in London may well have deliberately incorporated more Italianate melodic material in line with the J. C. Bach tradition there. Certainly Haydn, Gyrowetz and Pleyel in their London concertantes (a traditionally more relaxed genre) attempted to resolve genial melody into a symphonic framework. Gyrowetz featured similar elegant cantabile in his *Three Symphonies* performed at the Professional Concert and dedicated to the Prince of Wales. Haydn too makes conspicuous use of rounded melodic statements in his

London symphonies, even if they refer only obliquely to the Italianate tradition of Bach. This comment applies particularly to the earlier works: the Allegro of No. 96 (1791) even has an opening theme that could have served for a 'second subject', an impression reinforced by the texture (staccato inner parts, tonic and dominant bass). Almost all the Allegros, however, eschew formal fanfares in favour of soft melodic openings, a luxury allowed by the presence of slow introductions. These movements also play with the concept of a contrasting second tune, though it is often placed late and is liable to be brusquely interrupted. Even in his last symphony (No. 104) Haydn refers to the Italianate cantabile style, but as ever it furnishes material for the most intensive motivic examination as the movement progresses.

No composer in the 1790s could ignore Haydn's artistic or financial success, and Haydnesque tunes of pert innocence often sit alongside Italianate second subjects more reminiscent of Mozart (see, for example, Clementi's single surviving piano concerto). Yet the London school of the 1790s was not content with imitative pastiche. The cantabile Italian idiom developed into a grander simplicity in Viotti's London violin concertos in a transformation of his Parisian risoluto manner. London pianists developed a similar melodic grandeur, especially a vein of nobly expressive Adagio melody that looks to the nineteenth century (as does the high filigree decoration with which they embellished it). At the same time, new kinds of lighter melody evolved. A characteristic second-subject type was the coyly innocent tune in dotted rhythms, as in Dussek's Second Piano Concerto of 1794 (C. 104); this post-Mozartian concept looks to Weber and other neo-classicists of the next century. In an interesting relation of ideas, Dussek in his Grand Military Concerto (C. 153) transforms a military orchestral theme into just such a naive contrast for the soloist. Some rondos also display a new jaunty swagger, more striking than graceful and often using dotted or polacca rhythms. Even Pleyel, in his London concertante for two violins (B. 114), finds a catchy finale-tune with offbeat accents, already far distant from Haydn's rondo style.

Expression: the Adagio and the minor mode

The term 'expression' had traditionally been restricted to the process of musical communication, but Avison's *Essay on Musical Expression* (1752) accelerated the acceptance of new implications behind the concept. It now began to adopt emotional connotations, even if in fact Avison scarcely departed from a traditional view of mimesis. Two types of music – slow movements and music in the minor mode – came to be regarded as particularly expressive, and London's attitude towards them deserves special consideration.

The British prided themselves on their good taste in the cultivation of the Adagio. The word could be used in many contexts. In general it was applied to the finely drawn-out Italianate cantabile. Often it was associated with solo playing, where it implied a warm singing tone and restraint in ornamentation, as will be seen in the next section. It also became a critical cliché in connection with artistic discernment. A 1788 newspaper article about the musical nobility focussed almost entirely on their attitudes towards the Adagio.[28] In similar vein, John Marsh related the three movements of J. C. Bach's symphonies to opera-audience taste-levels: 'The first or principal movements seem to be calculated for the meridian of the pit, (where the Critics generally assemble) the middle strain for that of the boxes, (where people of a more refined taste usually sit) and the last strain for that of the galleries.'[29] Audiences ostentatiously paraded their good taste by regularly encoring Haydn's slow movements. In fact the movements most popular there – those in Symphonies Nos. 53, 94 and 100 – are all of an Andante/Allegretto type. Nevertheless Haydn also developed another kind of Adagio that had resonances with London audiences, in movements of a rapt visionary quality marked by major-key diatonicism and chordal textures. The idiom can be traced back to hymn-like symphony and quartet movements of the late 1780s: in London Haydn enriched it in such fine pieces as the slow movement of the 'Rider' quartet, and the serene Largo aria in the *Scena di Berenice*. Both of these are characteristically set in E major, the key of morning innocence in *The Creation* and of Beethoven's vision of the starry heavens in Op. 59 No. 2.

This anti-galant trend towards a pure classical simplicity was not, of course, unique to London. But throughout this period London maintained some allegiance to slow music of unadorned but profound expression, and this allegiance was strengthened in the last two decades of the century by the clear preference of the Concert of Ancient Music for such music. An extraordinary number of those Handel airs favoured there and at oratorio selections are of this Largo or Larghetto type, often in triple time (though ironically 'Handel's Largo' was virtually unknown). Among these airs are deeply moving expressions of pathos such as 'Total eclipse' and 'Farewell, ye limpid springs'. 'Angels, ever bright' is a beautifully restrained prayer in diatonic idiom, while 'Pious orgies' adds bitter-sweet minor-mode inflexions. In several airs Handel achieved a quite exceptional mood of rapt serenity: for example, 'Dove sei', 'Rendi 'l sereno al ciglio' and 'Verdi prati'.[30] The last named, as well as 'I know that my redeemer liveth' and several others of this type, are written in E major, the key Handel also selected for a vision of heavenly bliss in 'Farewell, ye limpid springs'. It is not suggested that Haydn adopted this key-association from Handel (he had already used it in a similar way in other works), but London would certainly have been familiar with the sonority of a quiet visionary E major before his arrival. By the early nineteenth century such pieces could even be called sublime, breaking through the word's strong association with choruses. Handel's 'I know that my Redeemer liveth' received this accolade from John Crosse, and Burney even included Haydn's instrumental Adagios: 'sublime in ideas and the harmony in which they are clad'.[31]

Some other pieces popular in London throughout the period adopted a similar mood of major-key chordal tranquillity or pathos: music as varied in origin as Gluck's 'Rasserena il mesto ciglio' (in triple-time E major), the opening of Jommelli's Chaconne (suggestive of a slow minuet), Boyce's 'Softly rise, O southern breeze' in a mood of rapturous enchantment. This was an idiom less often attempted within the galant lingua franca, although Abel was especially partial to a richly expressive four-part harmonic string texture. But, as charm and decorative elegance began to give way to a deeper style of slow movement, London soloists sometimes adopted the diatonic chordal texture, as (superimposed on the *romance*) in the E major Andante of Viotti's Concerto No. 23.

Many of these examples convey a mood of uplifting spirituality, sometimes allied to a Christian message. Even the instrumental Adagio became directly linked with the church when a solemn theme from a Pleyel quartet (B. 349) was popularised as a 'German hymn'. But the widespread usage of the unadorned chordal texture suggests that it did not maintain a specifically liturgical connotation. Furthermore, the texture could also be enrolled to summon up images of the ancient world in Philidor's *Carmen Seculare*.

It is evident, therefore, that music of pathos and expression was not necessarily that of a high emotional temperature, nor need it use the minor mode or chromatic intensity. Seldom was Handel's minor-key music selected for public performance: a rare exception was the selection of part of the mournful Funeral Anthem for Queen Caroline at the 1784 Commemoration, though even here the audience was most affected by the pathos of the treble voices in 'She deliver'd the poor that cried'. The overt emotionalism of C. P. E. Bach's *empfindsamer Stil* was little regarded in London and in general, as the traditionalist Hawkins complained, the minor mode was avoided by galant composers. Indeed they rarely essayed powerful minor-key symphonies, even by comparison with their continental counterparts. This is unfortunate in the light of the high quality of works in G and C minor by J. C. Bach (Op. 6 No. 6), Sacchini (Periodical Overture No. 49) and Barthelemon (Op. 6 No. 4). The nervous expressionism of Haydn's 'Sturm und Drang' idiom seems to have had relatively little success. Some of his minor-key symphonies written around 1770 arrived in London in the early 1780s (preceded by those of Vanhall). Yet the 'Farewell' symphony seems to have received only a single performance in 1785, and the poignant and dramatic *Stabat Mater* was heard only once outside the Nobility Concert (London evidently preferred the more melancholy pathos of Pergolesi's setting).

London did prove more susceptible to minor-key music written in the later Classical style. The London school showed a new leaning towards more overtly expressive music, encouraged by the new capacities of the piano. Two of the most impressive sonatas of Clementi's concert years, written after his exposure to the music of J. S. Bach as well as that of Haydn in Vienna, are in minor mode: the F minor Op. 13 No. 6 and the F sharp minor Op. 25 No. 5.[32] In both, suppressed agitation flares up with unaccustomed dramatic intensity: the latter includes a profound B minor Lento, the impact of which derives no longer from galant melodic decoration but from pungent dissonance and yearning chromatic harmony. Depth of expression could itself be enhanced by apparent simplicity, drawing attention to dramatic and harmonic effect. Almost as striking is Dussek's passionate A minor Sonata (C. 80), although as often with this composer there is no slow movement. Dussek made a speciality of exaggeratedly stormy *minore* sections; and even in his major mode music he developed a Schubertian predilection for sentimental harmonic colouring, often using the flattened sixth of the scale. Certainly by 1800, by which time they had ceased to play sonatas in public concerts, both Clementi and Dussek were writing sonatas of an early Romantic depth of expression.

Few concertos of the period adopt the minor mode and seldom do they attempt the inner seriousness of the piano sonatas, for all their dramatic *minore* passages. J. B. Cramer's Second Piano Concerto (Op. 16) provides an arresting D minor exception: even the rondo is in unusually earnest mood. But one concerto-composer showed a clear predilection for the minor mode. Out of the nine concertos Viotti wrote in London in the 1790s four are in the minor mode. This tendency had already surfaced in his Parisian concertos, with their driving orchestral style and grand violin lines; but in his new concertos Viotti clearly attempted to moderate this style, by blending the dramatic orchestral idiom into a more melodic whole. Almost all the London concertos begin with a cantabile statement from the orchestra: in the outstanding A minor Concerto No. 22 the orchestral subject is transformed by the violinist into a lyrical parody of the risoluto French solo entry, and the whole movement is suffused with a tender yearning quality that was much admired by Brahms.

During the 1780s and early 1790s London imported from Vienna a surprising amount of minor-key music in a high-Classical idiom (symphonies by Haydn and Kozeluch, numerous chamber works by Pleyel in *furioso* manner). How these were received is open to question, but the Beethovenian urgency of Vogel's F minor *Démophon* overture was certainly in vogue from 1792. Evidently London was prepared to accept certain minor-mode idioms. But continued ambivalence is reflected in Haydn's London output. It is striking that he chose to write a C minor symphony for his first season, though he eschewed the driving *minore* style and took care to palliate discontinuity with rounded major-key tunes. But London never took to the work and it proved Haydn's last symphony in the minor mode. Instead he matched current practice by incorporating stormy sections in slow movements and rondo finales; and three symphonies open with an ominous minor-mode introduction, an idea perhaps learnt from a Pleyel symphony (B. 147) performed at the Professional Concert in 1791. Elsewhere, however, Haydn did return conspicuously to the minor mode: in the 'Rider' quartet, in the *Storm* chorus, in the *furioso* F minor ending of the *Scena di Berenice* (following the example of *Arianna a Naxos*). When Thomas Robertson rejected Hawkins's strictures against modern music, it was the return of the minor mode in Haydn's music that he called as a primary witness.[33]

Virtuosity and ornamentation

Writers and press-reviewers alike complained repeatedly of the dependence of instrumentalists and singers on virtuoso trickery. The English prided themselves on their discernment in rejecting empty virtuosity and excessive embellishment, preferring instead melodic directness and music that 'spoke to the heart'. Such reviews as the following were commonplace, with their antitheses between surprise and pleasure, between execution and pathos:

A great deal of the [vocal] music of the present day, is calculated more to astonish than to please. Expression and simplicity are often sacrificed to execution.

[The cello solo and oboe concerto] were, what Solos and Concertos usually are, admirable for most brilliant *Execution*; – but why should the best Portion of the Art be unaccomplished? – Why with Execution should there not be *Pathos* likewise?

Weichsel's *maiden* Concerto shewed wonderous rapidity of execution; but [it] was calculated not so much to affect the heart of the hearer with pleasure and delight, as to excite admiration and astonishment.

I will venture to say *solos* and *solo concertos* have done but little good to the cause of MUSIC. LA MOTTE's great merit was to figure away in *alt*, till at last, approaching to the bridge, he played himself, as it were, out of sight. The *dexterity* was *wonderful*, but for heaven's sake where was the *pleasure*?[34]

In fact such antitheses became pure clichés. Having heard Agujari sing at the Pantheon in 1775, Mrs Harris noted that it was the *ton* to say that she was 'more surprising than pleasing', though she herself did not subscribe to the view.[35]

  Features of modern instrumental virtuosity that caused most offence were flashy but vapid passage-work, excessive use of high registers, extravagant cadenzas and barn-storming passages in octaves and the like. Harpsichordists and pianists were particularly susceptible to the charge of note-mongering. For once Burney agreed with William Jackson, in his condemnation of chromatic scales:

Once in a year, perhaps, the rapid *ascent* in half-notes may be borne: but *downward*, the effect is as detestable as if the keys were swept with a broom, or as if the performer had taken an emetic; – and yet every *master*, and every *miss*, who is able to atchieve this feat, never omits it at a close, be the piece to which it is applied grave, gay, or graceful.[36]

The equivalent accusation levelled against violinists was that they over-extended the range of the instrument: 'The Violin players run the Treble Notes very high of late: I don't care says an old Musician, they are already got to the Bridge & my Comfort is they cannot get over it however.'[37] Some averred that such attempted brilliancies were simply ineffective, and that they resulted in impoverished tone. But we must assume that most virtuosi could give an accurate account of their own music, which was designed to show off their abilities. The real objection centred on a more fundamental point, namely that virtuosic display was by its nature a frivolous and mechanical avoidance of expression, that it focussed attention more on the performer than on the music. Thomas Twining thought that emphasis on 'trick, caprice and the difficulté vaincue' necessarily usurped expression and pathos: 'It seems to me as if no composer or player cou'd be in earnest, in altissimo.'[38] In the later part of the period reviewers began to distinguish performing skills from musical content. John Crosdill, for example, was praised for his performance but criticised for his composing ('he surprizes, but he does not elevate').[39] This is a significant shift, for it begins to suggest that the concerto could be regarded as a serious genre worthy the attention of composers not just executants.

Singers were also accused of excessive reliance on bravura passages and high tessitura, but the principal charge against them was excessive ornamentation. One Italian singer at Hanover Square was informed bluntly that she needed to be '*anglicised*', by discarding luxuriance and concentrating on the '*Mezzo Voce*'.[40] Even the celebrated castrato Marchesi was subjected to a sustained campaign of vilification. At his concert début on 14 April 1788 he was deemed acceptable only in recitative 'as it did not admit of that flourishing luxuriance to which the musical critics so vehemently object'. He must have succeeded in moderating his style of embellishment, for the following season reviewers noted approvingly that he had 'studied the taste of an English audience' with regard to the cantabile.[41]

This last comment reflects a widespread belief that England had a special taste in slow music. Another review put this more explicitly: '*Mons. Peiltein* on his Violin, did not want for brilliant Execution; – when England shall have taught him, and in Truth it is *the Property of England* so far to teach, "Perfection in the Adagio," Mons. Peiltein must be a very capital Performer.'[42] We have seen that understanding of the Adagio was regarded as a mark of the connoisseur. Its performance was likewise a sign of true artistry. Abel established a particular reputation in this regard: perhaps the viola da gamba, an ostentatiously elitist instrument by this date, encouraged this cultivation of an inner art. The violinist Barthelemon modelled his Adagio-playing on that of Abel, and his renown was such that the Prince of Wales sent his young protégé Bridgetower to him (rather than to Cramer or Salomon) to develop 'taste and feeling, in the *Andante* and *Adagio*'.[43]

The recurrence of criticisms of virtuoso performance is somewhat problematical. On the one hand it suggests that public taste was so low that concertos and bravura songs amounted to little more than acrobatic stunts to please an undiscerning crowd: John Marsh in his 1796 essay complained that instrumental cadenzas were often the only part to which the audience paid any attention. Many writers (even those otherwise sympathetic to modern music) castigated the London public for their poor taste in supporting such exhibitions and imitating them at home. Stevens in a lecture of 12 May 1802 shares out the blame in a series of clichés:

Suffer me to lament the revolution which of late years has taken place in the Musical taste of the public: and to regret the seemingly predominant ambition in our Instrumental performers, to excite astonishment, by violent rapidity on Keyed and other instruments; and in our singers, to surprize, by the difficult divisions of Bravura Songs; I much fear, that from these propensities in the public, and in public performers, we shall in time lose the elegance and Expression, which have so often charmed us, in a Cantabile Song; and that the exquisite delight which the *Adagio* movement of an Abel, or a *Barthelemon* has inspired will be unknown to us.

Even the newspaper reviewers cited above were, in effect, chiding their own readers in this respect. Yet almost in the same breath reviewers flatter their readers by suggesting that English audiences possessed an unrivalled refinement of taste that moulded any performer who came here.

The truth probably lay somewhere in between. Audiences were undoubtedly attracted by virtuoso display both at sophisticated fashionable concerts and at the gardens. But there was a line beyond which excess was unacceptable. Marchesi was able to draw back from the brink by moderating his style. In 1785 the internationally celebrated virtuoso Antonio Lolli was less fortunate. London laughed at his undisciplined compositions and his violinistic trickery, and he made an humiliatingly rapid departure. Again, the British congratulated themselves on their fine taste: 'LOLLI, as far outshone by Cramer and Giardini in the superior excellencies of the violin, *taste* and *pathos*, as he outdoes them in excentric oddity, trick, and voluble execution, is esteemed at the highest rate in some foreign countries.'[44] The most successful instrumentalists in London were those who steered a middle course, uniting a moderate virtuosity with a wide expressive range. Fischer and Cramer were praised for subjugating technique to 'the more superior Purposes of the Art, harmonious Composition and passionate Effect'.[45] At his last performance in 1792, Giardini 'did not aim at the *surprizes* of *execution*, but at a better quality – *expression*': Fanny Burney recorded touchingly that he played with 'a tone so meltingly melodious, so softly full, so smoothly pleasing, and so grandly commanding' that it still could not be rivalled.[46] It was on such qualities that innumerable comparisons were made – between Crosdill and Cervetto, Cramer and Salomon, Fischer and Parke, Giornovichi and Viotti. Madame Krumpholtz brought a similar vein of pathos to the harp, but only one pianist matched the reputation of the great violinists. Johann Samuel Schroeter's playing was regarded as a touchstone of exquisite sensitivity: '*Dusseck's* sonata on the piano forte, if it had less *affectation* of expression, would have resembled the affecting simplicity of the much lamented *Schroeter*.'[47]

The music published by London's virtuoso instrumentalists confirms a marked increase in technical demands during the period, following a general regression in the middle of the century. Virtuoso idioms suitable for each instrument were increasingly defined – broken tenths for the flute, long *messa di voce* notes for the oboe, string-crossing patterns for the violin, very high cello melodies, and so on. Pianists developed an expressive and bravura manner quite distinct from the harpsichord idiom; slightly later a separate harp style evolved (Dussek's Concerto Op. 30, C. 129, was published in idiomatic versions for both instruments). The repertoire also confirms that some virtuosi depended on technical tricks more than others. While Giardini and Cramer stressed a more melodic kind of figuration, other violinists (Franz Lamotte, Fisher, Lolli) reached pre-Paganinian heights of manual dexterity. The vacuous effect of technical gestures is frequently emphasised by a sharp distinction between melodic and virtuosic sections. A drastic example of such discontinuity is found in the cello sonata Op. 1 by Mara's husband, whose style of playing was deemed 'much more adapted to the taste of foreigners, than to that of Englishmen'.[48] Flights of virtuosic fancy were often described as wild or capricious. But in some cases such accusations are unjustified. Dussek's piano concertos were regularly criticised as the work of a dexterous madman; but they display a compositional control and virtuosic purpose lacking in most exhibition pieces of the period.

The most celebrated singers also united technical ability with expressive powers and restraint in ornamentation. In her single 1773 season Elizabeth Linley established a reputation for her 'soft, sweet, clear & affecting' voice, a reputation that persisted through her long years of public silence: as late as 1797 a critic advised modern singers to remember her 'soothing sounds' and reject 'superfluous *shakes* and *graces*' in Handel.[49] Dibdin rated her the finest soprano of her time, although most critics felt that Mara's stronger tone and depth of expression gave her the palm.[50] In the view of Edgcumbe, Mara and Billington both excelled in concerts thanks to their cultivated musicianship (he preferred Banti's natural theatricality on stage). With regard to male concert-singers, Edgcumbe and the Burney family agreed in singling out Gasparo Pacchierotti, whose singing was as legendary for exquisite feeling and pathos as for tasteful ornamentation.[51]

Undoubtedly a certain xenophobia lay behind much of the criticism of excessive virtuosity (compare the association of sensual Italian melody with Catholicism). John Byng facetiously allied himself with Fielding's Squire Western when he complained that he tired of 'difficult lessons, and hard concertos'.[52] Curiously perhaps, ornament and execution were frequently identified as French vices rather than Italian. Of course the word 'French' can be a blanket term for 'foreign', but some evidence suggests that by this date French audiences were indeed seduced by instrumental virtuosity. Cramer was amazed by the technical exhibitionism of French orchestral violinists, and his violin concertos were published in Paris rather than in London.[53] But in truth Britain could not claim a European monopoly on good taste. German critics repeatedly railed against technical excesses in similar terms to the British; nor did Lolli win over all critics in Vienna and Italy.

A specific area where ornamentation and displays of virtuosity were found offensive was ancient music. Anna Seward objected on principle to singers who 'gambol in the sacred songs',[54] but most criticisms were made on aesthetic grounds. Indeed simplicity in the singing of Handel became a byword. At the 1768 Covent Garden oratorios Tommaso Guarducci strove to match the English 'gravity of taste' with a plain but expressive style of performance (he added only a few embellishments on repeats).[55] Twenty years later Harrison sang 'Angels, ever bright' with 'that elegant and captivating simplicity ... which is so much to be preferred to the meretricious ornament of the Italian school'.[56] Cramer was lauded for playing Baroque music with 'reverential purity and simplicity'.[57] An extreme line was taken at the Concert of Ancient Music, where solo instrumental items were banned, outside concerti grossi like Geminiani's Op. 3 No. 1. Conspicuously avoided were such extrovert Handel songs as 'O had I Jubal's lyre' and 'Sweet bird', both of which were frequently performed elsewhere. The King had considerable influence in this direction: his approval of the engagement of Mrs Billington depended on her being persuaded 'to sing pathetick songs and not to over *grace* them'.[58] In fact, history was being rewritten. In Burney's view, Rubinelli sang 'Return, O God of hosts' so plainly at the Abbey that it was bald and insipid compared to Mrs Cibber's performance under Handel's direction. Indeed, Burney thought the whole British stand against ornamentation excessive, and fuelled only by envious musicians and dilettanti.[59]

The trend could be linked with the general move towards simplicity noted in connection with the Adagio. It would even be possible to argue that the tide of complaints against ornamentation in the 1780s indicates a heightened sensitivity against a practice already in decline. Certainly instrumentalists showed some reaction against shallow virtuosity. Sometime in the 1780s Clementi is supposed to have rejected displays of pianistic brilliance in favour of a 'more noble style of performance'; the change is in any case quite apparent in his sonatas from 1785 onwards.[60] Piano and violin concertos of the 1790s also show a more serious approach towards the genre. Viotti inspired a new style of appreciation altogether, normally reserved for Haydn: 'VIOTTI is original and sublime – he reaches at unattempted grandeur – and he never fails. What may be expected from him it is impossible to conceive. – He has a soul capable of magnifying Simplicity into the Wonderful. – His Music is yet better than his Performance.'[61] Soloistic display began to foreshadow the individualistic idiom of the next century, in the assertive fortissimo chords of the standard piano entry, in the noble singing line of the violin. The relationship between soloist and orchestra was dramatised. Even as brilliant passage-work and ornament were developed to new levels, these were subsumed into complex musical structures. The more serious sonata and concerto gave virtuosity a function other than vapid display.

Musical style: the learned, the sublime and the dramatic

The learned or scientific style

The terms 'learned' and 'scientific' appear in British musical literature in a variety of contexts. They may refer broadly to music of a serious, complex or sublime cast. When used by the supporters of the ancient cause, the terms are associated with sound taste and understanding, an appreciation of subtle musical qualities. For the detractors of such music, the same terms have a derogatory meaning indistinguishable from heavy or dull. A more technical association is with music not reliant on galant melody or virtuosic appeal, especially music in contrapuntal style. This section will be concerned with this last more specific usage.

Renaissance and Baroque music should not be equated absolutely with contrapuntal music. Some enduring madrigals were written in a light chordal idiom; many Handel airs were selected on the basis of their melodic appeal; and a number of well-known choruses relied largely on dramatic or pictorial interest. Nevertheless, some connoisseurs undoubtedly appreciated the compositional depths of ancient counterpoint. In a pamphlet of 1770 John Hawkins, a leading figure at the Academy of Ancient Music, proposed for study the music of great contrapuntists from Palestrina onwards, and at the Academy up until the 1770s members often heard complex motets and madrigals by Palestrina, Byrd, Victoria, Lassus and Marenzio. Contrapuntal madrigals were of course the backbone of the Madrigal Society repertoire and they were also performed, though infrequently, at the Concert of Ancient Music.

Eighteenth-century contrapuntal music was appreciated more widely. Even in the public venues, London maintained a penchant for fugal writing and Corellian trio textures well into the century. They could be heard in most of Handel's French overtures and in every one of the concerti grossi Op. 6, written for his 1739–40 oratorio season. The instrumental works of his London contemporaries, whatever their nationality, present a similar picture. Handel also continued to write massive contrapuntal choruses in oratorios as late as *Jephtha* (1752). In the view of Hawkins, Handel made a deliberate appeal to connoisseurs in such movements, knowing 'that he could attach to him the real lovers and judges of music by those original beauties, which he was able to display in the composition of fugue and chorus'.[1] These were, of course, the values that enabled Handel to enter the pantheon at both ancient societies. Even Charles Burney exonerated Handel's contrapuntal music from the charge of Gothic barbarism that he levelled at canons and fugues in which the words were obscured.[2]

London maintained some contrapuntal tradition into the 1750s, even as newer styles rapidly began to infiltrate instrumental music. For his benefit on 15 April 1752 the Dutch violinist Hellendaal, a virtuoso pupil of Tartini, advertised the performance of 'Grand Concertos, with Fugues, of his last Composition' (perhaps from his old-fashioned but accomplished Op. 3). Even Giardini took the precaution of including a lively fugal movement in the fourth of the overtures published in 1755. It may be significant that the first successful Mannheim composer in the late 1750s was the relatively conservative Richter: 'The first inventor of the style of the modern symphony is said to be Richter, whose compositions being more scientific than those of the generality of his immediate successors, (the last strains of many of them being short fugues) are therefore more pleasing to *connoisseurs*.'[3]

After Handel's death the contrapuntal tradition went into slow decline, though it was never entirely abandoned. In the first place, the unceasing performance of Handel oratorios meant that large fugal choruses never went out of circulation, despite shifts in popularity; similarly French overtures by Handel, Arne and Boyce continued to be popular at the gardens. Not surprisingly, Boyce's court odes retained formal Baroque counterpoint, and in the theatre the oratorios of Smith and Stanley stayed faithful to older orchestral and choral idioms. Even Arne in *Judith* adopts a Baroque idiom to illustrate the power of Jehovah ('Hell shrinks from th'impending stroke'); and it is striking that when he added the impressive 'Here sons of Jacob' for the 1773 revival he incorporated neo-Baroque contrapuntal sections. The young Thomas Linley, modern virtuoso violinist, paraded old-style counterpoint ostentatiously in his two Drury Lane works – the *Ode on the Spirits of Shakespeare* (1776) and the shorter *Song of Moses* (1777). The oratorio series also maintained the solid organ-concerto tradition, and J. C. Bach attempted to modernise the style at his peril. As late as 1784 Michael Arne was still able to improvise an organ fugue, albeit somewhat to the Haymarket audience's surprise.[4]

Some contrapuntal choral writing heard in London originated outside the Handelian line. Italian sacred music traditionally included fugues in a formal learned style. Liturgical music by Handel's Italian contemporaries was valued mainly at the Concert of Ancient Music, but newer Italian oratorios were heard at the theatres. Jommelli's *La passione* was performed several times between 1764 and 1771. All three choruses include sections in strict style, although one ends dramatically with the *sotto voce* repetition of the single word 'umanità'. For the choruses of his oratorio *Gioas, rè di Guida* J. C. Bach adapted music from liturgical music he had written in Italy during the 1750s. Significantly he not only made the orchestral parts much more colourful but he also altered fugal sections by inserting contrasting homophonic passages, thus approaching Handel's customary varied mix. Both French composers working in London in the 1770s used dignified contrapuntal writing to suggest the world of antiquity: Barthelemon in the oratorio *Jefte in Masfa* (already in the overture) and Philidor in his *Carmen Seculare* setting.

One older work that achieved a strikingly wide currency was Pergolesi's *Stabat Mater*, with its solemn duets in the Baroque learned idiom. It was heard at diverse venues, ranging from fashionable benefits in the 1750s (Giardini added four choruses in 1756), through oratorio series of the 1770s, to society concerts again up to 1800. But most of the music so far considered was directed at the English market; here there was some continuing appreciation of contrapuntal writing as well as a loyalty to English music of undecorated grandeur and religious association. All of these factors directly contradicted the values of fashionable concerts, where programmes were built round Italianate arias and symphonies. Fugal movements are indeed rare in London's modern instrumental music during the 1760s and 1770s, even by comparison with Austro-German music of the period. The neglect of counterpoint might appear to reflect a lack of the theoretical tradition that Fuxian studies provided on the continent. But in fact most composers arriving in London would have undergone a thorough contrapuntal training. J. C. Bach's impressive C minor piano fugue showed just what he could have achieved in this direction had he been called upon to do so.[5]

In the 1780s London witnessed a revival of interest in contrapuntal music, similar to that evident on the continent. By 1780 J. S. Bach's keyboard preludes and fugues (the '48') were known in London, if not performed in public. They had an immediate impact on Clementi, inspiring a number of piano fugues and influencing his style generally: his sonatas immediately display a new luxuriance of part-writing and harmony, for which there was no immediate precedent. Both Clementi and Dussek were partial to canonic writing. At the same time Handel's music was boosted by the activities of the Concert of Ancient Music. Unable to halt the decline of interest in the Old Testament oratorios, the directors took to selecting choruses, many of which found their way into the public domain via the Commemoration and *Redemption*. Often these grand choruses include substantial well-wrought contrapuntal sections, as for example 'From the censer' and 'The Lord shall reign'. Perhaps it was not the counterpoint that caused these to be preferred: the severe seventeenth-century fugue that Handel borrowed for 'Egypt was glad' was never introduced at public selections. Nevertheless, more contrapuntal music was enjoyed in London in the 1780s than in the previous two decades and when Reichardt's *La passione* was performed in 1785 it was specifically censured for its lack of Handelian counterpoint.[6]

Some London composers responded directly to the ancient revival. Ever the opportunist, Hook included in his organ concertos Op. 20 conspicuous stretches of counterpoint, including a fugato in No. 3. Borghi seems to have intended a witty comment on the ancient style in his symphony Op. 6 No. 6 (1787). A gentle rondo theme is brusquely swept aside by a lively unrelated fugue, which itself gives way to a galant coda underpinned by the fugue subject.[7] Others, however, had a more serious mission. Cooke's *Ode on the Passions* (1784) includes neo-Baroque and madrigalian choruses, while Charles Wesley's early organ concertos are pure Handel in style, even if the treatment of the orchestra by both composers saves them from accusations of pastiche. Wesley's brother was more receptive to new styles and his *Ode to St Cecilia*, performed in 1799, makes an individual response to the neo-Baroque. The combination of solid contrapuntal choruses with modern orchestral style and dramatic effects foreshadows nineteenth-century choral music. Indeed something of the same combination of old and new can be detected in choruses like 'The heavens are telling' in Haydn's *Creation*. When at one of Salomon's performances in 1800 Samuel Wesley played a Baroque-style organ concerto the audience must have appreciated a direct connection with Handel.

Glees, too, maintained an unobtrusive connection with the older traditions of Elizabethan madrigal and Anglican anthem. Newer glees performed in public varied greatly in their use of counterpoint and some are entirely chordal. Others, such as Cooke's pastiche 'In the merry month of May', make full use of madrigalian imitation in a tonal idiom; and a Handelian background is suggested in Callcott's 'Peace to the souls of the heroes'. Unfortunately, however, stiff phrasing and a pale harmonic background generally render the more polyphonic glees less successful than those of more varied textural sensitivity.

The influence of the counterpoint of both Fux and Bach on the Viennese masters is well known. Haydn's conspicuous fugues in the quartets Op. 20 and Symphony No. 70 were known in London from publications around 1780, though no reactions have been recorded. By the time of his arrival in London, freely contrapuntal manipulation of the simplest subject had become second nature to Haydn. In Symphony No. 95 the innocuous finale theme is subjected to the full glare of species counterpoint, perhaps Haydn's own ironic comment on ancient music. More typically, counterpoint is fully absorbed into the modern style, and it is liable to occur anywhere in a movement, as three examples from finales will show. In Op. 74 No. 1 Haydn replaces a 'contrasting second subject' with a quasi-learned disquisition on the opening motif, before dismissing it with an outrageously extended drone close. The recapitulation in Symphony No. 101 is the place for another fugato, this time in spectral pianissimo and fiddling away into distant keys before the full orchestra restores normality. Finally, in Symphony No. 103 Haydn forces the listener to address the question of counterpoint directly: the combination of simple horn-call and folk-tune has scarcely been stated when the latter is subjected to intensive motivic and contrapuntal examination. Indeed this colossal sonata-rondo is based on the dialectic between homophonic and learned presentations of material. Critics at last began to recognise the scientific qualities in Haydn's symphonies. Crotch saw that the modern symphonic style had been greatly enriched by the return of counterpoint:

While science was banished, the overture and concerto remained uninteresting; but when this was readmitted, and the sublime occasionally introduced, the modern style of instrumental music became, as such, much superior to what it had been.[8]

This was only one factor in a perception that modern symphonic music could after all make intellectual demands, involving not only the ability to disentangle complicated textures but also to follow an elaborate symphonic argument. The rise of dramatic discourse will be discussed in a later section.

The sublime

British aesthetics set the sublime in sharp contrast to the tender delicacy of the beautiful. The term sublime had many varied associations. It had not yet gained any connotation of meditative tranquillity; rather it suggested a lofty and awe-inspiring grandeur. In this primary sense, derived from Longinus, the sublime was found in majestic natural scenes, such as vast mountain ranges, precipices, deserts, expanses of water – and by extension in elevated emotions of courage, magnanimity and religious fervour. This soul-stirring quality, exalting and ennobling the human spirit, had an evident ethical dimension, which some closely allied to the contemplation of the Creator.

The sublime was soon perceived in Handel's music, especially in massive choruses on elevated sacred themes. In 1760 John Mainwaring rhapsodised about the sublime final choruses of *Messiah*, wherein 'the ear is fill'd with such a glow of harmony, as leaves the mind in a kind of heavenly extasy'.[9] This quotation also emphasises another important aspect of the sublime, namely that it inspired an abandoned emotional response. Many listeners at the Abbey Commemoration recorded that they were completely transported by the sublimity of the experience. Anna Seward countered William Cowper's objections by writing ecstatically of

> Those great designs attain'd, when, thro' the aisles
> Of the vast ancient fane, in torrents burst
> Those floods of harmony, that lift the soul
> Upon their swelling and tumultuous waves
> Up to the Throne of God.[10]

Undoubtedly, the emotional effect of the Commemoration was greatly increased by the unadorned grandeur and associations of Westminster Abbey. In addition, veneration for the greatness of a renowned artist was a recognised feature of the Longinian sublime.

To define musical images of the sublime more precisely is problematical. Aesthetic texts give only sketchy suggestions, usually mentioning long low notes and wind instruments such as the organ. A ready association was provided by the powerful simplicity of Handel's homophonic choruses; William Shield identified the sublime in slow choruses of stable harmony and rhythm.[11] John Gregory suggested that the following quotation could be directly applied to music: 'The main secret of being sublime, is to say great things in few and plain words: for every superfluous decoration degrades a sublime idea.'[12] Many popular Handel choruses included massive chordal sections, which are especially common in the celebratory royal anthems. This was music that unfolded on a grand scale with a strongly rhythmic background: Handel himself remarked to Gluck in 1746 that 'what the English like is something they can beat time to, something that hits them straight on the drum of the ear'. But sublime also were awe-inspiring effects such as the gradual build up to the first choral entry of *Zadok the Priest* or sudden contrasts from the mightiest fortissimo to a hushed unison. To similar ends the security of strong tonal progressions could be undermined by awesome plunges to unexpected harmony, for bold contrast was as much part of the sublime as grandeur; predictable regularity could not inspire the same sense of awestruck astonishment. A striking example of textural and harmonic contrast is found in 'O first created beam', a commentary on Samson's depravity expressed by reference to the story of the creation. Handel's contrast of undirected, halting chromaticism with a blazing rhythmic C major must surely have been known to Haydn.

Impressive choruses such as that beginning the Dettingen *Te Deum* revel in the full splendour of the Baroque orchestra, with a full wind section including brilliant trumpets. So too did Handel's most popular overture, the full-dress propagandist opening to the *Occasional Oratorio*. Loudness was taken to its inevitable extreme in the outsize festivals of the 1780s and 1790s, an exaggeration of the sublime that was recognised at the time. In the view of one commentator, 'the tasteful and cultivated ear sickens and withdraws' from the torrent of musical noise; and even John Marsh felt that *Redemption* contained too many grand choruses.[13] But the sublime in Handel had further connotations than mere noise and grandeur. It also implied multiplicity and diversity – a teeming activity suggested by contrapuntal or antiphonal use of chorus and by constantly shifting blocks of orchestral colour. Many of Handel's choruses mix the celebratory chordal style with vivid orchestral ritornello, fugue and free concertante interplay (for example, 'From the censer', 'Gird on thy sword', 'The Lord shall reign', 'Ye sons of Israel').

Yet another element of the sublime, elevated to a primary position by Edmund Burke in 1757, was terror, induced by the contemplation of battle-scenes, tempests at sea, and so on. Avison recognised that second-hand terror could be a pleasurable sensation: 'the Sense of our *Security* mixes itself with the terrible Impressions, and melts them into a very sensible Delight'.[14] This aspect of the sublime is clearly evident in Handel's descriptive choruses, where natural forces are used to illustrate Jehovah's power: whether physically over the Egyptians (in hailstones, fire and water) or symbolically (thunder in 'Fix'd in his everlasting seat', earthquake in 'He comes to end our woes', sea-storm in 'When his loud voice'). Anna Seward gave a graphic description of the images she saw in 'The horse and his rider hath he thrown into the sea' ('the clang of the trumpets, the thunder of the drums, the sounds of wild dismay, which burst in vollies from every part of the vast orchestra').[15] This chorus, like most of the examples cited, vividly portrays physical terror and spiritual awe within a context of praise and celebration, thus combining several different sides of the sublime.

None of these aspects – elevated grandeur, orchestral splendour, contra-puntal diversity, picturesque horror – are characteristic of the galant style, and during the 1760s and 1770s they were maintained only outside the lingua franca. Most English oratorio composers attempted to maintain the Handelian chorus tradition, both in terms of texture and in depiction of seascapes and the like. It is striking that the two biggest choruses in Arne's *Judith* are both concerned with the power of Jehovah; the new closing chorus of 1773 includes a furious minor-key section depicting the destruction of the enemies of the Lord. Even J. C. Bach included in his Italian oratorio *Gioas* a dramatic 'Baal' chorus, with tempestuous string figuration and operatic choral exclamations. The young Linley followed a different but related tradition in his *Ode on the Spirits of Shakespeare*. For the witches' scene in Part 2 he imports a supernatural stage idiom, complete with gloomy C minor, howling whirlwind effects and sudden drops to tremulous *piano*.

From the 1780s the notion of the sublime was gradually admitted to discussions of abstract instrumental music, but in a bewildering variety of contexts. In 1788 a paragraph in *The Times* praised Haydn's 'wildness of sublimity' (noting perceptively that Pleyel lacked this quality).[16] We have seen that Burney singled out his Adagios as sublime; while for Crotch this quality was found in such movements as Symphony No. 82's Allegretto (presumably the powerful *minore* section at bar 101) and also in majestic symphonic introductions.[17] In the last three symphonies in particular, written for a larger orchestra and hall, Haydn seems consciously to have aimed for a more grandiose effect, incorporating awesome contrasts between frenzied activity and solemn stillness. Contemporary reviewers frequently recognised the sublime in Haydn's London symphonies; it soon became a cliché, but the fact that a Haydn symphony could be reviewed in Handelian terms at all is significant. As we have seen in chapter 6, the term was also used in connection with scenes of horror in Haydn's *Storm* and the 'Military' Symphony. Echoes of this idiom recur throughout the later London symphonies, in tempestuous minor-mode outbursts which quickly give way to sunlit calm (see for example the slow movements of Nos. 99 and 102). One of the most shattering moments in all Haydn's œuvre is the complete collapse in No. 103 just when a pleasing codetta is expected; here Haydn uses disruptively 'Gothic' effects (*ff* diminuendos, drum-rolls, A flat minor chord) to prepare for the completely unexpected return of the introduction.

The term sublime could therefore be used in a wide variety of contexts, from a grandiose Handel chorus to a threatening Haydn military movement. All of these step beyond everyday urban experience and comforting pastoral make-believe into a world of deeper emotions, whether spiritual, inspirational or anxiety-ridden. Often these emotions are illuminated by images of the untamed physical world. Here was another opportunity for new music to assert its place in the intellectual framework of its time. In *The Creation*, which returns to many of the images discussed in this section, Haydn reinterpreted the sublime and placed it into a modern symphonic context.

Drama and contrast

The notion of drama within music is fundamental to any discussion of style change within the eighteenth century. Donald Tovey made a brisk distinction between Baroque architectural ritornello forms and Classical dramatic sonata procedures. While this analysis may require some refinement (Classical symphonies often retain ritornello elements), it remains a useful benchmark. Implicit in it is the difference between the older concept of 'single Affekt', an unchanging emotional state throughout a single movement, and the newer psychological drama propelled by flexible contrasts and emotional conflict or resolution. It is not suggested that London played any special role in this change, but the identification of a single repertoire enables a study of its effects and the views of contemporary critics.

Handel's music still adheres in broad terms to the Baroque concept. The drama of his great biblical oratorios, such as *Saul* and *Jephtha*, unfolds on the broadest scale over a succession of well-timed arias, accompanied recitatives and choruses. Where emotional transformation takes place within a single musical number, this is customarily achieved by manifest subversion of standard Baroque practice, rather than by any intrinsic change of musical language. In *Saul*, for example, one air is a violently interrupted da capo aria, another joins two short pieces together, another adds a passionately grieving coda. Internal conflict is created in the oft-extracted trio 'The flocks shall leave the mountains', where Acis and Galatea are threatened by the monster Polypheme: but this is really a duet and an aria sung simultaneously. There is more sense of dramatic contrast in some of the larger choruses, where it often contributes to the impression of the sublime. In 'Fall'n is the foe' the drama consists not so much in the vivid battle depiction as in boldly changing textures. Particularly arresting is the totally unexpected interruption of a fugato with hushed cries of 'fall'n' over throbbing strings, profoundly shifting attention away from the victor to the vanquished. Nevertheless such choruses still lack the concept of emotional transformation that is at the heart of the sonata and symphony. It is significant that in 'O first created beam' Handel could depict the change from darkness to light twice in succession, something Haydn would never have contemplated.

The essence of the new classicism lay only superficially in its lighter melodic idiom and its simple harmonic textures. More fundamental are the elements of contrast and emotional change. The quicksilver mood-shifts of the early Italian galant were known in London through opera overtures of the 1740s. The idiom was popularised in concerts by Giardini's overtures, with their playful exchange of motives and flexible alternation of brilliant orchestral tutti with short snatches of melody. It was exactly this idea of contrast that Burney singled out in the music of J. C. Bach, perhaps the finest composer of the later galant idiom: 'Bach seems to have been the first composer who observed the law of *contrast*, as a *principle*.'[18] His symphonies represent the ultimate refinement of the galant Italian idiom; indeed his first published set consisted of actual opera overtures, and several late symphonies also started life in the opera house. The galant ideal was an inventively varied interplay of contrasting ideas, and such invention must be the yardstick of originality in this repertoire. Thus in *ABC Dario Musico* (1780) Fischer's oboe music was described as original to the point of whimsicality, but nothing in his published concertos indicates more than a typical adherence to mid-Bach style. For all its agreeable transparency, however, Bach's music is not unsophisticated. He tackled the essential compositional problem of the new style: how to assemble a flow of diverse ideas into a meaningful coherence. Bach's success resided in his achievement of more-or-less satisfactorily balanced structures, within which melodies maintain a clear hierarchical function.

Bach's later music, more self-confident and public in manner, shows more breadth of melodic and structural conception. Many of the Op. 18 symphonies begin with a majestic call-to-attention, while chromatic prolongation and the delaying of cadences both contribute to a more spacious pacing of events. Bach also explores subtle ambiguities of function. The first of the set begins with a stock unison idea, but this straightway sounds again under bustling tutti material, and later it surprisingly underpins part of the second subject melody. Such textural argument is intimately connected with Bach's development of colourful instrumental timbres. He began to rely less on local dynamic effects, but exploited larger contrasts between richly varied sonorities; this applies in concertantes and chamber music, as much as symphonies. An early penchant for woodwind episodes can be seen in the operas of the 1760s and he soon transferred the idea to symphonies: Op. 9 No. 1 (published in 1773) includes soloistic episodes for two clarinets and bassoon. Three of the Op. 18 symphonies are scored for double orchestra (one with oboes, horns and bassoon, one with flutes), while many of the concertantes include solo parts for wind instruments. This emphasis was certainly in accord with British taste. Arne was particularly interested in unusual orchestral sonorities. *Artaxerxes* (1762) includes striking sections for woodwinds, such as the depiction of dawn in Act 1 with just oboes, bassoons, horns and double basses; and 'Water parted from the sea' features a wind-band of clarinets, bassoons and horns. Kelly shared this predilection. The *Maid of the Mill* overture (1765) and the Periodical Overture No. 17 (1766) both include passages for winds, the latter departing from his Mannheim models by substituting clarinets for oboes. Later in the century much the most interesting feature of Hook's songs is the variety of soloistic wind scoring, something that is not apparent from the printed vocal scores alone.

It has sometimes been suggested that London's 'new middle-class audience' should be credited with features of the later galant style, features designed to sustain the interest of the unsophisticated: the fast tempos, the emphasis on appealing melody, the striking tutti style, the colourful contrasts. But this view cannot be sustained, at least in this crude form. All of these audience-pleasing elements can be traced back to Italian opera overtures, which in London were the preserve of the élite Opera House. Even the undoubted connection between the symphony and the buffa idiom does not imply that symphonists directly moulded their style for a middle-class audience.

Until around 1780 London evidently preferred this appealing but relatively undemanding style to its more dynamic Austro-German variants. It seems that the initial enthusiasm for Johann Stamitz's excitable symphonies, with their bombardment of nervous dynamic contrasts and orchestral shock tactics, was short-lived. Even Bremner quickly looked elsewhere and his fourth set of Periodical Overtures (1767–8) consists entirely of Italian music. Suggestions of the Mannheim idiom, including the infamous crescendo, can certainly be detected in the early symphonies of Bach and Abel. But these were rapidly absorbed within the gracefully melodic Italian idiom. Bach is increasingly concerned with a sensual mix of melody and voluptuous sound, with contrast primarily used for pleasing variety, and he scarcely tapped the dramatic potential of the idiom. Even in an opera quartet performed at a concert in 1771 ('Deh torna'), the emphasis is on smooth melody rather than characterisation. Bach was certainly aware of the larger possibilities of symphonic argument: in his one minor-mode symphony, Op. 6 No. 6, a single motive is subjected to intensive harmonic examination, while in a late E major concertante the surprising D-natural in bar 6 has important structural consequences. But in general the motivic and tonal aspects of the dramatic symphonic idiom seem to have held relatively little interest for him.

Perhaps the high-galant style of Bach and his contemporaries had nowhere to go. The attenuated music of the late 1770s is not necessarily more interesting than that of the 1760s. One London work showed a way forward in its bold expansion of Bach's idiom. In Schroeter's impressive E flat major Piano Concerto Op. 5 No. 6 (1774), the style is enriched with chromatic inflexions, and the first movement includes a stirring development around minor keys, roving as far as a chord of F flat minor. Unusually this work was identified precisely in several concert advertisements. Similar enrichment of the galant idiom, transformed by other influences, was the secret of Mozart's mature style. But London, unable to appreciate Mozart's achievement, was ready for a new musical stimulus; in the heightened drama of Haydn's symphonies, contrasts formed an essential element of musical argument.[19]

Haydn's style is predicated on an exaggeration of unpredictable contrasts: striking rhythmic dislocations and changes of pace, quirky and comic use of rests, harmonic and dynamic shocks. Most novel of all were the mercurial lurches between idioms, from folk-style melody and rustic drones to grandiose fanfares, learned counterpoint and moments of sublimity. Indeed the unexpected is liable to turn up at any point, even in slow movements and minuets. To take one example, Haydn experimented ever more audaciously with tonal excursions. In the C major Quartet Op. 74 No. 1, both the opening Allegro and the minuet make conspicuous dives to A flat major, while the trio is in radiant A major. The Andantino in G goes much further, arriving by sleight-of-hand in distant C sharp minor before returning as easily to a now disturbingly innocuous tonic.

London reviewers frequently remarked on Haydn's fire and grandeur, but it was the quality of surprise and fantasy that they found particularly novel in Haydn's music. The following is a characteristic review of Haydn's third London symphony (No. 93), a review that in its clichéd way reflects closely the aesthetic concerns of the time:

Such a combination of excellence was contained in every movement, as inspired all the performers as well as the audience with enthusiastic ardour. Novelty of idea, agreeable caprice, and whim combined with all *Haydn's* sublime and wonted grandeur, gave additional consequence to the *soul* and feelings of every individual present.[20]

This symphony is indeed packed with unusual effects of scoring, harmony and construction: to list them here would be prosaic. The finale is a particularly fine example of Haydn's 'agreeable caprice', not only in the obviously playful treatment of the returning subject but also at a deeper structural level. Haydn toys with the conventions of both sonata and rondo, so that the listener loses track of whether he is in a recapitulation, a false-recapitulation or even a false false-recapitulation. Three times we are led to expect a return to the opening, but expectations are disappointed until a simplified closing reminiscence at bar 292. In this symphony Haydn recalls the D major brilliance of Symphonies Nos. 53 and 96 as well as those of Bach, but this element is only part of a much more ambitiously dramatic conception and the symphony ends with flamboyant theatricality. It perhaps represents Haydn's most direct attempt, after one season's experience, to match the English taste. Having achieved their enthusiastic approval in this and No. 94 he was free to press on with more subtle experiment in almost every direction, ranging from the structural use of woodwinds to examination of the very concept of the symphony.

A vexing question is whether the whimsical aspects of Haydn's style accorded with a latent and hitherto unrevealed English taste. They were certainly quite new to London in the early 1780s and at first British writers found the surprising juxtapositions incomprehensibly strange. Others complained of superfluity of material, the 'strong effusions of genius turned into frenzy', or of tonal diversions wherein 'sometimes the Key is perfectly lost, by wandering so far from it'.[21] However widespread such opinions were at first, they soon became a minority view. In 1784 Thomas Robertson, after an attack on 'unlimited modulation through a variety of Keys', exonerated the novelties of Haydn's music, in which uncommon modulations and discordant fermatas 'excite the happiest disorder and surprize'.[22]

One common critical prop was a perceived similarity between Haydn's music and the novels of Laurence Sterne (1713–68), a topic that has also received modern attention.[23] One link was a deliberate unconventionality, expressed in a vein of wit and caprice that can be both risqué and intellectually ingenious. Haydn matches Sterne in his ironic commentary on the nature of the symphony, focussing the listener on the form itself in a modern distancing effect. Indeed his eccentricities may have hit a particular nerve with the English, who were said to understand his music better than his countrymen. Certainly Haydn retained elements of the bizarre in his London music, after some initial caution; and reviewers there, unlike German critics, were not at all bothered by Haydn's popular tunes and musical humour (even the notorious bassoon 'raspberry' in Symphony No. 93 went unremarked). London seems to have had an instinctive feeling for Haydn's extraordinary blend of the grand and the trivial, of the inevitable and the incongruous, of the learned and the low – for his Sternian fantasies of intellectual wit and originality.

In 1791 Burney sarcastically remarked: 'We are not certain that our present musical doctors and graduates are *quite up* to Haydn yet.'[24] Aesthetic theory lagged way behind changes in musical style. Only in the 1790s was there an attempt to explain the whimsical contrasts of modern instrumental music, which accorded neither with the sublime nor with the beautiful. In 1794 Uvedale Price developed from landscaping theory a new aesthetic category, the picturesque.[25] The picturesque was perceived in paintings of quaint scenes such as ruins, gnarled oaks, cart-horses and peasants. One might perhaps link these with Haydn's rustic dances and folk-tunes, but more important attributes are capricious contrast and lack of symmetry. Price himself highlighted 'sudden, unexpected, and abrupt transitions', 'a certain playful wildness of character, and an appearance of irregularity' in the music of Haydn and Domenico Scarlatti.[26] The musical implications were amplified in William Crotch's discussion of the ornamental (his term for the picturesque), which he characterised by eccentric melody, broken rhythm and unexpected modulation.[27] Both writers recognised the value of mixing together the beautiful, the sublime and the picturesque. Yet a tendency remained to view the three as ultimately separable. In a letter to Crotch written in 1805, Burney still feels the need to excuse Haydn's caprice:

I have long ago said that Haydn's whimsicalities, which he sometimes introduced for the sake of variety, and sometimes in sport, had a great deal of wit in them; and knowing his natural temper to be playful, and music always good-humoured, regarded them as musical bons mots. But take away all these oddities, and does not enough remain of serious, beautiful & sublime, to constitute a truly great man?[28]

In a much more fundamental way it was the flexible combination of all three concepts that made up the dynamic modern symphonic style.

Haydn's achievement was, of course, far more than the apotheosis of the unpredictable, as his detractors eventually began to recognise. Counterbalancing the fantastical and disruptive tendencies was an overall coherent structural view. In the first movement of Symphony No. 102, one of Haydn's most tightly argued, Haydn brusquely dispenses with an ingratiating second theme in favour of a fortissimo unison and soft march-like answer in the 'wrong' key; yet this process both refers back to the introduction and introduces a new variant of the Vivace subject, as the composer subsequently demonstrates. Haydn virtually invented this concept of symphony and quartet as intellectual discourse. Each of the major London works follows an individual plan, to which generalisation would not do justice. Suffice it to say that Haydn typically works out a tonal, thematic or textural 'problem' in a drama leading to eventual resolution, as David Schroeder has demonstrated in connection with the symphonies.[29] In this sense, the symphonies form a commentary on musical procedures, focussing attention on the notion of musical communication and the role of the listener.

One example of Haydn's re-interpretation of norms is his adaptation of the slow introduction, which he had introduced in London both as a noise-killer and to heighten anticipation for the ensuing Allegro. Yet he increasingly uses it as a major element in the composition: by quotation and development later in the Allegro (Symphony No. 97), by direct thematic link (No. 98), by integration into the dramatic plan of the movement (No. 103), by intervallic derivation (No. 104). An essential feature of such processes was the Viennese concept of motivic manipulation, largely alien to the lingua franca of J. C. Bach. In addition to subtle thematic reference it enabled a revival of contrapuntal textures, now applied to folk materials in colossal development sections or sonata-rondos. Even Haydn's more Italianate melodies were constructed to offer innumerable possibilities for fragmentation and counterpoint. Sophisticated London listeners were quite well aware of what Haydn was doing; for example, this review after the first performance of the 'Clock' Symphony: 'Nothing can be more original than the subject of the first movement; and, having found a happy subject, no man knows like HAYDN how to produce incessant variety, without once departing from it.'[30] (Did the reviewer also catch the thematic connection with the D minor Adagio introduction?) By the time of the final symphony the concept was so familiar to London that Haydn was able to pare his materials down to a single ascending fifth, the violin's tuning notes.

Haydn's manner was naturally transmitted to his followers. Generally composers popular in London, such as Pleyel, Gyrowetz and Kozeluch, essayed a more relaxed and diffuse version of Haydn's style. Cantabile melodies are allowed to mingle with stock Haydnesque effects that can easily degenerate into ill-timed mannerisms. Pleyel's Symphony in D (B. 147), performed at the Professional Concert in 1791, is an effective if ultimately shallow imitation of Haydn's grand public manner. It begins promisingly with an urgently syncopated introduction in the minor, but the Allegro relies too heavily on vacuous fanfares. An elegant second melody is laid out on an expansive scale that Haydn would never have countenanced, while in the recapitulation it is followed by a pause and a quite gratuitous explosion on the inevitable flat submediant chord. Both Pleyel and Gyrowetz seem to have made some attempts to adapt to London's expectations, to judge from the symphonies and concertantes they composed for performance there. Yet London quickly came to realise that Haydn's followers were merely adopting the manner of the master but not capturing the imaginative or intellectual substance. None but Haydn retained any real presence in programmes of the later 1790s, the very time that Mozart was beginning to make an impact there.

The most enduring contribution by London composers in the last two decades of the century lay in the solo repertoire. We have already noted various factors that contributed to the more serious idiom of the London pianists and violinists. An additional component was their adoption of a more boldly dramatic approach. Bach and others had transferred galant orchestral idioms to the keyboard, but generally solo music had conservatively resisted conflict and symphonic argument. But Clementi's Op. 2 (1779) radically redefined a concert piano-style. The significance of the three solo sonatas lies not only in bravura pianism, but also in the use of vividly contrasting orchestral textures (the notorious octaves are really an attempt at a grand tutti). Indeed the two aspects are closely intertwined: Clementi's orchestral sonorities are in themselves virtuosic, and elsewhere pure pianistic brilliance is highlighted by deliberate discontinuities. This dramatic variety can result in a breathless search for effect, at the expense of more solid structural virtues. Alexander Ringer has linked this tendency of the London sonata towards 'short-range emotional effects' with the irrationality of the Gothic novel.[31] Clementi had to learn from Haydn how to incorporate drama into structures of expressive integrity. Nevertheless the combination of virtuosity and orchestral drama remains characteristic of many concert piano sonatas; it is also clearly related to the idiom of the public string quartet.

Many London concertos of the 1790s depart markedly from the easy-going styles of earlier decades. Long 'Mozartian' melodies were allied to Haydn's symphonic manner and to the bold or tempestuous style of the modern French overture (compare the arresting pauses, striking changes of texture and

grandiose chords in *Démophon*, mentioned above). While the French tur-
bulence was toned down for London, concertos written there show not only
more use of the minor mode, but also an impressive grandeur and heightened
drama. Solo parts include marked contrasts between forceful writing and
graceful cantabile episodes, between brilliant or agitated passage-work and
mock-naive subjects. Drama between soloist and orchestra is increased by the
bravura assertion of solo entries (pianists routinely opened with thick chords
followed by a flourish), by ever-longer cadential preparations delaying the
return of the orchestra, by alternations between orchestral fanfare and solo
virtuosity. Rarely, however, is there real symphonic development. Soloistic
drama takes the place of intense motivic working; often modulatory passage-
work is reserved for the central section of a movement or the episodes of a
rondo, the very places where a symphony would develop earlier material.

These London composers often follow Haydn's example in attempting
ambitious experiments with structure and tonality. Dussek made a speciality of
tonal explorations: settling on a flat key during a transition section, or diving
to a remote key in a second subject group, or migrating temporarily during a
cadential trill. Rather grotesquely in his F major Second Piano Concerto
(C. 104) the cadential trill veers off to a second tutti beginning in E flat instead
of the well-prepared C major. Particularly common is the juxtaposition of keys
a third apart, especially the jump to the flat submediant which threatens to
become a cliché. Similar key-relationships are to be found in Viotti's violin
concertos: in a particularly subtle variant the C major Concerto No. 27 has a
kind of recapitulation in serene E major, anticipating the key of the slow
movement.

All of these composers show a resistance to set patterns, and their openness
to formal experiment is a welcome feature in this age of so much conformity.
In his Third Piano Concerto (C. 125) Dussek experiments with the idea of a
slow introduction, which recurs (in Allegro transformation) both before the
first solo entry and at the recapitulation. An even more radical plan is found in
Viotti's Violin Concerto No. 25, which begins as follows:

Tutti	6/8	pastoral	A minor – A major
Tutti	4/4	stormy	A minor etc.
Solo	6/8	pathetic	A minor
Solo	4/4	lively	A major etc.

None of the four sections is thematically related, and the composer's aim is
evidently an irrational diversity. Also striking are experiments in finale design.
Some rondos are both serious in intent and large in dimensions: that in J. B.
Cramer's E flat major First Piano Concerto, Op. 10, is on a colossal scale, with
extreme contrasts of material and unexpected secondary tonal centres of D and
C. But it has to be admitted that rarely do these composers achieve the
satisfying coherence of Haydn's music, either in their musical timing or in
subtlety of motivic derivation. When Cramer in the first movement of the same

concerto interrupts the solo exposition with a fortissimo transformation of the Mozartian second theme, the effect is unwarranted and faintly ridiculous. The achievement of musical coherence with elements of similar diversity was left to Beethoven, a composer whose debt to the London school of the 1790s has been increasingly recognised.

Concert management and the musician

The finances of concert promotion

We have seen that concert promotion in this period took many diverse forms, ranging from traditional court patronage to commercial enterprises originated by musician-impresarios. This chapter focusses on the latter end of this spectrum, in an attempt to unravel the intricate web of concert finances, and to shed light on the varying fortunes of those who took part in these high-risk ventures.

Concert series and societies

Subscription concerts were by no means an assured route to prosperity, but there was no shortage of promoters willing to take the gamble. Most were professional musicians – Giardini and Frasi, Bach and Abel, Rauzzini and Lamotte, Salomon, Mara, Harrison and Knyvett – who were capitalising on established reputations. The aspiring Giuseppe Passerini and the inexperienced Jane Mary Guest from Bath were rewarded with indifference. A relatively new phenomenon was the promotion of concerts by non-musicians, including hall-managers (Hickford, the Willis brothers) and independent impresarios (Mrs Stuart, Lord Abingdon). Unusually, the owner of the Dean Street Rooms, Ogle, was the harpsichord soloist as well as promoter of the 1751–2 series; on the other hand, the singer Mrs Cornelys attracted patronage to her Carlisle House as a society hostess rather than as a musician. Two jointly owned halls also put on concerts: the Pantheon, owned by fifty shareholders and advised at various times by Burney; and the King's Theatre, which hosted the Opera Concert at its concert room during the later 1790s.

Some musicians were involved in experiments designed to share the risks. In 1788 Mara entered into an agreement with the Pantheon, whereby she received the subscriptions and paid the musical expenses, while the Pantheon received the takings from single tickets and paid for alterations to the hall.[1] A much more radical venture was the Professional Concert (1785–93), London's first self-managing orchestra: even the name is a manifesto of the change of status. It was run as a co-operative by the thirty or so orchestral members; any profits were shared out unequally 'according to the *average* prices', with Cramer taking the largest share. Singers and visiting soloists were hired in the normal way. Successful both financially and artistically for many years, the Professional Concert achieved an ideal balance between commercialism, patronage and professionalism. This precarious balance was upset by Salomon's success in recruiting Haydn; but the Professional Concert undoubtedly laid the corner-stone for the Philharmonic Society, another orchestral co-operative, even if changed circumstances in 1813 required members to subscribe rather than take profits.

Unfortunately no detailed financial accounts for major subscription concerts survive. Even the ledger of J. C. Bach's account at Drummond's Bank (1767–80) presents an inconclusive picture. It clearly bears some relation to the Bach–Abel concerts, with many payments to orchestral players of 15 guineas and higher fees to principals and soloists (in 1772 £63 to both Crosdill and Tacet, £105 to Cecilia Grassi). When expressed in either pounds or guineas, all of these sums are multiples of fifteen, the number of concerts in a season. Bach paid Gallini variable amounts (£420 in 1778), presumably for the use of the Hanover Square Rooms. In 1774 the concert receipts are itemised, 500 concert tickets bringing in £2,625. The figures do appear to confirm anecdotal evidence that the concerts brought Bach considerable revenue until the late 1770s, when his financial situation deteriorated rapidly.[2] But the account is clearly a personal one, rather than a coherent statement of concert finances, and it should also be remembered that Bach was involved in many other enterprises at the time, including the King's Theatre oratorios.

Subscription concerts were undoubtedly liable to vastly fluctuating fortunes on the winds of fashion. Though not such a financial headache as the Italian Opera, it was a precarious form of business, and musicians evidently promoted them for more reasons than immediate profit, such as future patronage and teaching. It seems that a substantial number of subscribers was needed to break even. When some 350 had subscribed to Mara's concert in 1787 this was regarded as adequate but somewhat disappointing, and only with a full subscription of 500 were reasonable profits achieved. Certainly there were some successes: with a whiff of scandal, Ann Ford is said to have made as much as £1,500 in 1760.[3] But there were also heavy losses. The case of the Professional Concert clearly illustrates the curve from disaster to boom and back again. After Abingdon's losses the previous two seasons, the Professional Concert in 1785 made hardly any profit for its members. But success soon followed, with full subscriptions and the conspicuous patronage of royalty, and in 1787 the performers were rewarded with nearly double their normal pay. Finally in the 1790s support dwindled as others came into fashion and the series collapsed after the 1793 season.

The question arises as to how many subscription series London could sustain. In the first half of the period there was generally only one major subscription series (except in 1753 when the Italian Opera House was still dark). By the later 1770s, however, two or three modern series were competing with the new Concert of Ancient Music. Social factors suggest that the market of potential subscribers could only grow modestly, and undoubtedly the growth in the number of concerts exceeded demand even in the boom years. Thus after a sustained period of success Bach and Abel were indeed harmed by competition before 1780. In the later 1780s, both the Concert of Ancient Music and the Professionals gained the ascendancy over the Pantheon and others, with Trew and Danby's Readings and Music reporting considerable losses.[4] Similarly the dual successes of Salomon and the Vocal Concert undoubtedly contributed to the demise of the Professionals. Salomon made a shaky start (he is said to have lost over £400 on his first two seasons) but he made good in 1793, even without Haydn. There is a danger of over-simplification, however. In 1783, even after he had dispatched a rival, Abingdon's Hanover Square series made little impact. This was simply a bad year for London's music, with the opera collapsing in disarray, and the single oratorio series poorly supported.

Expenses were very considerable, especially as series began to vie for special attractions to offer the public. Much the most expensive, of course, were star singers. Though one should beware of deliberate exaggeration in newspapers, there is reliable evidence of astronomic salaries being paid to a few international names, sometimes with free benefits thrown in. Whereas Bach's singers received little over £100 for the season, the Pantheon in the 1770s paid Agujari an astonishing £100 per night.[5] Their faith in her drawing-power proved entirely justified, and Charles Burney castigated the Pantheon managers for not pursuing this high-risk policy. Certainly he returned to it in 1790, engaging Pacchierotti for 1,000 guineas or more for thirteen concerts. This figure approached the annual salary of top principals at the Opera, but it may well have been necessary, since Pacchierotti's contract forbade him to sing elsewhere. By 1795 another factor had exacerbated the problems facing the impresario:

In the present situation of affairs on the Continent, Mr. SALOMON finds it impossible to procure from abroad any Vocal Performers of the first talents, but by the influence of terms which an undertaking like his could by no means authorize him to offer; and it would be a presumption, of which he is incapable, to solicit the Nobility and Gentry to an inferior entertainment.[6]

Only a new arrangement, in the Opera Concert, could provide a solution.

The 1780s saw the emergence of a new expense of comparable magnitude. The concept of star orchestral composer was unwittingly invented by Haydn, who was offered generous inducements to travel to London. Abingdon suggested 500 guineas and a free benefit (presumably he paid less for the music alone). The eventual terms of Haydn's agreement with Salomon are somewhat unclear, as they are intermixed with his operatic commitments. But according to one source Salomon paid £300 for the first six symphonies and £200 for their copyright; he also paid the expenses of a benefit, guaranteeing £200 profit. It was essential to Salomon that Haydn appear in person: as director with an international reputation Haydn in many ways resembled the jet-setting conductor of our own day. The Professionals attempted to lure him away with an offer 150 guineas above Salomon's fee, but they had to settle for his pupil, by way of imitation; Pleyel was reportedly dissatisfied with the £1,000 that he received.

Another heavy expenditure first became a burden in this period, for similar reasons. The concept of the travelling instrumental soloist was not in itself new: Bach and Abel are known to have engaged visitors for their concerts, and in 1789 the Professional Concert paid 5 guineas for single appearances. But in 1793 Salomon moved into a different league by engaging Viotti at an astonishing 550 guineas for the series (the fee taking into account the move from Paris). Violinists were as yet much more of a draw than pianists, and Viotti had been built up for some years as Europe's greatest violinist; his appearance must have compensated for the disappointment of Haydn's non-arrival, since this was Salomon's first season of financial success.

Almost all concert organisations involved an orchestra, a rising expense partly through new demands and partly through augmenting numbers. Giardini was credited with raising orchestral fees at top concerts from the customary half-guinea:

The Late Giardini suffered no inferior Musician to draw a Bow in any Orchestra where he himself was the Leader, for less than a Guinea per Night, and all the Performers in his Band were sure to be rewarded in the most liberal and generous Manner, whenever he had the musical Management of any Performance whether public or private.[7]

Since the leader and other principals might demand between 2 and 5 guineas, a typical nightly bill for a top 35-piece orchestra must easily have reached £60. This was what Lacy paid the orchestra even at his relatively humble Readings and Music series in 1786–7, and the 60-piece orchestras of the 1790s must have cost considerably more. Nor was it customary to reduce fees for a prolonged season, as the Opera did (here the basic fee was only 15/-, resulting in a nightly bill of £40).[8] Of the principal organisations, only the hard-pressed Academy of Ancient Music kept its fees at the former low level, paying the orchestral and vocal rank-and-file 10/6 or less. Even so the total performers' bill for a twelve-concert season came to £588 10s. (made up of 50 guineas to Cooke as musical director, 60 guineas to the Abrams sisters, £191 2s. to the other singers, £281 18s. to the orchestra).

A further significant expenditure for most promoters was the hire of a hall. Available figures are rather sporadic, but they also indicate generally rising costs. In 1754 the Dean Street Room cost 5 guineas a night; later in the century the middle-ranking Freemasons' Hall normally charged 10 guineas, though the impoverished Academy of Ancient Music negotiated a discount in 1784.[9] Other hall-owners took full advantage of the paucity of fashionable halls by charging much higher fees. Bach's account reveals annual payments of over

£500 to Almack when the concerts were held at his room, and Gallini's charges for Hanover Square were in a similar league. He himself claimed that Bach and Abel paid 50 guineas per concert; this figure is also cited in a report of 1783 which notes that lighting and refreshment were included. In 1786 the Concert of Ancient Music eased this burden by taking out a lease on the Tottenham Street Rooms at a rent of £210. They agreed also to pay £265 per annum for a wide range of minor expenses (coal and candles £82 14s. 6d., refreshments £63, beer for the performers £36, nearly £80 for royal servants, soldiers, constables, waiters and charwomen, etc.).[10]

Costs therefore rose dramatically in the last two decades of the century – through competition for the best performers and repertoire, through increasing orchestral numbers, through opportunism on the part of instrumentalists and hall-owners. The promoter without influence wishing to organise a twelve-concert series might easily face expenses of the order of £1,200 for soloists and new music; £720 for the orchestra; £550 for the hall and miscellaneous expenses (including advertising, printing and music-copying). Even a full subscription of 500, paying £2,625, would bring a profit of only £155, a meagre reward indeed for the risk involved.

Neither side of the equation offered much room for financial manoeuvre. Subscription prices hovered around the 5 guinea level throughout the period, even if the number of concerts gradually declined from twenty at Dean Street in 1751–2 (a double ticket), to fifteen (the Bach–Abel concerts up to 1780), to twelve in the last two decades. The 1780s saw some experimentation with price, including a rise to 6 guineas and a cut to 4 guineas, but the former could not be maintained and the latter may have merely implied an inferior product. Furthermore the number of subscribers was limited both by the exclusive price-levels and by the size of halls, with 500 regarded as a comfortable maximum at the Hanover Square Rooms. Only the opening in 1794 of the new King's Theatre concert-hall, seating 800, offered the possibility of greater income, but such a subscription level was probably unsustainable at this time.

Once the spiral of rising costs had been established it was extremely hard to reverse it, but attempts of various kinds were made. In 1786 the Professionals were said to have made economies in their provision of new music. Much more significantly they devised a scheme with Gallini to cut the expense of hiring international singers.[11] Gallini, owner of the Hanover Square Rooms, was in 1785 appointed manager at the Italian Opera, where his creative accounting eventually resulted in an extended law-suit with the proprietors. One of his underhand practices concerned opera singers' contracts. Gallini evidently allowed them to sing at various public and private concert series, in clear breach of normal exclusive practice which forbade such performance under threat of financial penalty. More seriously he surreptitiously included performance at the Professional Concert in several contracts – notably those of Rubinelli in 1787 and Marchesi in 1788. (This accounts for occasional references to the Professional as Gallini's concerts.) The precise financial implications of this

Table 3. *Balance-sheet for the Wesley concerts 1785*

Income				Expenditure									
	£	s.	d.		£	s.	d.	£	s.	d.	£	s.	d.
34 subscriptions	105	0	0	'Before it'				6	13	6			
mostly @ 3 gn.				'The Company'				10	4	0			
				'The Band'									
				5 string-players (7 nights @ 10/6)	18	7	6						
				2 horn-players (7 payments of 5/-)	1	15	0						
				Suppers	3	7	0						
				Rehearsals	0	9	0						
								23	18	6			
				[Unspecified				2	0	0]			
											42	16	0
				Profit									
				Family				11	9	6			
				Housekeeping				50	14	6			
											62	4	0
											105	0	0

Source: BL, Add. 35017, f. 53. The accounts were kept in a somewhat casual way and there are some inconsistencies. The unspecified expenditure of £2 may have included a further seven payments of 5/- to the horn-players.

shady dealing remain unclear. Gallini claimed that the singers had been paid the normal rate for their opera performances, and that singing at a few concerts was too trivial for any separate payment. He denied that he had himself benefited from any special agreement with the Professionals, even claiming to have charged them less for the Rooms than Bach and Abel. But his evidence is far from convincing. Gallini does seem to have defrauded the Opera by paying principal singers excessively to appear also at the Professional Concert (Rubinelli was lured away from Mara's concerts by the generous terms); and he must surely have received ample personal compensation in the form of high rent for his Rooms.[12] The Professionals, meanwhile, must also have benefited by getting the singers more cheaply. When in 1795 William Taylor required the opera singers to sing at the Opera Concert he was in effect publicly adopting Gallini's system, in response both to high expenses and the situation on the continent.

Attention was also turned to the wages of orchestral musicians. As a labour-intensive enterprise, concert promotion was prone to significant rises in costs as a result of small increases in wages. Now, as the process went into reverse, orchestral members proved the weakest link in the commercial chain. This situation had not arisen before, partly because 'fixers' were themselves influential instrumentalists and partly because London had only a small pool of top-quality players, who were powerful enough to resist reductions even without formal negotiating procedures. But the 1790s brought both a harsher financial climate and an influx of foreign musicians. Salomon was willing to break the unwritten rules of his profession by recruiting inexperienced players and foreigners 'at very low salaries': the young George Smart was paid only half a guinea in 1794.[13] Downward pressure on orchestral fees elsewhere followed inevitably. Indeed the Professional Concert might have survived into 1794 if the players had been prepared to accept lower wages when William Taylor offered them a joint contract for both Opera and concerts. Eventually in 1795 just such an arrangement was made in connection with the Opera Concert. Meanwhile, Harrison and Knyvett circumvented the problem by not hiring an orchestra at all for their Vocal Concert, at least in the early stages.

The one surviving complete set of accounts is of a special nature. The Wesley house-concerts were organised as a minute subscription series. The number of subscribers, paying 3 guineas for seven concerts, hovered around thirty-five. Expenses were low, since the minimal band consisted only of seven low-paid players in addition to the two Wesley boys. By way of example, table 3 is a summary of the 1785 balance-sheet. A profit of over £60 for the household must be counted a considerable success for such a modest undertaking.

Oratorio series

Little distinguishes the system of oratorio management from the series already considered, except that the managers laboured under the disadvantage of selling tickets nightly and could not therefore assess their income in advance. Most were again run by musician-impresarios, Englishmen following the Handel tradition at the playhouses: first Smith, Stanley and Arne, later Arnold, Linley, Harrison and Ashley (a specialist oratorio organiser bringing experience gained in the provinces). Only rarely were there attempts to court a different audience, as at Bach's two Italian seasons at the King's Theatre in the 1770s, and the Concert of Ancient Music's promotion of Handel oratorios in 1786–8. Generally the promoters simply hired the theatre, in the same way as subscription-concert organisers. The oratorio seasons were hardly ever part of the playhouse season itself (unusually in 1794 an impressive season was organised at Drury Lane, with the first concert chosen to open the fine new theatre). The performers were hired separately from the theatrical personnel, even if they often overlapped considerably: thus in 1775 the hire of the Drury Lane orchestra was regarded as a matter for negotiation. A crucial factor for Handel's musical heirs was the approval of George III. When Smith retired from partnership with Stanley, the succession was referred to the King, who recommended Sheridan (perhaps hoping that his wife, Elizabeth Linley, could be enticed back into public performance). Sheridan refused, but the King was

Table 4. *Receipts and expenditure at the Drury Lane oratorios 1779*

Receipts				Expenditure			
	£	s.	d.		£	s.	d.
Ticket sales	1,843	17	0	Vocal soloists	300	17	0
				Chorus	227	9	6
				Leader and instrumental soloists	81	0	0
				Orchestra	354	9	6
				Theatre and advertising	317	5	0
					1,281	1	0

evidently satisfied instead with Thomas Linley and his two other talented daughters.[14]

Some surviving records and anecdotes indicate again that both substantial profits and losses were to be made. The rivals to Handel and his successors often went financially unrewarded, despite undercutting with lower prices. Arnold's introduction in 1768 of playhouse prices, approximately half-price, certainly increased audience size. Yet there remained the danger of lowering the tone and this ploy did not result in lasting financial success in view of the high expenditure. At Drury Lane, Smith and Stanley reacted to playhouse prices with a compromise, retaining 10/6 for box tickets while reducing the price of the cheaper tickets; but here too audiences fell away before the revival of the mid 1780s.

Yet there were real successes. The financial basis of oratorio series was more favourable than that of the subscription concert, since audiences could be much larger and the general level of expenditure was lower. Certainly theatre charges were considerable: in the 1760s Covent Garden charged £35 per night, rising to 50 guineas in the 1790s, and the organ also had to be hired. Additional expenses included choral-singers and perhaps staging (in 1794 Drury Lane paid a carpenter £130 for this). But there were considerable savings on personnel. Although famous singers, even English ones, did not come cheaply, and celebrity instrumentalists were sometimes employed, salaries never remotely approached four-figure sums. In 1779 the highest fee for the eleven-night Drury Lane season was £115, while even in 1794 the equivalent figure for Harrison was £210 (Giornovichi was paid only £105 for his twelve concertos). The orchestra, too, was paid considerably less than its Hanover Square counterpart. Even more crucially, a full house, despite the range of prices, brought in a much larger sum than a normal concert. Oratorio takings could reach over £500 per night, giving a possible take for an eleven-night season of more than £5,500.

Such figures must have been achieved in the astonishing year of 1773, when the Linleys attracted everyone to Drury Lane. Accounts for other years show more modest, but nevertheless substantial takings. In 1761, for example, Smith and Stanley took a total of £2,720 6*s.* 6*d.* for the ten nights: receipts ranged from a high of £488 11*s.* for *Messiah* on 13 March (1,486 tickets) down to £108 16*s.* for Stanley's own *Zimri* on 20 February (411 tickets). By 1779, takings were down, and Stanley and Linley made only moderate gains on the season, as can be seen from table 4. The 1790s, on the other hand, saw a return to massive profits. The new Drury Lane in 1794 took £5,789 5*s.* for a twelve-night season, with audiences equally partial to *Messiah* and to Handel selections. By now expenditure was slightly higher, due to increased singers' fees: the company was paid £1,106 17*s.* for the season. Nevertheless the house must have cleared well over £4,000. It is easy to credit the view that in promoting oratorios John Ashley's 'only single object' was profit.[15]

Gardens

The finances of the pleasure gardens are outside the range of this inquiry, but some information on Marybone is directly concerned with concert management. Several musicians were proprietors there in various partnerships: Thomas Lowe (from 1763 to 1765), Pinto (1769) and Arnold (to 1774).[16] Newspapers suggest energetic enterprise and musical innovation during this period, but the frantic advertisement reflects insecurity rather than prosperity. All three musicians retired in financial ruin: Lowe claimed that he lost £2,000 in three seasons; Pinto lost a similar sum after a wet season and fled to Scotland; while Arnold is supposed to have lost around £10,000 as a result of embezzlement.

Accounts for the year 1768 show that Marybone was always a modest undertaking.[17] Income came from three sources: subscriptions (197 at $1\frac{1}{2}$ guineas would have brought in £310 5*s.* 6*d.*), individual tickets (daily totals during one week averaged £10 18*s.*); and takings at the bar (similarly, £15 15*s.* gross). Expenditure was also low, although musicians' fees accounted for a sizeable proportion. Lowe, now only managing the gardens on behalf of his creditors, received a weekly allowance of 5 guineas at the height of the season. Singers were paid from 2 to 4 guineas a week and the orchestra bill hovered around £28, suggesting an annual music-bill of some £850 for an eighteen-week season. The overall financial picture remains obscure, in the absence of the original documentation: receipts appear to have come to £2,085 1*s.* $7\frac{1}{2}d.$, expenses to £1,534 11*s.* 9*d.*, but one report recorded a deficit on the season.

A short summary of takings during a three-week period in 1774 (table 5) illustrates clearly the fluctuating fortunes of the different kinds of entertainment at Marybone. The profits on his benefit must have sweetened an otherwise bitter pill for Samuel Arnold.

Table 5. *Takings at Marybone Gardens in 1774*

Date	Day	Entertainment	Takings (town and field gate combined)		
			£	s.	d.
12.6	Sun.	Tea	21	15	0
13.6	Mon.	Concert of catches and glees, directed by Arne	38	2	6
14.6	Tues.	Concert, fireworks and Torre's exhibition	118	17	6
15.6	Wed.	Concert	3	10	0
16.6	Thurs.	Concert and burletta	17	19	0
17.6	Fri.	Concert, fireworks and Torre's exhibition	50	0	0
18.6	Sat.	Concert and burletta	10	1	0
19.6	Sun.	Tea	19	2	6
20.6	Mon.	[Rain]			
21.6	Tues.	[Rain]			
22.6	Wed.	[Rain]			
23.6	Thurs.	Ode set by Arnold, and other music	5	7	6
24.6	Fri.	Concert, fireworks and Torre's exhibition	86	15	0
25.6	Sat.	Concert and burletta	5	10	0
26.6	Sun.	Tea	17	3	0
27.6	Mon.	Ode set by Arnold, and other music	4	0	0
28.6	Tues.	Concert, fireworks and Torre's exhibition	63	0	0
29.6	Wed.	[Closed]			
30.6	Thurs.	Arnold's benefit: concert, burletta and fireworks	140	7	0
1.7	Fri.	Concert, fireworks and Torre's exhibition	30	10	0

Source: Abstracted from a single leaf in the Marylebone Library, with additional information from newspaper advertisements.

Benefits

Putting on a benefit concert was by no means as easy as it might appear. Innumerable excuses were offered for changes of date, and some began advertising as early as February, as much to reserve the date as to attract custom. The number of days available for benefits was strictly limited: most took place between late April and early June, and Opera and major concert-series sometimes obliterated all six days of the week. Sometimes a suitable hall could not be found or the main performers were unavailable: as early as 1754, Frasi complained that her performers were engaged every night from late March until mid May.[18] Not infrequently benefits were postponed so many times that the season ended before they could take place, or they were joined on a single day out of desperation. As usual, patronage could smooth the way: in 1761 the Duke of York directly interceded with the Ranelagh proprietors on Pasqualino's behalf.[19]

Leopold Mozart encountered just such difficulties after his arrival in London on 23 April 1764. His morning concert on 5 June was attended by over 200, but Mozart thought he could have attracted 600 earlier in the season.[20] Nevertheless, the expenses were a low 20 guineas, since many of the orchestra took no fee and the relatively minor Spring Garden Room cost only 5 guineas; so Mozart made a profit of some 90 guineas. The following year he was better prepared, taking benefits in both February and May, but both were still plagued with postponements. In February he changed the date to accommodate a performance of Arne's *Judith* at the Opera House, but it still clashed with rival attractions and the start had to be set at 6 o'clock. Profits, though respectable, were only slightly higher than in June 1764.

The promoter was himself responsible for all kinds of minutiae: newspaper-advertising, tickets and bills, staging and candles, refreshments for audience and performers, hire and tuning of keyboard instruments. He might have to engage bill-posters, organ-blowers, music-porters, attendants and constables. In 1757 a 'Widow under great Misfortunes by Losses at Sea' made a point of promising two doorkeepers 'whose Honesty may be relied on'; three years later Gambarini advertised that she had engaged two officers, twelve soldiers and six constables. At lesser venues, a ball was often provided after the concert, but this could incur the displeasure of the local magistrates, as happened after Isabella Vincent's overcrowded Marybone benefit in 1764. Even the concert itself could go disastrously wrong. When Walter Clagget opened his unauthorised Temple and Gardens of Apollo in October 1788, the platform was not ready at 6.30 p.m.; an hour later 1,000 people had taken advantage of the free tickets, and the organist Jonathan Battishill had to entertain the ill-disposed crowds before the concert eventually started at 8 o'clock. The standard of the performance apparently matched its organisation, and Clagget had to issue a public apology.

It was quite possible to make a loss on a benefit. In 1760 Gambarini advertised a third benefit to recoup the losses from the first two, losses caused by her assumption that unreturned tickets had been bought. Ten years later Barthelemon was plagued with forgery of Marybone tickets, a problem he counteracted by selling signed tickets at designated outlets. Even without these difficulties, a benefit entailed considerable outlay. An account sheet survives detailing the expenses involved in putting on an ode by Hook in 1772.[21] The total music-bill (see below) came to £62 16s., even without payments to the four vocal soloists and three instrumentalists, including the leader Giardini. In 1790 a German correspondent explained that an audience of 120 paying half a guinea was required just to cover the principal expenses – the hire of a hall at £20 and of an orchestra at (presumably) £43.[22] In fact, he underestimated the costs and even some well-publicised benefits undoubtedly failed. Despite the most extravagant press coverage the blind Miss Paradis received only a lukewarm response; in 1795 Mara (past her prime and out of favour because of an affair with a young singer) could only attract an audience of sixty.

	£	*s.*	*d.*
Choir (mostly @ 10/6)	7	17	6
Orchestra (mostly @ 1gn.)	33	12	0
Copying (375½ pages @ 1/-)	18	15	6
Porterage and tuning	2	11	0
	62	16	0

Wendeborn observed, on the other hand, that benefits could produce 'pretty handsome sums of money', which he equated with profits of 'an hundred and more guineas'.[23] Such sums perhaps required an audience of 400, an attainable target to judge from reviews. Haydn well exceeded this target, supposedly taking £350 at his 1791 benefit (the Hanover Square Rooms 'completely crowded' with some 666 persons?). Profits over £1,000 are mentioned in connection with both Mara and Sarah Harrop.[24] Such figures are seldom verifiable and they remain hard to interpret, since it is not clear whether donations are included, whether expenses were paid by a promoter, or whether all performers took a fee. Certainly newspapers often exaggerated: one journalist wrote that Cramer's benefit attended by 548 people made a profit of 550 guineas, a calculation for which he was roundly rebuked by a correspondent.[25] It is important to take into account the size of venue. Arnold's 1774 benefit at Marybone must have been attended by 802 people (paying 3/6) to produce gross takings of £140 7*s.* Harrop's £1,000 resulted from a Pantheon audience of 2,102: of course not all of these need have attended at the same time, and the numerous rooms of the Pantheon could absorb large crowds.

One awkward question concerns the payment of performers at benefits. Orchestral musicians certainly performed gratis on exceptional occasions, as did the entire orchestra at Clement's 1790 benefit.[26] By the 1820s this had undoubtedly become a more general practice, but it could not be assumed in the earlier period. The German correspondent quoted above warned that orchestral musicians charged £1 for benefits and the leader £5; that musicians expected a glass of wine does not mean that they renounced their fees.

Even charities were faced with substantial bills. Hall-owners might show compassion in special cases: the minutes of the Freemasons' Hall Committee reveal careful consideration for orphans, sufferers from fires and so on. Principals frequently gave their services. But in most ways charitable concerts were run as purely commercial fund-raising exercises. The detailed accounts of the Foundling and Lock Hospital concerts give a revealing view of variable profits (see table 6). The figures for the Foundling clearly illustrate initial enthusiasm, followed by a wane in interest after Handel's death, arrested temporarily by the engagement of the Linley sisters for a fee of £80 in 1773. The Lock concerts followed a less consistent pattern, but highest profits also came in the 1750s, when the concerts made a very significant contribution to the Hospital's finances: in the accounting year 1758–9 expenditure amounted

Table 6. The finances of Foundling and Lock Hospital benefits: a selection of available figures

Year	Foundling Hospital			Lock Hospital			Notes
	Receipts £ s. d.	Expenses £ s. d.	Profits £ s. d.	Receipts £ s. d.	Expenses £ s. d.	Profits £ s. d.	
1749	[401 3 0]	50 6 0]	351 3 0				
1750a	728 3 6]	[73 6 0]	969 7 0				
b	314 9 6						
1752	642 1 6	54 5 6	587 16 0			100 0 0	Concert at King's Theatre
1756	719 5 0	56 13 6	662 11 6			450 0 0	Concert at Drury Lane Theatre
1758	427 7 0	58 15 0	368 12 0	[497 17 3]	99 16 0	398 1 3	Concert at Drury Lane Theatre
1760	309 0 6	52 13 6	256 7 0				
1762	113 18 6	60 10 6	53 8 0	99 15 6	56 10 8	43 4 10	First concert at Lock Hospital Chapel
1763	153 16 6			232 11 1	102 9 4	130 1 9	First performance of *Ruth*
1769	226 5 6	88 0 0	138 5 6	95 4 5	57 11 6	[37 12 11]	*Ruth* at King's Theatre
1773	467 17 0	149 6 8	318 10 4	345 0 6	137 14 0	[207 6 6]	*Ruth* at Lock Hospital Chapel with Linleys
1777	156 19 6	67 13 8	89 5 10	325 12 0	114 17 6	[210 14 6]	*Ruth* at Lock Hospital Chapel
1780	—		—	202 1 6	107 19 0	[94 2 6]	*Ruth* at Lock Hospital Chapel

Notes: All the Foundling concerts took place at the Hospital Chapel; *Messiah* was performed every year except 1749. The Lock Hospital did not present the accounts in a consistent manner and there are some discrepancies between the various sources.

Sources: Foundling Hospital: minute-books of the General Committee (Thomas Coram Foundation for Children); minute-books of the Sub-committee and account-sheets in the Greater London Record Office (see also Burrows, 'Handel and the Foundling Hospital' and 'Handel's Performances of "Messiah"', 334).

Lock Hospital: Court and Committee Minutes, Cash-book (Royal College of Surgeons).

Table 7. *Expenses at Foundling Hospital benefits*

Year	Soloists	Chorus (including boys)	Orchestra and miscellaneous musical expenses	Other	Total
	£ s. d.	£ s. d.	£ s. d.	£ s. d.	£ s. d.
1754	17 6 6	9 19 6	24 13 6	6 18 0	58 17 6
1767	22 1 0	12 1 6	20 6 0	13 4 0	67 12 6
1769	12 12 0	19 19 0	39 18 0	15 11 0	88 0 0

to £1,392 and other income only £1,279, so the concert's profit of £398 was critical. During the 1760s *Ruth* and other oratorios achieved only moderate success; here too the Linleys inspired a revival in 1773, but profits never again matched those of the early years. While the abandonment of oratorio benefits may have been caused by personal friction, the Lock governors must have noted approvingly that two charity sermons in 1782 brought in £140 with a good deal less trouble.

A striking feature of these accounts is the rise in expenses. Most of the Foundling Hospital's expenses consisted of performers' fees. Those paid to vocal soloists, the Linleys aside, remained fairly static, but the general level of orchestral and choral fees rose significantly, largely through the influence of Giardini (see table 7). In 1769, Giardini's first year as leader here, the basic orchestral and choral fees immediately rose from around 10/6 to 1 guinea. When Giardini was not in control, fees were moderated to 15/-, bringing the total expenses back to £67 13s. 8d. in 1777.

The Lock Hospital accounts lack lists of performers, but they nevertheless furnish useful information about concert organisation. The level of expenditure was higher than at the Foundling Hospital, due to the hire of theatres in the 1750s, the erection of staging in the Chapel subsequently, and the role played here by Giardini. In 1776, for example, though all the principals performed gratis, the performers' bill came to £73 3s. 6d. out of total expenses of some £125. Interestingly, however, the Linleys were persuaded not to take a fee here, on being told that (unlike the Foundling) the Lock Hospital received no government funds.

An entirely special case was the Handel Commemoration. In 1784 tickets were priced at 1 guinea, and total receipts (including a donation from the King) amounted to £12,736 12s. 10d. Expenses were enormous (nearly £2,000 for staging, and controversially a similar figure to performers); yet the festival raised £6,000 for the Society of Musicians and £1,000 for Westminster Hospital.[27] When it was proposed to repeat the event in 1785, the cost and other difficulties connected with the Abbey prompted a search for another venue. Burney became involved in the negotiations, and his letters are

Table 8. *Expenses at benefits of the Royal Society of Musicians*

Year	Venue	Takings, including royal donation			Expenses			Profit		
		£	s.	d.	£	s.	d.	£	s.	d.
1792	St Margaret's, Westminster	1,097	7	0	702	11	1	394	15	11
1794	St Margaret's, Westminster	526	1	6	463	6	9	62	14	9
1796	Whitehall Chapel [Banqueting Hall]	796	4	0	789	11	2	6	12	10
1798	King's Theatre Room	397	11	0	151	18	0	245	13	0
1800	King's Theatre Room	448	4	0	88	7	8	359	16	4

revealing not only about such practical difficulties as organ pitches but also about the role of various figures influential in London's concert life: the King, Sandwich, Bates, Frederick Nicolay, Redmond Simpson. In the end the Abbey was preferred again, but even when the operation moved onto a smaller scale after 1791 the continuing high expenditure remained a millstone. By royal command the Ancient Music performers attended gratis, yet carpenters' bills could still exceed £300, and the presence of royalty itself pushed up bills for attendants, upholstery and the like. Though tickets remained at 1 guinea, numbers failed to justify the expenditure (see table 8), and removal to the King's Theatre Room in 1798 began a more prudent era.

Life as a professional musician

Advancement in the concert profession

For all except the foreign élite, entry into London's concert life was achieved only by arduous struggle; and for most musicians the struggle for material prosperity and for advancement within the profession continued to the end of their lives. This chapter will be concerned with the economic realities of life as a professional concert musician in London. First it is necessary to investigate how musicians made their way into the profession and the effect of patronage on the lives of individual musicians.[1]

At every stage in his career the musician was dependent on influence or interest of varying kinds, exerted by family, by professional musicians or by musical amateurs. This is not to assert that such a system was completely impervious to merit. The recommender's own judgment was on trial, and outside court posts few examples of manifestly unjust preferment have been found: the Professional Concert was charged with nepotism in advancing Miss Parke in 1790, but she was already an established singer. Nevertheless there was simply no system whereby musical achievement could be assessed after systematic training, nor whereby advancement in the profession could be achieved by audition. Only one reference to an impartial audition has been found, and this was part of a publicity campaign by Mrs Jordan, who herself organised a voice-trial with William Parsons, Master of the King's Musick.[2] Certainly many worthy musicians failed to reach their expected status in London's concert life through want of suitable connections. In 1784 the well-known singer Mrs Barthelemon (Arne's pupil Polly Young) took the extraordinary step of launching a bitter public attack on the entire system. Styling herself 'an English Woman, of an unblemished reputation', she complained:

She writes polite letters almost every autumn to every Manager, viz. to the Opera-House ... REFUSED! the English Theatres, the SAME! Concerts, public and private; Ranelagh and Vauxhall, ALL excuses 'to the next season,' and 'that nothing can be done WITHOUT INTEREST:' 'they must not disoblige great people's recommendation' ... She humbly begs to know in what manner she should act in this unfortunate situation, having not the least misconduct or indecorum to charge herself with knowingly!³

Needless to say this did not produce an engagement, and Mrs Barthelemon continued to maintain only a peripheral place in London's concert life.

A very significant part in the upbringing of professional musicians was played by the family. In an analysis of musicians' families in the century from 1750, Deborah Rohr has estimated that the fathers of 80 per cent were musicians and that 86 per cent also married musicians.⁴ These figures suggest not only that children followed in family footsteps, but also that fathers played a major role in training them and making professional contacts. London's musical life spawned numerous musical dynasties: the Arnes and Youngs, the Linleys, the Cramers, the Weichsells, the Mahons, the Ashleys. In all of these cases the concert or theatre activity of older family members enabled the next generation to appear in public. Marriage could also enhance the career of a woman, provided that it was to another musician: the singer Sophia Corri, already instructed by her father, was undoubtedly assisted by her marriage in 1792 to Dussek, through whom she also became well known as a pianist and harpist.

London still lacked a central training scheme for British musicians, despite a series of proposals during the eighteenth century. Burney's 1774 plan for a conservatoire at the Foundling Hospital came closest to fruition, but even this would not have provided a respectable professional academy for middle-class students, as the Royal Academy of Music was intended to do in 1823. The only thorough musical education for children was that received by choirboys at the main choral foundations; they were housed and educated by eminent cathedral-musicians such as Cooke at Westminster Abbey and Nares at the Chapel Royal. The boys were regularly hired out to concert organisations, providing invaluable experience in the secular music world. As a St Paul's choirboy, Stevens performed at the Castle Society, at Bach's Italian oratorios, at Mrs Cornelys's 'Threnody' and at Sharp's private concerts, as well as at the Madrigal Society and on the opera stage. Some choirboys were also taught keyboard skills in the cathedral tradition, skills which gave an unusually solid basis for concert work. Many English tenors and basses came up through this route, as did other influential figures in London's concert life. Samuel Arnold, a choirboy and subsequently organist at the Chapel Royal, became not only a theatre composer but also a prominent director of oratorios and concerts. Sir George Smart, pillar of early Victorian music, received his first concert experience as a Chapel Royal boy at the Ancient Concerts.

A more universal route into London's concerts emphasised the artisan nature of the career. This was the apprentice system, which was also open to girls. For a premium, which might exceed £100, a master would undertake to house and train an apprentice for a period of seven years. In 1768 Stevens was apprenticed to William Savage of St Paul's while still a choirboy, his father exceptionally paying £10 each year. After seven years Savage sent him into the world with 5 guineas, saying: 'I meant to give you twenty Guineas, but find that I cannot afford that sum' – words that must have been re-echoed through the years of Stevens's early career frustrations.[5] Other masters took their duties very lightly, even taking on apprentices they could not teach: the young Samuel Harrison was bound to one William Burton, who passed him over to Stevens for instruction on oratorio and concert songs. The unregulated system was prone to all kinds of further abuse. Since the master received any earnings from concert appearances, apprentices were inevitably subject to exploitation. Arne was notorious for using his apprentices as slave labour (and in Charlotte Brent's case for more intimate services); he was clearly guilty of forcing girls' voices to the detriment of their adult careers, as was recognised at the time.[6] Other apprentices he set to menial tasks. Burney recorded with irritation the drudgery he undertook for Arne in the mid 1740s: music-copying, coaching singers and so on.[7] Only by the fortunate intervention of a gentleman patron, Fulke Greville, was he able to escape and begin his move into higher circles. At the end of the century John Field was exploited by the more supportive but nevertheless avaricious Clementi, this time to show off pianos in the master's shop with his improvisations. For all its faults, however, the system could work effectively enough, and it provided some equivalent of qualification (some fathers bound their sons to themselves). Even at its worst it provided concert experience and contacts within the profession: Burney cannot have regretted Arne's finding him a place among the violas of Handel's oratorio orchestra, nor Field his concerto appearances at London's most prestigious concerts in the later 1790s.

An alternative to apprenticeship was private study, an expensive route that some thought preferable:

The youth in learning this science, is not to be put apprentice, but to attend different masters at the expense of his friends, till he has acquired great skill, both in the theory and practice; after which he may be employed as a Composer of Music: he may teach gentlemen and ladies to sing or play on Musical Instruments; may become organist to a church or gain a living by playing at one of the Theatres, Vauxhall, etc.[8]

Even Stevens took violin lessons after his apprenticeship ended, paying Barthelemon 5/3 for weekly lessons. He gained sufficient skill to be able to take part in a minor English concert, but a more important consequence was an engagement to sing at Arne's concerts of catches and glees (Arne was a relative of Barthelemon by marriage). Not all masters were equally suitable for the aspiring professional. Indeed Wilhelm Cramer actively discouraged Samuel Wesley, refusing to teach him any further when he learnt of his professional aims. Perhaps he simply intended to deflect Wesley from a frustrating career, but many teachers gave preference to wealthy and influential amateurs, thus contributing to the low standards of most native musicians. A few virtuosi, however, were active in training the next generation of professionals, and an important consideration for the student was the prestige of the teacher. When Edward Gibbon was asked in 1774 about singing teachers, he discovered that Parsons was recommended for the amateur, but that Bach was best for professional training as he was not only 'a much more finished Master', but also director of the Queen's concerts.[9] The career of his protégée Ann Cantelo amply backs up this opinion: Bach introduced her to the Queen's concerts and public concerts en route to a highly successful concert career as Mrs Harrison. Some such contact was essential for women musicians, for whom opportunities were very scarce if they wanted to avoid the social stigma of the stage. Women were barred from orchestral playing and only occasionally used in oratorio choruses, so they had to compete as solo singers and pianists with the best of Europe. One pianist who did find a way through this eye-of-a-needle was Jane Mary Guest, daughter of a Bath tailor and another student of Bach. Guest was evidently able to present herself as a young lady of quality, for in 1780 Fanny Burney was invited to hear her play at her own house in Bath: she went on to achieve a more than satisfactory career in London as a solo pianist and teacher of royalty.

Very few British concert musicians studied abroad as yet. Apart from the expense and obvious dangers, study in Europe had the disadvantage that it did not establish musical contacts. Thomas Linley the younger, student of Nardini in Florence and friend of Mozart, could return to the security of the family connections; but when Charles Weichsell returned from Italy in 1790 it took him many years to build up a career, despite the fame of his sister Mrs Billington.

It is important not to underestimate the effect of this 'professional patronage', to use Rohr's useful phrase. Much employment came via other musicians, a system which exerted a rudimentary control over the profession. No evidence has been found for a deputy system in the orchestral sphere such as operated among organists and choristers, but influential musicians could always find ways into the profession for relatives and apprentices, by employing them at their own concerts or obtaining other engagements. The prodigy J. B. Cramer was often heard at the Professional Concert, and Giardini's student Wilton (later a well-known festival leader) appeared at an early age in string quartets at the Pantheon. Some prominent musicians showed self-confident disinterest in promoting potential rivals; Mara, for example, received much praise for employing at her concerts the little-known soprano Mrs Stuart. Particularly powerful within the profession were 'fixers' deputed by concert promoters to engage the musicians – men such as Storace *père* and Redmond Simpson, who attracted the perpetual wrath of Dibdin for exerting 'injury to the cause of *real genius*'.[10] The importance of professional connections emerges clearly from the autobiography of Giacomo Ferrari (one of the new breed of freelance non-performing composers): they had to be established before lucrative patronage could be expected to follow. Ferrari arrived in London in 1792 with only an introduction to the composer Pozzi, but he soon called on his 'old friends' Attwood (a fellow-student in Naples), J. B. Cramer and Dussek (both of whom he knew from Paris). At one of Domenico Corri's house-concerts he met Salomon, leading to the public performance of a scena, which 'raised my name here considerably'; he was to become one of London's leading singing-teachers and his operas were performed at the King's Theatre.

A more institutional kind of professional patronage stemmed from the Society of Musicians. Though in essence a benefit scheme, the society wielded considerable influence. Most of the principal concert musicians were members, as were many of lesser standing. Thus the society brought together musicians of all kinds, foreign and native, vocal and instrumental, theatre and church. At first its influence was primarily felt through the annual concerts, organised by a committee of musician-members and a showpiece for the profession. Later, connections with the Concert of Ancient Music and with George III brought added status, if also an enforced change of artistic policy: in 1785 the King allowed the use of the title 'Royal Society of Musicians', five years before official confirmation with a royal charter. The society made no attempt to help musicians enter the profession, to regulate standards or to improve working conditions; and it had its critics, some of whom set up the New Musical Fund in 1786. But it did provide musicians with some sense of corporate identity and a measure of control over their own profession. Even Dibdin, one of the fiercest critics, acknowledged that it was a nursery for wind players which had benefited the two Parkes in particular.

One final aspect of professional patronage concerns the various spheres of professional influence in London. Most obviously these followed national boundaries. The Italian cabal at the Opera was notorious for its opposition to interlopers such as J. C. Bach or Haydn, Mara or Michael Kelly. Such clannishness undoubtedly extended to concerts, even if Italians could no longer afford to isolate themselves: Italian singers were accused of forming a claque in leading applause for their own at public concerts.[11] Nor were German musicians slow to help each other, aided by the obvious partiality of Queen Charlotte. Thus Bach went out of his way to assist Schroeter, helping him to get music published and introducing him at court; on Bach's death Schroeter succeeded him as the Queen's music-master. The royal preference for German musicians culminated in the Duke of York importing an entire 24-piece German band in 1783. Some of these foreign alliances were already forged abroad before arrival in London: many German musicians arriving in London, including Cramer, Wendling, Ramm and Carl Stamitz, were former colleagues in the Mannheim court orchestra.

Other points of professional contact crossed national boundaries. Some London musicians actively maintained their Catholic faith through embassy chapels; Betty Matthews revealed an unexpected Catholic connection between J. C. Bach, the Davies sisters, the Mozarts and Mrs Garrick, though the impact of such relationships on concert life is impossible to determine.[12] A more concrete association was provided by freemasonry. A few concerts were primarily directed at masonic audiences, including annual concerts from 1794 to 1799 in aid of a freemasons' orphanage; sometimes such concerts listed performers in the form 'Brother Arnold'. More research is needed in this area, but it is evident that freemasonry did provide a web of connections that cut surprisingly across other distinctions. Members of the Grand Lodge in the 1770s included such prominent English musicians as Arnold, Fisher, Norris, Reinhold, Vernon and Simpson; the latter was responsible for organising fund-raising concerts in 1777–8. There were also foreign musical members. Wilhelm Cramer was admitted in 1777 on the recommendation of Simpson, and all the orphanage concerts were directed by Arnold and led by Cramer. One should not assume, however, that all musicians who performed at freemasons' concerts were masons themselves. Even when an ode by Fisher was performed at the dedication of the Hall in 1776 not all the sixty musicians were masons: those who were had to wear their aprons, and the others were requested to leave during the dedication ceremony itself.[13] Ordinary concerts at Freemasons' Hall were in no way masonic, as the hall was simply hired out on a commercial basis.

For all the importance of connections within the music profession, success at the highest level could still not be achieved without the patronage of the leisured classes. This patronage was not necessarily formalised as permanent employment, but interest was all in advancement within the profession; and each success could be used as a lever for the next. Stevens's professional career demonstrates strongly the continuing power of the patronage system. After disappointments as a choir-singer and as an organist, his career took an upward turn after two minor courtiers began to recommend him as a singing teacher. He obtained a post at a school for young ladies in Dulwich, where a fortunate meeting introduced him to Caroline Thurlow, daughter of the Lord Chancellor. Eventually Stevens met Lord Thurlow himself, and following an informal audition – an impromptu rendering of Purcell's 'Mad Bess' – the cloth-worker's son never really looked back. Thurlow's influence brought Stevens organist posts at the Inner Temple and at the Charterhouse; he supported Stevens's concerts and employed him for his own; and he brought about an introduction to Bates which led to a post at the Concert of Ancient Music. Stevens's touching but ultimately servile pride in the relationship is symbolised by an anecdote about Thurlow chatting to him in full view of the subscribers, a 'circumstance, tho' trivial, I thought so particularly kind at the time; that it is with pleasure I now mention it'.

The many different forms of patronage reached every corner of London's concert life. Foreign musicians had an in-built advantage, over and above a bias in their favour. Coming from foreign courts, they could present letters of recommendation from princes all over Europe; several formal testimonials to the Prince of Wales have survived. A rosy account of Salomon's life noted that:

his letters of introduction immediately made him known to all the amateurs of the day, among whom were numbered many of our nobility; and his cheerful disposition, united to great good sense, soon obtained for him the friendship of all who at first patronised him on account of his professional talents.[14]

The reality may not have been quite so straightforward, but such letters undoubtedly opened doors, and even Haydn came to London armed with letters to the Neapolitan and Austrian ambassadors. An established musician could provide an alternative route. Gyrowetz was much indebted to Giornovichi for introducing a string quartet at the Prince of Wales's concerts, resulting in speedy invitations from the nobility. At a somewhat less exalted level, Shield brought a letter from Dr Sharp of Durham to his brother William Sharp, gaining entry to the celebrated private concerts at which he accompanied 'all the instrumental performers of the first class then residing in London'.[15]

Sometimes patrons themselves 'discovered' musicians abroad or in the provinces. The Frenchman Barthelemon was encouraged to London by the Earl of Kelly, who obtained for him a position in the opera orchestra, as a first step on the road to eminence as a concert soloist. Three prominent musicians at the Concert of Ancient Music were protégés of the Earl of Sandwich: Joah Bates, the Cambridge-educated son of a wealthy Halifax inn-keeper, who wheedled his way into Sandwich's employment; Sarah Harrop, a Lancashire chorus-soprano, whom Sandwich encouraged to London for study with Bates and Sacchini; and Thomas Greatorex, who joined the Earl's household after a chance meeting in Leicester (he succeeded Bates at the Ancient Music in 1793). Different again was the case of Clementi, who was in 1766 bought from his father by Peter Beckford, in effect to provide cut-price entertainment at his Dorset residence; only in 1775 did the young Roman break away to make his début at London concerts.

There is a fine line between encouragement and exploitation. But many showed disinterested support of young musicians. The Prince of Wales took several young musicians under his protection. Attwood he sent abroad to study (Mozart was one of his teachers) and he 'rescued' the young black violinist Bridgetower from his irresponsible father. Other musicians were plucked from total obscurity. Sir Watkin Williams Wynn is said to have heard Edward Meredith singing in a cooper's workshop: he paid for his education and launched him into a modestly successful concert career. Less of a success, but nonetheless revealing, was the story of Sally Shilton, a collier's daughter and a domestic employed by Lady Newdigate of Cheverel Manor. Her naturally beautiful voice brought her into the drawing-room to entertain guests, and a professional career seemed a possibility.[16] Lady Newdigate's 1792 correspondence describes vividly the steps that she took to further this cause – consultations with Giardini and Bates, lessons with Mortellari, attendance at concerts, and a trial in front of discerning amateurs at a private musical party. But Sally's voice was thought to lack power, and 'everybody adds what a pity to send such a Sweet inocent Girl out of a happy & secure situation into such a Sea of Dangers as this town'. After this traumatic season the girl suffered some kind of breakdown; in the end she became a vicar's wife and her singing was heard no more.

Even well-established musicians continued to need influence to further their careers. It was assumed that places at court could only be obtained this way. Seeking the post of Master of the King's Musick, Boyce wrote to the Duke of Newcastle requesting his interest with the Lord Chamberlain, who was responsible for such appointments.[17] When Boyce died, Burney had the advantage of teaching the current Lord Chamberlain's four daughters and was even promised the place, but the King overruled in favour of Stanley. John Parke was admitted to the King's Band through the intervention of the Duke of Cumberland, but his brother only ever deputised there, remarking acidly that merit was nothing in an orchestra made up of 'noblemen's butlers and valets'; in 1788 the appointment of 'men of merit' rather than footmen and butlers caused ironic surprise in one newspaper article.[18] At a more everyday level, power was wielded by those further down the court list. An important figure for much of the period was Frederick Nicolay, an ambitious official and a minor violinist himself. In 1764, as principal page to the Queen, he was responsible for receiving distinguished foreigners who came to Court, and Leopold Mozart regarded him as a vital person to visit. By 1787 he had become overseer of court concerts, obtaining new music and engaging extra players;[19] and in 1800 he was still an active figure, being listed as 'Frederick Nicolay, Esq.' among the musical directors of the RSM benefit. Another important official later in the period was Madame Schwellenberg, Fanny Burney's draconian superior: Bridgetower '*fiddled* himself' into her good graces in order to play at court.[20]

Some public pressure could be exerted on the patronage system. The succession to the post of Master of the King's Musick was the subject of considerable speculation in the press. Newspapers could also be used for rudimentary self-promotion: on 28 April 1786 a paragraph appeared in *The Morning Herald*, noting that Miss Chanu had turned down public appointments 'with a view of rendering herself as acceptable as possible to Lady *Buckingham*'s visitors' (a coded application for engagement at private concerts). But these were only marginal attempts to inflect a pervasive system of largely aristocratic control. Even the Professionals were not immune. In 1787 the younger Parke took a place alongside his brother, the principal oboist; but even in this self-managing orchestra the appointment resulted only from the 'auspices' of the Duke of Cumberland, to whom Parke was a private musician.[21]

Fees and specialisation

The lack of comprehensive records inhibits a thorough study of London concert fees. Table 9 gives a selection of known figures, taken from sources of varying reliability. At the very least, these figures reveal an extraordinary range, reflecting marked variations both in concert types and in individual drawing-power. They illustrate clearly a widening gap between those in the highest and the lowest strata of London's concert life. The rise in fees for the fortunate reflected the ever-increasing demand during the 'rage for music' for the services of the very best soloists. At the same time these widening opportunities allowed the top performers an increasing specialisation in certain areas of musical life.

Specialisation was comparatively limited at the beginning of the period, when the available work was limited and London's musical culture was more unified. A top performer like the singer Giulia Frasi was employed in all kinds of music in London – at the Opera, at Handel's oratorios, at the Dean Street series, at the Castle Society, at Ranelagh. Burney implied that principals at both Hickford's in the West End and at City societies were largely indistinguishable: certainly Festing was leader at most venues of any importance.[22] At the same time the relatively small number of foreign virtuosi could often be heard alongside local musicians, as witness the roster of soloists at the 1751–2 Dean Street series.

During the last quarter of the century, however, the dramatic expansion of London's concert life at its upper levels enabled the top performers to focus their activities on the principal organisations. This process was aided by the colossal sums that competitive series-promoters were prepared to pay to the most prestigious international singers, sums comparable to those paid by the Italian Opera for a whole season (in 1789 principals there were headed by Marchesi at £1,500 and Giuliani at £891, with most receiving a salary of around £200). The pattern was similar in the instrumental field. Even as early as the mid 1770s the violinist Cramer was able to renounce his membership of the Queen's Chamber Band because of 'the multiplicity of his engagements'.[23] Leaders in particular began to command higher fees, and the concept of the freelance instrumental soloist was born at the same time. In this context it is as inconceivable that Mara should have sung at Ranelagh as that Viotti should have played at a City tavern.

As suggested in chapter 5, oratorios and ancient music maintained a somewhat ambiguous position in this process. The Lenten oratorio seasons often hired one or two star singers and instrumentalists; but these were very much guest appearances to enliven a middle-ranking form of entertainment, with the most established stars able to move into lower levels without harming their reputations. The rise of ancient music to fashion in the 1780s, however, resulted in a realignment and much more cross-fertilisation between modern and ancient spheres. Top singers such as Mara, Billington and Banti were hired by the Concert of Ancient Music, and Mara even became closely associated with Lenten oratorio. The Academy's emulation meant that many of their singers coincided with those of the Concert. At the same time singers trained within the ancient orbit, including Harrison, achieved higher recognition. This

Table 9. Fees for concert performance

Type	Year	Fee (number of nights)	Performer	Source and notes
Solo singer				
Bach–Abel concerts?	1772	£105, £53 [15]	Sga Grassi, Savoi	Bach's account at Drummond's Bank
Bach–Abel concerts?	1777	£132 [15]	Savoi	Bach's account at Drummond's Bank
Pantheon Concert	1770s	£100 (nightly)	Sga Aguijari	Burney, *A General History*, vol. II, p. 882
Pantheon Concert	1774–5	1,200 gn. (13)	Sga Aguijari	Malcolm Elwin, *The Noels* (London, 1967), p. 46
Pantheon Concert	1784	£200 (6)*	Mme Mara	
Pantheon Concert	1785	1,000 gn. (13 [12])*	Mme Mara	
Pantheon Concert	1790	1,000 gn. (13) etc.	Pacchierotti	See McVeigh, 'The Professional Concert'
Professional Concert	1788	120 gn. [8]*	Mrs Billington	
Professional Concert	1790	400 gn. [6]	Mme Mara	
Professional Concert	1790	£10 (nightly)*	Sga Storace	
Concert of Ancient Music	1785	400 gn. (12)	Mme Mara	*PA* 21 September 1784
Concert of Ancient Music	[1780s]	£3, 5, 10 (nightly) or 3 gn., 10 gn.	Harrison	*WO* 11 and 13 February 1790 (i.e. increasing up to 1790)
Concert of Ancient Music	1790	£10 (nightly)*	Sga Storace	*WO* 26 February 1790
Academy of Ancient Music	1787–8	£63 (12)	Two Miss Abrams	'Academy'
Academy of Ancient Music	1787–8	£21 (12)	Gore	'Academy'
Covent Garden oratorios	1768	£600 (12 [11])	Guarducci	Burney, *A General History*, vol. II, p. 873
Drury Lane oratorios	1779	£115 (11)	Mrs Kennedy	*LS*, Part 5, p. 243
Drury Lane oratorios	1794	£210 (12)	Harrison	*LS*, Part 5, p. 1,573
Drury Lane oratorios	1794	36 gn. (12)	Dignum	*LS*, Part 5, p. 1,573
Marybone Gardens	1768	2 to 4 gn. (weekly)	[Various]	Clinch, *Marylebone*, p. 38
Foundling Hospital benefit	1754	6 gn., 1½ gn.	Sga Frasi, Wass	Deutsch, *Handel*, p. 751
Foundling Hospital benefit	1771	5 gn.	Mrs Weichsell	Court minute-book, 4 May 1771
Foundling Hospital benefit	1773	£100 less £20	Linleys	Court minute-book, 14 April 1773
Foundling Hospital benefit	1774	10 gn.	Norris	Court minute-book, 27 April 1774
Private concerts	1782	10 gn.	Pacchierotti	*PA* 18 May 1782
Private concerts	1788	10 gn. ('the customary')	Marchesi	*PA* 8 May 1788 (demanded 15 gn.)

Table 9 (*cont.*)

Type	Year	Fee (number of nights)	Performer	Source and notes
Choral singer				
Concert of Ancient Music	1785	15/- (nightly)	Stevens	Stevens, *Recollections*, p. 49
Academy of Ancient Music	1787–8	Most 6 gn. (12)	[Various]	'Academy'
Drury Lane oratorios (etc.)	c. 1780	£2 (weekly)	Holcroft	*Memoirs of the late Thomas Holcroft* (London, 1816), vol. II, pp. 24–5
Foundling Hospital benefit	1754	10/6	[Various]	Deutsch, *Handel*, p. 751
Foundling Hospital benefit	1769	1 gn.	[Various]	Sub-committee minute-book, 2 December 1769
Arne's Catches and Glees	1776	1 gn.	Stevens	Stevens, *Recollections*, p. 18
Director				
Academy of Ancient Music	1787–8	50 gn. p.a.	Cooke	'Academy' ('Conductor and Boys')
Marybone Gardens	1768	4 gn. (weekly)	Hook	Clinch, *Marylebone*, p. 38 ('Music Master')
Master of the King's Musick		£200 p.a.	[Various]	From 1765
Conductor of the Ball Musick		£100 p.a.	[Various]	
Private vocal concert	1799	5 gn. (from 3 gn.)	Stevens	Stevens, *Recollections*, p. 110 ('Conducting Glees')
Solo instrumentalist				
Salomon's Concert	1793	550 gn. (12 [13?])	Viotti	See McVeigh, 'The Professional Concert' (violin)
Drury Lane oratorios	1779	5 gn. (nightly)	Cramer	*LS*, Part 5, p. 243 (violin)
Drury Lane oratorios	1794	£105 (12)	Giornovichi	*LS*, Part 5, p. 1,573 (violin)
Queen's chamber musician	1764	£200 p.a.	Abel	*Grove's Dictionary*, 5th edn (viola da gamba, etc.)
Court appearance		24 gn.	Mozarts	Mozart, *The Letters*, p. 46
Private concerts	1789	40 gn. or 15 gn.	Mme Krumpholtz	*MP* 11 March 1789, *WO* 14 March 1789 (harp)
Private concerts	1789	10 gn. or 12 gn.	Giornovichi	*WO* 25 December 1789 (violin)
Private concerts	1795	3 gn.	Mlle Kirchgessner	*TB* 18 March 1795 (musical glasses)

Leader				
Academy of Ancient Music	1787–8	36 gn. (12)	Barthelemon	'Academy'
Drury Lane oratorios	1779	£40 (11)	D. Richards	LS, Part 5, p. 243
Foundling Hospital benefit	1754	1 gn.	Brown	Deutsch, *Handel*, p. 751
Mozart benefit	1764	3 gn.	[Unnamed]	Mozart, *The Letters*, p. 48
Benefit concert	1790	£5	[Unnamed]	*Musikalische Korrespondenz*, 1 (1790), 87
Queen's Band		£200 p.a.	Hay	*PA* 18 February 1785
Orchestral principal (sometimes with solos)				
Bach–Abel concerts?	1772	60 gn. [15]	Crosdill	Bach's account at Drummond's Bank (cello)
Bach–Abel concerts?	1773	30 gn. [15]	Eichner	Bach's account at Drummond's Bank (bassoon)
Salomon's Concert	1796	3 gn. (nightly)	W. Parke	Parke, *Musical Memoirs*, vol. I, pp. 303–4 (oboe)
Academy of Ancient Music	1787–8	12 gn. (12)	[Various]	'Academy'
Drury Lane oratorios	1779	£20 (11)	[J.] Parke	LS, Part 5, p. 243 (oboe)
Drury Lane oratorios	1794	£21 (12)	Ashe	LS, Part 5, p. 1,573 (flute)
Covent Garden oratorios	1790s	6 gn. (nightly); 10 gn. if concerto	S. Wesley	BL, Add. 27593, f. 139 (organ)
Mozart benefit	1764	3 to 5 gn.	[Unnamed]	Mozart, *The Letters*, p. 48
Orchestral rank-and-file				
Bach–Abel concerts?	1773	15 gn. [15]	Salpietro	Bach's account at Drummond's Bank (violin)
Wesley concerts	1785	3½ gn. (7)	Strings	BL, Add. 35017, f. 53
Salomon's Concert	1794	10/6 (nightly)	Smart	Smart, *Leaves*, p. 3 (violin/viola)
Academy of Ancient Music	1787–8	Most 4 to 6 gn. (12)	[Various]	'Academy'
Drury Lane oratorios	1794	9 gn. (12)	Asbridge	LS, Part 5, p. 1,573 (timpani)
Ranelagh Gardens	1788	7/- (nightly)	[Unnamed]	*TI* 5 June 1788 (reduced from 7/6)
Foundling Hospital benefit	1754	Most 8/- to 10/6, some 15/-	[Various]	Deutsch, *Handel*, p. 751
Foundling Hospital benefit	1769	Most 1 gn., some 2 gn.	[Various]	Sub-committee minute-book, 2 December 1769
Mozart benefit	1764	10/6	[Unnamed]	Mozart, *The Letters*, p. 48
Clark benefit	1776?	10/6	Stevens	Stevens, *Recollections*, p. 18 (violin)
Benefit concert	1790	£1	[Unnamed]	*Musikalische Korrespondenz*, 1 (1790), 87
King's Band		£40 p.a.	[Various]	£10 clothing allowance

Note. * And a benefit.

factor, together with the revival of English vocal music in the 1790s, resulted in a more open musical society which worked greatly to the benefit of English singers. This new openness should not be confused with a return to the limited opportunity of the 1750s; it reflects rather a broadening of the upper stratum to envelop a wider range of concert activity. The process also enabled a new type of high-status specialisation: the Harrisons, both former Hanover Square singers, chose to concentrate almost entirely during the 1790s on ancient and English concerts. The specialist oratorio singer was not far away.

Some specialisation also took place in the orchestral sphere, though it was less marked because poorly paid rank-and-file players could not afford to be too selective. Again it reflected perceived levels of concert activity, with fees matching these differentiations. Thus when in 1769 Giardini raised the Foundling Hospital fees to the top rate of 1 guinea, he did not simply pay more to the existing band, but brought in an almost entirely different set of players, many of them prominent at the Italian Opera. During the later 1780s the orchestral élite was clearly based round a tripole of Italian Opera, Professional Concert and Concert of Ancient Music. Reviews sometimes refer to these orchestras as one and the same, though they were in fact independently constituted. Closest were the Opera and Professional bands: of the thirty-one Professional members in 1785, twenty-one also played at the Opera.[24] The Professionals could presumably hope for the normal 1 guinea rate (at the Opera they received 15/- a night). Clearly this high pay and prestige attracted the very best players available; other orchestras were often criticised in comparison, and Salomon had actively to recruit quality players who would also accept lower fees. Slightly less prestigious was the orchestra of the Concert of Ancient Music: in 1790 only nine members also played with the Professionals, though this figure is distorted by the obligatory participation of the German musicians of the Queen's Band.

Other orchestras were not in the same league. While the Academy of Ancient Music might engage prestigious principals, they paid only basic rates of around 10/6 and their band was not of top quality. In 1790 only one player was engaged from the Professionals (Napier, propelled from the middle of the violas to the front of the first violins); eight others were shared with the Concert. Similarly, Harrison and Ashley employed at their oratorios this year some players from the Concert, but Ashley's son was elevated from principal viola to leader. In general, oratorio orchestras must have included many playhouse players, used to receiving around 5/- a night.[25] The band at Ranelagh went into serious decline in the 1770s: a pay-cut in 1776 resulted in a mass walk-out and the substitution of 'mere scrapers', while in 1788 the low pay (reduced from 7/6 to 7/-) caused many to play elsewhere before going on to Ranelagh later in the evening.[26] Doane's Directory of 1794, though scarcely to be trusted as an accurate record, confirms the relatively few overlaps between these various orchestras: only at concerts of the Society of Musicians and the New Musical Fund did such players naturally tend to come together.

We lack firm information on the subject of differentials within orchestras. The leader and principals were normally paid between two and five times the rank-and-file fee, solo performances included. Account sheets of the Foundling Hospital performances indicate some further variation, reflecting both instrument and position within the section. In 1754 the violinists received from 1 guinea down to 8/-; all the viola players were paid 8/-, but the cellists took 10/6 and the two double bass players as much as 15/- (perhaps reflecting scarcity or porterage costs); wind players received from 10/6 to 8/-. Giardini preferred an egalitarian 1 guinea all round, perhaps to emphasise the uniform excellence of his selection; in 1769 only two players, both cellists, received 2 guineas. At the Academy in 1787–8 the principal second violin, cello and double bass, and also the timpanist, were distinguished above the rank-and-file by double pay.

Such beginnings of specialisation should not be taken as indicating that there was no prospect of upward mobility within London's orchestral world. The career of William Parke provides an instructive example of a London musician reaching the pinnacle of his profession with no connections but those of his oboe-playing brother John. After experience on stage as a treble singer, his first orchestral work came at the age of fifteen as a viola player at Drury Lane Theatre and Vauxhall Gardens, where he moved to the oboe three years later. In 1783 he was appointed principal oboe at Covent Garden Theatre, and in 1786 was invited to play concertos at the Drury Lane oratorio series; in 1787 through the influence of the Duke of Cumberland he joined his brother at the Professional Concert. Thereafter he enjoyed a long and distinguished orchestral career, while (unusually) maintaining his place at Covent Garden.

The many who lacked Parke's talent and ambition had to be content with a much more menial existence. Indeed at the lower end of the profession it was scarcely possible to specialise at all, given the limitations of the market, and musicians took whatever work came their way. This is borne out by the large number of instruments that some professed. Applicants to the Society of Musicians often listed a whole range of disparate instruments. One of the many Kellners in the Queen's Band, Johann August, was not unusual in claiming to play the bassoon, cello, trombone and viola; Daniel Shutze simply 'plays all Instruments'. According to Angelo, the tenor Daniel Arrowsmith was not only a talented mimic, but he also played the violin, the cello and the flute at City concerts.[27] Presumably he was up to the comparatively modest demands of most repertoire of the period; even the clarinet soloist John Mahon was known as a reasonably accomplished orchestral violinist. But this kind of plurality was unthinkable at the very highest level: the celebrated oboist Fischer could have ruined his reputation at a stroke by indulging in public his skill on the violin.

Choral work presented rather a different situation. The nature of current choral singing – almost all in the Handelian cause – dictated a specialisation of repertoire, but the small amount of work meant that a few singers tended to monopolise it. Some singers at the Lenten oratorios were also theatrical personnel, but Doane's Directory confirms that many were specialist 'ancient' chorus-singers. Certainly most of the choir-members of the Concert and the Academy were singers from the cathedral tradition, often associated with the Chapel Royal, Westminster Abbey, or St Paul's. The two choirs overlapped more than the orchestras: in 1790 among the twenty-three men at the Academy twelve sang at the Concert. It was a relatively closed world which required special qualities. Stevens had to tell Lord Thurlow that he could not recommend Thomas Sedgwick to the Concert of Ancient Music because of his 'want of Science'.[28] The more secular equivalent was glee-singing, and many of the same performers were involved. Of the seventeen singers at the 1792 Vocal Concert all but two were engaged at either the Concert or the Academy around this time, as were most of the leading glee composers (including Webbe, Stevens, Danby and Callcott). These were the élite of the English singing world, newly risen to fashionable prominence through the changing tastes of the time.

The financial situation of the individual

No musician working in London for any length of time made his entire living from concert work, and the career of most musicians was an ever-varying cocktail of different enterprises. To this extent any specialisation within concert life was offset by deliberate diversification outside it, providing a measure of security against possible disaster. In any case a musician's career was always perceived as a whole, so that success in any one activity enhanced his general reputation and the possibility of further patronage.

Concert musicians were thus involved in all kinds of other performing milieus, ranging from theatre and church to glee clubs and military bands. The career of Samuel Arnold encompassed an extraordinary range: as well as a promoter of oratorios, gardens' manager, and concert director for the Pantheon, the Academy and the Royal Society of Musicians, he was also a prolific theatre composer, organist at the Chapel Royal and editor of ancient music publications. At a lower level, Hezekiah Cantelo introduced himself to the Royal Society of Musicians in 1785 as follows: 'Plays the Trumpet – Bassoon &c plays at Drury Lane Theater – Vauxhall, and the first Rigt. of foot Gaurds'; he became a well-known second trumpeter at top concerts. Singers and even orchestral players were often also church organists. In addition, most prominent performers were well-known composers. William Shield had regular employment as an orchestral violinist and viola player but he also composed many popular English operas, and in 1817 became Master of the King's Musick. But it was hard to make great riches from composition, and the real money was undoubtedly in light songs and piano music rather than in major concert music. It is salutary to read that Forster's edition of *The Seven Last*

Words, for which Haydn received 10 guineas, had sold only fifty copies by the late 1810s, despite the work's success at Salomon's concerts.[29]

A more reliable source of income was teaching; and, while some posts undoubtedly implied poorly paid hack-work, Hook received £600 per annum from two schools.[30] Furthermore the teaching of upper-class young ladies was prestigious as well as lucrative, and even Giardini appeared in Mortimer's 1763 directory not as a violinist but as a teacher of singing and harpsichord. An additional advantage was access to patrons, which might lead to further concert engagements. For some, though, teaching was a way of escape from the concert platform, either through failure or disillusionment. Burney built up a substantial practice, which enabled him to retire from performance: by 1780 he was charging 4 guineas entrance and half a guinea each lesson for the 'Masters & Misses', though he followed a punishing schedule, 'out every day before 9, & hardly ever at home before 11'.[31] Clementi abandoned his public career in 1790 at the height of his fame, and he was able to charge an exceptional 1 guinea per lesson. Perhaps more remarkably, the successful viola player Benjamin Blake started to learn the piano on the death of his patron the Duke of Cumberland; he became so sought after as a piano-teacher that he gave up orchestral playing.[32]

There is no way of assessing accurately the financial circumstances of any one musician, let alone the proportion of earnings contributed by concerts. Patrick Colquhoun's well-known assessment of average incomes, published in 1806, placed musicians alongside actors on £200, in effect towards the lower end of the middle classes.[33] This put them on a par with engineers and minor civil servants, and just above shopkeepers and tradesmen (£150), but clearly below members of other professions: doctors, artists and men of letters (£260), lawyers (£350). Rohr has estimated that a few musicians were in a much higher league (above £1,000), that some achieved comfortable incomes of between £200 and £1,000, but that the vast majority struggled to get anywhere near £200. Colquhoun's average figure certainly seems well on the high side, if it is intended to include all minor musicians across London.

Few figures of total income have been found, and often they appear distorted by exaggeration either upwards or downwards. Mara was clearly in the highest bracket during her early years in London. Some reported figures must be in the realm of fantasy (£2,500 in her first two weeks in London), but it is quite conceivable that in 1785 her concert income approached 3,000 guineas, even if this report was part of a campaign to discredit her. She apparently received from the Pantheon 1,000 guineas and a benefit, as well as 400 guineas from the Concert of Ancient Music, though she was only allowed to appear at two private concert series.[34] Such a level was not maintained, however: in June 1788 she let it be known that she required engagements totalling £1,000 if she were to remain for the ensuing season. German periodicals relayed high London incomes with astonishment:

	£
Rauzzini	2,000
Sacchini	1,800
Bach, Abel	1,500 each
Cramer	1,300
Giardini	1,200
Bertoni, Crosdill, Piozzi, Fischer	1,000 each
Parke	800
Dr Burney	750

But these figures were vigorously disputed, another writer suggesting that figures of £200 were more appropriate for Abel and Fischer, £300 for Bach.[35] Certainly a more sober assessment emerges from the following exchange from ten years earlier:

> GOLDSMITH. The greatest musical performers have but small emoluments. Giardini, I am told, does not get above seven hundred a year.
>
> JOHNSON. That is, indeed, but little for a man to get, who does best that which so many endeavour to do. There is nothing, I think, in which the power of art is shown so much as in playing on the fiddle.[36]

Yet even £700 would have put Giardini among the modestly wealthy – Colquhoun listed top civil servants and lesser merchants at £800, the lowest leisured classes at £700. Some prudent musicians were able to save enormous sums, if obituaries tell anywhere near the truth. Burton was said to have left £9,000, the centenarian Cervetto £20,000. Even Simpson died worth £10,000: essentially a second-rank oboist employed at such venues as the Castle Society, Vauxhall and Covent Garden, he was notably successful at finding his way into royal appointments.[37]

News of the riches to be made in London had spread across Europe by the early eighteenth century, and London was inundated throughout the century with foreigners attracted to this 'Peru for musicians'. Leopold Mozart marvelled greedily at the 'good catch of guineas' to be made there; Haydn is said to have left with a small fortune of some 15,000 gulden (£1,363). Neither could be persuaded to stay, but Archenholtz observed that 'the greatest part of the foreign musicians who visit London remain there', even if (as in the case of J. C. Bach) they had intended only a short visit. Some followed the advice of Wendeborn: 'Many foreign singers, fidlers, and dancers, are extravagantly paid; and, if they are the least frugal, they are enabled to retire to their own country, where they may live in affluence, enriched by English money.'[38] The flautist Karl Weiss achieved some renown for the 'handsome provision' he was able to take to Switzerland, while Giardini even managed to retain patronage after his departure. In 1784 he returned to Italy with annuities from all his royal patrons and from Lady Bingley's estate.[39]

British musicians were not entirely excluded from this bonanza, and some singers and instrumentalists reached the upper echelons of the profession. With the help of her successful benefit, Sarah Harrop's income for 1780 approached £2,000.[40] Even R. J. S. Stevens's comparatively modest career as a glee-singer and teacher took him to a position of some affluence. In a list appended to the first volume of his diaries he recorded his total income in 1778 as £62 15s.; by 1798 the comparable figure was £821 18s. 5d. Nevertheless British musicians constantly had to fight unjust prejudice, which bred resentment and led to sniping against foreigners. Without more consistent upper-class encouragement, they certainly faced an uphill struggle; there was never any suggestion that they should resurrect the protectionist measures that had been attempted around 1700.[41]

Moving further down the musical hierarchy, specific information about incomes becomes much scarcer. Undoubtedly the riches proved elusive for many, with even élite orchestral players working long hours for modest rewards, according to Giuseppe Baretti:

> As to the fiddlers and other Italians, who come here to play or to teach music, foolishly attracted by the great renown of English riches, they perform at the Opera and at Madam Cornely's, and trot about from house to house every morning, to give lessons for two guineas a dozen, while the winter lasts: but scarcely one in twenty has found himself twenty pounds the better at the year's end for these twenty years past.[42]

Baretti may have exaggerated somewhat, but there can be little doubt that in financial terms ordinary orchestral musicians reached only the lowest rung of the 'middle ranks'. Frederick James Messing was a far from unknown musician when at the age of twenty-seven he applied for membership of the Society of Musicians: 'I Profess the Violin Viola Violoncello & Guittar with Copying of Musick ... I have Play'd at ye Antient Concert at ye Crown & Anchor 10 Yrs I have play'd at His Majesty's Odes 7 Years.' His annual income was increasing and he was by no means impoverished, but £65 in 1779 put him only just above Colquhoun's artisans and labourers (£55), and £123 in 1781 still below shopkeepers and tradesmen (£150).

Many different factors combined to make a concert career precarious: intense competition, high living expenses, the short season, lack of job security, illness and old age. Competition was intense at all levels, given the very few permanent posts available and the small number of concerts even at the height of the 'rage for music'. The number of musicians always exceeded the available employment, as the proliferation of concerts was matched by the arrival of more musicians from the continent. The problem was less acute in the orchestral field, where some kind of work always seems to have been available even for quite modest performers. Three well-known musicians began their careers on the viola: Burney in Handel's oratorio orchestra in 1745, William Parke at Vauxhall in 1776, Smart at Salomon's concerts in 1794. But the highest quality was required to break into the élite orchestral ranks of the Italian Opera or the Bach–Abel concerts, especially on instruments other than violin or viola. Competition was exacerbated in the 1790s by the opening of the flood-gates to foreign arrivals, especially refugees from France. Excessive supply inevitably contributed to a general decline in fees, a situation made worse by the simultaneous fall in demand for concerts. Salomon could get away with paying low rates to foreigners; the Professionals resisted the trend at their peril.

Competition was even more fierce for soloists and leaders. While the best could command high fees, openings were few in number. There was also some sense of winner-takes-all, with the available work easily carved up between the few top performers. Thus Mrs Papendiek wrote, albeit not entirely accurately, that Salomon habitually led at private concerts, Giardini at the Opera, Cramer at 'the established concerts'. Barthelemon she regarded as a kind of substitute: another writer in 1785 suggested that he should try his luck in Dublin where 'with no rivalry, his success would be certain'.[43] A particularly raw system of competition was operated at Vauxhall, whereby engagement of singers for the next season was dependent on the number of encores received. Professional rivalries resulted in numerous outbreaks of outright, even public hostility between established artists: two singers in open dispute during a Vauxhall concert in 1765, Crosdill falling out with Cervetto after some unplanned embellishments in Abel's cello duet, Yaniewicz packing his violin rather than play a concerto under Salomon's leadership and so on. Mrs Weichsell haughtily refused to take part in *Ruth* at the Lock Hospital 'unless she had the part which Miss Lindley performed last year'.[44] A still more telling incident was related by Stevens, who recalled Harrison's apprehension at Kelly's London début and his relief at finding Kelly's style quite different from his own.[45]

A second cause of financial difficulty was the high cost of living in London, a disadvantage noted even by Leopold Mozart. Indeed foreigners, used to the relative comfort and ease of court life, must have found it surprisingly difficult to maintain their accustomed standards. One particular expense was clothing, since anyone involved with the aristocratic world had to dress with some style. It was also important from a professional point of view to live in the better areas of town. Giardini's changes of address reflect not only his own improving circumstances but also the fashionable trend westwards and then northwards: from Covent Garden via Soho to Mayfair and the Cavendish Square area. Instruments formed another great expense. While they could be regarded as a form of investment, the loss of uninsured instruments was disastrous. The King's Theatre fire of 1789 was catastrophic for those not playing at Napier's benefit: Cervetto is said to have lost a cello worth over 300 guineas.[46]

A third problem faced by London musicians was the short season. Any personal setback during the few winter months could be disastrous, since there was little time to recover lost fortunes. Then during the summer work prospects were often limited, since the only concerts in London after mid June were those at the pleasure gardens. As a consequence, while there was a natural link between the gardens and the playhouses, the shortage of other work did attract musicians from the winter concerts to the gardens. Thus Vauxhall audiences heard such well-known singers as Mrs Weichsell and Mrs Wrighten, and violinists of the calibre of Barthelemon and Pieltain. More unusually, the cathedral singer John Page joined the vocal ensemble there in 1790. Other musicians sought alternative summer employment outside London, perhaps touring provincial theatres and festivals or renewing connections abroad; only the lucky few received an invitation to the country seat of an aristocratic patron.

Fourth, London's concert life offered virtually no security. Only the King's Band involved a place for life, albeit with no direct prospects and an unchanging salary despite some inflation. Other orchestras did maintain some continuity: the six-man first-violin section of the Professionals remained constant throughout the organisation's nine-year existence. Similarly Stevens regarded a place in the chorus of the Concert of Ancient Music as his until he chose to relinquish it. But soloists were always engaged by the season, and nowhere was there any guarantee of continuing employment. As we have seen, Ranelagh in 1788 summarily abandoned vocal music and cut orchestral fees. In 1786 Stevens himself reduced the music bill at a charity dinner from £60 to 20 guineas simply by organising an ode without orchestra.[47] The life of J. C. Bach graphically illustrates the declining fortunes to which even the most famous musicians were susceptible. Wilhelm Cramer, perhaps the most secure of all instrumentalists of the period, was finally toppled in 1796 by Viotti. A year after his death, the ignominy of a benefit for his infant children was only avoided 'by the interposition of patronage, of the most exalted kind'.[48]

Allied problems were illness and old age. A sudden injury could spell disaster. For the entire 1789 season Borghi was incapacitated through 'a severe Malady in both Hands' and he had to advertise a special benefit. Declining powers in the twilight of a career meant increasingly minor engagements. The celebrated Thomas Lowe, Handel's oratorio tenor, was reduced after his unsuccessful Marybone venture to performance at Finch's Grotto and Sadler's Wells, while the once-celebrated prima donna Cecilia Davies sank into penury and dependence on charity. Older orchestral players must have felt constantly under threat: in 1786 after subscribers at the Opera recommended 'new and able hands' it was proposed to cut the pay of some older members.[49] Even Wendeborn confessed that he had heard of several foreign musicians dying in London 'wretchedly poor'.[50] Often it was pointed out that those who took benefit concerts were usually those least in need of them. The Society of Musicians provided a backup in cases of proven indigence: but the sums involved were tiny (an allowance in 1784 of 2 guineas per month, rising to 4 guineas in 1794). It is alarming to discover that one-quarter of its members made claims at some point in their careers.[51] Clearly few musicians were able or willing to save money against ill fortune and old age.

Success for the few, relentless hard work for the many, and the ever-present threat of unforeseen disaster: it is small wonder that musicians tried to amass as much as they could while the sun shone. If at times they appear selfish and mercenary, this has to be viewed against a background of low rewards and insecurity. Some bitterly regretted their career choice. Samuel Wesley in 1806 summed up the problems facing a serious musician:

I have every day more and more cause to curse the day that ever my poor good father suffered *musick* to be my profession. In this country experience continually shows that only impudent and ignorant wretches make any considerable emolument by it except a few singers ... but the whole is a degrading business to any man of spirit or any abilities ... If I had now three or four hundred pounds at my command, I would not hesitate to purchase a large share in a gin shop.[52]

Viotti did indeed become a wine-merchant, while others more conventionally went into music-related businesses, including publishing and instrument-dealing. Though such commercial activity took these musicians firmly into middle-class 'trade', the example of Clementi shows clearly that this was a step towards respectability by comparison with the career of piano virtuoso. For Joah Bates, the cultivation of music was a mere stepping-stone en route to the civil service, thanks to Sandwich, and at the Concert of Ancient Music he was universally regarded as a gentleman musician.

Another reason for leaving the public concert profession, or a means of escape from it, was provided by marriage to wealthy non-musicians. It was taken as a matter of course that a woman would forsake her public career on marriage, unless her husband was a musician. The most celebrated case was that of Elizabeth Linley, who as Mrs Sheridan could only be heard at private concerts; this decision must in fact have caused some debate, since it inspired Dr Johnson to pronounce his approval.[53] More surprisingly at first sight, the career of Sarah Harrop ended when she married Bates ('she, of course, gave up her performing in public'):[54] this clearly reflected, however, Bates's aspiration to be regarded as a musical amateur. A rare exception to the norm was provided by Isabella Young, who married the Hon. John Scott in 1757, but continued to sing for many years as either Miss Young or Mrs Scott. Two widely reported marriages affected men's careers, in quite different circumstances. John Crosdill seems to have landed the ideal catch, the seventy-year-old Mrs Colebrooke with £25,000 plus £1,500 per annum. He was able to abandon public performance and gave up all his pupils but the Prince of Wales.[55] The suave Schroeter, on the other hand, was bought off by an irate wealthy family, after a clandestine marriage to a young lady student: in return for an annuity of £500, he similarly agreed to give up his public career, playing only at the Prince of Wales's concerts. Schroeter's attractive widow was Haydn's close companion in London.

The social status of concert musicians

[Pacchierotti] is not only the first, most finished, and most delightful of singers, but an amiable, rational, and intelligent creature, who has given to himself a literary education, and who has not only a mind superior to his own profession, which he never names but with regret, in spite of the excellence to which he has risen, but he has also, I will venture to say, talents and an understanding that would have fitted him for almost any other.[56]

The financial situation of London's musicians evidently varied from luxurious affluence to abject poverty. But financial insecurity was only one aspect of musicians' low social status. Other factors included humble backgrounds, limited education and gauche social manners; musicians also shared the taint of immorality associated with the stage. In itself music was widely regarded as a trivial occupation, without social value, unworthy of someone of real accomplishment. Deborah Rohr has argued convincingly that, with the decline of the university church-music career, British musical life was dominated by low-status secular activity, a craft of artisans rather than a respectable middle-class profession with its own system of education, regulation of standards and financial strategy.

Musicians indeed remained dependent at every turn on patrons' support and approval, for all the outward appearance of a new commercial environment. Lacking any real alternative, musicians did their utmost to preserve this old-established relationship. Foreigners brought up in the obsequious atmosphere of continental courts were masters of the correct tone to adopt, cultivated yet respectful. British musicians on the other hand often lacked these skills. Arne can scarcely have endeared himself by his awkward manner and loose language, and Parry brought his career to an end by singing at the Ancient Concerts in a state of complete inebriation.[57]

A crucial issue for musicians was their reception in aristocratic houses. The very possibility that they might perform at private concerts in return for a supper or new connections confirms their traditional dependence, rather than any acknowledgment of social standing. Indeed musicians were often thoughtlessly exploited. Parke recalled playing at one noble household until 2.30 in the morning without any refreshment; and aristocrats were notorious for late payment (Haydn left the country still owed fees by the Prince of Wales for twenty-six concerts).[58] Regarding the correct attitude to adopt, Cousser's Machiavellian advice from 1704 still held good:

The usual honorarium for performing at the home of a nobleman is ten guineas. If afterwards you are invited to dinner and are expected to eat with the steward, make it clear that you would rather leave, then you will be seated at the nobleman's table ... If after the meal one is invited to remain when they begin to drink, one sometimes accepts but sometimes leaves, which pleases them, for although one mixes freely with them, one is not on equal terms. It is better if one joins the wives and drinks tea or coffee with them.[59]

In their assessment of their own status, musicians regarded social invitation into aristocratic circles as a critical litmus test. Parke wrote cringingly in his memoirs that George IV was the first to 'burst the barrier which had kept the arts at a chilling distance' by inviting men of talent to sit at his table.[60] For a humble chorus-singer like Stevens a mere public conversation with the Lord Chancellor was sufficient to call forth extravagant obeisance. Others aimed much higher. J. C. Bach was 'received in the higher circles of society as a visitor' as a result of his teaching;[61] the ambitiously vain Giardini cultivated such connections assiduously, to the extent that he began to expect a place at the dinner-tables of the great. But in reality dinner invitations were a badge of celebrity, rather than an acknowledgment of equal status. Perhaps only Charles Burney, by his literary endeavours outside the music profession, found a genuine acceptance among the leisured classes. Samuel Crisp wrote of Burney in 1781: 'He is now at the Top of the *Ton*. He is continually invited to all the great Tables, and parties, to meet the Wits and Grandees, without the least reference to Music.'[62] Certainly mere violinists like Giornovichi, however celebrated, were not expected to mingle with the audience at a public concert, and he was firmly rebuked.[63]

The most famous musicians therefore aspired to some familiarity with the aristocracy, who tolerated them and even befriended them on occasion. But ultimately musicians were left in no doubt as to their true status. Still less were they accepted into London's intellectual life, lacking as they did a broad education or an accepted theoretical basis for their art. Again only Burney as a writer made headway in this direction, as a somewhat peripheral member of Johnson's 'Club'.

London's concert life did, however, provide the prospect of the new status of a middle-class profession. Untainted by the unsavoury associations of either theatre or tavern, symphonic concerts in purpose-built concert-halls offered a more respectable version of secular music.[64] A significant step was the establishment of the Professional Concert. The organisation remained dependent on patronage, and aristocratic leverage was still applied behind the scenes. But it was essentially self-managing, with the highest possible standards achieved by careful assessment of merit. During its halcyon days it was financially sound and made handsome profits for the participants. Ultimately this momentum could not be sustained, because of the decline in aristocratic support for public concerts in general and the absence of a new bourgeois market. But the self-managing concept was not in itself invalid, and it was picked up again by the Philharmonic Society in 1813 with a more upper-middle-class audience. Another factor which had a significant effect on the status of the concert musician was the rise in the 1780s of the ancient movement, with its inbuilt pedigree. Ancient music had intellectual connotations (philosophical, aesthetic, antiquarian), and it was cultivated by gentlemen scholars of university education; indeed the music could itself be perceived as learned. There was also a direct or an acquired link with the church. Though paradoxically managed by amateurs, the movement gave new professional prominence to organist-directors and to cathedral singers, who could now use their art profitably but respectably in ancient and English concerts.

Composers were undoubtedly regarded as above executants: one commentator directly contrasted 'mere mechanical performers', their lives shortened by dissipation and debauchery, with long-lived composers, the real artists.[65] Respect increasingly attached to composers with doctorates, a degree achieved by composition in a cathedral idiom. The ancient revival brought many such figures into the public eye, and the doctors themselves founded an informal society. Another development of the 1790s enhanced their profile. This was the rise of the keyboard conductor, who (though not baton-waving) was a figure of authority, divorced from the mere mechanics of playing an instrument. George Smart, knighted in 1811, became an eminent figure of the early Victorian period as a conductor, and (in Cyril Ehrlich's assessment) 'even more remarkable is the fact that [unlike Burney] he achieved eminence without leaving the music profession'.[66]

Despite these positive changes in perception, public performance remained in some sense degrading. Adam Smith thought that the high fees paid to top performers were justified not only through market-forces but also as recompense for the prostitution of their talents in public.[67] Many musicians certainly preferred to attract lucrative private patronage where they could: indeed, some well-known performers hardly cultivated a public image at all. Nicolas Hüllmandel, a famous virtuoso pianist and a prolific composer, first came to London in 1771 and he settled there permanently in 1790; but only a handful of advertisements for his public performance have been found, and none at all from 1790 onwards. Viotti was preceded by a rumour that he 'will only play in select parties, as he is a man of good fortune':[68] though this rumour turned out to be false, clearly it was regarded as the highest accolade rather than a criticism.

The practicalities of concert promotion

Numbers and platform arrangements

Table 10 gives some figures for orchestra and choir sizes, based mainly on surviving lists of players. By contrast with steadily growing continental orchestras, London orchestras remained surprisingly static in numbers until the 1790s, when there was reaction both to the Handel Commemoration and to the musical demands of Haydn's symphonies. String sections were enlarged, and in 1792 the full 'Classical orchestra' (including a trombone to strengthen the bass line) was at last listed at the Professional Concert.[1] Before this date clarinet parts must often have been taken by flautists or oboists, with trumpeters and timpanist only employed as needed. Another factor was the size of concert-rooms. The larger orchestra used for Haydn's 1795 symphonies must have been in part designed for the King's Theatre concert-room, and Haydn is known to have doubled the woodwind parts.

Choirs at major public concerts were mostly professional, though at the Foundling Hospital the professional group was supplemented at least from 1771 by unpaid volunteers, and the massed forces of the Handel Commemoration were mainly amateur. Most choirs were entirely male, using boy trebles and male altos as in cathedral choirs; the Concert of Ancient Music maintained this practice until the end of the century. A change first occurred in the more secular world of Lenten oratorios at the theatres. At Covent Garden in 1773, women sopranos were introduced into the chorus alongside boys, following established practice at provincial oratorios; and a few women are listed among the choral sopranos (but not the altos) at the 1784 Commemoration. Nevertheless it was the difficulty of engaging boy trebles that proved an obstacle to choral music at Salomon's concerts in 1792. Glees were also traditionally scored for men only, reflecting their convivial origins: when soprano lines were added these could be taken by boys, but in public concerts women often took these parts.

Many questions about platform layout remain unanswered, even though some prints and verbal descriptions survive. The most specific information

Table 10. *Orchestra and choir sizes*

		Orchestra														Singers							
Organisation	Year	Flute	Oboe	Clarinet	Bassoon	Horn	Trumpet	Trombone	Timpani	Violin 1	Violin 2	Viola	Cello	Double bass	Continuo	Total	Solo	Treble	Alto	Tenor	Bass	Total	Source and notes
Wesley concerts	1785	0	0	0	0	0	0	0	0	2	2	1	1	0	hpd/org	9							BL, Add. 35017, f. 47
Professional Concert	1787	2	2	0	2	2	0	0	0	6	6	4	3	3	hpd	31							McVeigh, 'The Professional Concert'
Professional Concert	1793	2	2	2	2	2	2	0	1	6	6	4	3	3	pf	36							
Salomon's Concert	1793	2	2	0	2	2	2	1	1	—12–16—		4	5	4	pf	38–42							Estimate, adapted from Landon, *Haydn in England*, pp. 286–8
Opera Concert	1795	[4	4	4	4	4	2	1	1	10	10	6	5	4	pf]	c. 60							
Concert of Ancient Music	1788	—	4	0	4	4	2	3	2	—17—		4	4	2	[hpd/org]	47	9	15	8	9	8	49	BL, programme-book
Concert of Ancient Music	1800	0	4	0	4	4	2	3	1	—18—		6	4	4	[hpd/org]	51	12	16	10	12	11	61	BL, programme-book
Academy of Ancient Music	1789	0	3	0	3	2	2	0	1	—14—		4	4	2	[hpd]/org	36	5	c. 9	7	7	7	c. 35	CPL, programme-book Cf. *P.A* 26 January 1789
Sons of the Clergy Festival	1792	0	6	0	6	0	4	0	1	—24—		7	6	4	[org]	59							RSM minute-book of governors' meetings, 1 April 1792
Ranelagh Gardens	1752	0	2	0	0	2	1	0	1	3	3	1		—4—	org	18	2						Boyce Ode parts, Bodl., MS. Mus. Sch. c. 105; possible doubling
Ranelagh Gardens																c. 25							Estimate from a print showing the interior of the rotunda, for R. Wilkinson (BL, 840.m.28)
Vauxhall Gardens	c. 1790	0	2	0	2	2	0	0	0	3	3	1		—3—		16							Hook parts, CUL, Add. 6639 (see also Cudworth, 'The Vauxhall "Lists"', 27–8)
Foundling Hospital	1754	0	4	0	4	[2	2	0	1]	—14—		6	3	2	[hpd],org	40	5	[6]	—13—			?24	Court minute-book, 29 May
Foundling Hospital	1774	0	4	0	2	0	2	0	1	—15—		3	4	2	[org]	34	4	12	6	10	11	43	Court minute-book, 27 April
Handel Commemoration	1784	6	26	0	27	12	12	6	4	48	47	26	21	15	org	251	17	53	45	80	79	274	Burney, *An Account*, pp. 17–21

Table 10 (cont.)

Organisation	Orchestra															Singers						Source and notes
	Year	Flute	Oboe	Clarinet	Bassoon	Horn	Trumpet	Trombone	Timpani	Violin 1	Violin 2	Viola	Cello	Double bass	Continuo	Total	Solo Choir Treble	Alto	Tenor	Bass	Total	
New Year Ode	1771	0	2	0	1	0	2	0	1	3	3	1	}	—	4	17	3 3	3	4	5	18	Boyce Ode parts, Bodl., MS. Mus. Sch. d.325.b–c; possible doubling (King's Band nominally 24) Continuo parts: vc, db, db, hpd/vc
Queen's Band	1783	0	2	0	0	2	0	0	0	3	3	2	2	1	?hpd	16						C. F. Cramer, *Magazin der Musik*, 1:2 (1783), 1,037–9; also piano soloist

Note: In some cases it is clear that players doubled on other instruments. At the 1784 Handel Commemoration, women sopranos joined the treble line.

Abbreviations: hpd harpsichord; org organ; pf piano; vc cello; db double bass concerns choral performances, where some kind of amphitheatre arrangement was habitually adopted. A drawing of a Covent Garden oratorio performance (after Handel's time) clearly shows a tiered platform erected on the stage (see plate 4).[2] Chorus-singers as well as soloists are placed as usual in front of the orchestra, with the instrumentalists ranged around the director seated at the organ. Unfortunately the drawing has insufficient detail for the identification of the precise layout, but descriptions of 1785 and 1793 both confirm retention of the traditional seating of cellos and double basses near the keyboard, with violins and wind instruments fanning out behind.[3] The arrangement of singers solved natural problems of balance, even if it hampered visual communication between the performers. At one benefit concert in the King's Theatre, an experiment was evidently made in the layout, but the 'chorus singers were too much in the back ground, by which much of the effect was lost'.[4]

The 1784 Westminster Abbey arrangement, with elaborate staging built against the west window, was reminiscent both of oratorio performances and of the more elaborate events at the Chapels Royal. The plan and depiction in Charles Burney's *Account* show the ranks of choral singers disposed either side of the organ console, forming a double choir (see plan 1); all the bass instruments were clustered around the console, with the woodwind and upper strings higher up, and brass and timpani crowning the ensemble. First violins are placed on the left, seconds on the right. Both Academy and Concert of Ancient Music used staging to achieve a similar effect. According to Doane's detailed description of the Academy at the Freemasons' Hall in the 1790s, the main platform was some five feet above the floor, with three further platforms rising in a semi-circular plan towards the organ at the top (see plan 2). The arrangement of performers resembles that of the oratorios; Doane stresses the need for the singers to be able to see the conductor at the organ and harpsichord (his back to the audience), and for the instrumentalists to be able to see both conductor and leader. The Concert from 1785 was arranged in a similar amphitheatre plan, which was said to resemble the Drury Lane oratorio arrangement. A description by Reichardt replicates many of same points: soloists and chorus at the front, bass instruments around the central organ console, upper strings above, winds to the sides.[5]

Many prints depict concerts at the gardens, but most give only the sketchiest idea of the arrangement of players. In the cramped circular bandstand at Vauxhall the players sat below the organ in a semi-circular arrangement, leaving space for the singers to drape themselves over the parapet. The Ranelagh rotunda, on the other hand, contained a capacious tiered platform with the players ranged in four straight rows below the organ. A similar platform was also used for indoor concerts at Vauxhall.

Curiously enough, even less information survives about the lay-out at subscription concerts. There is no description of the orchestral arrangement at the Bach–Abel or Professional Concerts. At most concerts the orchestra must have sat on a flat floor: the purpose of the raisable orchestral platform at

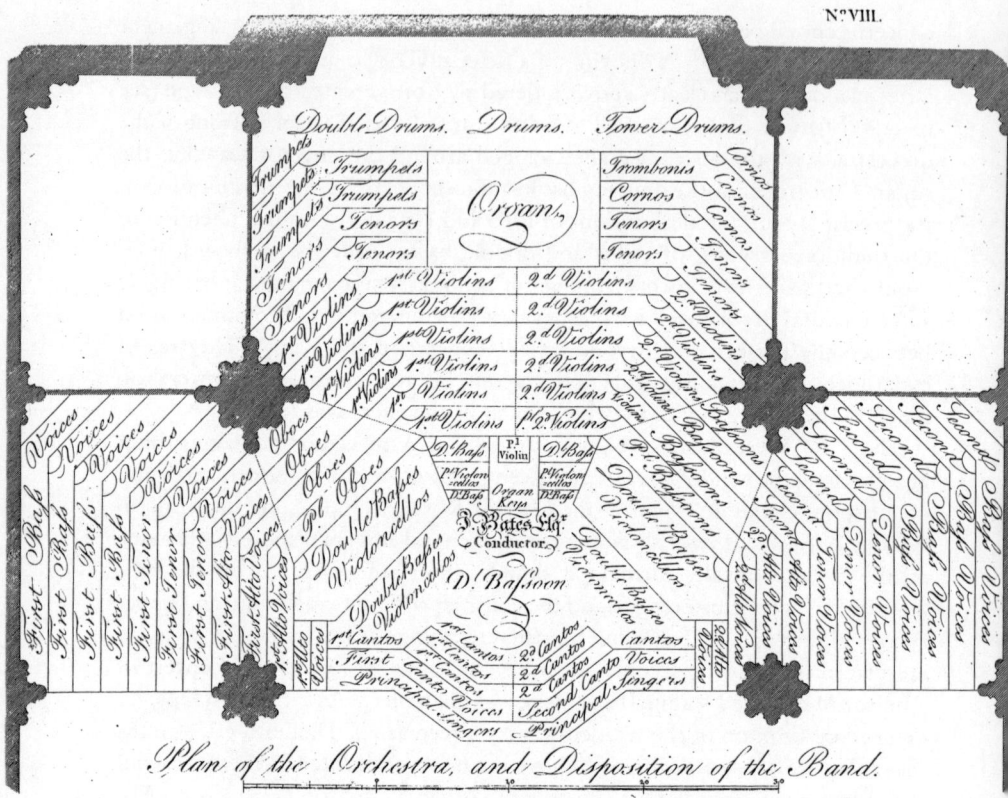

Plan 1   Plan of the performers at the Handel Commemoration at Westminster Abbey in 1784, from Burney, *An Account*

Hanover Square (mentioned in chapter 4) was purely to accommodate a larger audience, not to enable them to see better. Certainly this room was not designed for choral performance and there was no fixed organ. Salomon and Haydn were credited by Mrs Papendiek with arranging the orchestra in 1791 'on a new plan'. Quite what is meant by this is not clear. Both H. C. Robbins Landon and Neal Zaslaw have suggested that she was referring to an amphitheatre arrangement in itself, the players fanning out from the central director on rising platforms up to the timpani at the top.[6] But such an arrangement was already the norm for ancient music. Perhaps its transfer to the symphony concert was a novelty. In any case Mrs Papendiek's rather fanciful description suggests a much more significant novelty:

The pianoforte was in the centre, at each extreme end the double basses, then on each side two violoncellos, then two tenors or violas and two violins, and in the hollow of the piano a desk on a high platform for Salomon with his ripieno. At the back, verging down to a point at each end, all these instruments were doubled, giving the requisite number for a full orchestra. Still further back, raised high up, were drums, and on either

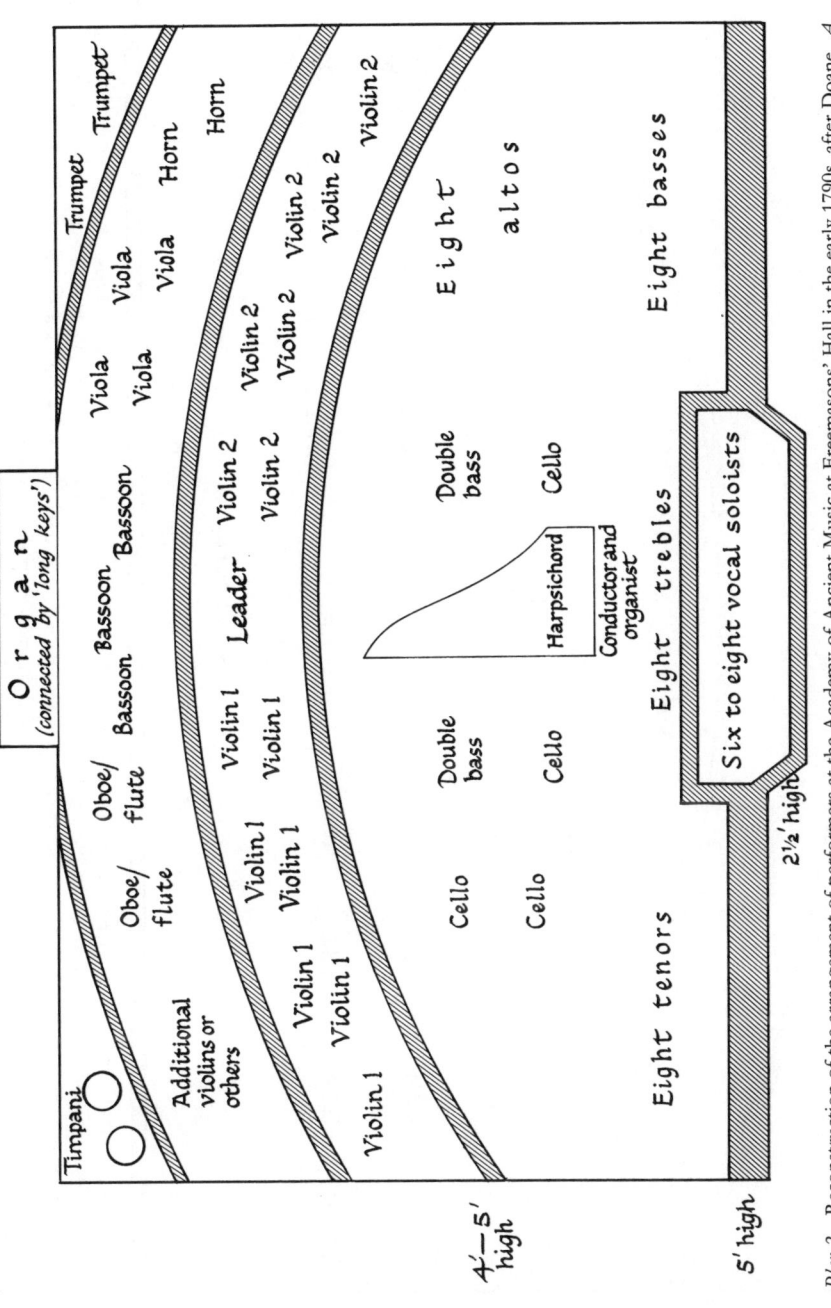

Plan 2 Reconstruction of the arrangement of performers at the Academy of Ancient Music at Freemasons' Hall in the early 1790s, after Doane, *A Musical Directory*, p. 81. This detailed description leaves only a few minor points to conjecture. The number of performers corresponds exactly with the list of personnel for the 1789–90 season in a programme-book in CPI, except that there were three oboists and only seven basses.

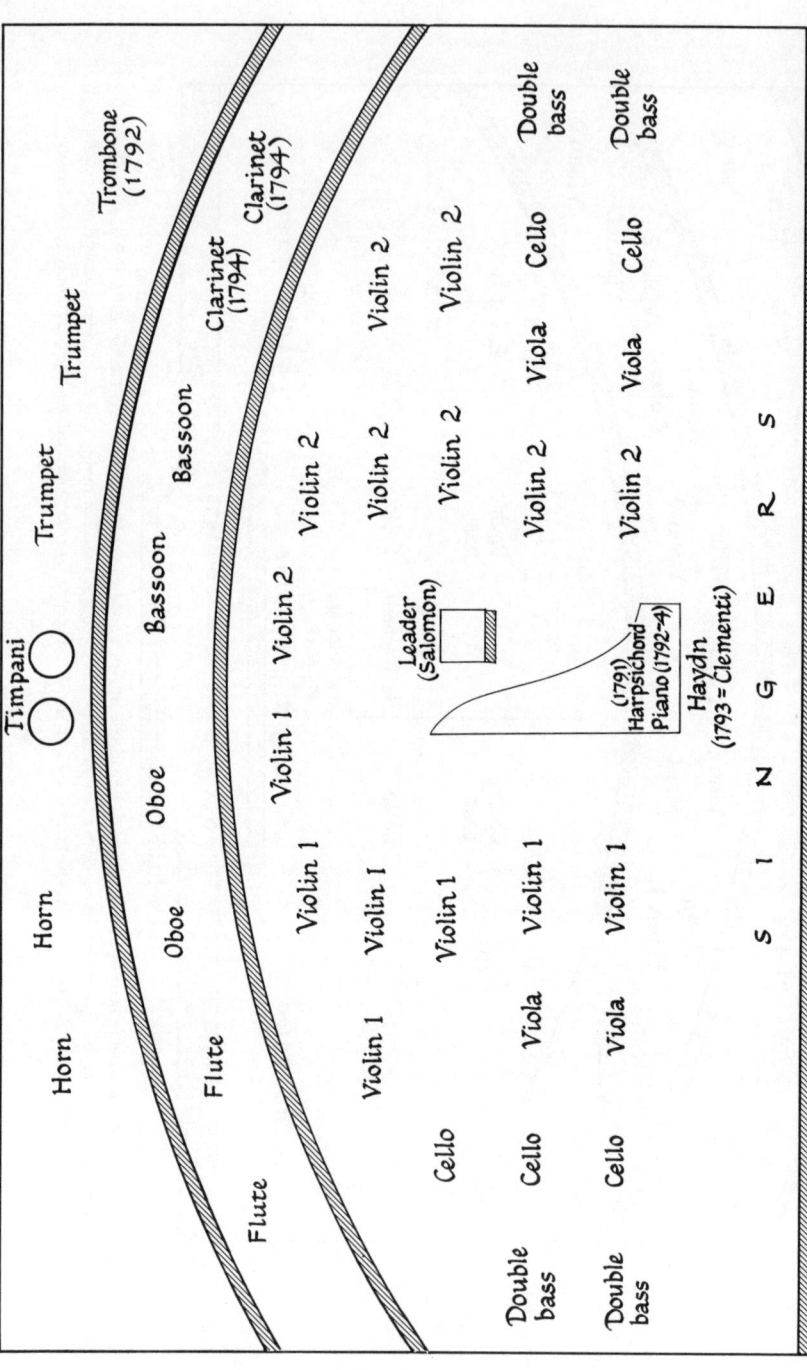

Plan 3 Hypothetical reconstruction of the orchestral arrangement at Salomon's concerts at the Hanover Square Rooms 1791–4, after the description in Papendiek, *Court and Private Life*, vol. II, p. 295 and the list of orchestral numbers for 1793 cited in McVeigh, 'The Professional Concert', 121. Mrs Papendiek describes the lay-out of the strings in some detail, but the number of platform-levels and the arrangement of wind-players are entirely conjectural. See also the slightly different interpretation in Zaslaw, 'Toward the Revival', 165; amended in *The New Grove Dictionary of Musical Instruments*, ed. S. Sadie (London, 1984), s.v. 'Orchestra'.

side the trumpets, trombones, bassoons, oboes, clarinets, flutes, &c., in numbers according to the requirements of the symphonies and other music to be played on the different evenings.[7]

The critical difference between this and the oratorio arrangement was the removal of the bass instruments (the former continuo) from centre-stage; the lower string sections are divided between left and right sides, foreshadowing a common nineteenth-century arrangement. A hypothetical reconstruction of this plan is reproduced as plan 3.

One further small point deserves a moment's consideration. Did performers stand or sit at London concerts in this period? Astonishingly, it is not possible to give a universal answer to this question, and circumstances may have varied. A number of descriptions of court concerts refer specifically to players (as well as courtiers) standing: when the Linleys performed for five hours at Buckingham House 'no one sat except the two performers who played the harpsichord and the violincello'.[8] Doane implies that the leader at the Academy stood. But other evidence points in a different direction. At Carlton House on one occasion Salomon was prevented from 'attempting to mount the leader's stool' by Yaniewicz.[9] At the Commemoration performances in 1784 'the band all stood' on the recommendation of Hay, to stop them flagging and to help them to see the leader; other reports confirm that all the performers had to stand throughout each act.[10] But to be worthy of mention this must have been regarded as an exception. Certainly singers at oratorios and 'ancient' venues normally sat down outside their own numbers, as we learn from controversy when prima donnas such as Mara refused to stand and join in the choruses.

Parts and instruments

One important aspect of concert promotion was the preparation of parts, and accounts frequently mention copying as an item of expenditure. Sometimes one of the performers would bring his own set of parts; it was expected of soloists, who would travel with jealously guarded material of their own favourite solo items. This applied to singers as well as instrumentalists: Handel's 'Nasce al bosco' could not be performed at a benefit in 1785 because Reinhold had left behind the orchestral parts.[11] Even an orchestral piece, Arnold's overture to *The Battle of Hexham*, was played at Vauxhall in 1791 from 'loose papers' brought by James Sarjant the trumpeter.[12]

It is important to remember that there would often be only one score and one set of parts in existence, material that was similarly guarded by its owners to protect against unauthorised performance. Handel and his amanuensis J. C. Smith kept a close watch on the oratorio scores, and copies were only lent out on the assurance that no further copies would be made, especially of the choruses. In 1757 Stanley told the Lock Hospital that he would do 'all in his power' to obtain the parts for *Alexander's Feast*.[13] Even Giardini's *Ruth*, which had lain unperformed at the Lock for some years, caused a ripple through the minute-books when the score and parts were surreptitiously appropriated for a Foundling Hospital benefit in April 1787. Some concert promoters, including Salomon, deliberately kept music in manuscript, since once a work was published the owner resigned all rights over its performance. Thus Stevens was annoyed but powerless when Greatorex added additional accompaniments to his trio 'O strike the harp'; in the end Greatorex's 'vanity, and presumption' did not prevent Stevens attending the public performance, and subsequently the composer made his own version.[14]

Little of the original performing material from this period has survived. Significant exceptions include complete sets of parts for Boyce's court odes, some for Bach sinfonie concertanti, a few for Haydn's London symphonies. Not much can be gleaned from these in terms of performance practice, since it was not customary to add markings such as phrasing or dynamics during rehearsal. It is also unclear whether string players normally shared a part or not. Illustrations tend to suggest one player to each part, but some evidence suggests otherwise. Three of the violin parts to Boyce odes from the 1750s have two names on them (and each ode was performed only once); for most odes sixteen or seventeen parts survive, suggesting a doubling of violins and violas if twenty-four players actually did take part. It may be significant that the string parts in the (unused) Foundling Hospital material correspond to about half the number of players in contemporary performances. Parts were clearly shared at the Commemoration, while a London viola part for Haydn's Symphony No. 101 has the two names 'Fiorilo & Slezak' on it.

When the composer was not present, most music would have been rehearsed without benefit of a full score. A few scores were published in the period, especially of ancient music by Corelli, Geminiani and Handel; but the closest approximation to scores of modern symphonies consisted in keyboard arrangements. Thus Haydn's middle symphonies simply arrived in parts, whether manuscripts from the composer or prints from a continental publisher. The parts would then be copied in manuscript or turned eventually into new printed editions.

The mechanism of the web of business relationships between impresarios, publishers and composers has yet to be fully determined. The whole process was complicated by the fledgling state of copyright laws and by the total lack of international agreements. In the simplest situation music would be performed in manuscript for one season and then sold to a publisher, as in the case of the Longman and Broderip edition of Haydn's Op. 54 quartets, performed at the Professional Concert in 1789. But sometimes the arrangement must have involved some collaboration between publisher and promoter: the Vienna composer Kozeluch offered his quartets Op. 33 in December 1790 to John Bland, but the following April (following Salomon's own visit to Vienna) Salomon performed one of them in manuscript in London, and Bland finally advertised his publication in June.[15] Other dealings with Haydn went far from smoothly, reflecting lack of negotiating procedures, difficulties in communication and some duplicity on the part of the composer. Probably none of the 'new music' he sent to the Professionals during the 1780s was in fact specially written (except for Symphonies Nos. 76–8, negotiations over which collapsed). But it was always unknown in London, until in 1788 Haydn blundered in sending the 'Paris' symphonies as new works.[16] The scandal was not so much that they had been written for a Paris concert series but that some of them were already available from a London publisher. During the 1790s Haydn showed level-headed appreciation of the new double market of public concerts and publication. He told Bland that he would send Salomon a new symphony (No. 92) only on the strict condition that it was not passed to any other entrepreneur or publisher; later he made an agreement with another London publisher, stipulating that if he took up residence in London he would be allowed to have quartets and symphonies performed at concerts prior to publication.[17]

The sources of Haydn's London symphonies illustrate eighteenth-century working practices vividly. The music itself went through various stages: Haydn continued to make alterations, both in response to the London performances and subsequently in Vienna. These changes are apparent in the various primary sources, which stand in complex relation to each other. The autograph scores (most of which Haydn took back with him to Vienna) and authorised copies by Johann Elssler have obvious pride of place. But many orchestral parts with corrections by Haydn also survive, while another important line of transmission derives directly from Salomon, who had his own scores copied before Haydn's departure.[18] Corrections in these scores presumably reflect performance alterations enshrined in his own set of parts (now regrettably lost). These versions therefore have some claim even over the autographs. Closely related, probably because derived from Salomon's orchestral parts, is the first complete English edition published by Robert Birchall around 1810. It differs markedly from the editions already published on the continent by André, Artaria and others. Though scarcely fundamental, a number of striking changes in scoring were made. Some are represented in the Salomon line only, and if authorised by Haydn they never found their way into the autograph: a new bassoon line in the first movement of Symphony No. 97, three bars of wind parts mistakenly omitted in the finale. On the other hand, revisions made by Haydn after he left London were never transmitted to Salomon. The portentous unison that opens Symphony No. 102 was originally scored for hollow strings, brass and timpani only: only later did Haydn add mellowing woodwind parts to the autograph.

Another factor in concert promotion was the provision of keyboard instruments, since a continuo instrument was always required in London (generally a harpsichord until 1791, subsequently a piano). For the young Mozarts' double concerto in 1764 Leopold Mozart had to pay 1 guinea to hire two harpsichords. In the 1790s Dussek himself hired pianos directly from Broadwood for his concerto performances; he is also remembered as the first pianist to show off his profile by placing the piano sideways, though whether this first occurred in London is not recorded. In some venues an organ was a fixture. The Vauxhall bandstand had a 'melodious toned finger organ' with eight stops, according to a sale catalogue of 1818. But for oratorios at the theatres a portable organ had to be installed on stage. The Lock Hospital paid Drury Lane 10 guineas for the use of the organ at its 1758 benefit; similarly in 1786 the Academy of Ancient Music agreed to pay 20 guineas a season for the new Freemasons' Hall organ and also to maintain it. Some promoters evidently had to make their own arrangements. Carl Stamitz hired an organ from Benjamin Flight for his Freemasons' Hall benefit in 1780; but he seems to have departed the country without paying for the hall, as the unfortunate Flight had to pay a ransom to get the organ back. In 1769 Smith and Stanley themselves bought a new Byfield and Green organ for Drury Lane: it boasted seven stops and a four-stop swell on the single manual.[19]

The keyboard instruments used at oratorio performances have been a source of debate. At performances of *Alexander's Feast* in 1736 Handel evidently sat at the harpsichord, with an assistant playing the organ. Three years later he introduced some new kind of organ, which seems to have enabled him to play both harpsichord and organ in oratorio performances.[20] Whether this innovation persisted is uncertain. At the Foundling Hospital Handel must have directed from the harpsichord, while Smith sat at the chapel's large fixed organ: at the performance shortly after Handel's death Smith took over the direction and Samuel Howard played the organ. At some stage, however, the organist became the dominant figure in choral performances, taking on the title of 'conductor'. This process was aided by another development with an equally obscure history. At Westminster Abbey in 1784, a contraption was installed enabling Bates to sit 19 feet away from the organ and some 20 feet below it. Edgcumbe noted in his *Musical Reminiscences* that this was the first usage of the so-called 'long movement', but Burney recalled a less ambitious version from Handel's day. In imitation, both ancient societies now adopted the device, with the organist-director also playing the harpsichord (Doane refers to the Academy's conductor sitting 'at the keys of the Organ and Harpsichord'). A cheaper alternative was the 'organized pianoforte' (both instruments in one case), the instrument used by Michael Arne at the Haymarket oratorios in 1784.[21]

Direction and continuo

The terms director and conductor need to be treated with some caution, since during this period either can refer to the musical manager or even to the financial promoter. Direction could also loosely mean overseeing or rehearsing: Haydn's Op. 64 quartets were published in London as 'Performed under his Direction, at Mr. Salomon's Concert'. The present section, however, is concerned with musical direction in performance.

Traditional systems of direction persisted in London during this period, though there were also signs of change. The functions of conductor were still shared according to context between leader (or 'first violin') and keyboard continuo-player. Orchestral works and solo arias were universally led from the violin. Other types of vocal music were directed from the keyboard: secco recitative by the harpsichordist, choruses by the organist. In the latter case the main role was the doubling of the choral parts, but at the Commemoration Bates also 'conducted by the motion of his head or his holding up a hand'.[22] In some circumstances the organist took the harpsichord part himself. Bates is known to have played the organ during choruses and at moments of special colour, but to have changed to the harpsichord elsewhere. This may have been Handel's own practice in his theatre oratorio performances.

Two variants on this pattern threatened the supremacy of the violinist-leader. England had long shared with Europe some tradition of time-beating for vocal performances. Stevens recalled that a parchment roll was used at the Madrigal Society in the 1770s, but the system was particularly associated with massed forces. Greene and Boyce wielded a roll of parchment at the Sons of the Clergy services, and the practice persisted here well into the nineteenth century. At a performance of his *Carmen Seculare* in 1782, Philidor followed French practice in beating time ('with great anxiety').[23] Similarly the New Musical Fund benefit in 1787 was performed 'under the direction of Dr. Hayes and Dr. Miller, who, with a large roll of parchment, beat time most unmercifully... Cramer led the band'.[24] Yet there was a widespread aversion to this system, with audiences finding it distracting and musicians regarding it as either ineffective or an affront to their professional pride. Indeed Handel's new instrument, whatever it was, specifically allowed him 'a better command of his performers', as he could sit at the keyboard throughout rather than beat time. At one of the Handel Festival performances Cramer is said publicly to have rebuked the parchment-wielding Hayes: 'Be so kind to tell the gentleman that when he has sat down I will begin.'[25] Burney commented that the 1784 Commemoration succeeded admirably with no need of a *manu-ductor* 'either with a roll of paper, or a noisy *baton*, or truncheon' (a clear dig at French practice). In a lecture given in 1827, Samuel Wesley described this form of conducting as old-fashioned, saying that it was 'totally discontinued at Oratorios'. He continued:

I confess that I never could perceive the Utility (much less the Necessity) of any third Person to keep an Orchestra singing & playing in just Time. The immediate and indispensable Province of the Leader, is to start the Band instantaneously together, upon all Occasions and in every Movement throughout the Performance. The Conductor at the Organ must be perfectly unanimous with him, more especially in the Choruses, where the Organ ought always to form a prominent Feature, and upon the Assistance of which the Voices very naturally and very rationally rely.[26]

A modern style of baton-conducting was introduced by the violinist Spohr at a rehearsal in 1820, but London retained a resistance to it for many years after that.

A more immediate development took place in the role played by the keyboard-player. Unobtrusive keyboard accompaniment continued throughout the period, even as Baroque figured bass became less and less relevant to the new music. While the continuo was clearly dropped from the more modern genres such as the string quartet, keyboard accompaniment was still needed for instrumental solos into the 1780s and in public performance of glees. The harpsichord was kept alive by ancient music and the King's preference; elsewhere it was replaced by the piano, as when in 1792 Haydn accompanied Mara 'all by myself at the pianoforte' in Purcell's 'From rosy bow'rs'. Certainly all orchestral and choral music in London continued to be performed with keyboard participation of some kind well past 1800. Indeed in the last decade of the century the keyboard-player received significantly more prominence. Haydn's arrival may have been partly responsible, together with the higher profile of ancient music. Before 1791, a keyboard player was scarcely ever advertised except in connection with solo performance. When benefits were given 'under the Direction of Mess. Bach and Abel', this was primarily a question of organisation. The Professional rosters up to 1790 unobtrusively include a harpsichordist, but the leader Cramer is always highlighted at the top. But when Haydn arrived in 1791 his name was prominently displayed in advertisements: 'Mr. HAYDN will be at the Harpsichord. Leader of the Band, Mr. SALOMON.' This was more than astute marketing. One anecdote suggests that Haydn himself rehearsed the opening of Symphony No. 92 until he was satisfied with the style of execution; during concerts he probably indicated the tempo before the start of each movement.[27] From 1792 he preferred to sit instead at a piano (on which he must have played the delightful 'cembalo solo' in Symphony No. 98), and the Professionals also abandoned the harpsichord in the same year.

Elsewhere too the keyboard-player acquired a new prominence. Not only do the Ancient Concerts and related benefits begin to list the keyboard conductor, usually Arnold or Greatorex, above the leader (this is hardly surprising in view of the organist's traditional role in oratorios); but a similar practice also obtained at many modern concerts after 1795, with Clementi often filling Haydn's shoes by 'presiding' at the piano. Clearly this was a move in the direction of the non-playing director (the pianist's duty was more to follow the full score than to contribute chords). Parke confirmed this change, recollecting that 'latterly the fashion crept in of having a leader and a conductor also'.[28] The dual system persisted well into the nineteenth century, to the disbelief of foreign visitors. Parke was himself aware of the potential conflict between the two roles, and it may be that the leader relinquished prestige in order to retain the real musical reins. Yet even if the violinist Spohr was the first baton-conductor in London, the concept of conductor there really originated with the keyboard-player. In his 1827 lecture Wesley noted the recent trend for organists to wave their arms or even to clap during choruses, rather than double the choral parts on the organ. This was the very route taken by the first celebrated English conductor, Sir George Smart: by 1834 he had adopted the baton, but he still kept his seat at the keyboard.[29]

Rehearsals and standard of performance

It is sometimes held that all eighteenth-century concerts were under-rehearsed and scrappily performed. The evidence from London in the second half of the century is very mixed in this regard, probably reflecting extremely variable standards of discipline and accuracy. Certainly the amount of rehearsal varied considerably. A club for performing gentlemen like the Castle Society would scarcely demand rehearsals: the programme was notified in advance but members were forbidden to take the parts home on pain of a heavy fine. But even a professional charity concert in 1795 could be put on without any rehearsal, a circumstance which led Haydn to withdraw his participation. The Academy of Ancient Music was also censured in the 1780s for its lack of rehearsals (formerly it had held rehearsals and concerts in alternation): even its professional orchestra was roundly criticised until rehearsals were reintroduced in 1789.

But these haphazard arrangements were evidently not the norm. Two rehearsals were held for *Israel in Egypt* at the 1786 Tottenham Street series, and this was thought a small number.[30] The Professional Concert rehearsed carefully, even attempting in 1790 to rehearse on Sundays until this was banned. Probably a single rehearsal was the norm here, as at the Concert of Ancient Music which in Stevens's time rehearsed each Monday morning before the Wednesday evening performance. There is no reason why limited rehearsal for a skilled band, well used to playing together in familiar idioms, should not have been sufficient. Normally one rehearsal must have been included in the fee (this was Stevens's experience). Only when something exceptional was required was the question of an additional fee raised. Cooke at the Academy received a higher salary when rehearsals were reintroduced in 1789, and the same season Cramer at the Concert negotiated more pay for additional rehearsals 'which are to be most religiously performed'.[31] Perhaps Mrs Billington's refusal to sing there in 1788 'on account of the hard duty of attending rehearsals' was a result of a breakdown of similar negotiations.[32]

Rehearsals could take many different forms. Mrs Papendiek recalled Abel informally going down to Bach's Richmond house each Wednesday to try out new pieces for the Queen's Chamber Band. During the 1740s Handel rehearsed his oratorios either at home or at the Prince of Wales's; Burney recalled that Handel was 'a blunt and peremptory disciplinarian', delivering his criticisms with a wit 'that was peculiar to himself, and extremely diverting to all but those on whom his lash was laid'. In another context Burney observed wrily that 'few composers are well treated by an orchestra, till they have used the performers roughly, and made themselves formidable'.[33] The private concert could in itself function as a kind of rehearsal, at which items could be tried out prior to public performance. Conversely, some rehearsals were open to the public. Thus court odes were often preceded by a so-called 'public rehearsal' at a tavern concert-room, itself prepared by the musicians' own practice; and rehearsals for the Handel Commemoration proved so popular that admittance was charged at half-price.

We can only guess at the nature of rehearsal often without benefit of a score and always without rehearsal-letters (Thomas Busby recognised the latter deficiency, far-sightedly suggesting the use of bar-numbers).[34] But we can indulge in some discussion of performance standards in comparative terms. Certainly London's orchestral standards rose during the period to rival the best in Europe, to judge from the opinions of German visitors. The initial impetus was given by the arrival in 1751 of Giardini, who, at the Opera in 1754, 'introduced new discipline, and a new style of playing, much superior in itself, and more congenial with the poetry and Music of Italy, than the languid manner of his predecessor Festing'.[35] Indeed Giardini acquired a reputation as a musical autocrat, banishing extraneous ornament and enforcing uniform bowing in clichéd analogy with the Prussian army. How he achieved this is less clear: contemporary orchestral parts lack any of the consistency of phrasing that would seem essential to modern standards.

When Burney visited Mannheim in 1772 he famously described the orchestra as 'an army of generals', a comment suggesting that such standards could not be matched in London. But in the next decade the Professionals, led by the Mannheim violinist Cramer, made a concerted effort at orchestral excellence. By 1790 they were 'the best disciplined band of which Europe can boast', according to one critic, while by contrast the Pantheon orchestra (deprived of any of the same players) required frequent rehearsal to achieve 'precision and firmness'. Even Salomon had problems with his new and disparate orchestra. The employment of Smart on the violin and viola after a few lessons from a double bass player is scarcely encouraging. But Salomon and Haydn together turned the orchestra into a virtuoso instrument, which could be exploited without compromise. In 1793 a correspondent reported to a German magazine: 'Salomon was always a good interpreter, but now one can say that he is superb. Perhaps, however, the presence of Haydn ... is in part responsible.'[36] In 1795 the Opera Concert united the achievements of the two orchestras, after initial difficulties caused by the increase in size had been overcome.

Standards elsewhere cannot have approached these levels. The King's Band was London's one stable orchestra, but its constitution as an orchestra of placemen certainly caused problems. Foreigners were excluded by law, while tenure resulted in members continuing to play well beyond their prime; furthermore the historical preference for strings meant that wind-players often had to be imported. At the English venues, virtually untrained players could obtain minor posts, and standards at the playhouses were often a source of complaint (Haydn in 1791 found the Covent Garden orchestra 'sleepy' under Baumgarten's leadership). Lenten oratorio performances were on the whole adequate rather than exceptional. Reichardt was none too impressed by the Drury Lane oratorio singers in 1785, and he rated Richards's leadership merely tolerable; another observer eight years later sardonically described the oratorio singing as 'not overdelicate'.[37] Opinions on the summer orchestras at the gardens varied markedly; perhaps Haydn's assessment of Vauxhall in 1792 ('the music is fairly good') is candid enough. Some excellent players did take part at Vauxhall. But entertaining comments by the programme-compiler reveal extraordinary deficiencies in any comparison with the top orchestras: 'Mr. Shaw afraid to lead Pleyel' (Stamitz was substituted); 'It is realy astonishing Mr. Mountain fail'd in Corelli & in his own Concertos he is a finish'd performer.' Some of the singers were frankly disastrous. Mrs Leaver drifted so sharp that the band ended a tone higher than they began, while Duffey was 'very imperfect, can't read – music'.[38] As for amateur gentlemens' concerts, Burney's pithy comment will suffice: 'The performers were sometimes in and sometimes out.'[39]

How well did the foremost virtuosi really play and sing? Some comments cited in chapter 8 might indicate that performance did not always match the brilliance suggested by the repertoire. But London's favourite singers – Elizabeth Linley, Mrs Billington, Madame Mara and Pacchierotti – were universally acclaimed for their technical agility and their tonal control. Some comments are quite specific. Stevens noted that Mara's voice filled the vast spaces of Westminster Abbey with ease; and he praised the Linley sisters: 'I never heard them sing in the smallest degree out of tune, even when performing without accompaniment.'[40] (In this they contrasted with Marchesi, who was widely accused of erratic intonation.) Still more importantly their singing had a profound impact on audiences. A detailed description of Mara's performance of 'I know that my Redeemer liveth' reveals a conscious emotional plan:

She opened it with great solemnity; hope was discernible; but it was only the dawn of hope, – as she proceeded, it brightened and expanded; but when she came to the last repetition of the sentence, the firm and animated confidence with which she uttered the words, 'I know,' and the jubilation of soul with which she pronounced the words, 'And in my heart I shall see God,' no language can adequately tell. The audience thought not of the air, or of the band, or even of the singer; they only felt the sentiment, and they felt it in all its sublimity.[41]

Instrumental playing was less often described, except in general terms of execution and tone. But it seems unlikely that Haydn would have taxed Salomon's quartet as he did without the highest expectations; and the London symphonies demand hitherto unattempted orchestral virtuosity. More specifically the oboist Fischer was celebrated for his control in swelling an astonishingly long note from pianissimo to forte and back again. Clementi was praised in 1784 for his unrivalled performance of passages in octaves and sixths, by a generally unsympathetic critic; while Pieltain on the violin was said to play double-stops 'perfectly in tune', indicating not only that this could be done, but also that others were deficient.[42] A final quotation makes an interesting comparison between two violinists, separating the merely good performance by Borghi from a spellbinding one by Cramer: 'Their Stile was different. That of the first was deep and nervous; whilst, from the second, the Ear listened to Notes *apparently* separated from the Instrument, and floating, amidst all the Brilliancy and highly tempered Modulation of Sound, in Air.'[43] Perhaps it would be fair to conclude that, surrounded by mediocrity or worse, just a few outstanding artists were heard whose qualities would be recognised in any age.

Epilogue

There are many factors to consider in any evaluation of a musical culture: the extent and range of its activities, its weight within the intellectual environment, the breadth of its social appeal, its role in the development of musical institutions, its artistic discrimination, the quality of the repertoire it inspires. Viewed from many of these perspectives London's concert life in the second half of the eighteenth century must be judged a striking success. In other regards, however, it is undoubtedly open to criticism, of the kind that was proffered at the time, although we should always beware of the biasses brought by the more aggressive critics.

Viewing London's early concert life from a historical perspective, one is immediately impressed by the prodigious growth of musical activity, which escalated dramatically during the second half of the eighteenth century. As striking as the diversity of London's musical life is the vitality of enterprise shown by musicians and impresarios alike. The rise of commercial concerts for a ticket-buying public reveals marked if sometimes superficial similarities with later patterns of concert management. While modern concert life ultimately stemmed from fashionable entertainments for West End society, concert symphonies and high-quality soloists did filter outside these élite venues to be heard by audiences of a much wider social spectrum. But the most significant feature of all in the long term was the establishment of concerts alongside opera within the social and cultural life of the capital. Two elements in particular contributed to this development. The first was the rise of the orchestral concert, based around semi-permanent orchestras such as the Professionals and around important new symphonic music. The second was the recognition of the notion of a canon of central masterworks. As yet, however, the two concepts scarcely overlapped, as they would in the next century. A core symphonic repertoire had only just begun to be established by the turn of the century, as orchestral music remained trapped in the ephemeral novelty-culture. The heritage of masterworks so far consisted largely of Baroque vocal music.

A direct consequence of these changes was a quickening of the trend towards a passive culture, which essentially excluded amateur participation except for ladies' drawing-room music. Partly this was a reflection of ever-rising professional standards, partly a result of the increasing technical demands of modern music (compare the symphony with the concerto grosso, the string quartet with the trio sonata). But above all it was a response to social pressures: as one writer inquired in 1788, 'what glory is it to a gentleman, even were he a fine performer, that he can strike a string, touch a key or sing a song, with the grace and command of an *hired* musician?'[1] Yet this need not be viewed entirely as a sorry tale of decline. The demise of universal participation (if such ever existed) need not necessarily lead to cultural frivolity, as has sometimes been argued.[2] It is more important to assess the extent to which audiences developed a discerning critical response and encouraged artistic growth.

A central issue here must be the effect of London's musical commercialism on the artistic environment. Evidently it did contribute directly to the vitality of London's concert life, but whether it led to fruitful creativity remains a more open question. Did London's artistic successes come as a result of the commercial background or in spite of it? Londoners at the time generally assumed that wealth could attract the best in the world and thus assured artistic achievement; while competition between promoters was always expected to encourage excellence. Furthermore, some measure of artistic influence was exerted at the upper levels of London's concert life by cultivated amateurs such as the Prince of Wales. At its best the system brought about a healthy alliance between musicians and discerning taste-leaders, who together guided the broader musical public. Viewed historically such an arrangement perhaps represents an ideal mid-point between despotic aristocratic control and the unfettered ravages of dubious public taste. Indeed the influence of an enlightened public was regarded by some as an unalloyed asset. Charles Burney thought C. P. E. Bach's compositional style would actually have benefited had he been forced to refine it for a London audience. More naively, John Marsh expounded the duty of composers to satisfy all three constituencies: 'Perhaps the proper test of excellence in this art should not be, that it affords pleasure to professors and connoisseurs only, but to the greatest number of *amateurs* indiscriminately taken.'[3] In this light, Parke's description of the crude system at Vauxhall whereby singers were re-engaged according to the number of encores is interesting. He does not regard it as intrinsically unjust, merely open to corruption from inferior performers; in general he assumed that the audience would have the discrimination to make fair artistic decisions.[4]

Yet this rosy and rather complacent view cannot represent the entire picture. There was no time during the period when the imperfect taste of the public was not under attack from some quarter: one could be forgiven for imagining that London's musical taste was in perpetual decline. Such comments are usually allied to accusations of vulgarisation associated with a broadening public. Thus middle-class audiences at the gardens were routinely castigated for their preference for sentimental songs, for their enjoyment of folk-melodies in concertos, for their delight in shallow displays of virtuosity. Nor were audiences at subscription concerts immune from criticism. Even here there was insufficient guidance from well-educated amateurs, according to John Gregory: 'The real effects produced by [music] are inconsiderable. This is entirely owing to its being in the hands of practical Musicians, and not under the direction of Taste and Philosophy ... No Science ever flourished, while it was confined to a set of Men who lived by it as a profession.'[5] Musicians were often accused of lowering their artistic aspirations to pander to the broad market. John Marsh admitted that J. C. Bach suited the different movements of a symphony to various segments of the audience, directing the finales towards those of least refined taste. Hawkins characteristically went further, in suggesting that Bach's 'coarse and artless' music represented only his public face: 'Like most of that profession who are to live by the favor of the public, both he and *Abel* had two styles of composition, the one for their own private delight, the other for the gratification of many.'[6] Indeed Bach's melodious and urbane craft, though more sophisticated than Hawkins allowed, seldom embraced deeper expressive or intellectual qualities. Lesser composers were all too content with more vapid versions of the same idiom: later gardens' songs, for example, too often lapse into maudlin sentimentality or empty show by contrast with the intimate textual response of cantatas from the middle of the century.

While the less knowledgeable middle-class audiences were especially open to accusations of poor taste, the public arena in itself undoubtedly contributed to a loss of refinement in musical language. To some extent this resulted purely from the demands of the larger concert-hall setting; but it also answered the need to please audiences of varying levels of musical sophistication, whatever their social background. Furthermore, the constant demand for new music inevitably encouraged haste at the expense of quality: 'Owing to the insatiable appetite of the multitude, composers of the first abilities are frequently obliged to rain down torrents of indigested compositions, which have nothing but novelty to recommend them.'[7] Clearly commercialism was to some degree a guilty party.

Rarely did musicians themselves openly bemoan their enslavement to public preference, and as a consequence professional taste and public taste seem rather suspiciously concordant. London's attitude towards Mozart provides a revealing exception. During the 1780s Mozart's music was promoted by several pianists, including his pupil Attwood and J. B. Cramer. But the predominance of private over public performances suggests that none of them was able to convert London's taste-leaders. London's two dominant composers of the period were much more successful in tailoring their product to audiences of diverse musical experience. Indeed both were extraordinarily successful in matching John Marsh's demand that music should appeal equally to the connoisseur, the professional and the average music-lover; and perhaps their achievement vindicates the notion of public taste guided by discerning amateurs. Even Hawkins recognised that Handel's success derived from his writing 'to two sorts of persons, the judicious and the vulgar', and he proceeded to identify airs that fell into each category.[8] The reception of Haydn's music in the early 1780s illustrates the system at its best: introduced to London's top concerts by connoisseurs like Abingdon, his symphonies quickly spread throughout London's concert structure. Haydn achieved an especially remarkable fusion of simplicity, grandeur and learning, since the flexibility of the Classical style could admit this mix even within a single movement. On his arrival in London, Haydn was able to develop this fusion to the most subtle ends. His use of artless melody and vivid effect for the most complex symphonic discourse brought sophisticated orchestral music a genuine popularity at all concert levels, accomplished without undue artistic compromise. It was a significant and rare success in the moulding of general public taste to a higher level of musical appreciation.

Superimposed on the debate about the decline of taste was the question of the relative worth of ancient (Renaissance and Baroque) music over modern music. The divide between ancient and modern appears to open up a chasm between serious and trivial musical cultures. Certainly this division was something that the Concert of Ancient Music wished to promulgate: the society's very existence was a manifesto for a reverential attitude towards art-music of lasting values, in explicit opposition to transient modernity. Opponents of modern music from Charles Avison to William Jackson mocked short-lived dependence on orchestral effect and enticing melody. Their most articulate ally was John Hawkins, who contrasted the two styles with scathing directness:

We hear no more of the solemn and pathetic Adagio, the artful and well-studied Fugue, or the sweet modulations of the keys with the minor third: all is *Allegro* and *Prestissimo*, and if not discord, such harmony as the ear sickens of hearing ... For reasons, which no one is willing to avow, Adagio-Music is exploded, and we are content to forego the Majesty and Dignity of the *Largo* and *Andante* movements, with all the variety arising from the interchange of different airs and measures, for the noise and rattle of the unisonus *Allegro*, to which no name can be given, or the intoxicating softness of that too oft iterated air, the *Minuet*.[9]

In truth one might sympathise with Hawkins's diatribes against the thin harmony and dull bass-lines of the music of the 1760s and 1770s. But the alliance of ancient music with serious art and modern music with superficiality was in part a propaganda ploy in the struggle for the artistic conscience of the nation. In reality, public concerts from Hanover Square to Vauxhall unselfconsciously mixed music from the light and unpretentious to the elaborate and demanding. Certain branches of ancient music simply remained in popular repertory, conforming to universal taste rather than consciously perpetuating artistic values. Even more to the point, the lightness of tone of modern orchestral music disguised genuine artistic aspirations, aspirations by no means inconsistent with the inbuilt ephemerality of the repertoire.

Thus to a large extent ancient and modern styles co-existed in the various public forums in the guise of entertainment. A hard-and-fast distinction could not yet be drawn between serious 'classical' concerts of older music and trivial modern programmes. Certainly broad-minded connoisseurs accepted both old and new as worthy of critical attention, and they resisted the attempts of extremists in the ancient camp to encourage the division. As Charles Burney agonised in connection with his account of the Handel Commemoration:

I will not deny my liberal principles – I will not abuse the lovers of the best Music of Italy & Germany, & say that they are only admired *through fashion*, & want of good taste & judgment ... [I] cannot, will not say that there is no other Music fit to be heard, or as well performed [as that of Handel].[10]

The recipient of this letter, Thomas Twining, had himself reacted angrily to the exclusion of modern music from the programmes of the Ancient Concerts, regarding it as an absurd act of retaliation.[11]

As it turned out, ancient music came into public fashion just as London's modern music was moving into a new phase, and something of a rapprochement occurred in the last two decades of the century. Changes in modern musical style resulted in a certain confluence of taste, as the deeper musical qualities of Haydn's symphonies began to be increasingly recognised. In 1796 John Marsh explicitly warned that, like Handel choruses, they required several hearings for a full appreciation of their qualities; in the same period, Richard Eastcott carefully distinguished the high standard of London's instrumental music from the decline he perceived in bravura songs.[12] Even soloists adopted a more ambitious musical agenda, and London's piano repertoire includes some of the most important music of the time. It is significant that a violin concerto could be reviewed in terms of a synthesis of idioms: 'Viotti played a concerto in a minor key, the composition and performance of which were alike masterly. In style it was neither perfectly ancient or modern, though it partook of the beauties of both.'[13] Burney also thought that Viotti's music recalled something of the solidity and pathos of the late Baroque.[14] It is no coincidence that the music of the 1780s and 1790s was the first in post-Baroque idiom to achieve any classical status in the early nineteenth century.

Meanwhile, the new music began at last to attract serious critical inquiry. Previously only the ancient cause had developed a coherent stance based on an understanding of the 'science' of music. The lack of an intellectual basis to modern music was undoubtedly an impediment to its general acceptance by men of letters: while the music of Handel was investigated in detail, no major studies were addressed to the works of J. C. Bach and Abel. This situation partly mirrored a prejudice against modern music amongst many British writers; but it also reflected a lack of appropriate aesthetic and analytical methodologies. Even Burney, fully in sympathy with modern music, seldom addresses the aesthetic issues it raised. His most revealing comments are side-swipes at traditionalists like Avison, as in his exasperated defence of Stamitz's symphonies:

It has long seemed to me as if the variety, taste, spirit, and new effects produced by contrast and the use of *crescendo* and *diminuendo* in these symphonies, had been of more service to instrumental Music in a few years, than all the dull and servile imitations of Corelli, Geminiani, and Handel, had been in half a century.[15]

Around the turn of the century modern music was at last adopted into the theoretical mainstream. Early in the 1800s William Crotch attempted to reconcile Haydn's symphonies with current aesthetic theory by his adoption of the category of the picturesque. Meanwhile, A. F. C. Kollmann in his *Essay on Practical Musical Composition* (1799) showed how the study of modern periodic structures and larger forms could lead out of the traditional disciplines of counterpoint and figured bass.

Viewing London's concert repertoire in this period as a whole, there remains a nagging doubt as to whether the brilliance and vitality of London's public concert life disguise a more fundamental lack of creativity. Concern was expressed at the time about the encouragement of performance at the expense of composition, with worries that neither foreign nor British composers in London measured up to the standard of the executants there.[16] Nor was the revival of ancient music received with universal approval, since it was already perceived as the first step towards a museum culture, to borrow the modern phrase: the effect of Lully-veneration on French music earlier in the century did not go unnoticed. In 1784, even before the Commemoration, Stanley had bemoaned the uselessness of trying to compete with the oratorios of Handel.[17] Furthermore, one can argue that London was a cultural magpie, merely reflecting European trends by importing and imitating the Italian opera, the Italian and German symphony, the French concerto and *symphonie concertante*. Even Haydn's London symphonies were in the last analysis something of an artistic accident, a bought-in Viennese culture that chanced to produce a set of enduring masterpieces. One strand in this concern was always the demise of British music: 'There is positively no Nation in Europe, where Music is so generally patronized and so little professed, as in our own.'[18] Indeed, only the older generation of Arne, Boyce and Stanley made a lasting contribution in the field of concert music, and some of their most enduring music dates from the 1740s. Younger British composers encountered indifference and discouragement: in 1762 John Potter referred to 'the cold reception' that any English music was bound to receive,[19] and influential patrons conspicuously neglected to redress the situation. Nor were British composers able to seize those few chances that came their way. A manuscript symphony by Storace, one of the most talented contenders, was dismissed at the Anacreontic Society as a 'wretched composition', in which 'almost every passage might evidently be traced to other authors'.[20] Clearly any concept of a national style had already been lost; by 1799 Kollmann regarded the Scots song as Britain's only distinctive musical idiom. Many factors contributed to this artistic stagnation and decline of opportunity, but undoubtedly high among them was public infatuation with Handel oratorios and Haydn symphonies, beside which all else seemed to pale in comparison.

But it would be parochial to view London's concert repertoire solely through a veil of laments about missed opportunity. London deserves credit for its artistic achievements when these are viewed in a wider international context. The continued appreciation of Handel and the new enthusiasm for older masters show a commendable discrimination in the face of fashion, and in this regard London led the way. As Burney wrote with understandable pride, 'there is, perhaps, no country in Europe, where the productions of old masters are more effectually preserved from oblivion, than in England'.[21] Some English repertoire from the 1750s and 1760s can stand comparison with almost any music by contemporary European composers. The orchestral music of Boyce is of particularly high quality, and Arne continued to write memorable vocal music; indeed, in *Judith* he produced an oratorio of real distinction. Furthermore, the liberal encouragement of foreign musicians was repaid by significant compositional achievements. If London nurtured no C. P. E. Bach, nevertheless the galant symphonies and concertantes of his half-brother J. C. Bach represent some of the best music of the comparatively thin 1760s and 1770s. Then during the next decade, well before his arrival in the capital, Haydn was acclaimed there with an enthusiasm unmatched even in Germany and Austria. Finally, towards the end of the century, London's public concert platform inspired a truly innovative creative surge in the music of several leading instrumentalists. In their sonatas and concertos, Clementi, Dussek and Viotti display an individuality and artistic integrity that set them above all but the greatest masters of their day.

Appendices

Concert venues – Abbreviations

A   Almack's Rooms, King Street (later W)
Cas   Casino, Great Marlborough Street
CG   Covent Garden Theatre
DL   Drury Lane Theatre
DSt   Great Room, Dean Street
FMH   Freemasons' Hall, Great Queen Street
H   Hickford's Room, Brewer Street
Hay   Little Theatre (New Theatre, Theatre Royal), Haymarket
HHo   Hatton House, Cross Street
HSq   Hanover Square Rooms
KT   King's Theatre, Haymarket (Italian Opera House)
KTR   King's Theatre Room
P   Pantheon, Oxford Street
Roy   Royalty Theatre, Well Street (now Ensign Street)
SSq   Carlisle House, Soho Square
TSt   Tottenham Street Rooms
W   Willis's Rooms, King Street (formerly A)

Appendix A
Subscription and oratorio series

Subscription series

Season	Promoter	Place	Number	Dates	Usual day	Notes and price of subscription
1749–50	Manfredini	H	5?	?–6 Mar.	Tue.	Individual tickets 5/-.
1750–1	Miss Robinson	H	10	28 Jan.–?	Mon.	2 gn. single, 3 gn. double; individual tickets 5/-.
1751–2	Ogle	DSt	20	14 Dec.–25 Apr.	Sat.	3 gn. single, 5 gn. double; individual tickets 10/6.
1752–3	Mrs Ogle?	DSt	12	20 Jan.–7 Apr.	Sat.	2 gn. single, 3 gn. double, 4 gn. treble; individual tickets 10/6.
1753–4	Giardini, Vincent	DSt	[12]	23 Jan.–24 Apr.	Tue.	1 gn.; individual tickets 10/6 or 5/-.
	Passerini, the two Plàs	DSt	6	15 Mar.–17 May	Thu.	Twelve concerts projected; 2 gn. single, 3 gn. double; individual tickets 5/-.
	Passerini	DSt	5	17 Jan.–14 Feb.	Thu.	
1754–5	Giardini, Sga Frasi	DSt	12	13 Jan.–[21 Apr.]	Mon.	3 gn. single, 5 gn. double.
1755–6	—	—	—	—		
1756–7	—	—	—	—		
1757–8	—	—	—	—		
1758–9	—	—	—	—		
1759–60	Miss Ford	Hay	5	18 Mar.–22 Apr.	Tue.	Individual tickets 10/6 and 5/-.
1760–1	—	—	—	—		
1761–2	Schuman	DSt	3	18 Feb.–5 May	—	1 gn. (one gentleman or two ladies); individual tickets 10/6 or 5/-.
1762–3	—	—	—	—		
1763–4	Mrs Cornelys (with Cocchi)	SSq	?	15 Feb.–8 May	Wed.	At least nine concerts.
1764–5	Mrs Cornelys (with Bach, Abel)	SSq	10	23 Jan.–27 Mar.	Wed.	5 gn.; possibly more concerts subsequently.
1765–6	Mrs Cornelys (with Bach, Abel)	SSq	15	8 Jan.–7 May	Wed.	
1766–7	Hay	H	?	9 Jan.–?	Fri.	
	Mrs Cornelys (with Bach, Abel)	SSq	15	14 Jan.–13 May	Wed.	
1767–8	Bach, Abel	A	15	13 Jan.–4 May	Wed.	3 gn. (ladies), 5 gn. (gentlemen).
	Hay	H	?	?–?	Fri.	See P.A 9 and 29 Jan.
1768–9	Bach, Abel	A	15	11 Jan.–17 May	Wed.	As previous season.
	Hay	H	?	16 Jan.–?	Mon.	
1769–70	Bach, Abel	A	15	17 Jan.–16 May	Wed.	
	Hay	H	?	22 Jan.–9 Apr.	Mon.	
	Giardini, Vento	[SSq]	?	29 Jan.–?	Mon.	
1770–1	Bach, Abel	A	15	9 Jan.–8 May	Wed.	Operatic 'Harmonical Meetings', then four concerts (14 Mar.–16 Apr.)
	Mrs Cornelys	SSq	?	24 Jan.–?	Thu.	

Season	Promoter	Venue	No.	Dates	Day	Remarks
	Giardini, Vento	[SSq]	?	28 Jan.–?	Mon.	10/6 (one gentleman or two ladies); individual tickets 5/-.
	Bromley	H	3	28 Mar.–19 Apr.	—	
1771–2	Bach, Abel	A	15	22 Jan.–20 May	Wed.	
1772–3	Bach, Abel	A	15	13 Jan.–12 May	Wed.	
1773–4	Bach, Abel	SSq	15	12 Jan.–4 May	Wed.	
1774–5	Pantheon	P	12	24 Jan.–25 Apr.	Mon.	6 gn. for twelve tickets.
	Pantheon	P	13	12 Dec.–4 May	Mon.	Individual tickets (not less than two); additional concert on 23 May.
1775–6	Bach, Abel	HSq	15	1 Feb.–24 May	Wed.	
	Bach, Abel	HSq	15	17 Jan.–8 May	Wed.	Individual tickets (not less than two).
	Pantheon	P	12	29 Jan.–13 May	Mon.	
1776–7	Barthelemon, Mrs Stuart	Cas	12	2 Feb.–26 Apr.	Fri.	4 gn.
	Pantheon	P	14	18 Nov.–28 Apr.	Mon.	Individual tickets 10/6 (not less than two); additional concert on 13 May.
1777–8	Bach, Abel	HSq	15	22 Jan.–14 May	Wed.	Ten concerts projected; 5 gn.; only three concerts advertised.
	Mrs Stuart	TSt	10?	20 Feb.–?	Thu.	
	Pantheon	P	16	24 Nov.–3 June	Mon.	Individual tickets 10/6 (not less than two).
	Bach, Abel	HSq	15	21 Jan.–13 May	Wed.	
	Rauzzini, Lamotte	HSq	5	27 Mar.–1 May	Fri.	2 gn.
	Casino	Cas	4	4 June–?	—	2 gn.
1778–9	Pantheon	P	12	25 Jan.–26 Apr.	Mon.	Individual tickets 10/6 (not less than two).
	Bach, Abel	HSq	15	27 Jan.–18 May	Wed.	
	Rauzzini, Lamotte	HSq	8	19 Mar.–14 May	Fri.	
1779–80	Bach, Abel	HSq	15	19 Jan.–10 May	Wed.	3 gn.
	Pantheon	P	8	24 Jan.–13 Mar.	Mon.	5 gn.
1780–1	Pantheon	P	10	29 Jan.–2 Apr.	Wed.	Individual tickets 10/6.
	Bach, Abel	HSq	12	31 Jan.–9 May	Wed.	Individual tickets 10/6.
	Rauzzini	HSq	4?	30 Mar.–27 Apr.	Fri.	5 gn.
1781–2	Pantheon	P	8	4 Feb.–8 Apr.	Mon.	Five concerts projected; 2 gn.; fifth concert postponed, perhaps indefinitely. Ten concerts projected; 3½ gn.; individual tickets 10/6.
1782–3	Abel	HSq	12	6 Feb.–8 May	Wed.	5 gn.
	Earl of Abingdon	HSq	12	19 Feb.–21 May	Wed.	6 gn.
	Baron Kaas	FMH	1	10 Mar.	Mon.	Nine projected; 3 gn.; individual tickets 10/6; only one took place.

Subscription series (*cont.*)

Season	Promoter	Place	Number	Dates	Usual day	Notes and price of subscription
1783–4	Earl of Abingdon	HSq	12	11 Feb.–19 May	Wed.	6 gn.
	Miss Guest	TSt	5	23 Mar.–24 May	—	2 gn.
	Pantheon	P	6	29 Mar.–11 June	Thu.	Individual tickets 10/6.
1784–5	Pantheon	P	12	27 Jan.–5 May	Thu.	4 gn.; individual tickets 10/6; additional concert on 12 May (benefit for Mme Mara).
1785–6	Professional Concert	HSq	12	2 Feb.–11 May	Wed.	5 gn.
	Professional Concert	HSq	12	6 Feb.–8 May	Mon.	
1786–7	Salomon	HSq	4	2 Mar.–23 Mar.	Thu.	2 gn.
	Professional Concert	HSq	12	5 Feb.–7 May	Mon.	
	Mme Mara	HSq, W	6	8 Feb.–24 May	Thu.	3 gn.; three concerts at each venue.
1787–8	Professional Concert	HSq	12	11 Feb.–5 May	Mon.	5 gn.
	Mme Mara, Pantheon	P	10	21 Feb.–5 June	Thu.	Twelve concerts projected; 5 gn.; individual tickets 10/6.
1788–9	Professional Concert	HSq	12	2 Feb.–4 May	Mon.	5 gn.
1789–90	Pantheon	P	12	28 Jan.–29 Apr.	Thu.	5 gn.; individual tickets 10/6; additional concert on 6 May.
1790–1	Professional Concert	HSq	12	15 Feb.–17 May	Mon.	5 gn.
	Professional Concert	HSq	12	7 Feb.–2 May	Mon.	5 gn.
	Salomon	HSq	12	11 Mar.–3 June	Fri.	5 gn.
1791–2	Harrison, Knyvett – Vocal Concert	W	12	11 Feb.–4 May	—	Eight concerts on Sat. for 3 gn.; four additional concerts on Fri. for 1½ gn.
	Professional Concert	HSq	12	13 Feb.–7 May	Mon.	5 gn.
	Salomon	HSq	12	17 Feb.–18 May	Fri.	5 gn.; additional concert on 6 June.
1792–3	Harrison, Knyvett – Vocal Concert	W	10	7 Feb.–25 Apr.	Thu.	4 gn.
	Salomon	HSq	12	7 Feb.–2 May	Thu.	5 gn.; additional concert on 27 May.
1793–4	Professional Concert	HSq	12	18 Feb.–13 May	Mon.	5 gn.
	Salomon	HSq	12	10 Feb.–12 May	Mon.	5 gn.
	Harrison, Knyvett – Vocal Concert	W	10	13 Feb.–1 May	Thu.	4 gn.
1794–5	King's Theatre – Opera Concert	KTR	9	2 Feb.–18 May	Mon.	4 gn.; additional concerts on 21 May and 1 June.

	Harrison, Knyvett – Vocal Concert	W	10	5 Feb.–23 Apr.	Thu.	4 gn.
1795–6	King's Theatre – Opera Concert	KTR	10	1 Feb.–30 May	Mon.	4 gn.
	Salomon	HSq	12	18 Feb.–12 May	Thu.	5 gn.
1796–7	King's Theatre – Opera Concert	KTR	12	6 Feb.–5 June	Mon.	5 gn.
1797–8	King's Theatre – Opera Concert	KTR	12	5 Feb.–11 June	Mon.	
1798–9	W. Cramer – Professional Concert	W	6	14 Mar.–6 May	Mon.	3 gn.
1799–1800	Willis brothers?	W	11	14 Feb.–16 May	Fri.	Twelve projected; 5 gn.; twelfth not advertised. Managed by Raimondi.

Notes

1 Principal sources: *GA*/*PA* (to 1780), other newspapers thereafter. For further details and programmes for the period 1783–95 see McVeigh, 'The Professional Concert', and Landon, *Haydn in London*.

2 Subscription series were generally held in the latter part of the season, which lasted at the outside from September to June. Thus, for example, Giardini's concerts in the 1752–3 season took place between January and April 1753.

3 Only the standard ticket-prices are given; sometimes reduced subscriptions were offered later in the season, as well as tickets for subscribers' friends and so on.

4 The distinction between the subscription series and the society or private series is not always clear. For the purpose of this list, organisations which did not advertise extensively (such as the two ancient societies or the Wesley concerts) have been excluded, as have the Castle Society and other gentlemen's clubs.

Oratorio series

Year	Promoter	Place	Number	Dates	Usual days	Price Box	Pit	Galleries	Notes
1750	Handel	CG	12	2 Mar.–12 Apr.	Wed., Fri.	10/6	10/6	5/- 3/6	The performance on 20 Mar. was probably cancelled.
1751	Handel	CG	7	22 Feb.–15 Mar.	Wed., Fri.	10/6	10/6	5/- 3/6	
1752	Handel	CG	13	14 Feb.–26 Mar.	Wed., Fri.	10/6	10/6	5/- 3/6	
1753	Handel	CG	11	9 Mar.–13 Apr.	Wed., Fri.	10/6	10/6	5/- 3/6	
1754	Handel	CG	11	1 Mar.–5 Apr.	Wed., Fri.	10/6	10/6	5/- 3/6	
1755	Handel	CG	11	14 Feb.–21 Mar.	Wed., Fri.	10/6	10/6	5/- 3/6	
	Arne	DL	4	12 Mar.–21 Mar.	Wed., Fri.	10/6	5/-	3/- 2/-	Subscription terms for first three nights. Music mainly by Arne.
1756	Handel	CG	11	5 Mar.–9 Apr.	Wed., Fri.	10/6	10/6	5/- 3/6	
	Barbandt	Hay	3	18 Mar.–1 Apr.	Thu.	10/6	10/6	3/- 3/-	Subscription 1 gn. Music mainly by Barbandt.
1757	Handel	CG	11	25 Feb.–1 Apr.	Wed., Fri.	10/6	10/6	5/- 3/6	
1758	Handel	CG	10	10 Feb.–17 Mar.	Wed., Fri.	10/6	10/6	5/- 3/6	
1759	Handel	CG	11	2 Mar.–6 Apr.	Wed., Fri.	10/6	10/6	5/- 3/6	
1760	Passerini	DSt	6	18 Jan.–10 Apr.	—	10/6	5/-	—	Included music by the King of Prussia.
	Smith, Stanley	CG	10	22 Feb.–28 Mar.	Wed., Fri.	10/6	10/6	5/- 3/6	Included music by Smith and Stanley.
1761	Barbandt	Hay	3	28 Jan.–19 Feb.	—	10/6	3/-	2/- 2/-	Subscription 1 gn. Music mainly by Barbandt. Additional benefit on 26 Feb.
	Smith, Stanley	CG	10	6 Feb.–13 Mar.	Wed., Fri.	10/6	10/6	5/- 3/6	Included music by Smith and Stanley.
	Arne	DL	3	27 Feb.–6 Mar.	Wed., Fri.	10/6	10/6	5/- 3/-	Music mainly by Arne.
1762	Smith, Stanley	CG	10	26 Feb.–2 Apr.	Wed., Fri.	10/6	10/6	5/- 3/6	
	Arne	DL	10	26 Feb.–2 Apr.	Wed., Fri.	7/-	5/-	3/- 2/-	Subscription 3 gn. Included music by Arne.
1763	Smith, Stanley	CG	10	18 Feb.–25 Mar.	Wed., Fri.	10/6	10/6	5/- 3/6	Included selection, The Cure of Saul.
1764	Smith, Stanley	CG	11	9 Mar.–13 Apr.	Wed., Fri.	10/6	10/6	5/- 3/6	
1765	Smith, Stanley	CG	11	22 Feb.–29 Mar.	Wed., Fri.	10/6	10/6	5/- 3/6	
1766	Smith, Stanley	CG	11	14 Feb.–21 Mar.	Wed., Fri.	10/6	10/6	5/- 3/6	
1767	Smith, Stanley	CG	11	6 Mar.–10 Apr.	Wed., Fri.	10/6	10/6	5/- 3/6	

Year	Composers	Theatre	No.	Dates	Days	Prices	Notes
1768	Smith, Stanley	CG	11	19 Feb.–25 Mar.	Wed., Fri.	10/6 10/6 5/- 3/6	Promoters from *PA* 30 Jan. Included music by Arnold and Piccinni.
	Arnold, Toms	Hay	11	19 Feb.–25 Mar.	Wed., Fri.	5/- 3/- 2/- 1/-	
1769	Smith, Stanley	CG	11	10 Feb.–17 Mar.	Wed., Fri.	10/6 10/6 5/- 3/6	Included music by Piccinni and Arnold.
	Arnold, Toms?	Hay	11	10 Feb.–17 Mar.	Wed., Fri.	5/- 3/- 2/- 1/-	
1770	Bach	KT	6	1 Mar.–5 Apr.	Thu.	10/6 10/6 5/- 3/-	Music mainly by Jommelli and Bach. Additional performance on 12 June.
1771	Smith, Stanley	DL	11	2 Mar.–6 Apr.	Wed., Fri.	10/6 5/- 3/6 2/-	Included music by Arnold, Jommelli and Piccinni.
	Arnold, Toms	CG	11	2 Mar.–6 Apr.	Wed., Fri.	5/- 5/- 3/- 2/-	
	Bach	KT	5	10 Jan.–7 Mar.	Thu.	10/6 5/- 3/- 2/-	Intermittent. Music mainly by Bach and Jommelli.
1772	Smith, Stanley	DL	11	15 Feb.–22 Mar.	Wed., Fri.	10/6 5/- 3/6 2/-	Included music by Arnold and Piccinni.
	Arnold, Toms?	CG	11	15 Feb.–22 Mar.	Wed., Fri.	5/- 4/- 3/- 2/-	
	Smith, Stanley	DL	11	6 Mar.–10 Apr.	Wed., Fri.	10/6 5/- 3/6 2/-	Promoters from [John Potter], *The Theatrical Review*, 2 (1772), 207–8. Included music by Arnold.
	Arnold, Toms	CG	11	6 Mar.–10 Apr.	Wed., Fri.	5/- 4/- 3/- 2/-	
1773	Smith, Stanley	DL	11	26 Feb.–2 Apr.	Wed., Fri.	10/6 5/- 3/6 2/-	
	Arne	CG	11	26 Feb.–2 Apr.	Wed., Fri.	5/- 4/- 3/- 2/-	Included music by Arne.
	Arnold, Toms?	Hay	11	26 Feb.–2 Apr.	Wed., Fri.	5/- 3/- 2/- 1/-	Included music by Arnold.
1774	Smith, Stanley	DL	11	18 Feb.–25 Mar.	Wed., Fri.	10/6 5/- 3/6 2/-	Included music by Smith and Stanley.
	Barthelemon	Hay	11	18 Feb.–25 Mar.	Wed., Fri.	5/- 3/- 2/- 1/-	
1775	Stanley, Linley?	DL	11	3 Mar.–7 Apr.	Wed., Fri.	10/6 5/- 3/6 2/-	Included music by Stanley.
	Bach, Abel	KT	11	3 Mar.–7 Apr.	Wed., Fri.	10/6 10/6 5/- 3/-	
1776	Stanley, Linley	DL	11	23 Feb.–29 Mar.	Wed., Fri.	10/6 5/- 3/6 2/-	Included music by Linley, jr.
	Arnold, Hook?	CG	11	23 Feb.–29 Mar.	Wed., Fri.	7/6 5/- 3/- 2/-	Included music by Arnold and Hook.
1777	Stanley, Linley	DL	11	14 Feb.–21 Mar.	Wed., Fri.	10/6 5/- 3/6 2/-	
	Arnold	CG	11	14 Feb.–21 Mar.	Wed., Fri.	10/6 5/- 3/6 2/-	Included music by Arnold.
1778	Stanley, Linley	DL	11	6 Mar.–10 Apr.	Wed., Fri.	10/6 5/- 3/6 2/-	
	Hook, Arnold?	CG	11	6 Mar.–10 Apr.	Wed., Fri.	10/6 4/- 3/- 2/-	
1779	Stanley, Linley	DL	11	19 Feb.–26 Mar.	Wed., Fri.	10/6 5/- 3/6 2/-	Included music by Hook and Arnold.
	Philidor	FMH	3	26 Feb.–12 Mar.	Fri.	— 10/6 — —	Music mainly by Philidor.
1780	Barthelemon	Hay	6	3 Mar.–26 Mar.	Wed., Fri.	5/- 3/- 2/- 1/-	
	Stanley, Linley	DL	11	11 Feb.–17 Mar.	Wed., Fri.	10/6 5/- 3/6 2/-	
1781	Stanley, Linley	DL	11	2 Mar.–6 Apr.	Wed., Fri.	10/6 5/- 3/6 2/-	
1782	Stanley, Linley	DL	10	15 Feb.–22 Mar.	Wed., Fri.	10/6 5/- 3/6 2/-	
1783	Stanley, Linley	DL	9	14 Mar.–11 Apr.	Wed., Fri.	10/6 5/- 3/6 2/-	

Oratorio series (cont.)

Year	Promoter	Place	Number	Dates	Usual days	Price			Notes
						Box	Pit	Galleries	
1784	Stanley, Linley	DL	10	27 Feb.–2 Apr.	Wed., Fri.	10/6	5/-	3/6 2/-	For 3 Mar., see *MC*.
	M. Arne, Barthelemon	Hay	7	3 Mar.–2 Apr.	Wed., Fri.	5/-	3/-	2/- 1/-	For 12 Mar., see *MC*. Included music by T. A. Arne. Additional benefit on 27 Apr.
1785	Stanley, Linley	DL	9	11 Feb.–18 Mar.	Wed., Fri.	10/6	5/-	3/6 2/-	
1786	Arnold, Linley?	DL	11	3 Mar.–7 Apr.	Wed., Fri.	5/-	3/-	2/- 1/-	Included music by Arnold and the Handel selection, *Redemption*.
	Concert of Ancient Music	TSt	6	3 Mar.–7 Apr.	Fri.	—	—	—	By subscription 3 gn. Complete Handel oratorios.
1787	Linley, Arnold, Mme Mara	DL	11	23 Feb.–30 Mar.	Wed., Fri.	10/6	5/-	3/6 2/-	Promoters from *MC* 5 Feb. Included music by Arnold.
	Concert of Ancient Music	TSt	6	23 Feb.–30 Mar.	Fri.	—	—	—	By subscription 3 gn. Complete Handel oratorios.
1788	Linley, Arnold	DL	11	8 Feb.–14 Mar.	Wed., Fri.	10/6	5/-	3/6 2/-	Included music by Arnold.
	Concert of Ancient Music	TSt	6	8 Feb.–14 Mar.	Fri.	—	—	—	By subscription 3 gn. Complete Handel oratorios.
	Hindmarsh	Roy	6	8 Feb.–12 Mar.	Wed.	5/-	3/-	2/- 1/-	Advertised in *MP*. Promoter from *MP* 12 Mar.
1789	Linley, Arnold	DL	11	27 Feb.–3 Apr.	Wed., Fri.	10/6	5/-	3/6 2/-	
	Harrison, Ashley	CG	6	27 Feb.–3 Apr.	Fri.	5/-	3/-	2/- 1/-	
1790	Linley, Arnold	DL	11	19 Feb.–26 Mar.	Wed., Fri.	5/-	3/-	2/- 1/-	
	Harrison, Ashley	CG	11	19 Feb.–26 Mar.	Wed., Fri.	5/-	3/-	2/- 1/-	

Year	Performers	Venue	No.	Dates	Days					Notes
1791	Linley, Arnold	DL	11	11 Mar.–15 Apr.	Wed., Fri.	5/-	3/-	2/-	1/-	
	Harrison, Ashley	CG	11	11 Mar.–15 Apr.	Wed., Fri.	5/-	3/-	2/-	1/-	
1792	Linley, Arnold?	KT	11	24 Feb.–30 Mar.	Wed., Fri.	6/-	3/6	2/-	1/-	
	Harrison, Ashley	CG	11	24 Feb.–30 Mar.	Wed., Fri.	5/-	3/-	2/-	1/-	
1793	Linley, Arnold	KT, Hay	11	15 Feb.–22 Mar.	Wed., Fri.	6/-	3/6	2/-	—	Subscription 2½ gn. Transferred to Hay at lower prices. Subscription 2½ gn.
1794	Ashley	CG	11	15 Feb.–22 Mar.	Wed., Fri.	6/-	3/6	2/-	1/-	
	Ashley	CG	11	7 Mar.–11 Apr.	Wed., Fri.	6/-	3/6	2/-	1/-	
	Linley, Storace	DL	12	12 Mar.–12 Apr.	Wed., Fri.	6/-	3/6	2/-	1/-	
1795	Ashley	CG	10	20 Feb.–27 Mar.	Wed., Fri.	6/-	3/6	2/-	1/-	
	Arnold	KT, KTR	3	20 Feb.–13 Mar.	Fri.	10/6	10/6	5/-	5/-	Six intended: transferred to KTR, then probably abandoned. Included music by Guglielmi.
1796	Ashley	CG	10	12 Feb.–18 Mar.	Wed., Fri.	6/-	3/6	2/-	1/-	
1797	Ashley	CG	10	3 Mar.–7 Apr.	Wed., Fri.	6/-	3/6	2/-	1/-	
1798	Ashley	CG	10	23 Feb.–30 Mar.	Wed., Fri.	6/-	3/6	2/-	1/-	
1799	Ashley	CG	10	8 Feb.–15 Mar.	Wed., Fri.	6/-	3/6	2/-	1/-	
1800	Ashley	CG	10	28 Feb.–4 Apr.	Wed., Fri.	6/-	3/6	2/-	1/-	Included Haydn, *The Creation.*
	Barthelemon	HHo		3 Mar.–?	Mon.	—	7/-	—	—	Six intended, with subscription terms; price reduced later. Unclear how many took place (*TI* 22 Feb., etc.).

Notes

1 Principal sources: *GA/PA* (to 1780), other newspapers thereafter. Most of these performances are listed in *LS*, which gives full details of performers and programmes. The names of the promoters were rarely advertised until the 1790s, but they were sometimes given in reviews and memoirs, or can be inferred from the repertoire (see also *LS*). The source is cited above only in exceptional cases.

2 The repertoire was dominated by oratorios and similar works by Handel. Occasionally from 1763, and frequently from 1786, complete works gave way to selections, sometimes adapted to new libretti. Performances of major works by other composers were comparatively rare (these are noted in the right-hand column above); a few individual items were introduced into selections.

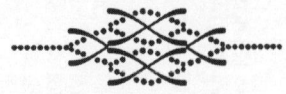

Appendix B
Concert programmes: a selection

Titles of vocal music apart, some light editing has been applied in the interests of consistency. The order of each item has been standardised in the form composer–genre–performer–title. For other examples, see plates 9 and 10.

Principal subscription series

Ogle's series at the Dean Street Room, 1751–2: 9th concert (8 February 1752)

7 p.m.
By subscription for 20 concerts (3 gn. single, 5 gn. double); 10/6 for non-subscribers
Source: *GA* 8 February 1752

1	Handel	Overture	—	
	Stanley	[Cantata]	Miss Sheward	'Who'll buy a heart' [from Op. 8]
	Handel	[Song]	Sga Francesina	'The morning lark' [from *Semele*]
	—	Solo (cello)	Pasqualino	
	—	[Song]	Sga Galli	'So che pergiolo'
	Handel	[Song]	Sga Francesina	'Myself I shall adore' [from *Semele*]
	Geminiani	Concerto	—	
2	—	Concerto (oboe)	Vincent	
	Lampugnani	[Song]	Miss Sheward	'Bel piacer saria d'un core'
	Ciampi	[Song]	Sga Galli	'Pastorella'
	—	Solo (violin)	Giardini	
	Barsanti	[Song]	Sga Francesina	'Ritorne al caro bene'
	Ciampi	[Song]	Sga Galli	'Quel rusceleto'
	Corelli	Concerto – 8th	—	[From Op. 6]

(Abingdon's) Hanover Square Grand Concert, 1784: 3rd concert (3 March 1784)

8 p.m.
By subscription: 6 gn. for 12 concerts
Source: *PA* 3 March 1784, review in *PA* 5 March 1784

1	Mozart	Overture	—	
	—	Quartet (horn)	Pieltain [P.-J.]	
	—	Song	Sga Dorcetti	'Ah se in ciel'
	—	Sonata (piano)	Clementi	
	Sarti	Song	Miss Cantelo	'Un amanti sventurato'
	Graf	Concerto grosso (flute, violin, viola)	Decamp, Cramer, Blake	
2	Haydn	Symphony (new)	—	
	—	Song	Harrison	
	Stamitz	Concerto (oboe, bassoon)	Ramm, Schwarz	
	Rauzzini	Duet	Harrison, Miss Cantelo	'Calma lisinga'
	—	Lesson (harp)	Mme Clery	
	—	Full piece	—	

Opera Concert 1797: 1st concert (6 February 1797)

King's Theatre Room
By subscription: 5 gn. for 12 concerts
Source: *OR* 16 January and 6 February 1797, review in *TB* 7 February 1797

1	Cherubini	Overture	—	
	Tritto	Song	Braham	
	Lindley	Concerto (cello)	Lindley	
	Cimarosa	Song	Viganoni	
	Viotti	Concerto (violin)	Viotti	
2	Haydn	Symphony (grand MS.)	—	One of Haydn's 'London' symphonies, made available by Salomon
	Paisiello	Duet	Viganoni, Mme Banti	
	Steibelt	Concertante (harp, piano)	Mme Krumpholtz, Steibelt	
	Haydn	Cantata	Mme Banti	
	—	Full piece	—	

English subscription series

Harrison and Knyvett's Vocal Concert 1792: 1st concert (11 February 1792)

Willis's Rooms, 8 p.m.
By subscription: 3 gn. for 8 concerts
Source: *TI* 31 January and 11 February 1792

1	Rogers	Glee	—	'Come all noble souls, who skill'd in music's art'
	Jackson	Trio	—	'In a vale clos'd with woodland'
	Atterbury	Glee	—	'Come let us all a maying go'
	Boyce	Song	Harrison	'Softly rise, O southern breeze' [from *Solomon*]
	J. S. Smith	Glee	—	'While fools their time in stormy strife employ'
	Arne/Jackson	Quartet	—	'Where the bee sucks'

Andreozzi	Song	Mrs Harrison	'Nel ved[e]rmi'
Webbe	Catch	—	'To the old long life and treasure'
Callcott	Glee	—	'Peace to the souls of the heroes'
2 Callcott	New glee, composed expressly	—	
Danby	Round		'O let the merry peal go on'
Majo	Song	Harrison	'A morir se mi condanna'
—	Duet	—	'From morn till night'
Stevens	New glee	—	'To be gazing on those charms'
Ravenscroft	Glee	—	'We be soldiers three'
Handel	Song	Mrs Harrison	'Angels ever bright and fair' [from *Theodora*]
Webbe	Glee (double choir)	—	'To love I wake the silver string'
Webbe	Hunting glee	—	'Away, away, we've crown'd the day'

Ancient societies

Academy of Ancient Music 1756–7 (5 May 1757)

[Crown and Anchor Tavern]
Source: programme in Leeds Public Library

1 Lassus	Motet a4		'Parce mihi, Domine'
Lotti	Motet a4 with instruments		'Confitebor tibi, Domine'
2 Pepusch	Motet a4		'Beatus vir'
Handel	Anthem a4 with instruments		'My song shall be alway'
3 Purcell	Anthem a4		'O give thanks unto the Lord'
Negri	Motet a4 with instruments [mass-movement]		'Gloria in excelsis Deo'
Byrd	Canon		'Non nobis, Domine'

Academy of Ancient Music 1790–1: 2nd concert (6 January 1791)

Freemasons' Hall
Source: programme in CPL

1 Handel	Overture and march	—	From *Saul*
Boyce	Air and chorus	Carr	'Softly rise' from *Solomon*
Webbe	Glee a4	—	'Swiftly from the mountain's brow'
Handel	Recitative and song, with violin	Miss [H.] Abrams, Salomon	'First and chief', 'Sweet bird' from *L'Allegro*
Handel	Chorus	—	'He gave them hailstones' from *Israel in Egypt*
Handel	Recitative, air and chorus	Sga Storace	'He chose a mournful muse', 'He sung Darius', 'Behold Darius' from *Alexander's Feast*
Boyce	Recitative and air	Kelly	'Who quits the lilly's', 'Balmy sweetness' from *Solomon*
Handel	Air and chorus	Sga Storace	'Tyrants would' from *Athalia*
2 Arnold	Overture	—	From *The Battle of Hexham*
Vinci	Song	Sga Storace	'Vo solcando'
Handel	Song	Kelly	'Piangero' [from *Giulio Cesare*]
Jackson	Canzonet	The Miss Abrams	'Do not unbind'
Corelli	Concerto – 8th	—	[From Op. 6]
Hasse	Song	Miss T. Abrams	'Pallido il sole'

Handel	Chorus	—	'For unto us' from *Messiah*
Bertoni	Song	Miss [H.] Abrams	'Non temer'
Handel	Air	Miss T. Abrams	'Pious orgies' from *Judas Maccabaeus*
Pergolesi	Chorus	—	'Gloria in excelsis Deo'

Concert of Ancient Music 1789: 3rd concert (4 March 1789)

Tottenham Street Rooms
Source: programme in BL

1	Avison	Concerto	—	
	Handel	Duet and chorus	The Miss Abrams	'Caro, bella', 'Ritorni omai' [from *Giulio Cesare*]
	Graun	Song	Harrison	'Un cosi grand' ardire'
	Morley	Glee	—	'Now is the month of maying'
	Hasse	Song	Miss Cantelo	'Or che salvo'
	Handel	Chorus	—	'He gave them hailstones' from *Israel in Egypt*
	Handel	Recitative and song	Sga Storace	'O worse than death', 'Angels, ever bright and fair' from *Theodora*
	Handel	Introduction and chorus	—	'From the censer' from *Solomon*
2	Handel	Overture	—	From *Amadis* [*Amadigi*]
	Purcell	Scene	—	'Woden, first to thee' from *King Arthur*
	Handel	Song	Harrison	'Oft, on a plat' from *L'Allegro*
	Bond	Concerto – 3rd	—	
	Handel	Recitative and chorus	Harrison	'Search round the world', 'May no rash intruder' from *Solomon*
	Handel	Song	Sga Storace	'What though I trace' from *Solomon*
	Handel	Chorus	—	'Gird on thy sword' from *Saul*

Pleasure gardens

Marybone Gardens 1768 (7 September 1768)

6.30 p.m.
1/-
Source: *PA* 7 September 1768

1	Bach	Full piece	—	
	—	Song	Taylor	
	—	Song	Miss Davies	
	Abel	Overture	—	
2	[Arne]	Overture	—	From *Artaxerxes*
	—	Song	A gentleman	First appearance in public
	[Arne]	Overture	—	From *Thomas and Sally*
	—	Song	Wooller	
	—	Song	Phillips	
	—	Song	Miss Froud	
	Arne	[Glee]	—	'Which is the properest day to drink'
	—	Song	Lowe	
	—	Song	Master Brown	
	—	Concerto (violin)	[J.] Collett	

3 —	Concerto (organ)	Hook	
—	Ode	—	In honour of the King of Denmark
Howard	Cantata	Wooller	
—	Song	Taylor	
—	Song	Miss Davies	
—	Solo (flute)	Blanck	
—	Scots song	A gentleman	
Handel	Overture	—	From *Ariadne* [*Arianna in Creta*]
—	Song	Phillips	
—	Song	Miss Froud	
Abel	Symphony	—	
—	Song	Master Brown	
Handel	Coronation Anthem	—	

Vauxhall Gardens 1791 (29 June 1791)

[8 p.m.]
[1/-]
Source: Vauxhall 'Lists', Lambeth Archives Department

1 Fisher	Full overture	—	From *The Syrens*
[Hook]	Song	Duffey	'Let philosophers prate'
Handel	Overture	—	From *Berenice*
[Hook]	Song	Miss Leary	'O dearly do I love to rove'
Stamitz	Symphony	—	
[Hook]	Song	Miss Milne	'Not long before the close of day'
Haydn	Full symphony	—	
[Hook]	Song	Darley	'Tho' the muses ne'er smile'
—	Concerto (organ)	[Hook]	
[Hook]	Song	Mrs Addison	'Lord what a fuss'
[Hook]	Serious glee and laughing catch	—	
2 [Hook]	Song	Duffey	'Ah! tell me ye swains'
—	Concerto (oboe)	[J. Parke]	
[Hook]	Song	Miss Leary	'As cross the fields'
[Hook]	[Finale]	—	*The Feast of Anacreon*

Benefits: (a) Principal

Society of Musicians: Fund established for the support of decayed musicians and their families (25 April 1763)

King's Theatre, 6.30 p.m.
Pit and boxes 10/6, first gallery 5/-, second gallery 3/6
Source: *PA* 25 April 1763

1 Bach	Overture	—	
—	Solo (mandolin)	Leone	
Piccinni	Song	Sga Cremonini	'Furia di donna irata'
—	Concerto (bassoon)	Miller	
Ciampi	Song	Ciardini	'Vedi amor nel mio sembiante'
Traetta	Song	Sga De Amicis	'Quando saprai chi sono'
2 —	Concerto (cello)	—	
Galuppi	Song	Quilici	'Saro qual e il torrente'
Piccinni	Song	Giustinelli	'Destrier che al arme uiate'
—	Concerto (oboe)	Simpson	
Piccinni	Song	Sga Cremonini	'Misero pergoletto'
Galuppi	Song	Ciardini	'State lungi sol per poco'

3	Jommelli	Song	Quilici	'Fieri tormenti'
	Traetta	Song	Giustinelli	'Di quanto cor le pene'
	—	Concerto (violin)	—	
	Zingoni	Song	Sga De Amicis	'Madre non mi conosci'
	—	[Chorus]	—	'God save the King'

Fischer (3 April 1778)

Freemasons' Hall, 7.30 p.m.
[10/6]
[Directed by Bach and Abel]
Source: *PA* 3 April 1778

1	Bach	Overture	—
	—	Song	Amantini
	—	Solo (cello)	Crosdill
	—	Trio (violin, viola, cello)	Cramer, Giardini, Crosdill
	—	Song	Piozzi
	—	Concerto (violin)	Cramer
2	—	Concerto (piano)	Bach
	—	Concerto (oboe)	Fischer
	—	Song	Sga Balconi
	[Bach?]	Concerto (oboe, violin, viola, cello)	Fischer, Cramer, Giardini, Crosdill
	—	Solo (viola da gamba)	Abel
	Abel	Symphony	—

Salomon (11 April 1799)

Willis's Rooms, 8 p.m.
10/6
Source: *TB* 11 April 1799

1	Haydn	Grand overture MS.	—	
	Haydn	Quartet (two violins, viola, cello)	—	
	Cimarosa	Aria	Benelli	
	—	Concerto (violin)	Salomon	
	—	Aria	Mme Mara	
	Haydn	Favourite military movement	—	[From Symphony No. 100]
2	Haydn	Grand overture MS.	—	
	—	Recitative and aria	Benelli	
	—	Concerto (piano)	Dussek	
	—	Scena	Mme Mara	
	—	Duet concertante (violin, viola)	Salomon, Master Pinto	His pupil
	Haydn	Grand march MS.	—	
	—	Finale	—	

Benefits: (b) English/mixed

Master Arne (5 February 1751)

New Theatre, Haymarket, 6.30 p.m.
Pit and boxes 10/6, galleries 5/-
'The Whole to be disposed in the Manner of an Oratorio'
Source: *GA* 5 February 1751

1	Arne	New overture – No. 3 —		
	—	Italian song	Sga Frasi	
	—	Song	Sga Galli	'Chi non ode i miei sospiri'
	—	Solo (oboe)	Loge	Lately arrived
	Handel	Song	Mrs Arne	'Di cor mio' from *Alcina*
	Palma	Song	Master Arne	'Spesso mi sento dir'
	Arne	New concerto (organ)	Master Arne	
2	Arne	New overture – No. 6 —		
	—	Italian song	Sga Frasi	
	—	Song	Sga Galli	'Non a ragione ingrata'
	Handel	Song	Mrs Arne	'Torna mi a vagghegiar' from *Alcina*
	Hasse	Song	Master Arne	'Che furia, che mostro'
	Arne	New pastoral scene	Sga Frasi, Sga Galli, Lowe, Master Arne, chorus	From *As You Like It*
3	Arne	New overture – No. 5 —		
	Arne	Serenata	Sga Frasi, Sga Galli, Mrs Arne, Lowe, Master Arne, chorus	*The Judgment of Paris* (with alterations and improvements)

Mathews, of Bath (24 September 1789)

Crown and Anchor Tavern, 8 p.m.
3/6
Source: *MP* 23 September 1789

'Calculated to please Ladies and Gentlemen, and not offend the most delicate Ear'
Pieces, catches, glees, madrigals and new songs (ancient and modern):

T. Billington	[Cantata]	—	*The Soldier's Farewell on the Eve of a Battle* (11 airs and a duet)
Harington	Glee MS.	—	'Oh should'st thou, gentle zephyr!'
Harington	Glee	—	'At the close of the day; or, Ba, ba, ba'
Harington	Celebrated stammering glee	—	'Old goody groaner'
[Stevens]	Favourite glee	—	'Sigh no more, ladies'
[Arnold]	Glee and catch	—	From *The Battle of Hexham*
[Arnold]	[Song]	Edwin	'Moderation and alteration' from *The Battle of Hexham*
[Carter]	[Song]	Bannister	'Stand to your guns, my hearts of oak' [from *The Milesian*]
—	Glees and catches	—	'Hail, social pleasure', 'Joan said to John', 'The lawyer'
Dibdin	Songs	Mathews	'The siege of Troy', 'The stone-eater' [?], 'A sweet little cherub; or, Poor Jack'
Harington	Ode	Mathews and others	*Ode for a Lord Mayor's Feast; or, The Alderman's Thumb*

Harrison (27 April 1798)

King's Theatre Room, 8 p.m.
10/6
Source: *TB* 26 April 1798

1	[Haydn]	Overture: grand military symphony	—	[No. 100]
	Purcell	Air and chorus	Harrison	'Come, if you dare' [from *King Arthur*]
	Webbe	Glee a8	—	'To love I wake the silver string' (with new accompaniments)
	Bach	Song	Nield	'Non so d'onde viene'
	Storace/Corfe	New glee MS. a4	—	'Poor Zelica'
	Mozart	Duet MS. (piano)	Miss Greatorex, Miss A. Greatorex	
	Webbe	Glee MS. a4	—	'The mansion of peace'
	Haydn	Favourite canzonet, with harp	Mrs Harrison, Meyer	'My mother bids me bind my hair'
	Paisiello	Celebrated sextet MS.	Mme Banti, Mrs Harrison, Master Elliot, Harrison, Nield, Bartleman	From *Pirro*, never performed in this kingdom
	Handel	Recitative and chorus	Nield	'O thou bright orb' from *Joshua*
2	Pleyel	Concertante MS. (two violins, viola, cello, two horns)	Cramer, F. Cramer, Shield, Lindley, the Leanders	
	Stevens/ [Greatorex]	Favourite glee, arranged a5 with harp and piano	Meyer, Greatorex	'O strike the harp' (cf. p. 214)
	Sarti	Song, with oboes, horns and bassoons	Harrison	'Son qual nave'
	Arr. Greatorex	Portuguese hymn MS.	—	'Adeste fideles' (quartet and chorus)
	Corelli	Solo (violin) – 11th	Cramer	[From Op. 5]
	Pergolesi	Song	Bartleman	'O Lord! have mercy upon me'
	Webbe	[Glee] a6	—	'Ode to melancholy'
	Paisiello	Song	Mme Banti	
	[Purcell]	Finale	—	'To arms', 'Britons, strike home' [from *Bonduca*]
	—	[Chorus]	—	'God save the King' (with chorus)

Appendix C
Concert accounts: a selection

The material has been lightly edited and re-ordered for the sake of clarity; some items have been amalgamated.

(i) Foundling Hospital benefit: Messiah (24 April 1761)

Source: Court minute-book, 6 May 1761 (Thomas Coram Foundation for Children); separate account sheet (Greater London Record Office).
Similar accounts for 1754 and 1758 are reproduced in Deutsch, *Handel*, pp. 750–1, 800–1.

Income

			£ s. d.	£ s. d.
436 tickets [@ 10/6]				228 18 0

Expenditure

			£ s. d.	£ s. d.
Soloists	Sga Frasi	6 gn.		
	Mrs Scott	3 gn.		
	Beard	—		
	Quilici	4 gn.	13 13 0	
Choir	6 [9?] boys	£4 14s. 6d.		
	Men	Three 1 gn., ten 10/6	13 2 6	
Orchestra	Violins	Leader 1 gn., one 15/-, ten 10/-		
	Violas	Three 8/-		
	Cellos, double basses	[Three and two] 10/6		
	Oboes	Two 10/6, one 10/-, one 8/-		
	Bassoons	Two 10/6, two 8/-		
	Trumpets, horns	[Two and two] 10/6		
	Timpani	One 10/6	17 1 0	
Others	Servants	Four 10/6		
	Music-porters	£1 11s. 6d.		
	[J. C.] Smith, sr.	5 gn.	8 18 6	
				52 15 0
Profit				176 3 0

(ii) Lock Hospital benefit: Ruth (3 April 1776)

Source: Committee minute-book, 2 May 1776; Court minute-book, 18 April 1776, 17 April 1777; cash-book (Royal College of Surgeons)

Income

	£	s.	d.	£	s.	d.
62 tickets sold at the door [@ 10/6]	32	11	0			
Received [for tickets] from governors and coffee-houses	275	16	0			
Later receipts	50	8	0			
240 books of the oratorio [programmes @ 1/-]	12	0	0			
				370	15	0

Expenditure

	£	s.	d.	£	s.	d.
[The five soloists and four others performed gratis]						
Orchestra [and choir]	73	3	6			
Carpenter	23	16	0			
'For Painting the Scenes'	12	12	0			
Advertisements, etc.	7	9	8			
Printing of tickets	1	18	0			
Tea, coffee, rusks, etc.	6	0	8			
Dr Nares		10	6			
				125	10	4

Profit 245 4 8

(iii) Royal Society of Musicians benefit: Handel selection, St Margaret's Church, Westminster (30 May 1793)

Source: Concert account-book (Royal Society of Musicians)

Receipts

	£	s.	d.	£	s.	d.
King's donation	105	0	0			
577 tickets @ 1 gn.	605	17	0			
Rehearsal tickets	23	12	6			
Books [programmes]	33	16	0			
				768	5	6

Expenditure

	£	s.	d.	£	s.	d.
[Singers and orchestra performed gratis]						
Carpenter	170	16	$11\frac{1}{2}$			
Advertising	124	0	1			
Upholsterers, painter	58	18	6			
Organ-builder	10	0	0			
Church-wardens	50	0	0			
Vestry attendants, door-keepers, programme-sellers	29	4	0			
Church-officers, pew-keepers, bell-ringers, porters, watchmen, scaffolding	24	4	10			
High constable, peace-officers	11	2	0			
Music-porters	13	15	0			
Music-copying	8	19	7			
Dr Arnold for loss of books [music]	5	5	0			
Sga Galli, compensation for Mme Mara's performance	26	5	0			
Refreshment for performers not members of the society	18	3	6			
Miscellaneous (ticket-stamper, lamp-lighter, matting, etc.)	14	9	$7\frac{1}{2}$			
				565	4	1

Profit 203 1 5

Notes

1. Prologue

1 *MH* 14 March 1786.
2 *MC* 1 April 1788.
3 Letter of 7 May 1788 in *Journal des Luxus und der Moden*, 3 (1788), 218.
4 *MC* 13 February 1792 (routs and levees omitted). For a typical newspaper list of regular musical events in 1791 ('as Music will be the chief pleasure of the season'), see Landon, *Haydn in England*, p. 41.
5 Letter of 4 July 1791 in *Dear Miss Heber*, ed. Francis Bamford (London, 1936), p. 101.
6 Roger North, quoted in Tilmouth, 'Some Early London Concerts', 17.
7 Hawkins, *A General History*, p. 808.
8 *Memoirs of Dr. Charles Burney*, pp. 90–3.
9 Burney, *A General History*, vol. II, p. 1,008.
10 *MP* 15 December 1789.
11 *PA* 11 May 1780.

2. 'An exclusive principle': subscription and ancient concerts

1 'Aldermen and Big Bourgeoisie of London Reconsidered', *Social History*, 6 (1981), 362.
2 *Observations*, p. 33.
3 Quoted in *Survey of London*, vol. XXXI, p. 275.
4 *Journeys*, p. 47.
5 Burney, *A General History*, vol. II, pp. 1,013–14.
6 *An Inquiry*, p. 418.
7 Rouquet, *The Present State*, p. 113.
8 See Ehrlich, *The Music Profession*, pp. 6–7; Leppert, *Music and Image*, pp. 40–2; Charters, 'Abel in London', 1,226. A 'last appearance' was advertised on 23 January 1761 (but see p. 39).
9 Description of the assembly on 26 November 1761 in Kielmansegge, *Diary*, p. 196.
10 Archenholtz, *A Picture*, vol. II, pp. 177–80.
11 Originally twenty-one concerts were planned for the 1764–5 season, directed by Bach, Cocchi and Abel (Mrs Harris's letter of 19 October 1764 in Malmesbury,

Letters, vol. I, p. 115).

12 See a card to Miss Banks from the Duchesses of Ancaster and Northumberland in the Banks Collection, J9.541.

13 Letter of 3 February 1775 in Malmesbury, *Letters*, vol. I, p. 287.

14 Burney, *A General History*, vol. II, p. 1,017. See also *The European Magazine*, 5 (1784), 366.

15 Letter of 21 March 1775 in Malmesbury, *Letters*, vol. I, p. 297.

16 Entry of 28 May 1783 in *The Diary*, p. 304. For full references concerning subscription concerts from 1783 to 1793 the reader is referred to McVeigh, 'The Professional Concert'.

17 *Musical Memoirs*, vol. I, p. 103.

18 *A General History*, vol. II, p. 883.

19 *WO* 25 February 1793.

20 *DI* 4 January 1793, *OR* 1 January 1793.

21 *MP* 15 December 1789.

22 *TI* 13 February 1792, *OR* 1 January 1793.

23 Advertisement for the Vocal Concert in *OR* 5 January 1793.

24 *MH* 1 March 1781.

25 *WO* and *MP* 8 March 1788.

26 *MP* 15 April 1785.

27 *WO* 10 February 1790.

28 *MP* 25 April 1788, *WO* 26 April 1788.

29 *TI* 29 January 1790.

30 *Reminiscences*, pp. 221–2.

31 *MP* 6 February 1798.

32 Landon, *Haydn in England*, p. 23.

33 *QMMR*, 3 (1821), 65–6.

34 Papendiek, *Court and Private Life*, vol. I, pp. 133, 236; Wesley, 'Reminiscences', f. 40.

35 This paragraph is indebted both to this book and to Weber's articles on the subject. I am most grateful to him for letting me see sections of the book in progress.

36 *DUR* 29 September 1785.

37 *MP* 12 February 1788.

38 Letter of 23 March 1786, BL, Egerton 2159, f. 57.

39 Burney, *An Account*; John Crosse, *An Account of the Grand Musical Festival* (York, 1825), p. 174; Gardiner, *Music and Friends*, vol. I, p. 150. Several descriptions are quoted in Myers, *Handel's Messiah*, chapter 5. See also Johnstone, 'A Ringside Seat' and Weber, 'The 1784 Handel Commemoration' (revised as chapter 8 of *The Rise of Musical Classics*).

40 Letter of 13 August 1786 in *Journals and Correspondence of Thomas Sedgewick Whalley* (London, 1863), vol. I, pp. 489–90.

41 Weber, *The Rise of Musical Classics*, p. 233.

42 See Colley, 'The Apotheosis of George III', 104–6.

43 Drummond, 'The Royal Society', 282–3.

44 *Observations*, pp. 28–32. Dibdin proposed this idea at an early stage (*MP* 17 September 1785): see also *The Professional Life*, vol. II, pp. 161–4.

3. Other types of concert

1 For clarification of the legal position on Lenten performance, see Joel Sachs, 'The End of the Oratorios', in *Music and Civilization: Essays in Honor of Paul Henry Lang*, ed. E. Strainchamps and M. R. Maniates (New York, 1984), pp. 168–82. From 1753 all theatres were closed during Passion Week.

2 Dean, *Handel's Dramatic Oratorios*, p. 134.

3 [John Potter], *The Theatrical Review*, 2 (1772), 209.

4 Letters of 1 March 1771 and 10 March 1775 in Malmesbury, *Letters*, vol. I, pp. 217, 293.

5 *Westminster Magazine*, quoted in *LS*, Part 4, p. 1,697.

6 *MC* 23 March 1786.

7 Busby, *Concert Room*, vol. I, p. 102.

8 Burney, *A General History*, vol. II, p. 1,015.

9 *The European Magazine*, 5 (1784), 371–2.

10 Coxe, *Anecdotes*, pp. 52–3.

11 *Westminster Magazine*, March 1775, quoted in *LS*, part 4, p. 1,875.

12 Parke, *Musical Memoirs*, vol. I, p. 55. See also Stevens, 'Lectures', No. 44.

13 *PA* 23 and 28 February, 2 March 1782.

14 'Hints', 60.

15 *PA* 26 March 1784.

16 *MC* 15 December 1785.

17 *Hanoverian London*, p. 76.

18 See L. D. Schwarz, 'Social Class and Social Geography: The Middle Classes in London at the End of the Eighteenth Century', *Social History*, 7 (1982), 167–85.

19 On this and other City societies, see further McVeigh, *The Violinist*, pp. 28–31, and McLamore, 'Symphonic Conventions'. The reduction did not take place before 1764.

20 Archenholtz, *A Picture*, vol. I, p. 125; Kielmansegge, *Diary*, p. 248.

21 See McLamore, 'Symphonic Conventions', pp. 162–6, on this interesting debate.

22 This paragraph is largely derived from Kelly, *Reminiscences*, p. 225; Parke, *Musical Memoirs*, vol. I, pp. 80–4; Stevens, *Recollections*, pp. 24–8; *DI* 25 December 1789. The first president was a solicitor, the last the banker Richard Hankey. Though not strictly speaking in the City, the Crown and Anchor Tavern in the Strand was used for bourgeois concerts.

23 *MH* 4 February 1785; Stevens, *Recollections*, p. 27.

24 Kelly, *Reminiscences*, p. 165; *OR* 6 January 1792.

25 Hawkins, *An Account*, pp. 10–11. The later history of the society is taken from Doane, *A Musical Directory*, pp. 79–83, and from programmes in CPL.

26 *OR* 6 January 1792.

27 *OR* 23 January 1796, *TB* 27 March 1797.

28 *GZ* 11 January 1788, *MP* 14 December 1786.

29 *TI* 23 February 1788, *MC* 15 December 1791.

30 *Reminiscences*, vol. I, pp. 277–8.

31 Archenholtz, *A Picture*, vol. II, p. 175.

32 *TI* 28 March 1792.

33 *GZ* 13 May 1788.

34 Entries of 27–28 May 1783 in *The Diary*, p. 304.

35 See Edward Miller, *Letters on behalf of Professors of Music Residing in the Country* (London, 1784); also Dibdin, *The Musical Tour*, pp. 162–9. The first concert took place in 1787.

36 On the Foundling performances see Burrows, 'Handel and the Foundling Hospital'; on the Lock, see McVeigh, 'Music and Lock Hospital'.

37 Entry of 13 February 1765 in *The Journal of the Rev. John Wesley, A. M.*, ed. N. Curnock (London, 1909–16), vol. V, p. 106. *Ruth* was first performed in 1763 in a setting by Avison and Giardini; by 1768 Giardini had taken over the entire work.

38 *MC* 19 April 1781.

39 Note on BL, Add. 27636, f. 129v.

40 Smart's first season took place in 1751–2. Dibdin began his London entertainments in 1789, the most famous being 'The Oddities' and 'The Wags' (for an idea of the nature of these see *The Musical Tour*).

41 Archenholtz, *A Picture*, vol. II, pp. 176–7.

42 Kielmansegge, *Diary*, p. 24. Information in the following paragraphs is indebted to the work of McGairl, Sands, W. S. Scott, Southgate, Southworth and Wroth cited in the bibliography.

43 Burney, *A General History*, vol. II, p. 1,011.

44 Some minor gardens, notably Finch's Grotto, were able to offer music later.

45 *MC* 30 May 1786.

46 *Reminiscences*, vol. II, p. 1.

47 *GZ* 1 September 1780.

48 Entry of 8 June 1767 in *The Diary*, p. 10.

49 *PA* 22 April 1785, 15 April 1786.

50 *MC* 14 April 1788 (cf. *MH* 19 February 1787).

51 Quoted in Southworth, *Vauxhall Gardens*, p. 77.

52 *Musical Memoirs*, vol. II, pp. 318–19.

53 *Recollections*, pp. 16–17.

54 *A View*, vol. II, p. 235.

55 *Diary*, p. 279 (cf. p. 245). The instrument was probably a harpsichord.

56 Malmesbury, *Letters*, vol. I, pp. 107, 293–6.

57 See Stanley Sadie's discussion in Johnstone and Fiske, *The Eighteenth Century*, pp. 316ff.

58 Entry of 15 March 1784 in *Mary Hamilton*, ed. E. and F. Anson (London, 1925), p. 172.

59 Letter of 15 July 1784 in *The Queeney Letters* (London, 1934), p. 164.

60 These ranged from the aristocratic Noblemen and Gentlemen's Catch Club and the opposition Je ne sais quoi Club to the bourgeois Anacreontic Society and the Harmonists' Society founded by Stevens and others.

61 Stevens, 'Lectures', Nos. 9 and 46.

62 John Ella, *Record of the Musical Union*, 1 (1845), 13, also quoted in Rohr, 'A Profession', p. 249. The reference is clearly to chamber music in the modern sense.

63 This and the following references are from Parke, *Musical Memoirs*, vol. II, pp. 16–17, vol. I, p. 239.

64 *A General History*, vol. II, pp. 1,013–14.

65 *PA* 24 February 1783.

66 Letter of 22–23 February 1791 in Granville Leveson Gower, *Private Correspondence*

1781 to 1821 (London, 1916), vol. I, p. 34.

67 *GZ* 12 March 1783.

68 *MC* 3 March 1788.

69 *PA* 21 September 1784.

70 *GZ* 5 April 1787.

71 *PA* 18 May 1782.

72 This paragraph is derived from Fanny Burney, *The Early Journals* and *Memoirs of Doctor Burney*, vol. II, pp. 101–13. The widowed Mrs Thrale later married Piozzi, to Johnson's disgust.

73 See the accounts and programmes in Wesley, 'Register'. For details of the printed proposals for 1781 and an 'apology' from Charles Wesley see Lightwood, *Samuel Wesley*, pp. 50–2.

74 Stevens, *Recollections*, p. 57.

75 *Musical Memoirs*, vol. I, p. 13.

76 Marsh, 'Memoirs', pp. 627–8; *GZ* 19 March 1785, *PA* 21 October 1785, *MC* 28 January 1792.

77 Burney, *A General History*, vol. II, p. 1,012.

78 *MH* 6 February 1784.

79 Entry of 6 May 1790 in Fanny Burney, *Diary and Letters*, vol. IV, pp. 373–5.

80 Entry of 3 November 1761 in *The Diaries of a Duchess* [Elizabeth Percy, Duchess of Northumberland], ed. J. Greig (London, 1926), p. 41.

81 Since concerts at these various venues are often discussed interchangeably, all are included in the following discussion. Lists of court orchestra members were printed in the *Court and City Register*.

82 Charters, 'Abel in London', 1,225.

83 Papendiek, *Court and Private Life*, vol. I, p. 65. The chronology of this is somewhat unclear: Cramer only arrived in London in 1772, but both Bach and Abel had styled themselves 'Chamber Musician to the Queen' in 1764.

84 *The London Magazine*, n.s. 4 (1785), 141. See also *MC* 29 July 1783; Carl Friedrich Cramer, *Magazin der Musik*, 1:2 (1783), 1,037–9.

85 *Diary*, pp. 225–6.

86 Angelo, *Reminiscences*, vol. I, p. 445.

87 *Court and Private Life*, vol. I, p. 94.

88 Letter of 9 November 1785 in *The Autobiography*, vol. VI, p. 309. In 1799 Burney attended a concert at the music-room in the Castle, for which the King had prepared a list of music by Handel to be performed (Scholes, 'George the Third', 79–80).

89 Entry of 2 August 1786 in Fanny Burney, *Diary and Letters*, vol. II, p. 417, one of several references to court concerts.

90 Lady Macartney's letter of 7 April 1789 in *Gleanings from an Old Portfolio*, ed. G. Clark (Edinburgh, 1895–8), vol. II, p. 122.

91 Rice, 'The Blind Dülon', 30. See also *QMMR*, 1 (1818), 154–6.

92 *Court and Private Life*, vol. I, pp. 65, 106.

93 Letter of 29 October 1779 in *The Autobiography*, vol. V, pp. 478–9.

94 Black, *The Linleys of Bath*, p. 97.

95 Letter of 28 May 1764 in *The Letters*, p. 47.

96 Parke, *Musical Memoirs*, vol. I, p. 121, vol. II, p. 189.

97 Papendiek, *Court and Private Life*, vol. I, p. 200; also vol. I, pp. 133, 234.

98 *MH* 5 May 1786, *PA* 11 January 1787.
99 *MC* 20 January 1791. The remainder of this section is derived from Landon, *Haydn in England*, pp. 283–5. No Haydn symphony was performed at the annual Handel concerts as suggested by Griesinger.

4. The concert in London life

1 McKendrick, Brewer and Plumb, *The Birth of a Consumer Society*, chapter 3.
2 *A Polite and Commercial People*, p. 574.
3 Rogers, *Literature and Popular Culture*, p. 6.
4 *MP* 15 April 1785.
5 Letter of 6 March 1793 in *Dear Miss Heber*, ed. F. Bamford (London, 1936), pp. 150–1.
6 No. 128 (reply in No. 130). The wife with pretensions to culture appears to be Mrs Fox Lane (cf. Burney, *A General History*, vol. II, pp. 1,013–14).
7 Potter, *Observations*, p. 106.
8 Elizabeth Mure, quoted in A. F. Scott, *An Age of Elegance* (Old Woking, 1979), p. 47. The reference is to Scottish imitation of English manners.
9 *TI* 23 February 1788.
10 Licences for Hickford's Room 1770–2 survive in the Greater London Record Office (MR/LMD/1/20–22); for Marybone, see Sands, *Marylebone*, pp. 129–31. The unlicensed concert is mentioned in *PA* 27 August 1756.
11 Nevertheless it is impossible to credit the figure of 1,500 for Haydn's 1792 benefit.
12 Reichardt's report of 1785 in *Musikalisches Wochenblatt*, p. 137.
13 Letter of 2 January 1791 in *Journal des Luxus und der Moden*, 6 (1791), 68.
14 Entry of 26 November 1761 in Kielmansegge, *Diary*, p. 196.
15 *Memoirs* (London, 1930), p. 52.
16 *PA* 1 January 1783.
17 *MC* 19 May 1788.
18 *GZ* 25 June 1772.
19 *TB* 31 May 1796.
20 *Correspondence*, ed. W. S. Lewis (New Haven and Oxford, 1937–83), vol. XXIV, p. 310.
21 Letter of 12 May 1792 in *The Journals*, vol. I, p. 144.
22 Entry of 27 March 1775 in *Diary of a Visit to England in 1775*, ed. J. L. Clifford (Cambridge, 1947), pp. 63–4.
23 Burney, *An Account*, p. 40; *MH* 31 January 1792.
24 *TB* 3 March 1796.
25 *MP* 23 April 1785.
26 Angelo, *Reminiscences*, vol. I, p. 445; Parke, *Musical Memoirs*, vol. I, p. 172.
27 Robertson, *An Inquiry*, p. 429.
28 *MC* 26 March 1791.
29 *Observations*, p. 14.
30 *Court and Private Life*, vol. I, p. 215, vol. II, pp. 296–7.
31 *MC* 8 March 1791.
32 *MC* 13 March 1784.
33 *Journal des Luxus und der Moden* (1794), cited in Landon, *Haydn in England*, p. 246.
34 Giacomo Gotifredo Ferrari in *The Harmonicon*, 8 (1830), 371.

35 *A View*, vol. II, p. 233; *An Inquiry*, p. 431.
36 *A Social History*, p. 119.
37 'A Comparison', 163.
38 See Schueller, 'The Use and Decorum of Music'.
39 Quoted in Deutsch, *Handel*, p. 773.
40 See chapter 3 note 37.
41 *PA* 18 December 1784.
42 Eastcott, *Sketches*, pp. 195–6; see LeHuray and Day, *Music and Aesthetics*, pp. 118–19.
43 Thomas Noel's letter of 7 February 1772 in Malcolm Elwin, *The Noels and the Milbankes* (London, 1967), p. 31.
44 Letter of 19 November 1764 in *Correspondence*, ed. P. Toynbee and L. Whibley (Oxford, 1935), vol. II, p. 853.
45 Entries of 25 May 1783 and 25 May 1790 in *Diaries*, ed. L. Bettany (Oxford, 1929), pp. 41, 74.
46 Quoted in Weber, *The Rise of Musical Classics*, p. 166.
47 *PA* 28 April 1786. See also the satirical letter from 'NO MUSICIAN' in *MH* 29 June 1787.
48 Malcolm, *Anecdotes*, pp. 187–8. The first point recalls an article in *PA* 27 August 1756.
49 See, for example, *The European Magazine*, 23 (1793), 28–32, 103–5.
50 See Castle, *Masquerade and Civilization*, pp. 53–5.
51 *Letters*, vol. I, pp. 228–9.
52 See Andrews, *An Inquiry*, especially from p. 77; *MC* 1 April 1788.
53 See the report and a letter from 'THEATRICUS' in *PA* 15 March 1782; *PA* 19 January 1787.
54 Andrews, *An Inquiry*, p. 3.
55 *Thoughts*, pp. 43–8; *Memoirs of the Late Mrs Robinson* (London, 1930), pp. 51–4.
56 *TI* 14 May 1788.
57 *The European Magazine*, 14 (1788), 482.
58 Parke, *Musical Memoirs*, vol. II, p. 327, vol. I, p. 281, vol. I, p. 185; Malcolm, *Anecdotes*, pp. 424–5. Further on this decline see Milligan, *The Concerto*, pp. 18–20, where 1792 is seen as the peak of activity.
59 *DI* 20 July 1793.
60 See Joanna Innes, 'Politics and Morals: the Reformation of Manners Movement in Later Eighteenth-Century England', in Hellmuth, *The Transformation of Political Culture*, pp. 57–118.
61 *OR* 22 February 1792.
62 *Reminiscences*, vol. I, pp. 283–4.
63 See 'Memoir of Johann Peter Salomon', *The Harmonicon*, 8 (1830), 46; *QMMR*, 1 (1818), 342.
64 Parke, *Musical Memoirs*, vol. II, p. 160.
65 'Reminiscences', ff. 122–3.

5. The musical product: novelty and familiarity

1 See the conscious attempt at such a spread in a list of advertisements placed by the Academy of Ancient Music in 1790 (Paris, Bibliothèque Nationale, Conservatoire Collection, Res. F.1507, f. 6).

2 *MP* 9 November 1785, *MP* 6 February 1789.

3 *MP* 21 January 1786.

4 See John Taylor, *Records of My Life* (London, 1832), vol. II, p. 101.

5 *WO* 13 April 1790.

6 According to *MP* 24 March 1789; the offending review has not been located.

7 *MC* 12 April 1788.

8 'The Contemporaneity', 192.

9 Letter of 10 December 1750 in *The Autobiography*, vol. II, p. 626 (referring to Dublin).

10 Fanny Burney, *The Early Journals*, vol. I, p. 249.

11 *GZ* 13 February 1788.

12 McKendrick, Brewer and Plumb, *The Birth of a Consumer Society*, chapter 2.

13 *Court and Private Life*, vol. I, pp. 215–16.

14 Ibid., vol. I, p. 185. She must mean the Decayed Musicians' Fund, not the New Musical Fund; the account of Salomon's début is inaccurate in several respects.

15 *MH* 20 February 1783, *PA* 13 March 1783.

16 *MH* 13 April 1787.

17 *Memoirs of Dr. Charles Burney*, pp. 91–2.

18 Kelly, *Reminiscences*, p. 161.

19 Burney, *A General History*, vol. II, p. 896.

20 *GZ* 1 March 1793.

21 *PA* 25 May 1758.

22 *MC* 15 February 1793.

23 Malmesbury, *Letters*, vol. I, p. 297.

24 *The European Magazine*, 5 (1784), 366. Cramer was hired as leader from 1773: as a German from Europe's finest symphony orchestra, he had exactly the right credentials and was able to provide much-needed continuity.

25 Georg Christoph Grosheim, *Das Leben der Künstlerin Mara* (Kassel, 1823), p. 34.

26 *WO* 25 June 1787.

27 *DI* 28 April 1791.

28 *MP* 18 April 1788.

29 *WO* 10 March 1789, *MP* 24 March 1789, *DI* 5 April 1791.

30 *MP* 6 October and 5 May 1786, *MC* 25 May 1787.

31 *MC* 16 May 1786. Though her father was German, Mrs Billington was universally regarded as the great British soprano of the late eighteenth century.

32 Letter of 6 November 1786 in *The Manuscripts of the Earl of Carlisle*, Historical Manuscripts Commission, vol. XLII, p. 651.

33 Neville, *The Diary*, pp. 305–6; *The European Magazine*, 9 (1786), 328–9.

34 *DI* 12 March 1791.

35 Entry of 17 February 1790 in *Thraliana*, p. 757.

36 *MC* 8 March 1785, *MC* 14 February 1792.

37 *PA* 9 March 1785.

38 *MP* 12 March 1791.

39 See Leppert, *Music and Image*, pp. 39–40.

40 Very exceptionally, on 26 March 1792 the violinist Madame Hartog advertised that she would be 'Leader of the Band' at her benefit.

41 Entry of May 1789 in *Thraliana*, p. 748.

42 *MC* 15 March 1791 (of Agathe-Elisabeth-Henriette Larrivée).

43 Burney in Rees, *The Cyclopaedia*, s.v. 'Vogler, George Joseph'.

44 *MC* 17 February 1795.

45 *MH* 21 March 1783, *DI* 6 March 1792.

46 *MH* 8 July 1785 (the performers' names inferred).

47 Burney in Rees, *The Cyclopaedia*, s.v. 'Violoncello'.

48 *The European Magazine*, 5 (1784), 363–4.

49 *PA* 5 April 1783.

50 For a recent discussion of the early years, see Maunder, 'J. C. Bach and the Early Piano'. The Pasquali 'Piano e Forte Concerto' of 1752, mentioned by Roger Fiske (Johnstone and Fiske, *The Eighteenth Century*, p. 217) was not written for the instrument.

51 Wesley, 'Reminiscences', f. 85; *QMMR*, 2 (1820), 309–10.

52 Advertised for Sophia Dussek's performance on 21 March 1800 (after her husband had left the country).

53 *OR* 25 February 1794.

54 Parke, *Musical Memoirs*, vol. II, pp. 239–42.

55 Review in *MC* 27 January 1792.

56 *PA* 14 March 1785.

57 Sung in his one-man shows in the 1780s (printed in *The Musical Tour* after p. 310).

58 *MC* 8 February 1780.

59 *MH* 15 May 1783. For analysis of the symphonic repertoire here in 1786 and 1790–1, see McGairl, 'The Vauxhall Jubilee', and Cudworth, 'The Vauxhall "Lists"'.

60 *A General History*, vol. II, pp. 1,017–18.

61 See especially Roscoe, 'Haydn and London'; Oldman, 'Haydn's Quarrel'; McVeigh, 'The Professional Concert'. The quotations are in *MH* 25 November 1782 and *MP* 8 October 1788.

62 Leopold Mozart's letter of 1–2 March 1787 in *The Letters*, p. 906.

63 *The European Magazine*, 9 (1786), 320–1.

64 Letter of 2 March 1792 in Landon, *Haydn in England*, p. 141.

65 *The Concerto*, p. 46. Early in his career J. B. Cramer played Mozart's concerto K. 414 'repeatedly' at the Anacreontic Society (*MP* 17 January 1786).

66 *TI* 27 September 1788.

67 *GZ* 4 February 1785, *PA* 27 March 1778.

68 *MC* 1 May 1784. The works concerned were a clarinet concerto and 'Pleasure! my former ways resigning' from Handel's *The Triumph of Time and Truth*.

69 *Music and Friends*, vol. I, p. 21.

70 See Fiske, *English Theatre Music*, p. 259.

71 'Memoirs', p. 331; unidentified cutting in BL, L.R. 282.b.7.

72 *A General History*, vol. II, p. 1,009.

73 For a detailed analysis of the repertoire of the Ancient Concerts, see Weber, *The Rise of Musical Classics*, chapter 6, to which this paragraph is indebted.

74 Letter of 26 May 1784 in *The Letters*, vol. I, p. 417.

75 Quoted in Hogwood, *Handel*, p. 245.

76 *PA* 21 March 1785, *DI* 27 February 1793.

77 *MH* 19 February 1793.

78 *A General History*, vol. II, p. 1,013.

79 *GZ* 13 February 1788.
80 'A Comparison', 164.
81 *WO* 25 April 1789.

6. The musical product: programming

1 *Roger North on Music*, pp. 353, 305.
2 On 17 February 1786 (*MC* 11 February).
3 See William Weber in Peyser, *The Orchestra*, pp. 365–6. In *Letters*, vol. I, pp. 221–3, Charles Davy launched an interesting attacked on casual programme-planning.
4 In one review J. B. Cramer was informed that he should have omitted some repeats in a piano concerto (*MH* 22 May 1787), while on another occasion Mara was advised that her programme needed more songs (*PA* 10 February 1787).
5 *PA* 17 April 1782.
6 Angelo, *Reminiscences*, vol. I, p. 275.
7 Letter of 25 February 1772 in Malmesbury, *Letters*, vol. I, pp. 253–4.
8 'Lectures', ff. 119–21, with an example of such a programme.
9 *A General History*, vol. II, p. 389.
10 This quartet (as Op. 25 No. 1) is discussed in Hickman, 'Haydn and the "Symphony in Miniature"', 17–21. See also his 'The Flowering of the Viennese String Quartet in the Late Eighteenth Century', *MR*, 50 (1989), 157–80. The French division between the amiable amateur *quatuor concertant* and the first-violin dominated *quatuor brillant* is largely irrelevant to the London professional repertoire, which was based on concertante writing for ensembles of virtuosi.
11 See Landon and Jones, *Haydn*, pp. 289–96; Somfai, 'The London Revision'. For discussion of the reception of Opp. 54–5, see McVeigh, 'The Professional Concert', p. 11.
12 'The *Symphonie Concertante*'; *Observations*, p. 21.
13 *PA* 25 April 1783.
14 Letter of 21 April 1784, quoted in Williams, 'The Life and Works of John Stanley', p. 56.
15 *Letters upon the Poetry and Music of the Italian Opera* (Edinburgh, 1789), pp. 88–9.
16 *A General History*, vol. II, p. 638.
17 *MC* 8 March 1791.
18 *Pace* Landon, *Haydn in England*, p. 47, it was not performed at the New Musical Fund concert in 1791.
19 Dibdin had pioneered this genre at Sadler's Wells in the 1770s.
20 'Memoir of Johann Peter Salomon', *The Harmonicon*, 8 (1830), 46.
21 Parke, *Musical Memoirs*, vol. II, p. 133; *DI* 5 May 1792.
22 Jackson, *Observations*, p. 14; *MC* 21 January 1786.
23 *MH* 6 April 1785.
24 *PA* 20 March 1789. On 5 March the paper had expressed surprise when the audience joined in.
25 *Henry Purcell and the London Stage* (Cambridge, 1984), pp. 117–25.
26 See the analysis of such songs performed at Vauxhall in 1790 in McGairl, 'Music at Vauxhall', pp. 51–2.
27 Unidentified cutting of 19 May 1790 in Bodl., G.A. Surrey c.22.
28 Fiske, *Scotland in Music*, pp. 25–9.

29 *MP* 15 March 1798.
30 *PA* 26 March 1784.
31 *Music and Friends*, vol. I, p. 6, vol. III, p. 302.
32 *The Musical Tour*, p. 199.
33 *PA* 21 March 1785.
34 *OR* 13 March 1794.
35 *TB* 17 March 1800. Some Hindustani music was published in westernised garb around this time (see Owain Edwards, 'Captain Williamson's Compositions', *MR*, 42 (1981), 116–29; Raymond Head, 'Corelli in Calcutta', *EM*, 13 (1985), 552). 'Favorite Indostan Airs' were performed by the Duke of York's band at Vauxhall's Oriental Gala in 1800 (*TI* 24 July).
36 See Rimmer, 'Edward Jones's Musical and Poetical Relicks'.
37 *WO* 1 February 1787. Kotzwara's infamous *Battle of Prague* is the apotheosis of the banal in this line. Only a child could have performed this in a public concert, as Sophia Hoffman (aged 6) did in 1793, accompanied by her brother (aged 4) on the kettledrum, in a neat definition of social roles.
38 *MH* 21 May 1785.
39 *OR* 24 March 1792. The first advertisements to use the nickname 'Surprise' were those for Andrew Ashe's benefit on 6 June 1796.
40 *DI* 25 February 1792, *TI* 27 February 1792.
41 See Noske, 'Sound and Sentiment'.
42 *OR* 22 March 1793.
43 *MC* 5 May 1794. A more vivid, but less accurate, description of the 'horrid sublimity' of the movement is found in *MC* 9 April 1794. See also Johnson, '"Giant HANDEL"', 528–9.

7. Taste and national idioms

1 *PA* 5 October 1753, *PA* 5 March 1779.
2 Landon, *Haydn in England*, pp. 140–1, 187–8.
3 *An Account*, p. iv.
4 'The London Revision', *Haydn and the Enlightenment*.
5 *A General History*, vol. II, pp. 849, 1,015.
6 Rouquet, *The Present State*, p. 111.
7 Jackson, *Observations*, p. 16; [Gregory], *A Comparative View*, p. 146.
8 *A Comparative View*, p. 146.
9 Letter of 3 February 1776 in *The Letters*, vol. I, p. 201.
10 *Boswell in Holland*, ed. F. A. Pottle (London, 1952), p. 52.
11 *A General History*, vol. II, p. 958. See also Jones, 'Haydn's Music in London'.
12 *MH* 21 March 1783.
13 *GZ* 24 February 1787.
14 Plantinga, *Clementi*, pp. 79–83.
15 *A General History*, vol. II, p. 1,004.
16 The choruses in *Zimri* are lost.
17 *The European Magazine*, 6 (1784), 172.
18 The massive, often contrapuntal chorus 'Here sons of Jacob' in BL, Add. 11517, ff. 58–73v, was added for a revival in 1773.
19 BL, G.800.m.(55).

20 *A Tour to London* (London, 1772), vol. II, p. 113.

21 Letter of 10 December 1750 in Delany, *The Autobiography*, vol. II, p. 626; Rees, *The Cyclopaedia*, s.v. 'Viotti'.

22 *A General History*, vol. II, p. 955. The sentiments are attributed to Abel in Rees, *The Cyclopaedia*, s.v. 'Bach, Charles Philip Emanuel'.

23 *The European Magazine*, 9 (1786), 321.

24 Quoted in Landon, *Haydn in England*, p. 121. For information about Mozart publications in London I am indebted to David Wyn Jones.

25 *MC* 14 November 1788, *MC* 4 February 1789.

26 See, for example, the entry of 4 November 1798 in *Memoirs of the late Thomas Holcroft* (London, 1816), vol. III, p. 61.

8. Musical style: 'music intended to reach the heart'

1 *An Essay*, p. 70. Extracts from this and several of the texts quoted in this chapter and the next are reproduced in Lippman, *Musical Aesthetics* and in LeHuray and Day, *Music and Aesthetics*.

2 *A Comparative View*, p. 130.

3 Published in *Essays*, pp. 461–71.

4 *A General History*, vol. II, p. 261 (cf. Grant, *Dr. Burney*, pp. 30–1, 44–5). In 'Affective Unities', Peter W. Cosgrove offers a contentious view of this dichotomy, allying it to political and religious polarisation.

5 *The Musical Tour*, pp. 265, 182.

6 A. Peter Brown, 'The Earliest English Biography', 345.

7 Letters of 4 May 1781, 5 July 1783, 22 October 1783 in BL, Add. 39929.

8 This discussion of aesthetic issues is considerably indebted to the clarification provided by Larsson, 'The Beautiful', which is also the source of some relevant citations. See also Neubauer, *The Emancipation*.

9 *Substance of Several Courses*, p. 35.

10 *Memoirs*, p. 167.

11 *An Essay on Taste* (London, 1759), pp. 64–5.

12 *An Essay on the Sublime* (London, 1747), p. 33.

13 Rouquet, *The Present State*, pp. 112–13.

14 *WO* 25 May 1787.

15 *A Comparative View*, pp. 147–8.

16 *An Inquiry*, pp. 401, 434.

17 Fiske, *Scotland in Music*, p. 61.

18 See Robert Hoskins, 'The Theatre Music of William Shield', *Studies in Music*, 21 (1987), 91; Temperley, 'The London Pianoforte School', 27.

19 Letter of 27 October 1785 in *Letters*, vol. I, p. 88.

20 Rosen, *The Classical Style*, part 6, chapter 1.

21 Further on the role of such song-versions in nurturing British appreciation of Haydn's music, see Wheelock, 'Marriage à la Mode'.

22 'The Vocal Style of Thomas Augustine Arne', 87.

23 Smither, *The Oratorio in the Classical Era*, p. 251.

24 It was also known (from *Redemption*) as 'He layeth the beams'.

25 See especially Eric Weimer, *Opera Seria and the Evolution of Classical Style, 1755–1772* (Ann Arbor, 1984), chapter 1.

26 Malcolm Cole, 'The Vogue of the Instrumental Rondo in the Late Eighteenth Century', *JAMS*, 22 (1969), 425–55.

27 Letter of 18–20 May 1776, BL, Add. 39929, f. 99v.

28 *MP* 18 January 1788.

29 'A Comparison', 162.

30 These were also known (from *Redemption*) as 'Holy, holy, Lord God Almighty', 'Lord, remember David' and 'Where is this stupendous stranger'. Sometimes 'Farewell, ye limpid springs' was listed by the title of the preceding recitative, 'Ye sacred priests'.

31 John Crosse, *An Account of the Grand Musical Festival* (York, 1825), p. 299; Rees, *The Cyclopaedia*, s.v. 'Haydn, Joseph'.

32 For an attempt to relate Clementi's sonatas to current theories of expression, see Klaus Hortschansky, 'Clementi und der musikalische Ausdruck', *Chigiana*, 38 (1987), 59–85.

33 *An Inquiry*, pp. 433–4.

34 Eastcott, *Sketches*, p. 159; *PA* 18 February 1782; *PA* 12 March 1790; Dibdin, *The Musical Tour*, p. 199.

35 Letter of 21 March 1775 in Malmesbury, *Letters*, vol. I, p. 297.

36 Quoted in Landon, *Haydn in England*, p. 103.

37 Entry of 1777 in *Thraliana*, p. 129.

38 Letter of 22 October 1783, BL, Add. 39929, f. 322.

39 *PA* 2 March 1782.

40 *PA* 20 February 1784.

41 *GZ* 4 February 1789, *WO* 10 February 1789.

42 *PA* 21 February 1782.

43 *WO* 15 April 1790.

44 *PA* 18 February 1785.

45 *PA* 17 April 1782.

46 *MH* 24 May 1792; *The Journals*, vol. I, p. 159.

47 *GZ* 18 April 1791.

48 *PA* 4 September 1784.

49 Fanny Burney, *The Early Journals*, vol. I, p. 249; *The Monthly Mirror*, 3 (1797), 179.

50 *The Professional Life*, vol. II, p. 114.

51 *Musical Reminiscences*, pp. 116–17, 23–6.

52 Entry of 8 July 1781 in *The Torrington Diaries*, ed. C. B. Andrews (London, 1934–8), vol. I, p. 56. The reference is to *Tom Jones*.

53 Parke, *Musical Memoirs*, vol. I, p. 278.

54 Letter of 5 June 1786 in *Letters*, vol. I, p. 153.

55 Burney, *A General History*, vol. II, p. 872.

56 *GZ* 12 April 1788. The allusion is to Marchesi.

57 Burney, *An Account*, p. 67.

58 Letter of 23 March 1786, BL, Egerton 2159, f. 57.

59 *A General History*, vol. II, pp. 899, 888.

60 See Plantinga, *Clementi*, p. 98.

61 *OR* 20 February 1793.

9. Musical style: the learned, the sublime and the dramatic

1 *A General History*, p. 889.
2 *An Account*, p. 34. Cf. Grant, *Dr. Burney*, pp. 24–6.
3 Marsh, 'A Comparison', 161. This does of course represent a view from the 1790s.
4 Stevens, *Recollections*, pp. 8, 46–7.
5 Part of Op. 5 No. 6, but probably written before his arrival in London.
6 *The European Magazine*, 9 (1786), 320–1.
7 See the transcription and discussion in Sickbert, 'The Symphony'.
8 *Substance of Several Courses*, pp. 76–7.
9 *Memoirs*, pp. 190–1. This discussion is indebted to Larsson, 'The Beautiful'; see also Johnson, '"Giant HANDEL"'.
10 *The Poetical Works* (Edinburgh, 1810), vol. III, p. 9.
11 *An Introduction to Harmony* (London, 1800), pp. 34–6.
12 *A Comparative View*, p. 138, quoting [Hugh Blair], *A Critical Dissertation on the Poems of Ossian* (London, 1763), p. 69.
13 *GZ* 2 June 1790; 'Hints', 70.
14 *An Essay*, p. 6.
15 Letter of 9 August 1786 in *Letters*, vol. I, p. 168. The reference is to the final chorus in *Israel in Egypt*.
16 *TI* 8 May 1788.
17 Larsson, 'The Beautiful', part 3, chapter 2.
18 *A General History*, vol. II, p. 866.
19 Symphonies by Haydn published in London up to 1786 include Nos. 10, 20, 31, 35, 41–3, 45, 47, 49, 53, 62–3, 66–71, 73–81. Later symphonies quickly became available there, and many earlier works were added to the catalogues.
20 *TI* 20 February 1792.
21 Dibdin, *The Musical Tour*, p. 182; Jackson, *Observations*, pp. 16–17.
22 *An Inquiry*, pp. 360, 434.
23 See Irving, 'Haydn and Laurence Sterne'; Bonds, 'Haydn, Laurence Sterne'.
24 Quoted in Landon, *Haydn in England*, p. 103.
25 See Larsson, 'The Beautiful', part 3.
26 *An Essay on the Picturesque*, rev. edn (London, 1796–8), vol. I, pp. 55–6.
27 *Substance of Several Courses*, p. 36.
28 Quoted in *A General History*, vol. II, pp. 1,033–4.
29 *Haydn and the Enlightenment*, chapter 12.
30 *MC* 5 March 1794.
31 'Beethoven and the London Pianoforte School', 744.

10. The finances of concert promotion

1 All information here about subscription concerts in the period 1783–93 is derived from McVeigh, 'The Professional Concert', where full references will be found.
2 Bach's Drummond's Bank ledger reveals total credits for 1777 of £2,861 10*s.*, for 1778 £1,890, for 1779 £1,058; in 1780 an overdraft of £43 18*s.* 11*d.* was paid off. The figures given in Terry, *John Christian Bach* are somewhat inaccurate.
3 Highfill, Burnim and Langhans, *A Biographical Dictionary*.
4 Freemasons' Hall Committee minute-book, 6 May 1788.

5 For details of fees see table 9 below. An example of Charles Burney's correspondence on behalf of the Pantheon is in *The Letters*, vol. I, pp. 255–6.

6 *MC* 14 January 1795.

7 Wesley, 'Reminiscences', f. 133.

8 *MC* 16 December 1786; *MP* 21 December 1786, *MH* 11 December 1786.

9 *LS*, part 4, p. 419; Freemasons' Hall Committee minute-book, 28 August 1784.

10 See Elkin, *The Old Concert Rooms*, pp. 85–9.

11 This paragraph is derived from the Chancery testimony in the case between Gallini and William Taylor of the King's Theatre, especially Public Record Office C31/248 no. 285 and C107/201 (1788–9). I am most grateful to Curtis Price for bringing this revealing material to my attention.

12 In a single concession to the Opera, Marchesi was required to sing four times there before appearance at the Professional Concert (*MP* 19 March 1788); the start of Salomon's 1791 season was delayed for a similar reason.

13 Smart, *Leaves*, p. 3.

14 See Sheridan's letters to Linley dated 31 December 1775 and 17 November 1774 in *The Letters*, ed. C. Price (Oxford, 1966), vol. I, pp. 95, 85–6. Financial information in this section is derived from *LS*.

15 Busby, *Concert Room*, vol. III, pp. 105–6.

16 For further details, see Sands, *Marylebone*. Note that the advertisement cited in Sands, p. 65, is in fact in *PA* 28 September 1768, not 1765.

17 Figures assembled from the selections in Clinch, *Marylebone*, pp. 38–9; typescript by Edward S. Foot in Marylebone Library; Sands, *Marylebone*, p. 70.

18 *PA* 29 March 1754.

19 Lock Hospital Committee minute-book, 27 June 1761. The Duke was George III's brother, not his son.

20 Information on Mozart's concerts is taken from *The Letters*, pp. 46–56.

21 The occasion was the opening of a new exhibition room for the Society of Artists. The accounts, now held by the Royal Academy of Arts, are found in SA/40/7–8. I am very grateful to Tony Trowles for bringing this source to my attention.

22 *Musikalische Korrespondenz*, 1 (1790), 87.

23 *A View*, vol. II, p. 239.

24 C. F. Cramer, *Magazin der Musik*, 2:1 (1784–5), 234; letters quoted in Weber, 'London', 312, and Matthews, 'Joah Bates', 750.

25 *PA* 13 and 17 April 1784.

26 Robert Haas, 'The Viennese Violinist, Franz Clement', *MQ*, 34 (1948), 18. In 1845 John Ella claimed to have performed gratis at 280 concerts in the preceding twenty years (*Musical Record*, 1 (1845), 23).

27 Accounts for 1784 in Burney, *An Account*; for 1792 onwards in the archives of the Royal Society of Musicians (copy of the 1792 accounts in Matthews, *The Royal Society … List of Members*, pp. 208–9).

11. Life as a professional musician

1 This chapter is indebted to the pioneering work of Ehrlich (*The Music Profession*) and Rohr ('A Profession'). I have used the term 'profession' without any specific implication.

2 *DI* 22 February 1791.

3 *MP* 2 November 1784.

4 'A Profession', pp. 49–50. As the author points out, these statistics are inevitably skewed by the nature of the sources.

5 Stevens, *Recollections*, p. 15.

6 *MC* 11 April 1785.

7 *Memoirs of Dr. Charles Burney*, pp. 42–50.

8 Joseph Collyer, *The Parent's and Guardian's Directory* (1761), quoted in Ehrlich, *The Music Profession*, p. 9.

9 Gibbon's letter of 16 February 1774 in *The Letters*, ed. J. E. Norton (London, 1956), vol. II, p. 4.

10 *The Musical Tour*, p. 169. Dibdin's comments reflect a private feud with Simpson, but others shared his view.

11 *MP* 7 May 1789.

12 'The Davies Sisters, J. C. Bach and the Glass Harmonica', *ML*, 56 (1975), 156.

13 Hall Committee minute-book, May 1776. There is much information here about the organisation of the music, including a lengthy dispute with Fisher about payment and rights to the Ode. An account of the ceremony was printed in *The Gentleman's Magazine*, 46 (1776), 218–20. See also John Morehen, 'Masonic Instrumental Music of the Eighteenth Century: a Survey', *MR*, 42 (1981), 222.

14 'Memoir of Johann Peter Salomon', *The Harmonicon*, 8 (1830), 45.

15 Prince Hoare, *Memoirs of Granville Sharp*, 2nd edn (London, 1828), appendix 6.

16 See Newdigate-Newdegate, *The Cheverels*, especially chapters 8 and 9. The story was used by George Eliot for the second of her *Scenes of Clerical Life*.

17 Letter of 26 November 1755, BL, Add. 32861, f. 102.

18 *GZ* 19 May 1787; Parke, *Musical Memoirs*, vol. I, pp. 269–71, vol. II, p. 129; *MP* 10 June 1788.

19 *PA* 11 January 1787.

20 *The British Mercury* (Hamburg), 11 (1789), 287.

21 Sainsbury, *A Dictionary*, s.v. 'Parke, William Thomas'.

22 Burney, *A General History*, vol. II, pp. 1,008, 1,012.

23 Papendiek, *Court and Private Life*, vol. I, p. 76.

24 Based on a comparison of lists in *PA* 11 and 20 January 1785. The opera list is slightly defective, as the double basses are listed as bassoons. Players at the Concert of Ancient Music are listed in programmes from 1788, at the Academy from 1789.

25 See the figures for Covent Garden in 1760–1 and 1767–8 in *LS*, Part 4, pp. 815 and 1,271. Many of the players listed here were employed at the (pre-Giardini) Foundling Hospital performances.

26 *MP* 9 April 1776, *TI* 5 June 1788.

27 *Reminiscences*, vol. I, pp. 275–8.

28 Manuscript 'Recollections', vol. I, p. 128.

29 Landon, *Haydn in England*, p. 82. For further information on fees for non-concert activity in London, see Rohr, 'A Profession'.

30 Parke, *Musical Memoirs*, vol. II, p. 254. The most detailed study of the music-teaching profession is Leppert, 'Music Teachers'; see also Stevens, *Recollections*.

31 Lonsdale, *Dr. Charles Burney*, pp. 234, 253, 272. One teacher advertised reduced rates for those coming to his own house (*MP* 4 May 1798).

32 Sainsbury, *A Dictionary*.

33 *A Treatise on Indigence* (London, 1806), pp. 23–4. Compare also a similar assessment for 1759–60 in Peter Mathias, 'The Social Structure in the Eighteenth Century: a Calculation by Joseph Massie', *The Economic History Review*, 2nd ser., 10 (1957–8), 42–3.

34 *DUR* 28 October 1785, *PA* 21 September 1784. The following year (as prima donna at the Opera) her income was said to have exceeded £4,000 (*PA* 7 March 1786).

35 [C. L. Junker?], *Musikalischer und Künstler-Almanach auf das Jahr 1783* (Kosmopolis [Leipzig], 1783), p. 142, repeated with slight variations in [J. N. Forkel], *Musikalischer Almanach ... auf das Jahr 1784* (Leipzig, 1784), p. 220, disputed on p. 221.

36 Entry of 15 April 1773 in James Boswell, *Life of Johnson*, ed. G. B. Hill, rev. L. F. Powell (Oxford, 1934), vol. II, pp. 225–6.

37 *WO* 25 June 1787.

38 *A View*, vol. II, p. 237.

39 *PA* 23 September 1784.

40 Mrs Henry Bates's letter of 13 April 1780, quoted in Matthews, 'Joah Bates', 750.

41 Daub, 'Music at the Court', p. 18.

42 *An Account of the Manners and Customs of Italy* (London, 1768), vol. I, pp. 149–50, a reply to the much more optimistic assessment by Samuel Sharp in *Letters from Italy* (London, 1766), p. 80.

43 *Court and Private Life*, vol. I, pp. 207, 149; *PA* 1 July 1785.

44 Lock Hospital Committee minute-book, 2 April 1770.

45 'Lectures', No. 47.

46 *MP* 19 June 1789, *PA* 20 June 1789.

47 *Recollections*, p. 56.

48 The concert was advertised for 12 May 1800; but see *The Monthly Mirror*, 10 (1800), 69.

49 *MH* 11 December 1786.

50 *A View*, vol. II, p. 239.

51 Rohr, 'A Profession', chapter 9. In 1814 the Society ceased to pay out for unemployment not caused by illness or old age.

52 Quoted in Lightwood, *Samuel Wesley*, p. 113.

53 Entry of 18 April 1775 in James Boswell, *Life of Johnson*, ed. G. B. Hill, rev. L. F. Powell (Oxford, 1934), vol. II, p. 369.

54 Stevens, 'Lectures', No. 47.

55 *PA* 26 July 1785. Mrs Colebrooke was the widow of Sir George Colebrooke's brother (*MH* 29 July 1785). Crosdill did occasionally perform in public subsequently.

56 Letter of 8 July 1780 in Fanny Burney, *Diary and Letters*, vol. I, pp. 435–6.

57 Stevens, *Recollections*, pp. 49–50.

58 *Musical Memoirs*, vol. I, p. 112; Griesinger, translated in Gotwals, *Joseph Haydn*, p. 34. Haydn subsequently submitted a claim for 100 gn., which was settled amid mutterings about avarice.

59 Samuel, 'A German Musician Comes to London', 592.

60 *Musical Memoirs*, vol. I, p. 241.

61 Papendiek, *Court and Private Life*, vol. I, p. 154.

62 Letter of 4 June 1781 in William Holden Hutton, *Burford Papers* (London, 1905), p. 63.
63 *MH* 11 May 1792.
64 This point is touched on by Rohr, *passim*, but her analysis underestimates some developments.
65 *The Gentleman's Magazine*, 59 (1789), 532.
66 *The Music Profession*, p. 42.
67 Quoted in Ehrlich, 'Economic History', 197.
68 *MP* 23 September 1789, repeated similarly in *DI* 20 November 1792.

12. The practicalities of concert promotion

1 The orchestra at the 1791 Pantheon Opera already had double woodwind according to *An Alphabetical List of the Subscribers*: 2–2–2–2 2–2 8–8–4–4–3 timpani and harpsichord (total 41). The list given in *LS*, part 5, p. 1,288 is incomplete.
2 Drawing by A. van Assen (see plate 4). The print from Ackermann's collection (reproduced in *Survey of London*, vol. XXXV, plate 47b) is not only later but also evidently less accurate. See also the descriptions of 1762 in Kielmansegge, *Diary*, p. 273 and of 1767 in Neville's manuscript diary, quoted in *LS*, part 4, p. 1,226.
3 Reichardt in *Musikalisches Wochenblatt*, p. 130; *Berlinische musikalische Zeitung*, p. 86.
4 *GZ* 13 June 1788 (of Napier's benefit on 11 June).
5 *Musikalisches Wochenblatt*, p. 137. See also descriptions in *PA* 5 and 15 February 1785.
6 *Haydn in England*, p. 53; 'Toward the Revival', 165. Both also refer to a letter of 1793 in *Berlinische musikalische Zeitung*, p. 86, but this description is simply a confirmation of the standard oratorio arrangement.
7 *Court and Private Life*, vol. II, p. 295.
8 Quotation in Black, *The Linleys of Bath*, p. 97.
9 Or Giornovichi (see Landon, *Haydn in England*, p. 288).
10 *MC* 7 June 1784.
11 *The London Magazine*, n.s. 4 (1785), 301.
12 Vauxhall 'Lists', 19 August 1791.
13 See the Earl of Shaftesbury's letters of 1756–7 in Betty Matthews, 'Handel – More Unpublished Letters', *ML*, 42 (1961), 129–30; Lock Hospital Committee minute-book, 18 June 1757.
14 Stevens, *Recollections*, pp. 109–10.
15 McVeigh, 'The Professional Concert', 9. Kozeluch was of course free to publish his own edition in Vienna.
16 See ibid., 64; Oldman, 'Haydn's Quarrel'; Roscoe, 'Haydn and London'; also Poole, 'Music Engraving Practice'; Radice, 'Haydn and his Publishers'.
17 H. C. Robbins Landon, 'More Haydn Letters in Autograph', *Haydn Yearbook*, 14 (1983), 200–2; Jens Peter Larsen, 'A Haydn Contract', *MT*, 117 (1976), 737–8.
18 See Searle, 'The Royal Philharmonic Society Scores'.
19 Williams, 'The Concertos of John Stanley', 111.
20 Dean, *Handel's Dramatic Oratorios*, pp. 109–12. Donald Burrows ('Some Thoughts Concerning the Performance of Handel's Oratorios', *Händel-Jahrbuch* (1989), 67) has cast doubt on the suggestion that Handel's new instrument was a

composite harpsichord-organ. See also Barry Cooper, 'The Organ Parts to Handel's "Alexander's Feast"', *ML*, 59 (1978), 159–79; Alfred Mann, 'Handel's Successor: Notes on John Christopher Smith the Younger', in Hogwood and Luckett, *Music in Eighteenth-Century England*, pp. 135–45.

21 Stevens, *Recollections*, p. 47.

22 Mrs Henry Bates's letter of 7 June 1784 quoted in Matthews, 'Joah Bates', 751.

23 Entry of 13 May 1782 in Neville, *The Diary*, p. 293.

24 Parke, *Musical Memoirs*, vol. I, p. 98.

25 Parke, *Musical Memoirs*, vol. I, p. 39. The detail of this anecdote is somewhat suspect.

26 'Lectures', ff. 44–44v.

27 See Landon, *Haydn in London*, pp. 54–5, 103.

28 *Musical Memoirs*, vol. II, pp. 150–1.

29 Koury, *Orchestral Performance Practices*, p. 73.

30 *MC* 3 April 1786.

31 Resolution dated 7 April 1788 in a programme in CPL; *MH* 27 November 1788.

32 *GZ* 10 January 1788.

33 *A General History*, vol. II, p. 1,010; *Musical Tours*, vol. II, p. 155.

34 *Concert Room*, vol. II, p. 134.

35 Burney, *A General History*, vol. II, p. 853.

36 Quoted in Landon, *Haydn in England*, p. 189.

37 *Musikalisches Wochenblatt*, pp. 130–1; *Berlinische musikalische Zeitung*, p. 86.

38 Vauxhall 'Lists', 19 July 1790, 3 August 1791, 15 June 1790, 28 June 1791.

39 *Musical Tours*, vol. I, p. 72.

40 Stevens, 'Lectures', Nos. 46–7.

41 Charles Butler, *Reminiscences*, 4th edn (London, 1824), p. 395. The biblical text is slightly misquoted.

42 [Samuel Arnold] in *European Magazine*, 5 (1784), 366; *MH* 7 April 1786.

43 *PA* 7 May 1784.

13. Epilogue

1 Quoted in Loesser, *Men, Women and Pianos*, p. 260.

2 For example, Mellers, *Music and Society*, chapter 6.

3 'A Comparison', 161.

4 *Musical Memoirs*, vol. II, p. 15.

5 *A Comparative View*, pp. 111–12.

6 *Memoirs of Dr. William Boyce*, 102.

7 Eastcott, *Sketches*, p. 161.

8 *A General History*, p. 913.

9 *Memoirs of Dr. William Boyce*, 102; *An Account*, pp. 16–17.

10 Letter of 31 July 1784 in *The Letters*, vol. I, p. 425.

11 Letter of 18–20 May 1776, BL, Add. 39929, ff. 99–99v.

12 Marsh, 'A Comparison', 163; Eastcott, *Sketches*, pp. 158–61.

13 *MC* 19 February 1794.

14 Rees, *The Cyclopaedia*, s.v 'Viotti'.

15 *A General History*, vol. II, p. 945. See also his review of Jackson's *Observations* reprinted in Landon, *Haydn in England*, pp. 100–4.

16 *GA* 29 September 1786.

17 See p. 107.
18 *OR* 14 February 1792.
19 *Observations*, p. 105.
20 *TI* 18 January 1788.
21 *An Account*, p. v.

Musical sources

The following summary of musical sources is intended as an introductory guide rather than a comprehensive bibliography. Further identification of songs and other extracts from larger works will be found in the index.

Modern editions

Among important modern editions of London concert repertoire of this period are the following:

Individual composers

Abel, C. F. *Kompositionen*, ed. W. Knape (Cuxhaven, 1960–78)
    Six Selected Symphonies, ed. S. Helm, *Recent Researches in the Music of the Classical Era* III (Madison, 1977)
Arne, T. A. *Alfred*, ed. A. Scott, *Musica Britannica* XLVII (London, 1981)
    Six Favourite Concertos, ed. R. Langley (London, 1981)
    Four New Overtures, ed. R. Platt (London, 1973)
Bach, J. C. *The Collected Works*, general editor E. Warburton (New York, 1984–)
Boyce, W. *Solomon*, ed. I. Bartlett, *Musica Britannica* (forthcoming)
    Twelve Overtures, ed. R. Platt (London, 1970–2)
    Overtures, ed. G. Finzi, *Musica Britannica* XIII (London, 1957)
    Eight Symphonys, ed. M. Gobermann (Vienna, 1964)
Clementi, M. *Piano Sonatas* (see below)
    Two Symphonies, Op. 18, ed. R. Fasano (Milan, 1959–61)
    Piano Concerto, ed. R. Fasano (Milan, 1966)
Dussek, J. L. *Oeuvres* (Leipzig, 1813–17, repr. 1978)
    Piano Sonatas, ed. J. Racek, *Musica Antiqua Bohemica* 46, 53, 59 and 63 (Prague, 1960–3)
Field, J. *Piano Concertos*, ed. F. Merrick, *Musica Britannica* XVII (London, 1961)
Handel, G. F. *Werke*, ed. F. Chrysander (Leipzig, 1859–1903)
    Hallische Händel-Ausgabe, ed. M. Schneider and R. Steglich (Kassel, 1955–)
Haydn, F. J. *Werke*, ed. Joseph Haydn-Institut (Munich, 1958–)
    Editions of symphonies, quartets and vocal works by H. C. R. Landon
Linley, T., jr. *Ode on the Spirits of Shakespeare*, ed. G. Beechey, *Musica Britannica* XXX (London, 1970)

Viotti, G. B. *Four Violin Concertos*, ed. C. White, *Recent Researches in the Music of the Pre-Classical, Classical and Early Romantic Eras* IV and V (Madison, 1976)

Wesley, S. *Two Symphonies*, ed. R. Platt (London, 1974–6)

Collected editions

English Keyboard Concertos 1740–1815, ed. R. Langley, *Musica Britannica* (forthcoming), including works by T. S. Dupuis, J. Hook, J. Stanley, the Wesleys and others

The London Pianoforte School 1766–1860, general editor N. Temperley (New York, 1984–7), including the complete solo piano music of M. Clementi, and sonatas and duets by J. C. Bach, C. Burney, J. B. Cramer, J. L. Dussek, S. Wesley and others

Music for London Entertainment 1660–1800, Series F: *Music of the Pleasure Gardens*, general editor C. Hogwood (Tunbridge Wells, 1985–); four vols to date, music by T. A. Arne, W. Boyce and J. C. Bach

The Symphony 1720–1840, general editor B. S. Brook (New York, 1979–86); especially Series E, with works by C. F. Abel, T. A. Arne, J. C. Bach, F. H. Barthelemon, W. Boyce, J. Collett, J. A. Fisher, the Earl of Kelly, G. Rush, W. Smethergell, S. Wesley and others; some composers who visited London are represented elsewhere, including A. Gyrowetz (Series B, XI), A. Kammell (Series B, XIII), I. Pleyel (Series D, VI), F. X. Richter (Series C, XIV), A. Sacchini (Series A, III) and C. Stamitz (Series C, IV)

Contemporary editions

Much of the music cited in chapters 5 to 9 survives only in contemporary printed editions. For full bibliographical information the reader is referred to *Répertoire international des sources musicales*, especially Series A/I (Kassel, 1971–). Opus numbers follow the systems used there as far as possible; the works of Dussek and Pleyel are identified according to the catalogues of H. A. Craw (Ann Arbor, 1980) and R. Benton (New York, 1977) respectively.

Manuscripts

Significant works as yet unpublished in complete form include the following (the manuscripts are largely autograph unless otherwise noted):

Arne, T. A. *Judith*, BL, Add. 11515–17

Arnold, S. *Ode to Charity* (for the Choral Fund concert, 24 January 1799), Tenbury MS. 989 (copy), now in Bodl.

Barthelemon, F. H. *Jefte in Masfa*: Part 1, Library of Congress, Washington, ML 96.B326; Part 2, BL, R.M. 22.a.21

Boyce, W. Birthday and New Year Odes, Bodl.

Hook, J. Songs and other Vauxhall pieces: CUL, Add. 6632–40; BL, Add. 19647, 28971; RCM, MS. 295; Lambeth Archives Department, IV/162/9

Linley, T., jr. *The Song of Moses*, BL, R.M. 21.h.9 (copy)

Smith, J. C. *Paradise Lost*, Staats- und Universitätsbibliothek, Hamburg, MA/672

Stanley, J. *The Fall of Egypt*, RCM, MS. 596

Wesley, S. Symphonies, organ and violin concertos in BL, Add. 35007–11

Ode to St Cecilia, BL, Add. 14339 (also RCM, MS. 4017)

Select bibliography

ABC Dario Musico (Bath, 1780)

Academy of Ancient Music: 'Orders' and other documents relating to the Academy of Vocal Musick 1726–31, BL, Add. 11732

　Printed programmes in BL, CPL, Leeds Public Library

　Programmes 1768–73 and other documents, Paris, Bibliothèque Nationale, Conservatoire Collection, Res. F.1507

　The Words of such Pieces as are Most Usually Performed (London, 1761, 1768, *c.* 1775)

　'Academy of Antient Music' [payments to performers, 1787–8], *Notes and Queries*, 5th ser., 1 (1874), 63–4

Altick, Richard D., *The Shows of London* (Cambridge, Mass., 1978)

Andrews, John, *An Inquiry into the Manners, Taste, and Amusements of the Two Last Centuries, in England* (London, 1782)

Angelo, Henry, *Reminiscences*, 2 vols. (London, 1828–30)

Archenholtz, Johann Wilhelm von, *A Picture of England* (1785), tr. anon., 2 vols. (London, 1789)

Avison, Charles, *An Essay on Musical Expression* (1752), 2nd edn (London, 1753)

Ayrton, William, 'Diary' (1786), BL, Add. 60380

Banks Collection, British Museum, Department of Prints and Drawings (concert tickets and programmes)

Beattie, James, *Essays* (Edinburgh, 1776)

Beechey, Gwilym, 'Thomas Linley, Junior: His Life, Work and Times', Ph.D. diss., University of Cambridge, 1964

　'Thomas Linley, Junior. 1756–1778', *MQ*, 54 (1968), 74–82

　'Thomas Linley, 1756–78, and his Vocal Music', *MT*, 119 (1978), 669–71

Beedell, A. V., *The Decline of the English Musician 1788–1888* (Oxford, 1992)

Bennett, Clive, 'Clementi as Symphonist', *MT*, 120 (1979), 207–10

Berlinische musikalische Zeitung, ed. J. G. K. Spazier (Berlin, 1793–4)

Black, Clementina, *The Linleys of Bath*, rev. edn (London, 1926)

Bonds, Mark Evan, 'Haydn, Laurence Sterne, and the Origins of Musical Irony', *JAMS*, 44 (1991), 57–91

Borsay, Peter, *The English Urban Renaissance: Culture and Society in the Provincial Town 1660–1770* (Oxford, 1989) ed., *The Eighteenth-Century Town: A Reader in English Urban History* 1688–1820 (London, 1990)

Boyd, Malcolm, 'English Secular Cantatas in the Eighteenth Century', *MR*, 30 (1969), 85–97

'John Stanley and the Foundling Hospital', *Soundings*, 5 (1975), 73–81

Bremner, Robert, *Some Thoughts on the Performance of Concert Music* [1777], ed. N. Zaslaw in 'The Compleat Orchestral Musician', *EM*, 7 (1979), 46–57; ed. G. Beechey in *MQ*, 69 (1983), 244–52

Brook, Barry S., 'The *Symphonie Concertante*: Its Musical and Sociological Bases', *IRASM*, 6 (1975), 9–28

Brown, A. Peter, 'Critical Years for Haydn's Instrumental Music: 1787–90', *MQ*, 62 (1976), 374–94

'The Earliest English Biography of Haydn', *MQ*, 59 (1973), 339–54

Brown, John (1715–66), *A Dissertation on the Rise, Union, and Power ... of Poetry and Music* (London, 1763)

Brown, John (1752–87), *Letters upon the Poetry and Music of the Italian Opera* (Edinburgh, 1789)

Bruce, Robert J., 'William Boyce: Some Manuscript Recoveries', *ML*, 55 (1974), 437–43

Burden, Michael and Irena Cholij, eds., *A Handbook for Studies in 18th-Century English Music*, vols. I and II (Edinburgh, 1987, 1989)

Burney, Charles, *Memoirs of Dr. Charles Burney, 1726–1769*, ed. S. Klima, G. Bowers and K. S. Grant (Lincoln, Nebr., 1988)

The Letters (1751–84), ed. A. Ribeiro, vol. I (Oxford, 1991)

Musical Tours in Europe, ed. P. A. Scholes, 2 vols. (London, 1959)

A General History of Music (1776–89), ed. F. Mercer, 2 vols. (London, 1935)

An Account of the Musical Performances ... in Commemoration of Handel (London, 1785)

Articles in Abraham Rees, *The Cyclopaedia*, 39 vols. (London, 1819)

Burney, Fanny (later d'Arblay), *The Early Journals and Letters* (1768–77), ed. L. E. Troide, vols. I–II (Oxford, 1988–90)

Diary and Letters of Madame d'Arblay (1778–1840), ed. C. Barrett and A. Dobson, 6 vols. (London, 1904–5)

Evelina (1778), ed. E. A. Bloom (London, 1968)

Cecilia (1782), ed. P. Sabor and M. A. Doody (Oxford, 1988)

The Journals and Letters (1791–1840), ed. J. Hemlow, vol. I (Oxford, 1972)

Memoirs of Doctor Burney, 3 vols. (London, 1832)

Burrows, Donald, 'Handel's Performances of "Messiah": the Evidence of the Conducting Score', *ML*, 56 (1975), 319–34; see also *ML*, 66 (1985), 201–19

'Handel and the Foundling Hospital', *ML*, 58 (1977), 269–84

Busby, Thomas, *A General History of Music*, 2 vols. (London, 1819)

Concert Room and Orchestra Anecdotes, 3 vols. (London, 1825)

Caldwell, John, *English Keyboard Music before the Nineteenth Century* (Oxford, 1973)

Cannon, John, *Aristocratic Century: The Peerage of Eighteenth-Century England* (Cambridge, 1984)

Carse, Adam, *The Orchestra in the XVIIIth Century* (Cambridge, 1940)

Castle Society, *The Laws of the Musical Society, at the Castle-Tavern [at Haberdashers-Hall]* (London, 1731, 1751, 1759, 1764)

Castle, Terry, *Masquerade and Civilization* (London, 1986)

Charters, Murray, 'Abel in London', *MT*, 114 (1973), 1,224–6

Clark, J. C. D., *English Society 1688–1832* (Cambridge, 1985)

Clinch, George, *Marylebone and St. Pancras* (London, 1890)

Coggin, Philip, '"This Easy and Agreable Instrument": A History of the English Guittar', *EM*, 15 (1987), 205–18

Cole, Warwick H., 'The Early Piano in Britain Reconsidered', *EM*, 14 (1986), 563–6

Colley, Linda, 'The Apotheosis of George III: Loyalty, Royalty and the British Nation 1760–1820', *Past and Present*, 102 (1984), 94–129

    Britons: Forging the Nation 1707–1837 (New Haven, 1992)

Concert of Ancient Music, printed programmes in BL

Catalogue of repertoire 1776–92, BL, King's 318

Corfield, Penelope J., *The Impact of English Towns 1700–1800* (Oxford, 1982)

    'Class by Name and Number in Eighteenth-Century Britain', in *Language, History and Class*, ed. P. J. Corfield (Oxford, 1991), pp. 101–30

Cosgrove, Peter W., 'Affective Unities: The Esthetics of Music and Factional Instability in Eighteenth-Century England', *Eighteenth-Century Studies*, 22 (1988–9), 133–55

Court and City Register (London, 1750–1800)

[Coxe, William], *Anecdotes of George Frederick Handel and John Christopher Smith* (London, 1799)

Craufurd, J. G., 'The Madrigal Society', *PRMA*, 82 (1955–6), 33–46

Craw, Howard A., *A Biography and Thematic Catalog of the Works of J. L. Dussek (1760–1812)* (Ann Arbor, 1980)

Crotch, William, *Substance of Several Courses of Lectures on Music* (London, 1831)

Cudworth, Charles, 'The English Symphonists of the Eighteenth Century', *PRMA*, 78 (1951–2), 31–51

    Thematic Index of English Eighteenth-Century Overtures and Symphonies (London, 1953) (see also Hogwood and Luckett, *Music in Eighteenth-Century England*)

    'The English Organ Concerto', *The Score*, 8 (1953), 51–60

    'Boyce and Arne: "The Generation of 1710"', *ML*, 41 (1960), 136–45

    'R. J. S. Stevens 1757–1837', *MT*, 103 (1962), 754–6, 834–5; see also *MT*, 108 (1967), 602–4

    'The Vauxhall "Lists"', *GSJ*, 20 (1967), 24–42

Cuper's Gardens: John Tillingham's collection of cuttings in the Guildhall Library, London

Cyr, Mary, 'Carl Friedrich Abel's Solos: A Musical Offering to Gainsborough?', *MT*, 128 (1987), 317–21

Daub, Peggy E., 'Music at the Court of George II (r. 1727–1760)', Ph.D. diss., Cornell University, 1985

Davy, Charles, *Letters, Addressed Chiefly to a Young Gentleman*, 2 vols. (Bury St Edmunds, 1787)

Day, Thomas, 'A Renaissance Revival in Eighteenth-Century England', *MQ*, 57 (1971), 575–92

Dean, Winton, *Handel's Dramatic Oratorios and Masques* (London, 1959)

Delany, Mary, *The Autobiography and Correspondence*, ed. Lady Llanover, 6 vols. (London, 1861–2)

Deutsch, Otto E., *Handel: A Documentary Biography* (London, 1955)

Mozart: A Documentary Biography, 2nd edn (London, 1966)

Deval, Dorothy, '"Gradus ad Parnassum": The Pianoforte in London, 1770–1820', Ph.D. diss., University of London, 1991

Dibdin, Charles, *The Musical Tour* (Sheffield, 1788)

The Professional Life, 4 vols. (London, 1803)

'Lectures', BL, Add. 30968

Doane, J., *A Musical Directory for the Year 1794* (London, 1794)

Drummond, Pippa, 'The Royal Society of Musicians in the Eighteenth Century', *ML*, 59 (1978), 268–89

Drummond's Bank: ledgers, DR/427 (Drummonds Branch, the Royal Bank of Scotland plc, Charing Cross, London)

Eastcott, Richard, *Sketches of the Origin, Progress and Effects of Music* (Bath, 1793)

[Edgcumbe, Richard, 2nd Earl of Mount Edgcumbe], *Musical Reminiscences of an Old Amateur*, 2nd edn (London, 1827)

Edwards, Owain, 'English String Concertos before 1800', *PRMA*, 95 (1968–9), 1–13

Ehrlich, Cyril, 'Economic History and Music', *PRMA*, 103 (1976–7), 188–99

The Music Profession in Britain since the Eighteenth Century: A Social History (Oxford, 1985)

Eisen, Cliff, *New Mozart Documents* (London, 1991)

Elkin, Robert, *The Old Concert Rooms of London* (London, 1955)

Fiedler, Herma, 'German Musicians in England and their Influence to the End of the Eighteenth Century', *German Life and Letters*, 4 (1939), 1–15

Finch's Grotto: John Tillingham's collection of cuttings in the Guildhall Library, London

Fiske, Roger, *Scotland in Music: A European Enthusiasm* (Cambridge, 1983)

English Theatre Music in the Eighteenth Century, 2nd edn (Oxford, 1986)

Foot, Edward S., article on Marybone Gardens (typescript in Marylebone Library)

Ford, Boris, ed., *The Cambridge Guide to the Arts in Britain*, vol. V (Cambridge, 1991), vol. VI (Cambridge, 1990)

Forsyth, Michael, *Buildings for Music* (Cambridge, Mass., 1985)

Foster, Myles B., *History of the Philharmonic Society of London: 1813–1912* (London, 1912)

Foundling Hospital: minute-books of the General Committee (Thomas Coram Foundation for Children); minute-books of the Sub-committee and account-sheets (Greater London Record Office)

Freemasons' Hall: Committee minute-books (Library of the United Grand Lodge of England)

Frost, Tony, 'The Cantatas of John Stanley (1713–86)', *ML*, 53 (1972), 284–92

Gardiner, William, *Music and Friends*, 3 vols. (London, 1838–53)

George, M. Dorothy, *London Life in the Eighteenth Century* (London, 1925)

Giazotto, Remo, *Giovan Battista Viotti* (Milan, 1956)

Gibson, Elizabeth, 'Italian Opera in London, 1750–1775: Management and Finances', *EM*, 18 (1990), 47–59

Gillingham, Bryan, 'Social and Musical Matters Pertaining to J. C. Bach's Third Set of Keyboard Concertos', *MR*, 42 (1981), 225–37

Gladstone, Viscount, *The Story of the Noblemen and Gentlemen's Catch Club* (London, 1930)

Goodall, Richard, *Eighteenth-Century English Secular Cantatas* (New York, 1989)

Gotwals, Vernon, *Joseph Haydn: Eighteenth-Century Gentleman and Genius* (Madison, 1963) (translation of biographies by Griesinger and Dies)

Grant, Kerry S., *Dr. Burney as Critic and Historian of Music* (Ann Arbor, 1983)

Graue, Jerald C., 'Haydn and the London Pianoforte School', in *Haydn Studies*, ed. J. P. Larsen, H. Serwer and J. Webster (New York, 1981), pp. 422–31

[Gregory, John], *A Comparative View of the State and Faculties of Man with those of the Animal World*, 3rd edn (London, 1766)

Grove's Dictionary of Music and Musicians, 5th edn, ed. E. Blom (London, 1954); *The New Grove Dictionary of Music and Musicians*, ed. S. Sadie (London, 1980)

Gyrowetz, Adalbert, *Biographie* (Vienna, 1848)

[Hanway, Jonas], *Thoughts on the Use and Advantages of Music* (London, 1765)

Harley, John, 'Music at the English Court in the Eighteenth and Nineteenth Centuries', *ML*, 50 (1969), 332–51

Harris, James, *Three Treatises ... The Second Concerning Music, Painting and Poetry*, 2nd edn (London, 1765)

Hawkins, John, *A General History of the Science and Practice of Music* (1776), new edn, 2 vols. (London, 1853; facs. New York, 1963)

[Hawkins, John], *An Account of the Institution and Progress of the Academy of Ancient Music* (London, 1770)

  Memoirs of Dr. William Boyce (1788), ed. G. Beechey, in *MQ*, 57 (1971), 87–106

Haydn, Joseph, *The Collected Correspondence and London Notebooks*, ed. H. C. R. Landon (London, 1959)

Hayes, Deborah, 'Some Neglected Women Composers of the Eighteenth Century and their Music', *Current Musicology*, 39 (1985), 42–65

Hellmuth, Eckhart, ed., *The Transformation of Political Culture: England and Germany in the Late Eighteenth Century* (Oxford, 1990)

Herbage, Julian, 'The Vocal Style of Thomas Augustine Arne', *PRMA*, 78 (1951–2), 83–96

Herbert, Trevor, 'The Sackbut in England in the 17th and 18th Centuries', *EM*, 18 (1990), 609–16

Hickman, Roger, 'Haydn and the "Symphony in Miniature"', *MR*, 43 (1982), 15–23

Highfill, Philip H., Kalman A. Burnim and Edward A. Langhans, *A Biographical Dictionary of Actors, Actresses, Musicians, Dancers, Managers & Other Stage Personnel in London, 1660–1800*, 14 vols. to date (Carbondale, 1973–)

Hipple, Walter J., *The Beautiful, the Sublime, & the Picturesque in Eighteenth-Century British Aesthetic Theory* (Carbondale, 1957)

Hogwood, Christopher, *Haydn's Visits to England* (London, 1980)

  Handel (London, 1984)

  'The London Pleasure Gardens', general introduction to *Music for London Entertainment 1660–1800*, Series F, vol. I (Tunbridge Wells, 1985)

Hogwood, Christopher and Richard Luckett, eds., *Music in Eighteenth-Century England: Essays in Memory of Charles Cudworth* (Cambridge, 1983)

Hughes, Leo, 'The Mozarts' London', in *Paul A. Pisk: Essays in his Honor*, ed. J. Glowacki (Austin, 1966), pp. 103–15

Humphries, Charles and William C. Smith, *Music Publishing in the British Isles*, 2nd edn (Oxford, 1970)

Hunter, David, 'Music Copyright in Britain to 1800', *ML*, 67 (1986), 269–82

Irving, Howard, 'Haydn and Laurence Sterne: Similarities in Eighteenth-Century Literary and Musical Wit', *Current Musicology*, 40 (1985), 34–49

Jackson, William, *Observations on the Present State of Music in London* (London, 1791)

Jarrett, Derek, *England in the Age of Hogarth* (London, 1974)

Johnson, Claudia L., '"Giant HANDEL" and the Musical Sublime', *Eighteenth-Century Studies*, 19 (1985–6), 515–33

Johnstone, H. Diack, 'English Solo Song, *c.* 1710–1760', *PRMA*, 95 (1968–9), 67–80
'A Ringside Seat at the Handel Commemoration', *MT*, 125 (1984), 632–6

Johnstone, H. Diack and Roger Fiske, eds., *Music in Britain: The Eighteenth Century* (Oxford, 1990)

Jones, David Wyn, 'Robert Bremner and *The Periodical Overture*', *Soundings*, 7 (1978), 62–84
'Haydn's Music in London in the Period 1760–1790: Part One', *Haydn Yearbook*, 14 (1983), 144–72

Jones, William, *A Treatise on the Art of Music* (Colchester, 1784)

Kassler, Jamie C., 'Burney's *Sketch of a Plan for a Public Music-School*', *MQ*, 58 (1972), 210–34

Kaulitz-Niedeck [Anderson], Rosa, *Die Mara* (Heilbronn, 1929)

Kelly, Michael, *Reminiscences* (1826), ed. R. Fiske (London, 1975)

Kidd, Ronald R., 'The Sonata for Keyboard with Violin Accompaniment in England (1750–1790)', Ph.D. diss., Yale University, 1967
'The Emergence of Chamber Music with Obligato Keyboard in England', *Acta Musicologica*, 44 (1972), 122–44

Kielmansegge, Count Frederick, *Diary of a Journey to England in the Years 1761–1762*, tr. Countess Kielmansegg (London, 1902)

King, A. Hyatt, 'Frederick Nicolay, Chrysander and the Royal Musical Library', *The Monthly Musical Record*, 89 (1959), 13–24; repr. in *Musical Pursuits* (London, 1987), pp. 107–18; see also *Some British Collectors of Music, c. 1600–1960* (Cambridge, 1963)
'The Royal Taste', *MT*, 118 (1977), 461–3
'The London Tavern: A Forgotten Concert Hall', *MT*, 127 (1986), 382–5; repr. in *Musical Pursuits*, pp. 119–25

Knape, Walter, *Karl Friedrich Abel. Leben und Werk eines frühklassischen Komponisten* (Bremen, 1973)

Kollmann, A. F. C., *An Essay on Practical Musical Composition* (London, 1799)

Koury, Daniel J., *Orchestral Performance Practices in the Nineteenth Century: Size, Proportions, and Seating* (Ann Arbor, 1986)

Landon, H. C. Robbins, *Haydn in England 1791–1795* (London, 1976)
Haydn at Eszterháza 1766–1790 (London, 1978)

Landon, H. C. Robbins and David Wyn Jones, *Haydn: his Life and Music* (London, 1988)

Langford, Paul, *A Polite and Commercial People: England 1727–1783* (Oxford, 1989)
Public Life and the Propertied Englishman 1689–1798 (Oxford, 1991)

Langley, Leanne, 'The English Musical Journal in the Early Nineteenth Century', Ph.D. diss., University of North Carolina at Chapel Hill, 1983

Langley, Robin, 'Arne's Keyboard Concertos', *MT*, 119 (1978), 233–6

Larsson, Roger B. 'The Beautiful, the Sublime and the Picturesque in Eighteenth-Century Musical Thought in Britain', Ph.D. diss., State University of New York at Buffalo, 1980

'Charles Avison's "Stiles in Musical Expression"', *ML*, 63 (1982), 261–75

LeHuray, Peter and James Day, eds., *Music and Aesthetics in the Eighteenth and Early Nineteenth Centuries* (Cambridge, 1981)

Leppert, Richard, 'Music Teachers of Upper-Class Amateur Musicians in Eighteenth-Century England', in *Music in the Classic Period: Essays in Honor of Barry S. Brook*, ed. A. W. Atlas (New York, 1985), pp. 133–58

Music and Image: Domesticity, Ideology and Socio-cultural Formation in Eighteenth-Century England (Cambridge, 1988)

Lessem, Alan, 'Imitation and Expression: Opposing French and British Views in the 18th Century', *JAMS*, 27 (1974), 325–30

Lightwood, James T., *Samuel Wesley, Musician* (London, 1937)

Lipking, Lawrence, *The Ordering of the Arts in Eighteenth-Century England* (Princeton, 1970)

Lippman, Edward A., ed., *Musical Aesthetics: A Historical Reader*, vol. I (New York, 1986)

Lock Hospital: Court and Committee minute-books, cash-book (Royal College of Surgeons)

Loesser, Arthur, *Men, Women and Pianos: A Social History* (London, 1955)

The London Stage 1660–1800 [*LS*]: Part 4 (1747–76), ed. G. W. Stone (Carbondale, 1962); Part 5 (1776–1800), ed. C. B. Hogan (Carbondale, 1968); Index, ed. B. R. Schneider (Carbondale, 1979)

Lonsdale, Roger, *Dr. Charles Burney* (Oxford, 1965)

Lovell, Percy, '"Ancient" Music in Eighteenth-Century England', *ML*, 60 (1979), 401–15

Luckett, Richard, *Handel's Messiah: A Celebration* (London, 1992)

McCulloch, Derek, 'Mrs Papendiek and the London Bach', *MT*, 123 (1982), 26–9

McGairl, Pamela, 'Music at Vauxhall 1790–1791', M.Mus. diss., King's College, University of London, 1981

'The Vauxhall Jubilee, 1786', *MT*, 127 (1986), 611–15

McGuinness, Rosamond, '"A Fine Song on Occasion of the Day was Sung"', *ML*, 50 (1969), 290–5

English Court Odes 1660–1820 (Oxford, 1971)

'Newspapers and Musical Life in 18th Century London: A Systematic Analysis', *Journal of Newspaper and Periodical History*, 1 (1984–5), 29–36

McKendrick, Neil, John Brewer and J. H. Plumb, *The Birth of a Consumer Society: The Commercialization of Eighteenth-Century England* (London, 1982)

Mackerness, E. D., *A Social History of English Music* (London, 1964)

McLamore, Laura A., 'Symphonic Conventions in London's Concert Rooms, *circa* 1755–1790', Ph.D. diss., University of California, Los Angeles, 1991

McVeigh, Simon, 'Felice Giardini: A Violinist in Late Eighteenth-Century London', *ML*, 64 (1983), 162–72

'Music and Lock Hospital in the 18th Century', *MT*, 129 (1988), 235–40

The Violinist in London's Concert Life, 1750–1784: Felice Giardini and his Contemporaries (New York, 1989)

'The Professional Concert and Rival Subscription Series in London, 1783–1793', *RMARC*, 22 (1989), 1–135

Calendar of London Concerts 1750–1800, Advertised in the London Daily Press, database,

University of London Goldsmiths' College, 1990 (from which further references can be provided)

[Maddison, Robert], *An Examination of the Oratorios which have been Performed this Season, at Covent-Garden Theatre* (London, 1763)

[Mainwaring, John], *Memoirs of the Life of the late George Frederic Handel* (London, 1760)

Malcolm, James P., *Anecdotes of the Manners and Customs of London during the Eighteenth Century* (London, 1808)

Malmesbury: *A Series of Letters of the First Earl of Malmesbury, his Family and Friends, from 1745 to 1820*, ed. Earl of Malmesbury, 2 vols. (London, 1870)

Marsh, John, 'Memoirs' (1768–1828), CUL, Add. 7757; Huntington Library, MS 54457

   'A Comparison Between the Ancient and Modern Styles of Music' (1796), ed. C. Cudworth as 'An Essay by John Marsh', *ML*, 36 (1955), 155–64

   'Hints to Young Composers of Instrumental Music' [1807], ed. C. Cudworth, *GSJ*, 18 (1965), 57–71

Marshall, Dorothy, *English People in the Eighteenth Century* (London, 1956)

   Dr Johnson's London (London, 1968)

Marybone Gardens: collections of cuttings in BL (840.m.29), Marylebone Library (Ashbridge Collection) and RCM (Department of Portraits)

Matthew, James E., 'The Antient Concerts, 1776–1848', *PMA*, 33 (1906–7), 55–79

Matthews, Betty, 'Joah Bates: A Remarkable Amateur', *MT*, 126 (1985), 749–53

   The Royal Society of Musicians of Great Britain: List of Members 1738–1984 (London, 1985)

   The Royal Society of Musicians of Great Britain: A History 1738–1988 (London, 1988)

Maunder, Richard, 'J. C. Bach and the Early Piano in London', *JRMA*, 116 (1991), 201–10

Mellers, Wilfrid, *Music and Society*, 2nd edn (London, 1950)

Milligan, Thomas B., *The Concerto and London's Musical Culture in the Late Eighteenth Century* (Ann Arbor, 1983)

Mingay, G. E., *English Landed Society in the Eighteenth Century* (London, 1963)

Moritz, Carl Philipp, *Journeys of a German in England ... in 1782*, tr. R. Nettel (London, 1965)

Morrow, Mary Sue, *Concert Life in Haydn's Vienna* (Stuyvesant, 1989)

Mortimer, Thomas, *The Universal Director* (1763), extracts in 'An Eighteenth-Century Directory of London Musicians', *GSJ*, 2 (1949), 27–31

Mozart: *The Letters of Mozart and his Family*, tr. E. Anderson, 3rd edn (London, 1985)

Mullan, John, *Sentiment and Sociability: The Language of Feeling in the Eighteenth Century* (Oxford, 1988)

Musikalisches Wochenblatt (1791–2), in *Studien für Tonkünstler und Musikfreunde*, ed. F. L. A. Kunzen and J. F. Reichardt (Berlin, 1793)

Myers, Robert Manson, *Handel's Messiah: A Touchstone of Taste* (New York, 1948)

Nettel, Reginald, *The Orchestra in England* (London, 1946)

   'The Oldest Surviving English Musical Club [the Madrigal Society]', *MQ*, 34 (1948), 97–108

Neubauer, John, *The Emancipation of Music from Language: Departure from Mimesis in Eighteenth-Century Aesthetics* (New Haven, 1986)

Neville, Sylas, *The Diary of Sylas Neville 1767–1788*, ed. B. Cozens-Hardy (London, 1950)

New Musical Fund: printed programmes and handbills in BL and the Banks Collection (British Museum, Department of Prints and Drawings)

New Oxford History of Music, vols. VII and VIII (London, 1973 and 1982)

Newdigate-Newdegate, Lady, *The Cheverels of Cheverel Manor* (London, 1898)

Newman, William S., *The Sonata in the Classic Era*, 3rd edn (New York, 1983)

North, Roger, *Roger North on Music*, ed. J. Wilson (London, 1959)

Noske, Frits, 'Sound and Sentiment: The Function of Music in the Gothic Novel', *ML*, 62 (1981), 162–75

Oldman, Cecil B., 'Haydn's Quarrel with the "Professionals" in 1788', in *Musik und Verlag: Karl Vötterle zum 65. Geburtstag*, ed. R. Baum and W. Rehm (Kassel, 1968), pp. 459–65

Page, Janet K., 'The Hautboy in London's Musical Life, 1730–1770', *EM*, 16 (1988), 359–71

Papendiek, Charlotte, *Court and Private Life in the Time of Queen Charlotte*, ed. V. D. Broughton, 2 vols. (London, 1887)

Parke, William Thomas, *Musical Memoirs*, 2 vols. (London, 1830)

Pearce, Ernest H., *The Sons of the Clergy*, 2nd edn (London, 1928)

Petty, Frederick C., *Italian Opera in London 1760–1800* (Ann Arbor, 1980)

Peyser, Joan, ed., *The Orchestra: Origins and Transformations* (New York, 1986)

Pickering, Jennifer M., *Music in the British Isles 1700 to 1800: A Bibliography of Literature* (Edinburgh, 1990)

Piggott, Patrick, *The Life and Music of John Field 1782–1837* (London, 1973)

Pixley, Zaide E., 'The Keyboard Concerto in London Society, 1760–1790', Ph.D. diss., University of Michigan, 1986

Plantinga, Leon, *Clementi: His Life and Music* (London, 1977)

Pleasants, Virginia, 'The Early Piano in Britain (*c.*1760–1800)', *EM*, 13 (1985), 39–44

Plumb, J. H., *England in the Eighteenth Century*, rev. edn (Harmondsworth, 1963)

The Commercialisation of Leisure in Eighteenth-Century England, Stenton Lecture 1972, reprinted in McKendrick, Brewer and Plumb, *The Birth of a Consumer Society*

Pohl, C. F., *Mozart und Haydn in London*, 2 vols. (Vienna, 1867; facs., New York, 1970)

Poole, H. Edmund, 'Music Engraving Practice in Eighteenth-Century London', in *Music and Bibliography: Essays in Honour of Alec Hyatt King*, ed. O. Neighbour (London, 1980), pp. 98–131

Porter, Roy, *English Society in the Eighteenth Century* (Harmondsworth, 1982)

Potter, John, *Observations on the Present State of Music and Musicians* (London, 1762)

Price, Curtis, 'The Small-Coal Cult', *MT*, 119 (1978), 1032–4

'Italian Opera and Arson in Late Eighteenth-Century London', *JAMS*, 42 (1989), 55–107

Price, Curtis, Judith Milhous and Robert D. Hume, 'A Royal Opera House in Leicester Square (1790)', *Cambridge Opera Journal*, 2 (1990), 1–28

The Impresario's Ten Commandments: Continental Recruitment for Italian Opera in London 1763–64 (London, 1992)

Pritchard, Brian W., 'The Musical Festival and the Choral Society in England in the Eighteenth and Nineteenth Centuries: a Social History', Ph.D. diss., University of Birmingham, 1968

'The Provincial Festivals of the Ashley Family', *GSJ*, 22 (1969), 58–77

Radice, Mark A., 'Haydn and his Publishers', *MR*, 44 (1983), 87–94

Ranelagh Gardens: collections of cuttings in BL (L.R. 282.b.7 and 840.m.28)

Rees, Abraham, *The Cyclopaedia*: see Burney, Charles

Reid, Douglas J. and Brian Pritchard, 'Some Festival Programmes of the Eighteenth and Nineteenth Centuries', in *RMARC*, 5 (1965) to 8 (1970)

Rennert, Jonathan, *William Crotch (1775–1847)* (Lavenham, 1975)

Rice, Albert, 'The Baroque Clarinet in Public Concerts, 1726–1762', *EM*, 16 (1988), 388–95

Rice, John A., 'The Blind Dülon and his Magic Flute', *ML*, 71 (1990), 25–51

Rimmer, Joan, 'Edward Jones's Musical and Poetical Relicks of the Welsh Bards, 1784: A Re-assessment', *GSJ*, 39 (1986), 77–96

Ringer, Alexander L., 'Beethoven and the London Pianoforte School', *MQ*, 56 (1970), 742–58

Robertson, Thomas, *An Inquiry into the Fine Arts* (London, 1784)

Robinson, Michael F., 'The Decline of British Music, 1760–1800', *Studi musicali*, 7 (1978), 269–84

Roe, Stephen, 'J. C. Bach, 1735–1782: Towards a New Biography', *MT*, 123 (1982), 23–6

  'J. C. Bach's Vauxhall Songs: A New Discovery', *MT*, 124 (1983), 675–6

  The Keyboard Music of J. C. Bach (New York, 1989)

Rogers, Pat, *Literature and Popular Culture in Eighteenth Century England* (Brighton, 1985)

Rohr, Deborah A., 'A Profession of Artisans: The Careers and Social Status of British Musicians 1750–1850', Ph.D. diss., University of Pennsylvania, 1983

Roscoe, Christopher, 'Haydn and London in the 1780's', *ML*, 49 (1968), 203–12

Rosen, Charles, *The Classical Style*, rev. edn (London, 1976)

Rouquet, Jean André, *The Present State of the Arts in England* (London, 1755)

Royal Society of Musicians: admission-book, personal files, minute-books of Governors' meetings (from 1785), minute-book of the concert-committee, concert account-book (from 1792)

  Printed programmes in BL (Royal Music Library)

Rudé, George, *Hanoverian London 1714–1808* (London, 1971)

Rule, John, *Albion's People: English Society, 1714–1815* (London, 1992)

Sadie, Stanley, 'The Wind Music of J. C. Bach', *ML*, 37 (1956), 107–17

  'British Chamber Music, 1720–1790', Ph.D. diss., University of Cambridge, 1958

  'Concert Life in Eighteenth Century England', *PRMA*, 85 (1958–9), 17–30

[Sainsbury, John], *A Dictionary of Musicians* (London, 1824)

Salmen, Walter, *Johann Friedrich Reichardt* (Freiburg, 1963)

Samuel, Harold E., 'A German Musician Comes to London in 1704', *MT*, 122 (1981), 591–3

Sands, Mollie, 'Music as a Profession in Eighteenth-Century England', *ML*, 24 (1943), 90–2

  Invitation to Ranelagh 1742–1803 (London, 1946)

  The Eighteenth-Century Pleasure Gardens of Marylebone (London, 1987)

Schlesinger, Thea, *Johann Baptist Cramer und seine Klaviersonaten* (Munich, 1928)

Scholes, Percy A., 'George the Third as Music Lover', *MQ*, 28 (1942), 78–92

  The Great Dr. Burney, 2 vols. (London, 1948)

Schroeder, David P., *Haydn and the Enlightenment* (Oxford, 1990)

Schueller, Herbert M., '"Imitation" and "Expression" in British Music Criticism in the 18th Century', *MQ*, 34 (1948), 544–66

'The Use and Decorum of Music as Described in British Literature, 1700 to 1780', *Journal of the History of Ideas*, 13 (1952), 73–93

'The Quarrel of the Ancients and the Moderns', *ML*, 41 (1960), 313–30

Scott, Hugh A., 'London Concerts from 1700 to 1750', *MQ*, 24 (1938), 194–209

Scott, Marion M., 'Maddalena Lombardini, Madame Syrmen', *ML*, 14 (1933), 149–63

'The Opera Concerts of 1795', *MR*, 12 (1951), 24–8

Scott, Walter S., *Green Retreats: The Story of Vauxhall Gardens 1661–1859* (London, 1955)

Searle, Arthur, 'The Royal Philharmonic Society Scores of Haydn's "London" Symphonies', *Haydn Yearbook*, 14 (1983), 173–86

Sekora, John, *Luxury: The Concept in Western Thought* (Baltimore, 1977)

Seward, Anna, *Letters* (Edinburgh, 1811); see also *Journals and Correspondence of Thomas Sedgewick Whalley*, ed. H. Wickham (London, 1863)

Sickbert, Murl J., 'The Symphony in England: A Contribution to 18th-Century Musical Scholarship', Ph.D. diss., University of Colorado at Boulder, 1979

Simon, Edwin J., 'A Royal Manuscript: Ensemble Concertos by J. C. Bach', *JAMS*, 12 (1959), 161–77

Simon, Jacob, ed., *Handel: A Celebration of his Life and Times 1685–1759* (London, 1985)

Slatford, Rodney, 'Domenico Dragonetti', *PRMA*, 97 (1970–1), 21–8

Smart, George, *Leaves from the Journals of Sir George Smart*, ed. H. B. and C. L. E. Cox (London, 1907)

Smither, Howard E., *The Oratorio in the Classical Era* (Oxford, 1987)

Society of Artists: minute-books (Royal Academy of Arts)

Society of Musicians: see Royal Society of Musicians

Somfai, László, 'The London Revision of Haydn's Instrumental Style', *PRMA*, 100 (1973–4), 159–74

Southgate, T. Lea, 'Music at the Public Pleasure Gardens of the Eighteenth Century', *PMA*, 38 (1911–12), 141–59

Southworth, James G., *Vauxhall Gardens* (New York, 1941)

Speck, W. A., *Stability and Strife: England 1714–1760* (London, 1977)

Spitzer, John, 'Improvised Ornamentation in a Handel Aria with Obbligato Wind Accompaniment', *EM*, 16 (1988), 514–22

Stevens, R. J. S., 'Recollections of the Life of Richard John Samuel Stevens', MS. in CPL; as *Recollections*, ed. M. Argent (Basingstoke, 1992)

'Lectures', MS. in the Guildhall Library, London

Stone, Lawrence, *An Open Elite? England 1540–1880* (Oxford, 1984)

Supičić, Ivo, 'Early Forms of Musical "Mass" Culture', in *Music in the Classic Period: Essays in Honor of Barry S. Brook*, ed. A. W. Atlas (New York, 1985), pp. 249–57

Music in Society: A Guide to the Sociology of Music (Stuyvesant, 1987)

The Survey of London, 41 vols. to date (London, 1900–)

Temperley, Nicholas, 'Handel's Influence on English Music', *The Monthly Musical Record*, 90 (1960), 163–74

'Mozart's Influence on English Music', *ML*, 42 (1961), 307–18

'The London Pianoforte School', *MT*, 126 (1985), 25–7

'London and the Piano, 1760–1860', *MT*, 129 (1988), 289–93

Terry, Charles S., *John Christian Bach*, 2nd edn (London, 1967)

Thompson, F. M. L., ed., *The Cambridge Social History of Britain 1750–1950*, 3 vols. (Cambridge, 1990)

Thrale, Hester L., *Thraliana*, 2nd edn, ed. K. C. Balderston (Oxford, 1951)

Tilmouth, Michael, 'Some Early London Concerts and Music Clubs, 1670–1720', *PRMA*, 84 (1957–8), 13–26

'A Calendar of References to Music in Newspapers Published in London and the Provinces (1660–1719)', *RMARC*, 1 (1961), 1–107

Todd, Janet, *Sensibility: An Introduction* (London, 1986)

Trowles, Tony A., 'The Musical Ode in Britain *c.* 1670–1800', D.Phil. diss., University of Oxford, 1992

Turberville, A. S., ed., *Johnson's England*, 2 vols. (Oxford, 1933)

Tutenberg, Fritz, *Die Sinfonik Johann Christian Bachs* (Wolfenbüttel, 1928)

Twining, Thomas, Letters, BL, Add. 39929

Recreations and Studies of a Country Gentleman of the Eighteenth Century, ed. R. Twining (London, 1882)

Ullrich, Hermann, 'Maria Theresia Paradis in London', *ML*, 43 (1962), 16–24

Vauxhall Gardens: *A Description of Vaux-Hall Gardens* (London, 1762)

Collections of cuttings in BL (Cup. 401.k.7), Bodl. (G. A. Surrey c.21–25) and Lambeth Archives Department, London (formerly the Minet Library)

'Lists' (registers of programmes) for 1790–1 (Lambeth) and 1792–3 (Harvard Theatre Collection, Cambridge, Mass.)

Wainwright, David, *Broadwood by Appointment* (London, 1982)

Walker, Ernest, *A History of Music in England*, 3rd edn, rev. J. A. Westrup (Oxford, 1952)

Weber, William, *Music and the Middle Class* (London, 1975)

'Mass Culture and the Reshaping of European Musical Taste, 1770–1870', *IRASM*, 8 (1977), 5–22

'The Muddle of the Middle Classes', *19th Century Music*, 3 (1979–80), 175–85

'Intellectual Bases of the Handelian Tradition, 1759–1800', *PRMA*, 108 (1981–2), 100–14

'The Contemporaneity of Eighteenth-Century Musical Taste', *MQ*, 70 (1984), 175–94

'The 1784 Handel Commemoration as Political Ritual', *Journal of British Studies*, 28 (1989), 43–69

'The Eighteenth-Century Origins of the Musical Canon', *JRMA*, 114 (1989), 6–17

'London: A City of Unrivalled Riches', in *The Classical Era*, ed. N. Zaslaw (Basingstoke, 1989), pp. 293–326

The Rise of Musical Classics in Eighteenth-Century England: A Study in Canon, Ritual, and Ideology (Oxford, 1992)

Wendeborn, Friedrich August, *A View of England towards the Close of the Eighteenth Century* (1785–8), tr. author, 2 vols. (London, 1791)

Werkmeister, Lucyle, *The London Daily Press, 1772–1792* (Lincoln, Nebr., 1963)

Wesley, Charles, sr., 'Register of Concerts by C. and S. Wesley, 1779–1785', BL, Add. 35017 (copy)

Wesley, Samuel, 'Lectures', 1811–1830?, BL, Add. 35014

'Reminiscences', collected *c.* 1836, BL, Add. 27593

Wheelock, Gretchen A., 'Marriage à la Mode: Haydn's Instrumental Works "Englished" for Voice and Piano', *Journal of Musicology*, 8 (1990), 357–97

White, Joseph A., 'The Concerted Symphonies of John Christian Bach', Ph.D. diss., University of Michigan, 1958

Williams, A. Glyn, 'The Life and Works of John Stanley (1712–86)', Ph.D. diss., University of Reading, 1977

'The Concertos of John Stanley', *MR*, 42 (1981), 103–15

Wolff, Konrad, 'Johann Samuel Schroeter', *MQ*, 44 (1958), 338–59

Wright, Josephine R. B., 'George Polgreen Bridgetower: An African Prodigy in England 1789–99', *MQ*, 66 (1980), 65–82

Wroth, Warwick, *The London Pleasure Gardens of the Eighteenth Century* (London, 1896)

Young, Percy M., *The Concert Tradition from the Middle Ages to the Twentieth Century* (London, 1965)

A History of British Music (London, 1967)

Zaslaw, Neal, 'Toward the Revival of the Classical Orchestra', *PRMA*, 103 (1976–7), 158–87

Mozart's Symphonies: Context, Performance Practice, Reception (Oxford, 1989)

Index